AF145508

Communism in Philosophy

Historical Materialism Book Series

The Historical Materialism Book Series is a major publishing initiative of the radical left. The capitalist crisis of the twenty-first century has been met by a resurgence of interest in critical Marxist theory. At the same time, the publishing institutions committed to Marxism have contracted markedly since the high point of the 1970s. The Historical Materialism Book Series is dedicated to addressing this situation by making available important works of Marxist theory. The aim of the series is to publish important theoretical contributions as the basis for vigorous intellectual debate and exchange on the left.

The peer-reviewed series publishes original monographs, translated texts, and reprints of classics across the bounds of academic disciplinary agendas and across the divisions of the left. The series is particularly concerned to encourage the internationalization of Marxist debate and aims to translate significant studies from beyond the English-speaking world.

For a full list of titles in the Historical Materialism Book Series available in paperback from Haymarket Books, visit: www.haymarketbooks.org/series_collections/1-historical-materialism.

Communism in Philosophy

Essays on Alain Badiou and Toni Negri

Alberto Toscano

Haymarket Books
Chicago, IL

First published in 2025 by Brill Academic Publishers, The Netherlands
© 2025 Koninklijke Brill NV, Leiden, The Netherlands

Published in paperback in 2026 by
Haymarket Books
P.O. Box 180165
Chicago, IL 60618
773-583-7884
www.haymarketbooks.org

ISBN: 979-8-88890-795-5

Distributed to the trade in the US through Consortium Book Sales and
Distribution (www.cbsd.com) and internationally through Ingram
Publisher Services International (www.ingramcontent.com).

This book was published with the generous support of Lannan
Foundation, Wallace Action Fund, and the Marguerite Casey Foundation.

Special discounts are available for bulk purchases by organizations and
institutions. Please call 773-583-7884 or email info@haymarketbooks.org
for more information.

Cover art and design by David Mabb. The cover art is a development of
Long Live the New! no. 42, Kazimir Malevich drawing on Morris & Co. design,
paint and wallpaper on canvas (2016).

Printed in the United States.

Library of Congress Cataloging-in-Publication data is available.

For Matteo Mandarini and Ray Brassier

In memory of Marina Vishmidt (1976–2024)
and Joshua Clover (1962–2025)
Chi ha compagni non morirà

∴

Contents

PART 2
Toni Negri, or, the Communist Tendency

The Communist Differend

Philosophy is like the attic where one accumulates resources, lines up tools and sharpens knives in difficult times.
ALAIN BADIOU

• • •

Communism is a joyous ethical and political collective passion that fights against the trinity of property, borders and capital.
TONI NEGRI

• •
•

Communism and philosophy.[1] The reader could be forgiven for thinking of this as an anachronism or an antinomy. Generously, one could borrow Deleuze's non-dialectical formula: a disjunctive synthesis. After all, hadn't Marx, now almost two centuries ago, heralded philosophy's realisation in the guise of its practical termination, shadowing the proletariat's own self-abolition – and famously prompting Adorno's melancholy observation, according to which philosophy's survival was an effect of having missed its rendezvous with history? If, among an active minority, the phrase 'communism and philosophy' does not sound like a nonsense – or as the heading for an antiquarian inquest into Soviet speculations – it is no doubt largely thanks to the efforts of the two thinkers whose thought I track throughout these pages.

My own encounter with both of them – that is, with their books, and to be precise, at first, with Negri's *The Savage Anomaly* and Badiou's *Deleuze*, and shortly thereafter his *Being and Event* – was marked from the outset by the uniqueness of their position within the philosophical field. (Parenthetically, and retrospectively: To have two teachers – *maestri* or *maîtres* – is perhaps as good a way as any to avoid becoming a disciple.) In the immediate wake,

1 I am very grateful to Svenja Bromberg for her indispensable editorial help in compiling this collection. Thanks also to Jason Smith for his acute comments on an earlier version of this introduction.

but also the protracted eve, of the 'obscure disaster' of historical communism – which both thinkers, who had glimpsed shoots of emancipatory revolt
in the opposition to the regimes of the European East, did not conceive as
an *event* but rather the inevitable consequence of a long history of reversals
and putrefactions – it took some theoretical audacity to assert that the revolutionary negation of the capitalist order was an intimate ingredient of thinking
about being and truth. What to most apologists of the transition to capitalism appeared as reckless nostalgia proved intensely invigorating to someone
beginning his apprenticeship in philosophy in the mid-1990s with an intuitive
attachment to the politics of equality and an instinctive repulsion for the spectacle and propaganda of neoliberalism.

There were no doubt other, less intransigent, less militant, philosophical
interrogations of communism to hand – Agamben, Nancy, Derrida, as well as
numerous reiterations of the classical Marxist vision – but Negri and Badiou
were alone in tying an unapologetic affirmation of communist politics with an
equally 'innocent' assertion of the need for philosophy, and more precisely for
philosophy not (just) as a historical body of thought, but as an active practice –
an attitude for which I'd been primed by my first and formative philosophical encounter with Gilles Deleuze (and more specifically with his *Nietzsche
and Philosophy*), who served in the long run as a kind of intercessor (to use a
term of his coinage). In an initially inchoate way, philosophy appeared as an
indispensable vantage point from whence to reinvent what communism may
have meant for a present in which all its emblems had been dispatched to the
scrapyard (more than the dustbin) of history; but communism was also a kind
of orientation, however minimal, however abstract, without which philosophy
appeared mired in sterility and its synthesis of universality and intellectuality beset by the most glaring performative contradictions. It was only later, as
I became more attuned to the trajectories of these two thinkers, that I really
grasped how their philosophical inventiveness was bound up with their political defeats as well as with their own creative tenacity – not by chance are some
of their most speculative works the product of enforced retreats.

Following in the path treaded by many insurrectionaries before him, Negri
produced *The Savage Anomaly* and *The Constitution of Time* (this latter's first
draft having been destroyed, pissed on and set on fire by prison guards[2]) in the
cells to which he was confined by the Italian state after a notorious confected
indictment; years later, after returning to Italy in order to trigger (unsuccess-
fully) an amnesty for the political prisoners of the 1970s, he would once again

---

2   Negri 2003c, p. 130.

seize the occasion of captivity for intense speculative effort in *Kairòs, Alma Venus, Multitudo*. Badiou himself, experiencing the 'winter years' (Negri), or what he himself would later dub 'the Restoration', with his civil freedoms still intact, nevertheless repeatedly theorised his philosophical activity – for all of its 'eternal' orientation – as a response to political defeat, as evidenced in our epigram. Even more pointedly, in the prefatory note to his seminar on *Parmenides* from the mid-1980s, he talks of building a 'philosophical carapace' to shelter the political truths of communism from the hostile, inclement environs of reaction.[3] Both thinkers would register their opposition to the regressive or defeatist philosophical consensus that settled into place in Italy and France (Negri's own place of exile throughout the 80s and early 90s) in important diagnostic and polemical interventions.[4] They would do so on the basis of very different 'images' of philosophy: for Badiou, the demand for an 'expatriation' (see Chapter 2 in this volume) of Marxism would be followed by that of philosophy's 'desuturing' from its conditions, especially politics;[5] Negri's identification of philosophical truth with (social and political) action means that any separation, even in principle, between philosophy and politics is to be rejected.[6]

This staggered time or *décalage* of communism and philosophy has its own historical models – the most striking of all perhaps being Lenin's retreat into Hegel's *Science of Logic* (and Clausewitz's *On War*) after European socialism's political catastrophe in 1914 – but it also suggests that, even for figures who never accepted the deep *anti*-philosophical strains of historical materialism, *communist philosophy* is not a simple syntagm. To treat philosophy solely as communism's strategic retreat would of course not just be brutally reductive – of what remains, especially for Badiou, its more than relative autonomy – it would also mislead us into thinking that its function is a consolatory or utopian one. Badiou's metaphor of a 'shelter' for political thought and future practice is intended to orient us toward the notion that philosophy can also serve as an intellectual laboratory or anticipatory space for the 'desire for revolution' – which he identifies as an inextricable dimension of philosophy itself, pairing up revolutions in thought with the thinking of revolution.[7]

---

3 Badiou 2014b, p. 8.
4 See Negri 2013a, Part II: 'The Decline of "Weak Thought"'. On Badiou's abiding concern with reactionary thought, see Power and Toscano 2009, pp. 27–46. Badiou's book-length debates with Alain Finkielkraut, Jean-Claude Milner and Marcel Gauchet underscore the importance of this concern throughout his oeuvre.
5 See Badiou 1999.
6 'A truth is a collective action on the part of persons who campaign together and who transform themselves'. Negri 2004, p. 26.
7 Badiou 2015b, p. 11.

Notwithstanding the deep divisions between their respective images of philosophy, I think the resonances and parallels between Badiou and Negri's articulations of philosophy and communism cannot be gainsaid – while we must also recognise that they are external not immanent analogies, ones not just largely inoperative from within these two styles and systems of thought, but which also require a temporal and political distance to be discerned. It is not an accident then that these figures of communist philosophy could serve as conjoined inspirations for some of us who came of speculative age in the 1990s, and who did so at a considerable remove from the political conjunctures and identities that shaped Negri and Badiou. Moreover, as the publication of this collection itself more than verifies, this distance is deeply marked by a relatively unprecedented (if deeply uneven) 'globalisation' (which is also to say 'Americanisation') of the field of radical intellectual thought – not just a distance, but a kind of abstraction from its antagonistic contexts of production. It is through Anglo-American publishing and the mediations especially of US academia that these articulations of communism and philosophy have circulated across the planet. Notwithstanding a very strong Hispanophone presence, Negri and Badiou are by and large read in English (and their translators, myself included, also circulate through this curious and problematic arrangement). Communism and philosophy, in other words, circulate via cultures of thought which, notwithstanding important exceptions, have been deeply hostile to communism and to (non-analytical and non-pragmatist) philosophy. The intransigent and partisan affirmation of a politics against and other to capitalism has its distribution centres in the system's heartlands. For both philosophers this is a relatively recent phenomenon, and so are the rather surface polemics between them – especially the one that saw them lock horns at the second *Idea of Communism* conference in Berlin's Rosa Luxemburg Platz, to which I'll return below.

For the rest of their careers, notwithstanding the short-circuits and potential analogies that may be glimpsed in their respective manners of relating communism and philosophy, Badiou and Negri have not been rivals but existed in separate if at times contiguous but rarely communicating theoretical and political universes. Indeed, if someone were to resurrect Plutarch's biographical framework for today's radical thinkers, Badiou and Negri would nicely qualify for *Parallel Lives*. Born just four years apart in the 1930s, their trajectories are not just conjoined by their contemporary standing as the two foremost European communist philosophers of the early twenty-first century. Both had very precocious entrances into intellectual life, Negri being the youngest full professor in Italy when he took up his position, Badiou already both a published fiction writer and public philosopher in his 20s; both never belonged to Communist parties, coming of age politically in socialist formations (the Italian PSI and the

French PSU respectively), with early experience of electoral politics; both also encountered the rupture of the 'long 1968' not as youths but in their 30s, becoming leaders of far left political formations that, in very different ways, responded to the 'Leninist' (in Badiou, 'Marxist-Leninist') turn that followed what Henri Lefebvre called 'the explosion'[8] – Potere operaio and Autonomia operaia for Negri, the Union des communistes de France marxiste-léniniste (UCFML) for Badiou. And, as I've already sketched out, both of their mature positions are profoundly shaped by their analyses of and response to the counter-revolution without a revolution that we are still today trying to escape. Such parallels, combined with their rise to international philosophical and political prominence, would seem to warrant an ampler contrast of concepts and positions.[9]

Comparative philosophy, however, is an eminently problematic pursuit: not only can it generate rather dry correlations, pedantic exercises in conceptual auditing, it also presumes a neutral vantage or a homogeneous space in which otherwise distinct approaches can be forced into an encounter none of the parties really envisaged. If we think that philosophy is not just the invention of concepts but perhaps even more so the delineation of certain *problems*, as Deleuze himself suggested in *Bergsonism* and *Difference and Repetition*, we could propose that the only legitimate comparative effort would require at least a contiguity, or some kind of resonance and interference, between the respective problematisations attached to the proper names of philosophers – or perhaps, it might demand identifying the problems repudiated by different philosophers for dissimilar reasons. In a more limited vein, the comparison of positions can be a fruitful regional exercise, bringing different systems of thought to bear on the analysis of very specific problems or texts, possibly drawing from them third ways or positions neither had envisaged.

In this vein, I can envisage potentially fruitful conjunctions, clashes or parallaxes between Negri and Badiou on an ample number of issues, mirroring the humbling amplitude of their respective writings, but also their contemporaneity, however distant. Thus, we could anticipate much material for reflection in playing their forays into the history of philosophy against one another: Negri's multi-faceted immersion into Spinoza, and its reinvention of the historical-materialist method in philosophy, over against Badiou's far more limited but very significant dissension from the outlines of contemporary left Spinozism, complemented by their crucially divergent estimations of the legacy of the

---

8 Lefebvre 1969.
9 We can now read Negri and Badiou's memoirs and autobiographies in tandem to confirm these resonances and divergences. Negri 2015, 2017, 2020; Badiou 2023.

Cartesian subject.[10] Even a glance at the texts in question reveals a methodological chasm, between an approach that steeps conceptual analysis in conjunctures of class struggle and capital, in Negri's profoundly influential and
heterodox politicisation of the history of philosophy, his recovery of subversive materialist currents in and against modernity, and Badiou's proudly neoclassical schematisation of philosophies in terms of their modes of making the
truths of their time compossible (which introduces history at a very different
level, that of rupture and event). But the dossier could be much expanded,
to consider their lateral but indicative relationship to Heideggerian ontology
(and the Left Heideggerianisms of Nancy, Lacoue-Labarthe, Agamben, Cacciari and others), their response to Derridean deconstruction, their readings
of Althusser, their antipodal relation to Deleuze, their defining attempts first
to revive and then to transcend Leninism.

Such comparative work would also serve to reveal the notable and asymmetrical absences, for instance Badiou's telling indifference (or even hostility) to
the tradition of political and legal philosophy (from Machiavelli and Hobbes all
the way to normative, jurisprudential and constitutional questions), or Negri's
distance from Freudian-Lacanian psychoanalysis.[11] A welter of keywords of any
radical political thought for the present also receive contrasting formulations
in their work: democracy, the people, the state, revolution, organisation, and
so forth. A 'distant reading' of their work would also likely track the emergence
and circulation of certain terms which, while they receive a radically different
cast in their philosophies, nevertheless signal their participation in the same
broad community of radical European philosophy (and of its reception), more
recently crystallised under the 'Idea of Communism' rubric, but readily grasped
as the metaphysical translation of the rupture of '68': singularity, multiplicity,
subjectivity, event (or novelty and invention), and the opposition to representation (terms not by accident crucial to the thought of their intercessor Deleuze).
A generic, 'ideological' analysis would no doubt regard these as speculative
inscriptions of a Marxist self-criticism, shared by Negri and Badiou with those
among their contemporaries seeking to rescue communism from its historical
wreckage. Indeed, in the course of their polemic, Negri, whilst refusing any of
their consequences, conceded that he shares the starting points of Badiou's
philosophical reinvention of communism: the break with 'real socialism' and

---

10   See Mandarini and Toscano 2006.

11   Badiou would likely deem the fact that Negri, in one of his rare engagements with Lacan,
      treats his work in terms of a linguistic turn, as further proof of the thesis of democratic
      materialism. See, in *The Winter is Over*, the review of Roudinesco's biography of Lacan
      (Negri 2013a).

the suspicion of any identity between communist movements and capitalist development. We'll return to the second point, since it is on their diametrically opposed estimations of the link between communism and capitalism (and philosophy) that their differend is in the end to be located.

As to the opposition to real socialism, this is not simply a function of their lifelong distance from and antagonism to their national Communist parties, it also speaks to their very different responses to the 'crisis of Marxism' of the 1970s, both nevertheless sharing a need to radicalise the content of communism against any social-democratic dilution, to abandon developmentalist teleologies and to attack most instantiations of 'the Left'. Notwithstanding Negri's assertion – against what he perceives as Badiou's communism without Marxism (to which Badiou, perhaps predictably, retorted that he'd rather be a non-Marxist communist than a non-communist Marxist) – of the enduring necessity of the critique of political economy, we can also note what is perhaps the most glaring affinity between these otherwise antagonistic thinkers, an affinity of temperament rather than concept, it could said: their common conviction that, in spite of its destructive dimension, communism, *philosophical* communism, is essentially *affirmative*, that there is a joy or beatitude to thought, albeit in largely opposed Platonist and Spinozist figures.[12] Hence the distance – notwithstanding episodic engagements with the likes of Marcuse – from the negative dialectics of the Frankfurt School, with its asseverations against affirmative thought, and a shared 'critique of critical criticism', that suggests convergent judgments on the profound political limitations of the critical stance.[13]

Hence also their complex struggles with the dialectic, with negativity, with Hegel. Doing justice to them would require a sustained and nuanced engagement that far transcends the purposes of this introduction. Negri's anti-Hegelianism, which combines an early critical engagement with the philosophy of right, an absorption of the critique of Hegel that traversed Italian Marxism, and his own encounter with Deleuze – culminating in an unequivocal response to Pierre Macherey's alternative: 'Hegel or Spinoza?' – can

---

12   We might also contrast the recovery and subversion to which they subject their tutelary philosophical figures; it is notable that the conjunction of philosophy and communism demands such seemingly paradoxical entities as a *Platonism of the multiple* and a *Spinozism of insurrection*.

13   See, among many other loci in Badiou, Badiou and Kakogianni 2015, pp. 17–18 and Badiou 2014a, p. 330; for Negri, see 2009b. But note also the irony of Negri diagnosing the absoluteness of Badiou's event as a by-product of a paralysing totalisation of capitalist society, *à la* Adorno or Debord, in his intervention at the second Idea of Communism conference (Negri 2011).

be fruitfully contrasted with Badiou's combination of a fidelity to Hegelian thought with a seemingly devastating abandonment of totality and teleology. But we could also note that both have sought to nuance what might have appeared as their departures from the dialectic, Badiou in particular treating Negri as an antagonist in the great ideological combat between democratic materialism ('there are only bodies and languages') and his own materialist *dialectic* ('there are only bodies and languages, except there are truths').[14] To my mind, the almost equal prominence but thoroughly incommensurable significations given to the term *ontology*, and to the imperative to think being beyond the One and towards the multiple – for Badiou through the mathematical resources of set theory, for Negri via Spinoza's discovery of the ontology of the modes in the writing of the *Ethics* – would need to pass through this dialectical filter to attain intelligibility.[15] Same for their differend over the philosophical meaning of 'life', with Badiou identifying vitalism with a capitulation of novelty before finitude and repetition, and Negri regarding the criticisms of his insistence on 'biopolitical production' as symptoms of a 'negation of class struggle'.[16] Negri's opposition of the common to the universal is also to be understood in this vein.[17]

Just as Badiou's preface to *Logics of Worlds*, from which these terms are taken, was couched in terms of ideology – not those of formalisation or the labour of the concept – so an introduction such as this can only trade in rough depictions of philosophical orientations, over-determined by political, or rather metapolitical, convictions. It is in this guise that I think we can depict the clash between Negri and Badiou as a kind of differend, to resurrect Lyotard's notion, a fundamental incompatibility of positions, or, in a more constructive

---

14   See Badiou 2008, pp. 1–8; and 2014a, pp. 427–50. It is worth noting that Negri himself, writing in the early 1990s with Jean-Marie Vincent, had penned a criticism of 'weak' or postmodern thought that partly chimes with Badiou, arguing that for the likes of Rorty in the US or Vattimo in Italy, capitalism had become language while social relations had turned into stories or multiple narratives, thereby anaesthetising social reality. See Negri and Vincent 1991.

15   The complex exercise of thinking Negri and Badiou's place within the proliferation of ontological discourses in post-1968 philosophy could prove fruitful: an unusual but potentially productive angle of entry would involve tackling their reflections on ancient materialism and atomism, perhaps triangulated with the very young Marx's dissertation on Democritus and Epicurus. For Badiou on atomism, see his *Theory of the Subject* (1982); for Negri's reflections on matter and the void, see *Kairòs, Alma Venus, Multitudo*, in Negri 2003c.

16   See Badiou's writings on Deleuze and Nietzsche for his opposition to all speculative and political vitalisms. For Negri's position, see Negri 2011a, p. 209.

17   Negri 2011a, p. 203.

vein – albeit one that would need to take a position *outside* their respective systems – as an *antinomy*. This is a clash that on its own terms, as it surfaced in the *Idea of Communism* conferences,[18] will leave a philosophical reader inevitably dissatisfied, not least because neither of the contenders appears to have engaged with any degree of depth in the other's work. And yet, even without the global reconstruction of their differend, or the local comparative investigations alluded to above, the recent crystallisations of these two lines, these two images of communism – whether polemically inscribed as the materialist dialectic against democratic materialism, or as communism without Marx against Marx without communism – foregrounds real fault-lines in our political moment, orientations that make contrary demands on partisans of a politics driven by the desire collectively to reinvent equality against the capitalist reign of equivalence.

The two rubrics around which I'd place this differend then – and they are tellingly not the concepts for which our authors are best known: event, fidelity, truth, or multitude, empire, *potentia* – are those of *tendency* and *separation*. Negri's spirited objection to Badiou, which revives the condemnatory Marxian language of idealism, supplemented by the Spinozist-Deleuzian attack on transcendence, is that the French philosopher's communism is not drawn immanently from within the class struggle and the mutations of production, that instead, in Negri's words, it is defined by 'the independence of reason, its guarantee of truth, the systematicity of an ideological autonomy'.[19] Contrariwise, it is only the presence of cooperative practices and communist desires in the present, in and against the bleeding edge of the revolutions of capital, that can define a Marxist communism, one that grounds communist rupture in present powers, following the schema of the *Manifesto*. Here, what Negri, in his justly famous seminar on the *Grundrisse*, elaborated as the 'method of the tendency'[20] – the discernment, grasping and intensification of the antagonistic vectors within capitalist development (what used to be termed its 'contradictions') – is for him the guarantee of materialism.

As I argue in Chapter 10, we could indeed draw out of Negri himself, namely from his writings of the *autonomia operaia* (workers' autonomy) period in the 1970s, a thinking of separation-as-autonomy, which is to say of an immanent separation, a position of the working class against the state of capital that is argued on the basis of the method of the tendency itself. As I put it: 'The subjectivation, singularisation and socialisation of living labour is thus the aim of

---

18   See Negri 2011a, p. 203 and Badiou's retort in Badiou 2011b.
19   Negri 2011a, p. 207.
20   See Chapter 10 of this volume for the relevant references.

a movement that seeks to force the separation from capitalist command'. Negri himself, delineating his own place in twentieth-century Italian radical political thought, has both asserted the importance of a 'separatist' moment to the political insurgencies of the 1970s (*autonomia* and radical feminism in particular) and presented a movement beyond separation as the signature of a contemporary communist philosophy. This is what in his essay 'The Italian Difference' he christens 'exodus', a term that nicely encapsulates something like a *tendency-to-separation*. 'What is at issue here', he writes, 'is really a caesura, a break, an ontological event. In this ubiquitous passage from separation to creative difference, from resistance to exodus, the movements and the consciousness of workers and/or women overcome the theme of the mere critique of the existent (a classical theme in the theories of organization of the modern era) and replace it with that of metamorphosis, of an inner and collective modification/transformation, both singular and ethical, led in the multitudes and by them. It is an exodus from this existence and from all its rules'.[21]

Now, while Badiou has repeatedly, and rightly to my mind, insisted on the superficiality of the criticisms of his conception of philosophy for depending on a miraculous notion of rupture, it is nevertheless evident – as I tried to argue at length in my first sustained interpretation of Badiou's political thought, 'Communism as Separation' (Chapter 1) – that his is a thinking of communism not as transitive to the status quo, even in its destruction, but as a separation, albeit a separation whose elements must be themselves drawn from the situation – and are thus in that sense immanent, but in a sense distinctly at odds with the Negrian idea of a tendency, or indeed the Spinozist or Deleuzian paradigm of immanence.[22]

The densely over-determined debate on communist subjectivity is thus anchored in two models of radical transformation, and indeed of 'emancipation', both of which possess their own Marxian matrices: Negri's in the notion that communist potentials are written into the materiality, the 'historical ontology' of capitalism, as expounded in the *Manifesto* or the *Grundrisse*, Badiou's in the utter rupture from capital and state that will allow the proletariat, as intimated by the Marx of the 'Introduction to the Critique of Hegel's Philosophy of Right' and crystallised in the *Internationale*, to go from *nothing* to *all* (or perhaps, in Badiou's Lacanian inflection, to 'not-all' ...).

---

21   Negri 2009a, p. 19.

22   The Platonist roots of communism as separation in the separability of forms are evident in Badiou 2014a, p. 357. Badiou will sometimes use notion of separation in ways that chime with the understanding of it as a name for statist and capitalist alienation (such as we may also encounter in Guy Debord's 'critique of separation'). See Badiou 2018b, 80–1.

Finally, it is in this grounding difference – the dialectic of separation against the dialectic of the tendency, both approaches stretching the very boundaries of dialectical thought to a potential breaking point – that we can find the sources of their very different interventions into the political problems of the present and the future of communism. Negri, in keeping with his long-held belief that capital will be broken at its *strongest* link, unfailingly emphasises the seeds of communism in the antagonistic development of capitalism, especially the increasing centrality of *subjectivity* itself (articulated as *common, singular, biopolitical, multitudinous*).[23] Whence the fact that his thinking can often appear improbably 'optimistic' in its efforts at a kind of materialist prophecy, wherein defeats themselves are signs of past and coming victories; but we can also consider, notwithstanding Negri's speculative hostility to the politics of state and parliamentary representation, his sympathetic estimations of the experience of Lula's Partido dos Trabalhadores in Brazil, or his polemics against the opposition to the Euro and the European Union across what he dismisses as the 'sovereigntist' left – these apparent recalibrations of the status quo being interpreted as political chances for the 'constituent power' of the multitude. Negri has never wavered from the conviction that we can find the 'prerequisites of communism' in our societies, that 'capitalist societies seem to survive by articulating themselves onto anticipations of communism'.[24] Contrariwise, for Badiou affirmation is not an affirmation of something in the sinews of the present, but only an affirmation of rupture. Hence his definition of communism as 'the *immediate* norm of any appreciation of conflicts' – communism not as the inbuilt tendency of these conflicts but as a principled standpoint of political and philosophical judgement, 'at a distance' from the established space of political possibilities.[25] Far from being driven by the strength of class struggle or opening up, in its reliance on subjectivity, untold potentials for revolution,

---

23   'Capitalism today needs subjectivity, it is dependent on it. It thus finds itself chained to what paradoxically puts it in danger: because resistance, the affirmation of an intransitive freedom of men, lies precisely in asserting the power [*potenza*] of subjective invention, its singular multiplicity, its capacity to produce the common on the basis of differences' (Negri and Revel 2008). For Negri, capitalism, in its responses to the creative insurgency of living labour, has incontrovertibly *increased* the possibilities of resistance. In a sense that is counter-intuitive to the vast bulk of left thought, Badiou included, the opposition to capital is *more* powerful (tendentially) than it was forty years ago. This is a perspective that is qualified in the final pages of Negri's autobiography (Negri 2020), where the conditions of contemporary anti-fascism are set out with combative sobriety. See Chapter 16 in this volume.

24   Negri 1990.

25   Badiou and Kakogianni 2015, p. 45.

contemporary capitalism is a reactionary, oligarchic reprise of nineteenth-century possessive predation. It is a world without subjects and without ideas, at least not ones visible in the bodies and languages that attain representation. Whence, irrespective of his sympathy for the 'invariant characteristics of movement communism' that can be glimpsed in the halting 'rebirth of history' since 2011, his ultimate estimation, in the face of the movements in Spain and Greece, of 'the manifest impotence of the progressive forces to compel even the slightest meaningful retreat' from the agencies of capitalist power.[26] From Badiou's perspective, capitalism is also to be understood from the partisan standpoint of the affirmation of communism, but unlike for Negri, there is no immanence of communism to capitalism – though communism can be understood as an intervention into capitalism's Real. As Badiou writes: 'The access to the real of capitalism is the affirmation of equality; it is deciding, declaring that equality is possible, and making it exist as much as this is possible through action, organisation, the conquest of new places, the propaganda and construction, in disparate circumstances, of new thoughts, insurrection and war if must be'.[27]

In the final analysis, for the one, communism is a living potentiality pervading the increasingly 'socialised' character of contemporary production and reproduction, for the other, it will only be reinvented at the 'point of the impossible' of our current situation, in a separation from our extant political bodies and languages. For the one, subjectivity, as the metamorphosis and cooperation of productive 'singularities' (not mere individuals) is *always already* at work in the ontology of capitalism, for the other, subjects are rare and communism straddles the eternity of its 'invariants' and the incalculable chance of its insurgence, in the mode of the *not yet*, which is also that of the wager of the 'future anterior': *it will have been the case that these actions were in keeping with communist principles*. In other words, for Negri revolutionary novelty must be articulated with the novelty, the innovations, of cooperative production and the metamorphoses of its relations; for Badiou, anything truly new in the domain of politics (or indeed any other field of truthful practice) will, by definition, be radically *other* to capital.

The essays collected in this book, written at different times, occasioned by different demands (some endogenous to my research, some contingent on invitations), can all be fruitfully approached, I hope, with this differend over the very meaning of communism as their horizon, but they do not address it head on. While they all are driven by the conviction, inherited from Negri

---

26   Badiou 2013. Contrast with Negri's own intervention on Greece in the same issue of *Radical Philosophy* (Negri 2013b).

27   Badiou 2015a, p. 36.

and Badiou, that communism and philosophy must be thought together, they remain local inquiries, whose method, to the extent that they have one, is not that of affirmation but of the immanent critique of certain elements or components of these two thinkers' political (or metapolitical) thought. I hope they can serve the reader to reconstruct for themselves the stakes and prospects of communist philosophy today.

PART 1

Alain Badiou, or, the Communist Separation

∵

Communism as Separation

Ordinary reality is a space of placements, a partitioned order, a network of rela-tions,[1] in short, a law-bound structure of representations. Thought is a two-fold operation: the separation, out of this structure, of an immanent excess and the rigorous application of this excess, this real kernel of illegality, back on to rep-resentation, to unhinge and transform its coherence.

This elementary image of thought – as a separation of and from reality, as the dysfunction of representation – has always been the crux of Badiou's work, yet it has also been subjected to a radical recasting, dividing his work into two distinct figures, of *destruction* and *subtraction*.[2] I would like to examine here the motivation behind this division, and to propose the thesis that it is on the basis of an exacting and unvarying commitment to a certain idea of what it is to think – an idea whose origin is exquisitely political – that Badiou has found it imperative to split his own thought in two, or, to use a formula that I will attempt to elucidate in the course of this essay: to split separation itself.

If thought is co-extensive with a practice of separation, what is it that comes to be separated? Or, if separation works out of the element of order and rep-resentation, what is the real – in the Lacanian sense – that emerges from this operation? The key to Badiou's entire intellectual enterprise is that *separation is aimed at bringing forth the inseparate*; that what cannot be assigned a part, that is to say, represented as an item within the structure of reality, is precisely what the operations which I have here summarised under the term 'separation' are designed to produce. A corollary to this affirmation is that in and by separ-ation, thought as capacity presents itself, or, which amounts to the same, that thought is the production of what cannot be 'taken apart', what cannot be rep-resented as a part, the name of which is *the generic* and which constitutes the cornerstone of Badiou's doctrine, as formulated in *Being and Event*.[3]

---

1   These three figures of the order of representation, which take the names of *esplace* (a neo-logism standing for 'space of placements'), state, and world, are elaborated, respectively, in *Théorie du sujet* (*Theory of the Subject*) (1982), *L'Être et l'événement* (*Being and Event*) (1988) and *Logiques des Mondes* (*Logics of Worlds*) (2006).

2   In *Being and Event*, Badiou himself subjected his earlier theory of the subject to criticism on the basis of this distinction. He has also made it into the principal schema through which to think both the glories and the ravages of subjectivation in the twentieth century, in *Le Siècle* (*The Century*) (2005).

3   Badiou's work from *Being and Event* onwards asserts that a non-representational, proced-

Yet the generic is a relatively late name in Badiou's philosophy, preceded by the name of the inseparate as a political project: communism. To consider the persistence, in Badiou's thinking, of the idea of communism, together with its rupture, or immanent destruction, is to understand what lies behind destruction and subtraction as the two principal figures of the thought of separation. Moreover, it is the only path allowing for the genuine comprehension of what might otherwise appear as a simple provocation, the idea that the highest task of thought (and of politics) lies in the production of Sameness – and not in the contagions of hybridity, the call of alterity or the experience of difference.

Admittedly, this path is rife with peril, the name of 'communism' eliciting, with almost physiological inevitability, the most ardent reactions, be they of hostility, or – rather seldom these days – of enthusiasm. Let us at once dispel or displace these reactions by considering, following Badiou himself, what divides the name of communism and allows for its philosophical examination.

In a dense and iconoclastic pamphlet from 1991,[4] Badiou ponders the significance for the thinking of politics of the then recent demise of the USSR. His verdict is stark: rather than constituting a veritable event this is but a second death, the death of the atrophied institutionalised body of communism, already bereft of any driving political subjectivity, of any sustained experimental invention of novel forms of organisation, watchwords and principles. No state, he argues, could function as the emblem of the politics of emancipation that once took communism as its name. This is not a matter of opinion but the consequence of a vital distinction within political ontology, between immanent and precarious processes of political subjectivation, on the one hand, and their fatal representation in the structures of the state, on the other. This distinction, which in Badiou's vocabulary is bound to the one between presentation and representation, is nevertheless not my immediate concern. The veritable *pièce de résistance* in this argument is the affirmation, in the wake of its incessantly represented death (of its death *in* representation, to follow Badiou), of the *eternity of communism*.

We enter here into the terrain of what Badiou names *metapolitics*.[5] Metapolitics is one of the figures taken by philosophy's qualified dependence on its conditions. Badiou's contention is that one must try to identify the effects

---

ural variety of separation is necessary to attain the in-separate or generic truth of being. See 'L'Ecriture du générique: Samuel Beckett', in Badiou 1992, p. 335 (translated in Badiou 2003a, pp. 6–7).

4   Badiou 1991a.
5   See Badiou 1998.

on thought, as registered and configured by philosophy, of singular sequences of non-philosophical subjectivation, the 'generic procedures' he divides into science, art, politics and love. The metapolitical – as opposed to the strictly intra-subjective (militant) or the represented (statist) – name of communism is constituted by a determination, for thought as such, extracted by philosophy from the aleatory invention and organisation of the politics of equality. The product of this extraction is an 'eternity'. As Badiou declares:

> The obstinate militant tenacity, elicited by an incalculable event, to sustain the aleatory being of a singularity without predicate, of an infinity with no immanent hierarchy or determination, what I call the generic, ... is – when its procedure is political – the ontological concept of democracy, or of communism, it's the same thing. ... [It is] the philosophical, and therefore eternal, concept of rebellious subjectivity. ... Every political event which founds a truth exposes the subject that it induces to the eternity of the equal. 'Communism', in having named this eternity, cannot be the adequate name of a death.[6]

That we are not in the presence of a nostalgic apologetics – the *ressentiment* of the defeated – will become clear in a moment, as we register the profound effects of Badiou's suspension of the destructive figure of politics, and of his stark diagnosis of Marxist-Leninism as the properly metaphysical stage of political ontology. For now, it is important to note that it is in such a metapolitical procedure – the philosophical extraction of a concept from the travails of subjectivation – that much of Badiou's often misapprehended Platonism lies. Eternity is thought here not as the intuition of an archetype, impassively anticipating its precarious manifestations, but as the fixation of a concept. Produced by the living thought of politics, punctuated by datable events and sequences, and bequeathed to posterity – as that which every singular political procedure reaffirms and rearticulates – the concept in this instance is that of 'the eternity of the equal'.

As Badiou himself notes in *Of an Obscure Disaster*, this 'formal' eternity (not the eternity of a transcendent substance but precisely that of the *idea* of communism) had already been the object of a co-authored tract of his (with François Balmès), *De l'Idéologie (On Ideology)*, in the guise of a theory of communist invariants.[7]

---

6   Badiou 1991a, pp. 13–15.
7   Badiou and Balmès 1976.

Still within the categorial ambit of the Marxist-Leninist tradition, the theory of communist invariants is articulated around two arguments: (1) Aspirations for radical equality, for the annihilation of property and the state, are present throughout the history of politics, revealed in the intermittence of revolts, in the specific figures of the antagonism between domination and the domin-ated.[8] These aspirations are essentially disjoined from any economic teleology and constitute the spontaneous thought of the masses in the face of the struc-tured objectivity of exploitation, as represented by the dominant ideology. There is, in other words, an 'immediate intelligence' of communism, which constitutes the antagonistic thought of the masses, the force of their resistance, and which is *unrepresentable* from the point of view of the state. (2) These com-munist invariants are only *realised* with the constitution of the proletariat, that is, with the advent of that figure that signals the transformation of the masses into the revolutionary class. The communist invariants, which had hitherto been structurally destined to defeat – forced to express themselves in the lan-guage of domination and serving the needs of *another* class – are now guided by the party and oriented by the divisive analysis of class. This conjunctural opportunity is, in the eyes of Badiou and Balmès, absolutely new, and bound to the fact that the invariants are no longer a demand of equality heterogeneous to the order of representation, but, albeit foreclosed, are structurally *transitive* to this order. In other words, with the advent of capitalism the unrepresent-able force that had driven revolt up to that point is capable, by means of the antagonistic conjunction of masses, class, and party, of assuming its role as the foreclosed *source* of order, of *taking power* in the clear knowledge that 'resist-ance is the secret of domination'.

Now, this contemporary figure of revolt, crystallised in what the authors refer to as the 'communism of production', is entirely sustained by the historico-political notion of *realisation*, whereby the unrepresentable excess that has always driven revolt can constitute itself not just as an intermittently recur-ring force, but, through class-antagonism and the appropriation of production, emerge as a transitional representation of the unrepresentable, a dictatorship of the proletariat. While this position is not the 'classical type' of a classist

---

8   The primacy of revolt – that is, the primacy of *practice* – is the militant *leitmotiv* of Badiou's writings in the seventies. See especially Badiou 1975, an intense and speculative comment-ary upon Mao's dictum 'it is always right to revolt against the reactionaries.' In it, we read the following: 'Revolt does not wait for its reason, revolt is what is always already there, for any possible reason whatsoever. Marxism simply says: revolt is reason, revolt is subject. Marxism is the recapitulation of the wisdom of revolt' (p. 21). Ergo, 'The real is not what brings together, but what separates. What advenes is what disjoins' (pp. 61–2).

politics – as testified to by the eternity of the invariants and the decisionist character of the antagonism directed by the party, which evacuates the tele-ological dimension of classism that inhere in the idea of the party as 'midwife' of communism – it does accord to class a crucial role, to wit that of providing the dialectical articulation of the unrepresentable demands of resistance ('the eternity of the equal') and the law that structures and orders representations (in this case the ideological expression of the relations obtaining under capital-ism). The transitivity of the excess (in the guise of resistance) to the structural totality (the capitalist mode of production and its ideology) is of the essence here; it sustains, in the domain of historical becoming, what Badiou will later refer to as the Marxist hypothesis, which posits the task of egalitarian politics as the domination of non-domination.

In *On Ideology*, Badiou and Balmès had written of the 'logical power' of the proletariat, its singular constitution, under the direction of the party, as the representative of the unrepresentable, the capacity to dominate the passage to non-domination. Badiou will examine this logical power in terms of a theory of the subject in his 1982 book. The effects of this examination upon the idea of a communism of production will prove considerable, leading the notion of a realisation of revolt to what can be seen as its point of extreme and ultimately unsustainable coherence.

Once again, the question is the following: how does the unrepresentable demand for non-domination, the invariance of communism, constitute itself as antagonistic to the structure of representation? How is political separation effected? In other words, what are the operations whereby a political subject comes to be? (A subject being, for Badiou, nothing if not the finite support of the irruption of the unrepresentable.) To answer these questions, we need to consider the nature and the extent of the transitivity obtaining between structure and subjectivation, or between representation and revolt. Unlike in *On Ideology*, in *Theory of the Subject* there seems to be no remnant of the Marxist-Leninist thesis of an appropriation of production. Indeed, there is no separation of production and ideology that would then allow for the constitu-tion of the former as autonomous domain; every being is constitutively split between itself and its indexical localisation by representation – what Badiou here calls the *esplace*, the space of placements. It is only this localisation, this place, which is allowed to appear; being 'itself', which is the real of the *esplace*, is unrepresentable, it is – in Lacanese – a lack-of-being [*manque-à-être*] (or, in Badiou's jargon, the *horlieu*, the out-of-place). 'Subject' names the organised capacity of this 'lack-of-being', this hidden force behind the structured process of localisation, to *turn* on the structure, to force representation to include its real.

The absence of any distinction between production – which would constitute the substance and power of the masses – and representation, means that the only way for 'the eternity of the equal' to be attested to is by purifying itself of the indexes of representation, of its inclusion in the totalising order of places. It might appear that in this model there is no place for the notion of transitivity, whether the logic of the latter be that of expression or that of appropriation. This impression would nevertheless be incorrect. Badiou's theory of the subject does in fact contain a notion of transitivity but it is one woven out of antagonism. This antagonism is to be understood in two ways: (1) the *structural* antagonism between place and force that constitutes determination as domination, as the indexing of every force to its proper place within the system of representation; (2) the *subjective* antagonism of a force bent on destroying its place, by crossing the limit imposed by determination and thus limiting representation itself, what Badiou, with some irony, calls 'the labour of the positive'.[9]

Indispensable to this figure of the thinking of non-domination – let us name it the *communism of destruction* – is 'the eternal antecedence of the subject to itself',[10] the idea that the force that organises itself as the destruction of representation 'was', always already, the real of representation itself, its foreclosed being. It is precisely because this transitivity is only given when the excess of the real turns on representation, and not on the basis of any autonomy of the masses that could be either assumed or appropriated (just as one would be said to appropriate the means of production), that its figure is a destructive one. The political subject proves its antecedence to itself by disarticulating the space of placement, and singularly by destroying its own place. Or: the masses are revealed as an antagonistic class by the organised destruction which is the only *raison d'être* of the party (let us not forget that party and subject are, for the Badiou of *Theory of the Subject*, quasi-synonymous terms). This communism of destruction can be seen as the ultimate, and perhaps terminal, figure of the politics of transitivity, a figure in which the absence of any actually existing autonomy from the domination of representation means that the transitivity of the subject to the structure can only be revealed by the never-ending destruction of the latter.

With the publication of *Can Politics Be Thought?* (1985) Badiou signals a break, at once philosophical and political, with the very idea of a dialectical transitivity between the politics of non-domination and the system of representation. At the heart of this rupture is a thorough rethinking of the very place

---

9   Badiou 1982, p. 30.
10   Badiou 1982, p. 163.

of the Two in political subjectivity, no longer to be configured as destructive antagonism but rather as a discontinuous and event-bound subtraction.[11] What happens to the idea of communism in this break, and in the series of works that draw out its considerable consequences for politics and ontology?

The first thing to note is that this break is not intra-philosophical but follows from the assumption of the end of a sequence of political militancy, from what Badiou calls 'the destruction of Marxism' (in this regard, the question that guides this chapter could also be formulated as: what is a communism that separates itself from Marxism?). In other words, the supplementation of the theory of the subject with a theory of the event is motivated by the need to hold true to the eternity of the equal whilst forgoing the tenets of transitivity. What, after all, is the 'function' of the event, if not that of allowing us to think the dysfunction of representation, the interruption of domination, without the compulsion of postulating the antecedence of the (political) subject to itself? Or, in more strictly political terms, to think the possibility of a communist politics, a politics of equality, which is not based on antagonism as the motor of representation?

It is precisely because of Badiou's untiring conviction, to which all his work bears witness, that the highest task of thought is to think communism – that is, to separate and configure the unrepresentable out of the structures of representation – that both the communism of production and the communism of destruction must be subjected to vehement criticism. What is deserving of the epithet 'metaphysical' in these doctrines is the idea that politics is somehow inscribed in representation, that what is foreclosed by domination is nevertheless endowed with a latent political force; which is to say, that the political subject that emerges out of the labour of the positive, whether this be the appropriation of production or the limitation and destruction of place, is its own obscure precursor. Even and especially in its destructive figure, the communism that depends on the transitivity of its subject to the structure of domination – a transitivity defined by antagonism as the foreclosed motor of representation – is cursed by its adherence to representation: it is forced both to manifest itself only in and by destruction *and* to endow itself with a representative, a referent, precisely in order to dominate non-domination (the decades of debate over the dictatorship of the proletariat are the history of this lure). Here lies the metaphysical impasse of the Marxist-Leninist figure of communist politics.

---

11   On Badiou's (post-Maoist) conception of antagonism, see his 'One Divides into Two' in Badiou 2002b.

The idea of communism that appears in Badiou's work in the wake of his deconstruction of transitivity in politics[12] – an idea of communism which, by way of contrast to the other two, I would like to call that of the *production of communism*[13] – is borne by a transformation in the very nature of separation, an emancipation from the dialectics and secret teleologies of antagonism.

In this regard, the concept of unbinding, *déliaison*, bears a decisive function, both critical and ontological.[14] It affects the ontological basis of the communist imperative to think politics from the side of the unrepresentable. The weakness or instability of Marxist-Leninism lies, in Badiou's eyes, precisely in the idea that a bond – the bond of class – could, via the antagonism concentrated by the party-form, undo binding as such.[15] The impasse of the destructive or dialectical figure of separation is constituted by its obstinate reliance, in order to sustain its attack on the domination of representation, on what Badiou calls 'entities of reference', objective crystallisations of antagonism.[16] Without these referents, and without the ontological support that they are accorded by the dialectical self-antecedence of the political subject, the movement of destruction, of the irruption of the unrepresented into the order of representation, is drained of all de facto consistency.

If, in the domain of emancipatory politics, 'the hypothesis of a domination of non-domination'[17] has been linked to the movement of destruction, it is to the extent that non-domination itself has been reduced to the fleeting real that flashes in the bloody interval between, on the one hand, the party's domination of an antagonistic struggle, and, on the other, the dominant structures of the socio-political order that demand to be destroyed. It is from this ant-

---

12   This is what Badiou castigates as 'the fiction of the political'. See Badiou 1985a, pp. 9–21. The date of this book's publication, two years after the recomposition of Badiou's Maoist party – the UCFML – as L'Organisation politique, under the aegis of a 'politics without a party', is a testament to the intimate link between Badiou's metapolitical reflections and his long experience of political militancy. The notion of a transitivity of the subject to the situation is explicitly attacked in Badiou 1992, p. 236.

13   The essential traits of this 'production of communism', formalized as the numericity proper to political subjectivation, are to be found in 'La Politique comme procédure de verité', in Badiou 1998.

14   See 'La déliaison politique' in Badiou 1998, pp. 77–87.

15   For a political balance-sheet of classism and how it may be overcome by a 'politics without party', the reader will refer to the (anonymous) analyses published in *La Distance politique*, the newsletter of L'Organisation politique.

16   Badiou 2005a.

17   Badiou 1985a, p. 27. This is where Badiou locates the (terroristic) paradox of a communist state.

agonistic, or negative, determination of the politics of non-domination that the 'double bind' of the communism of the twentieth century emerges. The primary imperative is: 'Act so as to realize non-domination!' But within this ontology of antagonism, 'the real, conceived as both contingent and absolute, is never real enough not to be suspected of semblance'.[18] Whence derives the second, 'binding', imperative: 'Suspect everything as an agent of domination!' The only resolution of this double bind – and it is indeed an incessant bind, so much so that it could almost be characterised as the veritable motor of much anti-systemic political action – is given by the continuous purification of both the subjective support of the party and the structure of representation itself. This movement of purification, whereby the only proof of the real of communism is provided by the step-by-step elimination of all instances of determination, provides the veritable form of *terror*, the notion that the unrepresentable is only given as a sort of infinite persecution of everything that dominates (e.g. classifies, ranks, places, divides, etc.) social being. It follows that the passive body of this destructive subjectivation – the party(-state) – can only persevere by perpetually sundering itself and laying waste to the intimate traces of the old order.

To avert the outcome of this lethal oscillation between the monolithic bond and the fury of destruction, whilst trenchantly holding on to 'the eternity of the equal', Badiou poses that the very material of politics is not to be sought in a consistent instance of antagonism (i.e. class), but precisely in the radical inconsistency, the infinite dissemination of what the order of representation forecloses. In this regard, communism is to be revitalised by traversing a certain nihilism, by giving up on the idea that its movement is inscribed in the structure of representation (the lure of class antagonism as the motor of history) or that it can refer to the consistency of a representative – however transitory – of the unrepresentable (the hypothesis of a dictatorship of the proletariat). So, while the thesis of unbinding – posing that the real of politics and representation is radically multiple and non-hierarchical, *ergo* that emancipation is

---

18   Badiou's critique of destruction is entirely immanent to his own conceptual and political trajectory, as evinced by the theoretical proposals of *Theory of the Subject*, but especially the lapidary and uncompromising pronouncements in the earlier *Theory of Contradiction*, such as: 'There are radical novelties because there are corpses that no trumpet of Judgment will ever reawaken' (Badiou 1975, p. 86). Or: 'To resolve is to reject. History has worked best when its dustbins have been the better filled' (Badiou 1975, p. 87). Arguably, it is precisely to the extent that his earlier writings provide us with the most extreme and consequent distillate of the destructive regime of thought that Badiou's later reflections on the century constitute a remarkable tool with which to orient ourselves in the present.

devoid of a substantial or embodied referent that would precede the invention of a practice – provides a far more unequivocal basis in abstract ontology for the idea of communism, it simultaneously removes any notion of a dialectical relation (be it genetic and/or destructive) between this real and the social reality in which it is inscribed, partitioned or regulated. It is crucial to understand that Badiou's hostility to a communism based on any variety of socio-economic immanence rests on the conviction that the eternity of the equal is not of the order of a new bond, of a new system of relations, but is instead an attempt to think and practise, in the specific domain which is that of politics, the radical demand of a singularity without predicate, of a multiplicity not ordained into property or determination. This is why all 'anticipations' of politics must be abandoned, why all political concepts that would make communism transitive to the genesis of order and representation must be forsaken. This is not only the case for socio-economic totality, for community,[19] or for the continuity of struggles,[20] but also for the terminal operation of transitivity – destruction – the production of a political substance through the infinite task of purifying representation.

At base, Badiou's diagnosis tells us, the metaphysical weakness as well as the very real disasters of communism are to be ascribed to a certain relationship to the political instance of representation, the state. This relationship is determined by the idea that the task of a communist thought and practice is to traverse the state by means of the analysis of class antagonism, with the aim of forcing communist subjectivity into the articulations of representation. But if antagonism is not the motor of political representation, what operation – that is, what form of subjectivation – can present the real of representation, can organise the communist demand to separate the inseparate out from its domination by the partial and hierarchical order of representation? What is certain, above all, is that the abandonment of class antagonism as the dialectical support of communist subjectivity affects it with a radical intransitivity to representation as well as making its manifestations discontinuous. The eternity of communism is now to be understood as a formal invariant (all forms of political subjectiv-

---

19   Much of Badiou's thought on the persistence of communism can be understood in its polemical divergence from the philosophical discourse of Jean-Luc Nancy and the latter's recourse to the category of community. See Nancy 1991, pp. 49–100, whose gist is elegantly encapsulated by its subtitle: *from the 'existence' of communism to the community of 'existence'*. Badiou's critique of the concept of community is to be found in 'Philosophie et politique', in Badiou 1992.
20   Badiou bases himself here on the concept of 'historical modes of politics', as developed in Lazarus 1996.

ity are communist) but not as a material one (there is no spontaneous drive to communism, which would be the precursor of its full-blown organised political subjectivation).

Though exclusion of the real remains a structural constant of representation, the figure of the Two, of the separation of the inseparate, is, each and every time, a singular invention. The rare and non-cumulative nature of political subjectivation is thus the consequence of the critical abandonment of the structural function of antagonism. Communism is here bereft of any assurance, and most importantly of any teleology – even the dark admixture of finalism and decisionism proposed by the figure of destruction. Since unbinding is an ontological given, albeit a foreclosed one, and not a force that must be liberated from representation, the problem of communism becomes precisely that of producing the inseparate; which is to say, it is neither that of realising it nor that of expressing it. One of Badiou's key metapolitical theses is that this production must take place *at a distance* from representation, at a distance from the state. What is at stake is precisely a non- or a-dialectical relation between the effective thinking of communism and the structures of domination, a relation that can no longer rely on antagonism as the hidden principle of the latter.

This theme introduces us to the crucial distance between Badiou's metapolitical inscription of his own 'politics without a party' and what he himself defines as the political project of 'generic communism', namely:

> an egalitarian society of free association between polymorphous workers, in which activity is not regulated by technical or social decrees and specializations, but by the collective mastery of necessities. In such a society, the state is dissolved as a separate instance of public coercion. Politics, inasmuch as it expresses the interests of social groups, and aims at the conquest of power, is itself dissolved. Thus, every communist politics has as its proper aim its own dissolution in the modality of the end of the separate form of the state in general, even if the state in question is a democratic one.

Badiou juxtaposes this 'Leninist' vision, founded on 'the ultimate end of politics [as] the in-separate authority of the infinite, or the coming to itself [*advenue à soi*] of the collective as such', to the idea of politics as a 'singular collective practice at a distance from the state', a politics in which the collective is a production of the formalising power of political prescription.[21] While we are

---

21   Badiou 1998, pp. 91, 92, 97.

keenly aware of the reasons behind Badiou's deconstruction of substantial or teleological varieties of communism, we must remark that the 'formal' criteria of this singular collective practice cannot – 'downstream', as it were – avoid the encounter with the materiality of 'necessities'. In other words, bereft as it may be of any transitivity to the dynamics of the social or any latency of the political subject, such a practice cannot but result in an *actual* production of communism, albeit a communism whose image can never be given in advance. While Badiou is indeed proposing something like politics for politics' sake (whence its autonomy as a generic procedure), the universalisable and egalitarian determination of such a politics cannot but have effects, 'communist' effects in the real.

This new image of communism also entails a new image of domination. The state, no longer split by antagonism (by its function as the placement or indexing of force), is in ontological excess of presentation, and forecloses the inconsistency or the void at the heart of reality; in specifically political terms, it forecloses unbinding as the real of social existence. As Badiou writes, 'the state is not founded on a social bond that it would express, but on unbinding, which it prohibits'.[22] Properly political subjectivation – politics as a truth procedure – begins with this real, with the infinity of unbinding, but, and this is essential, *it cannot rely on the internal dynamics of representation* to assure the possibility that unbinding may itself be applied back on to the bound structures of representation. Having abdicated the principle of (class) antagonism, politics thus depends on a wager regarding the dysfunction of representation, on holding true to the decision that something in representation has faltered, that at the edges of order the real of unbinding has made its irruption. It is therefore as the precarious point of a dysfunction of representation that the concept of the event allows for the construction of communism in the absence of structural antagonism.

In the dysfunction of which the event is the signal, political thought finds the rare chance to uphold, by means of the invention of principles and practices specific to the locus of this dysfunction, the eternity of the equal as the boundless capacity for universality. The invariants of *On Ideology* make a 'formal' return here, in the sense that every political truth, for Badiou, puts to the test the axiom that thought (i.e. the capacity to separate oneself from the hierarchies and determinations of representation) is the thought of all, that, in the vocabulary of Maoism, 'the masses think'. Yet, in contradistinction to the transitive, antagonistic forms of communism (of production and of destruction) this

---

22   Badiou 1988, p. 125.

position effectively removes the substantiality of the collective. The collective, it states, is a consequence of political subjectivation; it is the *effect*, on a situation, of the radically egalitarian demand that thought be universalisable.

The collective is thus not the starting-point of unbinding, whose ontological status is strictly pre-political, but the product of a two-fold process: on the one hand, the measurement of the infinite excess of the state, that is, of the untrammelled domination of representation prior to subjectivation; on the other, the constitution, on the basis of the event as dysfunction, of a *generic part* of the situation. To illustrate this formal delineation of political subjectivity, it is useful to consider its effects on the political concept of mass movement.

In the transitive forms of politics, the mass movement provides the 'spectacular' proof, not only that the hidden basis of political representation is antagonistic, but that the very motor of the dynamic of representation is constituted by the foreclosed power of the people and its drive to equality; in brief, that 'the masses make history'. The problem of political organisation is precisely that of realising – that is, of *dividing* – this force.[23] Whence the directive function of the party, as a power capable of appropriating and annulling representation, together with the operations that produce it.

This figure is deeply transformed in Badiou's work after 1985. While mass movements do remain a privileged site for the irruption of the real, providing what Badiou will call the 'inconsistent consistency of the multiple in historical presentation',[24] they are no longer continuous with political collectives, as the substantial precursors of political subjectivity. The mass movement, far from being this substance, is the problematic and pre-political sign that unbinding gnaws away under the hierarchical determinations of representation. The step from this manifestation of the unbound infinity of situations to the collective production of equality is instead founded on the two moments of separation which characterise political subjectivity: distance (or freedom) and subtraction (or equality).

Rather than being immanent to representation by way of antagonistic destruction, the production of communism depends on setting out a political space separate from that of the state, from its hierarchies and determinations. This space is constituted by fixing a stable measure to the otherwise errant excess of state domination. The means for this measurement is the political function of *prescription*.[25] A statement, drawn from the event-dysfunction,

---

23 See Badiou 1975, pp. 66–9, on the division within the masses as a possible site of the 'principal contradiction' pertaining to a political situation.

24 Badiou 1998, p. 81.

25 See Hallward 2005.

obliges the state to demonstrate its exclusion of presentation, its foreclosure of unbinding. In the practice of Badiou's *Organisation politique*, this prescription can take the form of a political principle such as 'everyone who works here is from here', a principle that manifests (in the repression, reluctance or indifference of the state) the (often abyssal) space which separates the order of representation from the communist demand that the subordination of thought and being to hierarchy and partition be suspended – a demand which in this case is anchored in the need to disqualify, once and for all, the so-called 'problem of immigration' and its nefarious exclusion of the principle of equality.

However, this moment of distance – the freedom of a political space at a remove from the state – might devolve into dualistic hysteria were it not for the construction, within this space, of an actual equality. If it is really to substitute antagonism as the key to subjectivation, the political function of distance must therefore be conjoined to the production of equality, to 'the production of some real under the egalitarian maxim'[26] (i.e., the maxim that thought is the thought of all). This production entails that, to use the terminology of *Being and Event*, a generic part be constructed by 'avoiding' the determinations imposed by the excess of the state. This generic part, made up of an infinite sequence of finite inquiries (of finite 'avoidances' of what the structure of representation would itself recognise as a part), is the precise concept of the separation of the inseparate, that is, of the real of a situation as it results from a truth procedure.[27] It is the real of a situation – it is its *truth* – to the extent that its only being consists in belonging to it; because it is woven out of inquiries at least one of which always avoids capture (domination) as a recognisable part. Equality is produced as a part whose only property is that of being *of* a situation, a part with no other trait but that of pure belonging to determine, to *separate* it.

We can see then how subtraction proves to be double: first, it is conceived as the unbound real of representation, as the unbinding subtracted from the order of representation, what representation cannot allow to appear; second, it is the procedure whereby this unbinding is configured at a distance from representation, by systematically subtracting it from this order, by constituting a generic part out of the systematic avoidance of the laws of representation. The distance between these two subtractions – the one foreclosed and ontological, the other enacted in subjectivation – sets out the temporality of the subject and accounts for the fact that the truth of being is always produced, and, moreover, that its dependence on the work of inquiries upon representation means that it

---

26   Badiou 1998, p. 165.

27   For the concepts of avoidance (*évitement*) and generic part, see Badiou 1988, in particular pp. 369–74.

is irrevocably situated (each of the inquiries is finite) at the same time as integrally universalisable (the truth of being is always that of a pure belonging, of a singularity not indexed by domination). With regard to politics, it is only this second subtraction that allows us to move from the infinite of unbinding to the equality of the same, in the space measured out by prescription; it completes the formal parameters of a communist politics, 'what singularizes the political procedure'.[28] Politics remains ineluctably 'against the state' – truth is still of the order of the Two, representation is forced to make place for the generic – but this opposition is no longer the engine of subjectivity. On the contrary, it is what subjectivity must create as the space of freedom and the collective 'body' of equality. Antagonism is a consequence, not a condition.

'The generic is *egalitarian*, and every subject, ultimately, is under the injunction of equality [*est ordonné à l'égalité*]'.[29] That is, every political subject takes the *form*, regardless of the names that call it forth, of a communist subject. Yet far from providing the subject with any density or substance, in light of Badiou's theory of the subject this means that there is nothing in the order of domination – that is, neither its production nor its representation – to guarantee the success, *or even the existence*, of a communist politics. Suspended to the event of dysfunction, to the freedom of prescription and the local inquiries into the generic, communism is presented here as bereft of the 'fiction' that it is somehow inscribed in the dynamics of the social. Or, equality is only eternal – as a formal requirement of every true instance of political subjectivation – to the very extent that it is nowhere latent. Alas, it is of the essence of Badiou's proposal that at this point metapolitics – that is to say, philosophy in its relation to political thought and practice – abandon any pretence of anticipating the precarious and situated fate of the production of communism. It is here that, in the words of *D'un désastre obscur*, politics really begins, and everything remains to be invented.[30]

---

28 Badiou 1998, p. 166.
29 Badiou 1988, p. 447. Perhaps the point of greatest distance between this philosophy of generic truth and Badiou's Maoist period revolves around the determination of political truth. Whilst the drive and the object of this earlier work also lay in the 'eternity of the equal', the separating truth itself was unequal in its address and its operation. As we read in *Theory of Contradiction* (Badiou 1975, pp. 16–17): 'Marxist truth is the reason that revolt makes its own in order to cut down the enemy. It repudiates all *equality* before truth. In a single movement, which is knowledge [*connaissance*] in its specific division into description and directive, it judges, pronounces the sentence, and immerses itself in its execution.'
30 Badiou 1991a, p. 56.

CHAPTER 2

Marxism Expatriated

Today's radical political (or metapolitical) theory is the offspring of a contorted dialectic of defeat and reinvention.[1] Though it is common to take contemporary ideas on emancipation and political subjectivity at face value, many of the defining characteristics of recent philosophical writing on radical politics are obscured if we fail to address how they emerged out of a reckoning with the failure or distortion of Marxist politics, and, moreover, if we disregard the extent to which they maintain an underlying commitment to the Marxist impulse from whence they arose. The mode of separation, as it were, from the organisational and theoretical tenets of Marxism (in whichever guise) can tell us a lot about the present resources and limitations of theoretical contributions to the contemporary thinking of politics that drew initial sustenance from that tradition, even if they are now allegedly 'beyond' Marx and Marxism. This is certainly the case with the work of Alain Badiou, whose knotty relationship to his own Marxist-Leninist militancy and to Marxist theory has been the object of rich and detailed investigation, above all in Bruno Bosteels's work. Bosteels's characterisation of Badiou's metapolitical trajectory in terms of 'post-Maoism'[2] already suggests that what makes Badiou's theoretical biography distinctive is at a considerable remove from the entire 'post-Marxist' tendency, chiefly

---

1   It is worth noting from the outset that Badiou – who does not seem to hold much truck with the term nowadays – put his work in the mid-eighties under the aegis of 'radicalism', often in terms redolent of a certain Kantian atmosphere that suffused the French debate on the retreat of the political and political judgement: 'What is a radical politics, which goes to the root, which refuses the administration of the necessary, which reflects on ends, upholding and practicing justice and equality, and which nevertheless assumes the time of peace, and is not like the empty wait for a cataclysm? What is a radicalism that is at the same time an infinite task?' (Badiou 1985a, p. 106) Showing the momentary influence of Lyotard, Badiou even links his notion of an axiomatic politics to Kant's treatment of aesthetic judgement in terms of 'reflective universality' (which, we could hazard, also affects the temporality of the future perfect, which is still at work in the concept of the generic). See Badiou 1985a, p. 76. It should also not be forgotten that *Can Politics Be Thought?*, like Lyotard's *L'enthousiasme. La critique kantienne de l'histoire* (1986), was occasioned by an invitation from Jean-Luc Nancy and Philippe Lacoue-Labarthe's Centre de recherche philosophique sur le politique and is in (polemical) dialogue with the problems identified by these philosophers.

2   Bosteels 2005, pp. 575–634. For a more extensive account, which incorporates and further develops this argument, see Bosteels 2011.

encapsulated in Ernesto Laclau and Chantal Mouffe's *Hegemony and Social-ist Strategy*, and compellingly dismantled in Ellen Meiksins Wood's *The Retreat from Class*.[3]

Having said that, the echoes of a common 'post-structuralist' theoretical conjuncture, and a critique of (or separation from) 'thick' Hegelian-Marxist versions of dialectics and social ontology, might make one suspect that 'the theoretical edifices of Laclau and Badiou are united by a deep homology'.[4] This 'deep homology', which Žižek identifies in the notion of a contingent, subject-ive rupture of ontological closure, is nevertheless offset, still according to the Slovenian philosopher, by a fundamental divergence, inasmuch as, in the last instance, Badiou's ' "post-Marxism" has nothing whatsoever to do with the fash-ionable deconstructionist dismissal of the alleged Marxist "essentialism"; on the contrary, he is unique in radically rejecting the deconstructionist doxa as a new form of pseudo-thought, as a contemporary version of sophism'.[5] Rather than either homology, or frontal opposition, it might be more precise to argue that Badiou's post-Maoism and the post-Marxism of Laclau and Mouffe inter-sect in manners that generate, from the peculiar perspective of contemporary radical thought, a kind of 'family resemblance', but that, when push comes to shove, they are really indifferent to one another, born of divergent assessments of the end or crisis of Marxism. To a certain extent, they connect the same dots, but the resulting pictures differ radically. In order better to delineate the spe-cific difference of Badiou's project, and of the problems that generated it, it is of considerable interest to examine the period between the highest speculat-ive product of Badiou's heterodox Maoism, *Theory of the Subject* (1982), and *Being and Event* (1988), in particular the book *Can Politics Be Thought?*, pub-lished in 1985, which is to say contemporaneously with Laclau and Mouffe's *Hegemony*.

Like many post-Marxists, and indeed anti-communists, Badiou attacks the 'metaphysics' that contaminate Marxist politics. In a Heideggerian pastiche, he even describes Marxism-Leninism as the 'metaphysical epoch of Marxist polit-ical ontology'.[6] Most 'deconstructions' of the Marxist canon have looked for this metaphysics in Marx's supposed reductionist 'economism' or in what they take

---

3   Laclau and Mouffe 1985; Wood 1998. As a future task, it would be very interesting indeed to gauge how well Badiou's own post-Leninist turn would fare under Wood's criticism – espe-cially insofar as Wood, rather than simply rehashing 'orthodox' criticism, is able, in a Marxian spirit, to foreground the importance of the Marxian critique of political economy to a defin-ition of such crucial concepts as freedom and equality.

4   Žižek 1999, p. 172.

5   Žižek 1998.

6   Badiou 1984, p. 8 and 1985, p. 61.

to be an imaginary constitution of the social, and of class structure in particular, whose correlate is the putative transparency of the post-revolutionary social bond. While some of these points may be registered in Badiou's texts from the mid-eighties, the emphasis is firmly on a conceptual dyad that persists even in later works like *Metapolitics*. This is the distinction between *politics* and *the political*. The thesis that lies at the core of Badiou's call to counter the supposed 'crisis' of Marxism by way of its 'destruction' and 'recomposition', is that Marxism has succumbed to the homogenising *political* fiction that imagines the possibility of measuring, anticipating and representing political action. According to this framework, '*the political* has never been anything but the fiction which *politics* punctures through the hole of the event'.[7]

One's initial impression is of a substantial overlap with Laclau and Mouffe in terms of the notions of working class, proletariat or people as fictions of the social bond, signifying fictions in which political action could find its guarantee. Indeed, the fundamental political fiction for Badiou is that of the 'alliance of the social relation and its measure' (where, as the treatment of the concept of 'state' in *Being and Event* suggests, measure is equivalent to representation). However, from the idea whereby the crisis of the political reveals that (in his vocabulary) *all sets are inconsistent*,[8] Badiou does not draw the customary post-Marxist lessons regarding the transcendental horizon of discursively generated identities and the *a priori* of antagonism as an intractable impediment to social revolution. In other words, he does not espouse the post-Marxist mix of strategic populism, sociological description, discursive ontology and cynical liberalism. Rather, the assault on the fiction of the social, and on Marxism's foundational commitment to a critique of political economy, is viewed by Badiou as the occasion for a renovation, and a kind of *purification*, of the *politics* of emancipation. Marxism, according to *Can Politics Be Thought?*, is unable to critique its own critique of political economy,[9] leaving its original political impetus cloaked and perverted, binding it to the mediations, however antagonistic, of economic and social relations. The maintenance of categories of totality and system within this approach is what imprisons the encounter and creation of a politics in the *fiction* of *the political*, which always comes down to 'the alliance of the social relation and its measure'.[10] Marxism – this is Badiou's verdict – was destroyed by its history, the subordination of politics to the fiction of a social measure.

---

7   Badiou 1985a, p. 12.
8   Badiou 1985a, p. 13.
9   Badiou 1985a, p. 14.
10   Ibid.

The political is a kind of metaphorical cloaking of the hiatus between state and civil society, representation and presentation. The aim of an emancipatory politics should not lie in the creation of a new bond; the inconsistency of the social does not open onto ever-renegotiated (and formally identical) disputes over its content, but on the idea of an autonomy and heterogeneity of politics, which occurs at a remove from any *relational* dialectic: 'What is dissipated is the thesis of an essence of the relations internal to the city, an essence representable in the exercise of a sovereignty, be it the dictatorship of the slaves, even if the relation is that of civil war within the class structure'.[11] So, while there is a convergence or homology around a certain anti-essentialism, what follows from Badiou's own attack on essential relations is a link between inconsistency and event, which still retains an emancipatory, rationalist reference to transmissible decision and a communist reference to the generic (in the axiom of equality) – rather than a generalised undecidability oscillating between a sociologistic account of discursive plurality and a political ontology of fundamental antagonisms. In other words, the 'destruction' of the political fiction that Badiou diagnoses within metaphysical Marxism is not an opportunity to affirm the *pluralism* of political struggles, but rather to argue simultaneously for their *singularity* and their prescriptive homogeneity. Badiou insists, during this period, in writing of the *recomposition* of Marxism, in putting his work under the aegis of 'Marxist politics', because of the unsurpassable character of the Marxist hypothesis, the hypothesis of a politics of non-domination that is irreducible to the state. Rescinding the fiction of the political, from within Marxism, is advanced as a kind of prolegomenon to the emancipation of (a Marxist) politics. In *Can Politics Be Thought?* we can thus observe, in a quasi-deductive manner, the passage from an internal dislocation of Marxism to a metapolitical thinking of the event: 'the determination of the essence of politics, unable to find a guarantee either in structure (inconsistency of sets, unbinding), nor sense (History does not make a whole), has no other benchmark than the event'. Note that it is through this 'ultra-one' of the event, that Badiou *maintains* 'the essence of politics': 'The firmness of essentialisation rests on the precariousness of what happens.'[12]

---

11   Badiou 1985a, p. 13. See also the Mallarmé quote from *Divagations* (1897) that Badiou adduces for this stance: '*le rapport social et sa mesure momentanée, qu'on la serre ou l'allonge, en vue de gouverner, étant une fiction*' ('since the social relation at any particular time, condensed or expanded to allow for government, is a fiction'). Mallarmé 2007, p. 290.

12   Badiou 1985a, p. 67. On the event as 'ultra-one', see Badiou 2006a, pp. 178–83.

Keeping this move in mind, we can elucidate several supplementary differences with the ideological attitude of post-Marxism, as well as shed some light on the direction taken by Badiou's further work. A particularly significant issue in this regard involves the difference between an ontology of the multiple and the kind of pluralist notion of hegemony put forward by post-Marxism. Whilst in both instances the undermining of unity (at the level of class identity and of party leadership, for instance, as well as in terms of the category of social totality) is used to articulate a movement beyond the supposedly Hegelian or totalising character of Marxist theory, Badiou's set-theoretical ontology of the multiple is of a wholly different order than the discursive pluralism of Laclau and Mouffe – indeed, the theme of the *generic*, running (explicitly or otherwise) through the whole of Badiou's work from the 1980s onwards, can be understood in terms of the need to maintain communism as an intrinsic property of truth and subjective fidelity. This is not an immanent critique of Marxism as a science of capitalism and revolution, but a displacement to a heterogeneous practical and theoretical framework (one in which politics and philosophy are de-sutured, as Badiou's 1989 *Manifesto for Philosophy* proposes) in order to retain a minimal Marxism conjoining the hypothesis of non-domination with the rational identification of the sites of subversion, without trapping politics in a teleological, revolutionary or programmatic framework.

We will inquire below as to whether maintaining the name Marxism is tenable once these theoretical options have been taken – especially bidding farewell to the concept of revolution. For the time being, it is worth noting that the emphasis on the subjective element in Marxist politics – already a prominent trait in Badiou's Maoism and still present in the 1980s concern with political 'forms of consciousness'[13] – is fully at odds with the post-Marxist concern with 'subject-positions' and the hegemonic negotiations of 'identity'. This anti-essentialist discursive ontology of the (empty) social is absent from Badiou, whose concern, as demonstrated quite consistently even in later books like *Ethics*, is not with the political interplay between identity and difference. Rather, Badiou's thought works at the interface between, on the one hand, the fact of identity-and-difference as a feature of the encyclopaedia of knowledges,[14] and, on the other, the production of the Same.[15] Despite the deceptive resonance, this is not to be confused with the two logics of Laclau and Mouffe, differential and equivalential. Why? Because in the latter these two logics remain transitive to one another and map out the transcendental horizon of political

---

13   See Sandevince 1984a.
14   Badiou 2006a, pp. 327–43.
15   Badiou 2001, pp. 25–7.

dispute, whilst in Badiou the production of sameness in the political field is a real production of truth that does not involve the strategic rearrangement and occupation of the language of the situation, but an organised subtraction from its very terms.

Instead of shifting the terrain from that of (the taking of) political power, of classical revolutionary politics, to the domain of discourse (the post-Marxist strategy whose fundamental 'electoralism' is persuasively ferreted out by Ellen Meiksins Wood), the shift made by Badiou and his political comrades is marked by the attempt, in order to maintain the hypothesis of non-domination, to consolidate and purify the subject of politics. In a distinction that would obviously strike the likes of Wood as spurious, since it characteristically bypasses the level of *class*, for Badiou it is not the state but proletarian capacity that lies at the heart of Marxist politics. Concerning the question of class struggle and antagonism as a crucial node in the so-called crisis of Marxism, and the possibility of a 'party of a new type', Paul Sandevince (a.k.a. Sylvain Lazarus) writes in *Le Perroquet* (a publication of Badiou's group, the UCFML), that: 'For Lenin, the essential is not struggle, but "antagonism against the entirety of the existent political and social order"'. This is read as a warning against the logic of the absorption of the party into the state, whilst the 'other path' involves assigning 'the process of politics to the masses/State contradiction grasped in terms of consciousness [*conscience*]'.[16] This is one of the sources of Badiou's own insistence on politics viewed not as strategy for power, or a way of ordering the social, but as an organised practice of *thought* (a 'truth procedure', in the later work). The link between the hypothesis of non-domination, the egalitarian and organised capacity for thought, and a separation from the state thus appears as one of the key tenets of this self-avowed 'Marxist politics'. This gives us an inkling as to why the appellations post-Maoism or post-Leninism (the one favoured by the various authors in *Le Perroquet*[17]) are more appropriate

---

16   Sandevince 1984b, p. 5. UCFML refers to the 'Groupe pour la formation d'une Union des communistes de France marxiste-leniniste'. In 1985, the UCFML disbanded and was succeeded by L'Organisation politique, a non-party organisation. See Hallward 2003 and Bosteels 2005 for more detailed information.

17   Sandevince 1984a. According to him, there is no positive meaning of Marxism-Leninism after the termination of the Cultural Revolution, and in the end 'one cannot extirpate Marxism-Leninism from its Stalinist matrix'. But the line taken by *Le Perroquet* is that it is necessary to maintain the Leninist break or division between social being and political consciousness. Thus, while moving beyond Lenin in terms of organisation (and indeed as concerns the link between class and revolution) there is a fidelity to a kind of Leninism of capacities, of thought. Politics under condition, in Sandevince-Lazarus's definition, is politics separated from the social. Can a certain Leninism be maintained beyond the

than post-Marxism. Having already concluded that Marxist politics is not the consequence of a critical analysis of capitalism, but is rather the means, within capitalist conditions, for the production of communism (so that the critique of political economy is wholly subordinate to the project of emancipation), the direction taken in the 1980s by Badiou and his comrades is primarily born out of the crisis of the Marxist political subject (i.e. the party), and not, as with 'traditional' post-Marxism, out of a critique of the metaphysical tenets and sociological shortcomings of Marxism as a science of capitalism. If Badiou's *Theory of the Subject* had declared that every subject is political and that subject equals party, what is at stake in this period (1982–88) which oscillates between the option for a 'party of a new type' and that of 'politics without a party'? Jameson contends that Marxism qua science of capitalism periodically gives rise to post-Marxism at moments of systemic crisis.[18]

Whatever the links between such crises and forms of political organisation, it is clear that for Badiou it is the party qua subject that is the focus of the crisis, not the ability of 'Marxism' to cope with social and economic transformations, or the shifts and turnabouts in class composition. Indeed, Badiou is generally rather sanguine about the Marxist understanding of capitalism and does not seem to think that Marx has really been surpassed in this domain. In any instance, Badiou is immunised against the stance according to which the failure of social ontology or economic analysis would debilitate Marxist politics. Indeed, he mocks this very possibility in a vicious piece caricaturing the 'old Marxist', the one who waits for the proper study of 'social formations' before acting, who thinks that 'one of these days the "workers' movement" will give us something to talk about'.[19] To the contrary, 'Marx starts, absolutely, not from the architecture of the social, in which he will, after the fact, deploy his assurance and his guarantee, but from the interpretation-cut of a symptom of social hysteria, uprisings and workers' parties. ... For the symptom that hystericises the social to be thus grasped, without pinning it to the fiction of the political,

---

party-form? Is the party-form a restraint on the virtuosity of political subjectivity? This of course raises the question of how political capacity can be fostered and rendered efficacious outside of the party-form.

18   Jameson 1996.

19   Peyrol 1983, p. 5. In *Can Politics Be Thought?*, Badiou puts the point as follows 'Communist politics must be wagered: you will never deduce it from Capital' (Badiou 1985a, p. 87). Of course, it could be argued that far from signalling a caesura, this 'long wager' (p. 90) is a feature of Marx's own thinking, which never held to such a chimerical 'deduction'. See Kouvelakis 2004. The idea of Marxism as promoting a 'deduction' of politics from the critique of capital runs the risk of converging with the 'straw-Marxism' denounced by Wood. See Wood 1998, p. 187.

proletarian political capacity – as a radical hypothesis of truth and a reduction to fiction of every foregoing notion of the political – must be excepted from any approach via the communitarian and the social'.[20]

By now, Badiou's philosophy is renowned as a philosophy of the event. But, in terms of what I referred to above as the dialectic of defeat and reinvention, could we also say that there are events of closure, failure, saturation? Without entering into doctrinal details, Badiou does overtly mark his treatment of the 'destruction and recomposition' of Marxism in terms of what he terms 'the end of referents', a position presaged by an article by the same titled in *Le Perroquet*, penned by Sandevince-Lazarus.[21] This passage through history is inexorable, inasmuch as 'Marxism alone presented itself as a revolutionary political doctrine which, if not historically confirmed ... was at least historically active'.[22] If Marxist politics, in its Marxist-Leninist phase, was crystallised around the figure of the party as subject, and suffused by an essential historicity, then this figure is seen to suffer from the collapse of its three primary referents: (1) *the statist referent*: the actual existence of Marxist states, as emblems of the possible victory of a Marxist politics, and of 'the domination of non-domination';[23]

---

20   Badiou 1985a, p. 20. This rethinking of the notion of capacity, it should be noted, is 'eventually' bound to the Polish workers' movement of the late 1970s and early 1980s. See the section of *Peut-on penser la politique?* entitled 'Universal meaning of the Polish workers' movement', Badiou 1985a, pp. 45–8, as well as Lebovici 1983, and many other pieces in the same publication throughout the 1980s.

21   However, Sandevince-Lazarus's way of posing the crisis is slightly more theoretical than historical. In fact, he too designates three referents but substitutes Marxism-Leninism itself for Badiou's focus on anti-imperialist wars: 'The referents are principally of three orders', he writes, 'the socialist State, the worker capacity to practice and formulate a revolutionary politics, and finally Marxism-Leninism'. Marxism-Leninism is also defined here as a 'precarious political amalgam', and there is a sense in some of the work in *Le Perroquet* of a political 'return to Marx', a (re)commencement of Marx that would sublate the Leninist experience. Moreover, Sandevince-Lazarus also emphasises that this is a *political* crisis: 'Marxism is in its nature a politics – as Marx himself clearly specifies in his letter to Weydemeyer – communist politics (for communism, the abolition of the wage, the reduction of great differences, the extinction of the State and political parties), a communist politics that is irreducibly antagonistic to bourgeois politics (for capitalism, imperialism, and the State). If there is a crisis of Marxism, it is the crisis of a politics, of a politics for communism, what we call, strictly speaking, Marxist politics.' Sandevince 1984, p. 10. But see especially UCFML 1983. The whole issue, under the heading '*Un Perroquet-Marx*', marking the hundredth anniversary of Marx's death, is devoted to these questions.

22   Badiou 1985a, p. 26.

23   Badiou 1985a, p. 27. Post-Leninism is thus defined by the break with 'reason of state' in all its forms, a break that draws its sustenance from the founding drive of Marxism itself: 'It is not the State that is the principle of universality of Marxist politics, but rather the communist process in the deployment of class struggles and revolutions'. Sandevince 1984c, p. 10.

(2) *wars of national liberation* as another emblem of actually victorious Marxist politics, and the 'fusion of the national principle and the popular principle'[24] in the invention of new ways of linking politics and war; (3) *the workers' movement*, especially in its incarnation in 'working class parties' with an explicit Marxist reference, 'mixed figures of a distant revolutionary Idea and the proximity of an oppositional activity'.[25]

Once again, it is not the analytical force of Marxism qua science of capital that is paramount for Badiou, but the collapse of its singularity as a revolutionary thinking and a politics that was fundamentally 'self-referential' (its instances were, to various degrees, homogeneous with its theory) and massively inscribed in historical reality. Though Badiou will always maintain (as he does in *D'un désastre obscur*) the 'eternity of communism', what is at stake here is the historicity of Marxism and the impossibility, in his view, for it to continue to draw any value from its actual history in the present. As Badiou puts it, 'its credit has run out'.[26] Note that, contrary to all specimens of post-Marxism, this has nothing to do with the explanatory capacity of Marxism (Badiou treats it strictly as a politics, not a doctrine, and only secondarily and strategically as an analysis of the social). The 'crisis of Marxism' is to be located in the collapse of its real referents: it is an immanent and thoroughly political crisis, for which the analytical force of the critique of political economy remains of little import. Along with this collapse of referents, this political death, which seems to suggest the separation of a communist hypothesis from moribund Marxist politics, Badiou also points to certain symptoms – larval and obscure political subjects which indicate that if a Marxist politics is to be 'recomposed', it can no longer be in terms of political processes that take it as an explicit reference-point. Marxism has not just lost its historical foothold; it is no longer an internal referent for nascent forms of emancipatory politics. This is what is meant by the *expatriation* of Marxism, as the key aspect of the crisis that we must destructively traverse (let us not forget that for the Badiou of *Theory of the Subject*, the becoming of a subject, and of a proletarian subject especially, is intimately linked to its own destruction, so that the call to be heeded here is for Marxism to truly subjectivise itself, after having gone through the 'subjective destitution' of its referents). In a piece from 1983, Badiou declares:

> Today, the referents of Marxist politics are not Marxist. There is a fundamental delocalisation of Marxism. Previously, there was a kind of self-

---

24   Badiou 1985a, p. 28.
25   Badiou 1985a, p. 29.
26   Ibid.

reference, because Marxism drew its general credit from States that called themselves Marxist, from wars of national liberation under the direction of Marxist parties, from workers' movements framed by Marxist trade-unionists. But this referential apparatus is gone. The great mass historical pulsations no longer refer to Marxism, ever since, at least, the end of the cultural revolution in China: see Poland, or Iran. Therefore, there is an expatriation of Marxism. Its historical territoriality is no longer transitive to it. The era of self-reference is closed. Marxism no longer has a historical home. All the political referents endowed with a worker and popular life are, with regard to Marxism, atypical, delocalised, errant. Any orthodox Marxist today will object that the Polish movement is national and religious, that the Iranian movement is religious and fanatical, that there is nothing there that fundamentally matters for Marxism. And this orthodox Marxism will be nothing but an empty object in the process of the destruction of Marxism.[27]

This theme of expatriation thus allows Badiou to maintain, albeit in a problematic register, the reference to 'worker and popular life', as well as the crucial (communist) hypothesis of non-domination, in the face of some of the very events that served as grist to the post-Marxist mill. By thinking in terms of the dislocation of Marxist politics and the tentative invention of new forms of consciousness, rather than with reference to the analytic and ideological failure of Marxism, Badiou can turn the political conjuncture of the 1980s – the death throes of historical communism and the birth of heterogeneous political forms – into an opportunity for the recomposition of a politics of emancipation.[28] Crucially, this is not done in relation to a return to logics of electoral alliance or the articulation of group demands outside of the working class referent, but in view of the possibility of a new workers' politics at a distance from the State, a non-classist, non-systemic experience of proletarian capacity. Rather than seeing the 'crisis of Marxism' as a chance for singing

27 Badiou 1984, p. 1. Badiou also refers to this issue in terms of the separation of Marxism from the history of the 'marxisation' of the workers' movement, now that it is no longer 'a power of structuration of real history', meaning that politics may be freed from 'the marxed [marxisée] form of the political philosopheme'. Hence the radical caesura vis-à-vis the previous periodisation of Marxist politics, and the proposal of the figure of (re)commencement. See Badiou 1985a, pp. 58–9.

28 Another crucial moment is of course to be registered in the death-knell of the sequence begun in the Chinese Cultural Revolution. See Bosteels 2005 and Badiou's Le Monde editorial on the trial of the Gang of Four, Badiou 2005b.

the praises of political plurality, Badiou seems to discern within it the possibility of a further singularisation of emancipatory politics. The wager then
is to look for the traits of a new politics of anti-statist emancipation in these
mass symptoms, these hysterias of the social. Though it transcends the limits of this chapter, it would be fruitful to follow the attempts – ultimately
frustrated by the religious and populist sclerosis of the Polish and Iranian
situations – made in *Le Perroquet* to track moments of organisational invention and worker capacity in non-Marxist political scenarios. Contrary to post-
Marxism, which sees in the rise of 'new social movements' a radical-democratic
pluralism beyond universalist[29] and communist hypotheses, Badiou's post-
Leninism is committed, from the 1980s onwards, to producing a metapolitical
framework for thinking the persistence of communism as a minimal, universalising hypothesis even in political scenarios where the name 'communism' is
anathema.

The requirement that the destruction and recomposition of Marxist politics
be internal – which is to say not dictated by its supposed explanatory shortcomings, its political disasters, or novel sociological facts – is motivated by
an appraisal of the subjectivity that dominates the post-revolutionary Restoration of the virtues of liberal capitalism and parliamentary democracy.[30] The
peculiarity of the reactive (or renegade) subjects that, from the mid-seventies
onwards, publicised the return to liberty on the basis of their own failures lies
instead in the fact that they perceived the 'crisis of Marxism' simply as the
subjective discovery of an objective fact (crystallised by Badiou in their typical utterances: 'we tried, it was a catastrophe' and 'I fail, therefore I am'): the
fact of the impossibility of emancipation. But for Badiou all that these failures
and disasters prove is that the opposition to existent society is a 'difficult' problem. Just like a mathematician who fails in a proof does not thereby declare as
inexistent the problem it stemmed from, so a political militant does not make
failure into either a necessity or a virtue: 'So that what is presented to us as a
conjoined progress of morality (liberating us from the totalitarian phantasm)

---

29   See, for instance, this characteristic pronouncement: 'The discourse of radical democracy
      is no longer the discourse of the universal; the epistemological niche from which "uni-
      versal" classes and subjects spoke had been eradicated, and it has been replaced by a
      polyphony of voices, each of which constructs its own irreducible discursive identity. This
      point is decisive: there is no radical and plural democracy without renouncing the dis-
      course of the universal and its implicit assumption of a privileged point of access to "the
      truth", which can be reached only by a limited number of subjects.' Laclau and Mouffe
      1985, p. 191.
30   Badiou's condemnation of the past two decades as a new post-revolutionary 'Restoration'
      is summed up in Badiou 2005a.

and of realism (seeing the objective virtues of the existent state of things) is in fact a confession of incapacity. The essence of reneging is incompetence'.[31]

Badiou here intervenes directly in the anti-Marxist philosophy of the Restoration, which sees the defence of the 'negative liberties' at the heart of parliamentary democracy (or capitalist parliamentarianism, as he will later dub it). He repeats the idea of a termination of the Marxist-Leninist sequence, of its manner of arranging certain political factors,[32] but, crucially, contends that we cannot disregard the fact that antagonism to the status quo is still at the heart of any politics of emancipation, and moreover that a return to the Enlightenment thematic of liberty is grossly insufficient, since the question of equality, which determines 'a *current* stage of the political question', cannot be evaded. In what concerns the legacy and destruction of what he dubs the Marxist/Leninist 'montage', the question is how to practice, under the conditions of a non-despotic State, a politics whose axiom is equality: a contemporary politics beyond the modern debate between the State of right and law (parliamentary constitutional liberal democracy, the *Rechtstaat*) and tyranny. We cannot turn away from 'contemporary' politics, initially marked by the entrance of the signifier 'worker' into the political field, for the sake of a merely 'modern' anti-despotic politics of democracy.

Following Badiou's hazardous 'de-socialisation' of Marxism, however, equality must not be thought in terms of equality of 'material positions' ('economistically'), but in strictly political terms. The maxim of equality becomes the following: 'what must the world be such that an inegalitarian statement is impossible within it?' Badiou here draws a crucial difference between the *modern* politics of liberty, which, ever since Saint-Just, functions in a symbolic register, as a form of non-prohibition, and a *contemporary* politics of equality, whose aim is to really make impossible the production of inegalitarian statements (this will remain the chief characteristic of Badiou's later concept of the generic). What is surprising here, especially in terms of the earlier commitment to a communist dialectic of destruction, is the idea of a complementarity between the politics of liberty and the politics of equality, along with the stipulation of the general problem of equality in 'times of peace', as detached from the revolutionary problematic of power, war and the state: 'under the general

---

31   Badiou 1987, p. 2. See also the section in *Can Politics Be Thought?* entitled 'The reactive
       meaning of contemporary anti-Marxism', Badiou 1985a, pp. 48–51.

32   'It is certain that [the Marxist] montage is exhausted. There are no longer socio-political
       subjects, the revolutionary theme is desubjectivated, History has no objective meaning.
       All of a sudden, the antagonism of two camps is no longer the right projection for global
       hostility to existing society'. Badiou 1987, p. 3.

conditions of a non-despotic State, how can one think and practice a politics whose overarching philosophical category is equality?'[33] A politics of equality, in this framework, works within the symbolic politics of prohibition for the sake of real-impossible equality. It is as if, albeit 'at a distance', Badiou sees the project of emancipation as conditioned to some extent by the apolitical (or anti-political) horizon of a liberal polity.

This bears two interesting, and problematic consequences. The first is that politics cannot be primarily or directly concerned with the betterment of the polity itself, since 'politics must be thinkable as a conjoined excess over the State and civil society, even if these are good or excellent'.[34] But the second consequence lies in the implicit suggestion that the politics of emancipation, having rescinded the project of power (in short, the dictatorship of the proletariat) is externally conditioned ('in times of peace') by a kind of liberal frame. Here lies the entire ambiguity of Badiou's problematic of 'politics at a distance from the State'[35] – which both maintains the antagonism against 'existing society' and, to an extent, the problem of how to change it, but (perhaps in a simply provisional way) combines this seemingly stark antagonism with the toleration of the symbolic framework provided by the very same society: 'We therefore continue to demand modern freedom (symbolic according to non-prohibition) from within which we work towards contemporary equality (real, according to the impossible)'.[36] Is this to say that Marxist politics can only persist from within a liberal envelope? Can we 'reformulate *from within politics* the synthetic vision of the backwards and nefarious character of our society and its representations' and maintain the 'difficult' problem of 'changing existing society', if we do not unequivocally pose the problem of the tension between liberty

---

33   Ibid.
34   Badiou 1985a, p. 20.
35   Badiou 2005c, pp. 150–1. It is worth noting that Badiou does maintain that this thematic of distance is not simply placed 'after' historical communism but is intrinsically post-Leninist. In an interview following the publication of *Being and Event*, he declares that his 'horizon remains that of the withering away of the State' and is driven by the attempt to generate an 'intra-popular democratic process'. See Badiou 1991b. But this withering away is detached from the question of taking power, as the state is transformed into a non-political referent in the field of politics, so that an intra-popular process does not issue into a Leninist notion of proletarian democracy, which would require not a distance from, but the *smashing* of the State.
36   Badiou 1987, p. 3. In the French revolutionary triad, equality always maintains precedence for Badiou. As 'the authority of the Same', it trumps freedom (which is too close to opinion) and fraternity (which flirts too much with the substance of community). In brief, the virtue of equality lies in its abstraction – the very abstraction that Badiou will describe in terms of a prescriptive axiom of equality. See also Badiou 1992, p. 248.

(in the state) and equality (in politics), together with their mediation by issues of power and authority? To put it otherwise, can a post-Leninist radical politics of equality afford to be entirely post-revolutionary?

At times, Badiou's 1980s 'expatriation' of Marxism, which already presupposes a distance between Marxist politics and the Marxist critique of political economy, seems entirely to dissolve any consistency characterising the Marxist project, casting doubt on the very possibility of holding onto the term Marxism. After all, won't Badiou, in *Metapolitics*, peremptorily declare that '*Marxism doesn't exist*',[37] in the sense that its political instances – its 'historical modes' to use Sylvain Lazarus's terminology – are absolutely inconsistent? And yet, throughout the 1980s, prior to the publication of *Being and Event*, Badiou seems to maintain the liminal validity of the notion of 'Marxist politics', at least in the sense that it is only by rigorously undergoing its destruction (and not its ironic deconstruction) that a new politics of emancipation will be 'recomposed'. What is at stake in this retention, *in extremis*, of the name of Marxism (or of 'Marxist politics')? If anything, the Anglophone vogue for post-Marxism was driven by a rejection of the articulation between social class and revolutionary politics, which reduced the idea of the proletariat to one contested and hegemonically posited identity among others. Once again, despite surface similarities, the move beyond class operated by Badiou and his cohorts is based on an intra-political and historical judgement, namely on the idea of a lost efficacy of the 'classist' mode of politics (dominated by the category of contradiction, and the transitivity between society and politics).[38] This also why Badiou declares that there are more things in the crisis of Marxism than anti-Marxism can dream of – in the main because anti-Marxism merely registers an objective crisis without being able to think through its primary, subjective aspect.[39] This means, on the one hand, that an orthodox defence of Marxism comes down to rehashing the old refutations of old objections, thereby remaining on the terrain of anti-Marxism, and, on the other, that the crisis must be experienced not as a way of merely pluralising or dissolving Marxism, but as an opportunity to radicalise its emancipatory, egalitarian core.[40] This radical-

---

37 Badiou 2005c, p. 58.
38 See Lazarus 2005. This theme of 'classism' is dealt with in numerous interventions in *Le Perroquet* and its successor publication *La Distance politique* and *Le Journal politique*.
39 Badiou, p. 51.
40 Which is why Badiou declares, paradoxically, that 'the contemporary being of what will articulate the new figure of politics, and which will still be able to call itself "Marxism" in being able to continue the emancipatory hypothesis, is nothing other than the complete thinking of its destruction'. (Ibid.) Badiou can say this to the extent that Marxism has always been for him synonymous with political militancy and not social analysis; it is

isation or purification of Marxism into a minimal, heterodox Marxist politics (what Badiou has elsewhere referred to as a communism of singularities), is all the more interesting inasmuch as it explicitly wards off the possibility of a post-Marxist turn. For whilst Badiou and his comrades appear definite about the end of the working class as a *socio-political* class (making no such claims for the end of social class per se), they are equally definite that no emancipatory politics can bypass workers.

This plea for a minimal Marxism can be observed in two steps. The first involves what Badiou, explicitly harking back to the Kant of the *Critique of Pure Reason*, calls a 'refutation of idealism'. If Marxist politics is detached from the social as the 'place of bonds' (*les lieux des liens*), what prevents the kind of idealist pluralism according to which any site and any subject, unbound from the requirements of transitivity with an ordered and ontologically grounded social structure, can be the locus of emancipation? Badiou is very aware that having abandoned a dialectics of social latency and political subjectivation he cannot depend on the 'substantial presupposition' of a political privilege of workers. And yet, he knows that a 'maximal' interpretation of his political axiomatic could lead to declaring the emergence of a political subject to be possible at any point whatever. To counter this prospect, Badiou engages in a minimal inscription of the egalitarian wager-intervention on an event, in what he calls 'pre-political situations'.[41] Whilst this minimal, anticipatory interregnum between the social and politics does not allow a pre-emptive *construction* of political subjectivity (e.g. the party of the working class), it allows, by analogy with Kant, a merely negative *reductio ad absurdum* of the maximal claim of political contingency (any subjects, anywhere). Forbidding himself any substantive resort to social ontology, Badiou nevertheless wants to argue that to elude 'worker singularities' in the formation of a political subject would be to suppose that a politics of emancipation could deploy itself without including in its trajectory any of the places or points where the *dominated* are the majority of the inhabitants. Whence the following 'theorem':

> Political intervention under current conditions, i.e. modern politics, cannot strategically avoid being faithful to events, whose site is a worker or popular site. Let us suppose that it can. Since the axiomatic hypothesis is

---

not a doctrine, but 'the life of a hypothesis', and this life can take the form of a protracted process of destruction and recomposition.

41   'I call *pre-political situation* a complex of facts and statements in which the collective involvement of worker and popular singularities is felt, and in which the failure of the regime of the One is discernible'. Badiou 1985a, p. 76.

that of a politics of emancipation, that is, of a non-statist subjective politics under the aegis of non-domination, it would follow that this politics
could deploy itself without ever including in its immediate field places
where the mass (whatever its number) of the dominated – in modern conditions – materially exists, i.e. in factories, in the estates in the *banlieues*,
in immigrant housing, in the offices of repetitive IT work. Especially if
we consider factories, the exception would be radical, since we can easily establish that factories are separated from civil society and from the
moderating laws that sustain its social relations. According to this suppos-
ition, the politics of non-domination would only exist, for the dominated
themselves, in the form of representation, since no event giving rise to an
intervention would include them in terms of its site.[42]

The point is not simply that an emancipatory politics must include the lowest
rungs, the excluded, the oppressed, but that they and their 'site' must be directly
involved – in other words 'presented' – by the emergent political subject. Otherwise, we remain at the level of the State, or, in Badiou's politico-philosophical
terms, of representation. So, this refutation of idealism does not simply attack
(or literally reduce to absurdity) the 'new social movements' ideology according to which emancipation may take place anywhere, anytime, by anyone. It
also undermines any Left (or even Marxist) notion that the dominated may
be *represented* in a political *programme* without partaking of political action
themselves.[43]

It is moving from this idea of a pre-political 'site' and warding off both an
idealist pluralism and any kind of 'speculative leftism',[44] that Badiou will give a

---

42 Badiou 1985a, pp. 81–2.
43 In this sense, though Wood's arguments against post-Marxism about the evacuation of
    power and exploitation from its political horizon might be thrown at Badiou, the latter is
    immune to the devastating conjunctural charge made by Wood against the post-Marxists,
    or new 'true' socialists, to wit that their 'deconstruction' of Marxist metaphysics is func-
    tional to an option for ideological battles and alliances focalised around electoral contests,
    and 'the logic of their argument is an electoralist logic' (Wood 1998, p. 190). While post-
    Marxism, with its sympathies for Austro-Marxism and the second International, signals a
    definite, if particularly elliptical, option for reform over revolution, Badiou's 'Marxist polit-
    ics' of the 1980s – and, we could argue, his later thinking and practice – appears entirely
    indifferent to this alternative. However, it is a stance founded on a drastic separation from
    the idea of a political 'programme' (as a mediation between subjective will and objective
    transformation) which renders his position inimical to the likes of Wood.
44 See Bosteels 2005b and 2011. See also, for background and analysis, Peter Hallward's
    chapter on politics in Hallward 2003 as well as his important article on 'The Politics of
    Prescription', Hallward 2005.

meta-ontological solution to these problems of Marxist politics in *Being and Event*. Starting from the intuition of a *reductio ad absurdum* of anti-worker political idealism, Badiou initially develops his theory of the event-site – a crucial component of his mature philosophy – in terms of the *factory* and of the worker as the subjective figure of politics. This is the second step, as it were, in the argument for a Marxist politics that would be capable of following its own metaphysical destruction. In 'The Factory as Event-Site', a text published in *Le Perroquet* in 1987 and originally intended for inclusion in *Being and Event*, we encounter both a potent distillate of Badiou's overall doctrine and his last explicit attempt to defend, in however minimal a fashion, a notion of Marxist politics.[45] That article's argument is philosophically far more intricate and challenging than the prescriptive and axiomatic positions rehearsed hitherto, showing a speculative daring far greater than the clever repetition of Kant's refutation. In a sense, what I have sought to do in this chapter is to demonstrate the internal theoretical and political necessity leading to this work on the event-site and, in so doing, to show how Badiou's intimate confrontation with Marxism is at the very foundation (albeit a vanishing one, since he eventually chose to omit this 'example') of the project crystallised in *Being and Event*. A closer investigation of the links between 'The Factory as Event-Site' and Badiou's further work should of course be carried out, but for now I would simply like to indicate the work that the concept of the event-site does in Badiou's attempt to maintain a minimal, liminal Marxism.

Far more than any of the other texts in *Le Perroquet*, this excised fragment of *Being and Event* pleads for a return to Marx (and Engels) that would even seem to bypass the post-Leninist reference. In 'The Factory as Event-Site' Badiou puts his metaontological and metapolitical investigation under the aegis of two conceptual inheritances of the Marxian thinking of worker politics, which the attempt to 'recompose' a Marxist politics seeks to weave together. These are *the void*, which in the Marxist apparatus is connected to the peculiarity of the proletarian (having *nothing* to sell but his labour-power, the proletarian is the bearer of a generic capacity), and *the site*, which Badiou links to Engels's inquiries into the localised material conditions under which exploitation is organised and resisted. In a pithy declaration, Badiou will define his philosophical undertaking in terms of a different articulation, a different dialectic, of these two terms, one that moves beyond the 'fictions' of orthodox Marxism: 'at the very heart of the objectivist version of the necessity of a worker reference, we

---

encounter two terms, the void and the site, which as we will see only acquire their full meaning once we decentre them in the direction of the subjective the vision of politics'.[46]

Without going into the details of Badiou's exposition, we should note that in asserting that a political event can only take place if it considers the factory as event-site, Badiou aims to provide a kind of minimal objectivity (i.e. another refutation of idealism) *without* making the intervention of politics and of political subjectivation transitive to a socio-economic datum. As he puts it: 'The paradoxical statement I am defending is finally that the factory, by which I mean the factory as a workers' place, belongs without doubt to the socio-historical presentation (it is counted-as-one within it), but not the workers, to the extent that they belong to the factory. So that the factory – as a workers' place – is not *included* in society, and the workers (of a factory) do not form a pertinent "part", available for State counting.'[47] This is the sense in which the factory is not the hidden abode of a production that could be reappropriated and disalienated, but a pre-political site 'at the edge of the void' (of the unpresented fact of domination), into which politics can intervene. The correlate of this notion is that the (proletarian) void itself is detached from an expressive logic of (dis)alienation and rearticulated to the notion of a production of the Same, a production of communism no longer immanently bound to a communism of production.[48] It is on the basis of the speculative trajectory laid out in 'The Factory as Event-Site' that Badiou can then reassert his (knotted, heterodox, errant) fidelity to Marxism:

> Reduced to its bare bones, Marxism is both the hypothesis of a politics of non-domination – a politics subtracted from the statist count of the count – and the designation of the most significant event sites of modernity, those whose singularity is maximal, which are worker sites. From this twofold gesture there follows that the intervening and organised experimentation of the hypothesis must ceaselessly prepare itself for the consideration of these sites, and that the worker reference is a feature of politics, without which one has *already* given up subtracting oneself from the State count. That is the reason why it remains legitimate to call oneself a Marxist, if one maintains that politics is possible.[49]

---

46   Ibid.
47   Ibid.
48   On these terms, and many of the issues having to do with the shifts in Badiou's thinking, see Chapter 1 in this volume.
49   Badiou 1986.

To the extent that Badiou's subsequent work remains more or less wholly consistent with the research programme of this 1987 article, we could consequently
hazard to read it as an attempt to think Marxism 'reduced to its bare bones'.

Inasmuch as the above has added some intelligibility to the vicissitudes of
Badiou's (meta)political thinking, its leave-taking from Marxism-Leninism and
its (re)commencement of Marxism, I hope it has also given rise to certain per-
plexities that can be made to resonate with the rest of Badiou's work and its
ongoing political interpretations. Simply by way of conclusion, I would like
to touch on two problems that are especially acute in this decisive phase of
Badiou's production.

The first concerns the manner in which Badiou remains faithful to a certain Marxian intuition about proletarian subjectivity and its political dynamics. Badiou, after all, defines the continuity-in-separation between the Marxian
legacy and his effort at its (re)commencement as follows: 'we (re)formulate
the hypothesis of a proletarian political capacity'.[50] However, the refutation
of idealism and maintenance of the 'worker reference' in other texts seems to
demand the evacuation of any pre-political subjective privilege to workers per
se (politics must touch on their sites, but they are not latent political subjects
qua workers). Can the void of the situation be equated with a political capacity?
And if this capacity is only the retroactive effect of a post-evental intervention (the politicisation of the factory axiomatically determines that 'workers
think') is the term 'capacity' really viable, considering its unavoidable links
to notions of disposition and potential and to the theory of (dis)alienation?
I would suggest that Badiou's philosophical conceptualisation of the concept
of the generic in *Being and Event* may be read as an attempt to transcend what
appear to be tensions in his earlier 'Marxist politics' by maintaining the link
between the void, equality and the subject without relying on any latency or
capacity whatsoever.

The second problem is connected to the sources, as it were, of emancipatory
politics. Badiou obviously wishes to purify and politicise the concept of equality, sever its dependence on merely material criteria. But, in his allergy to the
socialising fictions of orthodox Marxism, he seems to step back from contemporary criteria of politics to merely modern ones by framing his entire vision
of Marxist politics in terms of the politico-philosophical concepts of exclusion,
domination and representation. In a manner that is perhaps most obvious in
the section on the 'ontology of the site' in 'The Factory as Event-Site', Badiou
appears to deny the possibility that the concept of *exploitation* may be an uncir-

---

50   Badiou 1984, p. 8.

cumventable touchstone of any *contemporary* politics. As I argued in the next chapter, the difference between a politics at a distance from the state and a politics against capital might lie in the fact that the latter cannot be encompassed by the question of representation, inasmuch as capitalist power, while reliant on mechanisms of representation, also works 'directly' on singularities themselves, in ways that cannot be easily mapped in terms of exclusion, invisibility or domination. This is precisely what is at stake in the vicissitudes of the concept of value in the critique of political economy, a concept which I would suggest cannot be easily harnessed by the logic of re/presentation. The resulting (and rather formidable) challenge would be to combine the immediate politicisation of exploitation that characterises Marx's own work,[51] with some of the metaontological and metapolitical tools provided by texts such as 'The Factory as Event-Site'. A traversal of the logic of exploitation and its effects on our thinking of political subjectivity would also allow us to ward off the possibility of an 'aristocratic' solution, distantly reminiscent of Hannah Arendt's republican and councilist advocacy of the autonomy of politics against the disastrous impingements of the 'social question'.[52] This would of course force us to face head on one of the most arresting questions raised by Badiou's 'expatriation' of Marxism: is contemporary politics (the politics of positive equality) compatible with the continuation of modern, statist politics (the politics of negative freedom)? Or must it risk being 'anti-modern', and work on equality not just at a distance from, but *against* the State? This is not to suggest that Marx, like a political Odysseus, may soon be repatriated, and that we, faithful Penelopes warding off our post-Marxist suitors, can finally recognise him under unfamiliar garb. More modestly, let us suggest that Badiou's connection between the expatriation of Marxism and the (re)commencement of a Marxist politics is a salutary alternative to the quarrels between the antiquarians and the renegades, as well as a unique philosophical platform from which to (re)think Marx's politics.

---

51 See Kouvelakis 2004 and Tomba 2007.
52 Arendt 1963, especially Chapter 6: 'The Revolutionary Tradition and its Lost Treasure'.

CHAPTER 3

From the State to the World

What about the rest? The elephant-capital? It's the cement court on which the real game is played. Don't confuse the tarred surface with Bjorn Borg's run. The fact that the same man, Marx, is the cement engineer and the champion of the net heralds the new epoch of the polyvalent worker.

BADIOU 1982, p. 296

• • •

We can't defeat the system through isolated actions; we must engage it on all fronts – the university, the prisons, and the domain of psychiatry – one after another since our forces are not strong enough for a simultaneous attack. We strike and knock against the most solid obstacles; the system cracks at another point; we persist. It seems that we're winning, but then the institution is rebuilt; me must start again. It is a long struggle; it is repetitive and seemingly incoherent. But the system it opposes, as well as the power exercised through the system, supplies its unity.

FOUCAULT 1994

• •
•

It seems beyond dispute that the enthusiasm (as well as the hostility) that has greeted the thought of Alain Badiou in certain quarters within the Anglophone philosophical world is not only to be ascribed to the daunting originality and rare speculative force of his systematic project but also to its provocative political charge. In some respects this should be anything but astonishing; setting aside for the time being Badiou's own political militancy, the stringent demands of a militant intellect transpire from many, if not most, of Badiou's writings; whether directly, in the urgency of a metapolitical theorem or an ethical directive, or elliptically, as the formalised sediment of an endeavour to cognise the requirements of a novel philosophical figure of subjectivity. We should also not ignore the pressure exerted, in our intellectual conjuncture, by an often-stagnant politico-philosophical landscape, one rendered even more debilitating when it is punctuated – but certainly not punctured – by a concern with ethics and subjectivity devoid of anything but an imaginary relationship to political emancipation. Furthermore, the strenuous conviction with which the singularity of the political, and of its dignity as an immanent mode of thought (and not just a 'practice' that would serve as the occasional or occasioning object of philosophical reflection), is treated in Badiou's work has struck a chord, uncertain as its resonance may still be. And yet, as some have intimated, the core of Badiou's thought seems in many regards to be remarkably indifferent to what over the past few years has appeared as the floating referent of a politics whose retreat – whether 'empirical' or philosophical – might be drawing to a close, for better or worse. This referent is that of 'anti-capitalism'.

Both in its informational circulation and in its assumption as the watchword of a growing host of demonstrations of antagonism and refusal, many effects of indeterminacy have attached themselves to this unstable and symptomatic syntagm, turning it into a veritable lure for political practice. The reasons for the conspicuous absence of an explicit channel of communication between Badiou's current doctrine and the set of struggles gathered under the banner of anti-capitalism are certainly complex and must be sought in some of the fundamental tenets of Badiou's doctrine. An investigation of their sources may offer valuable clues about Badiou's metapolitics. What is more, it might lead us to question whether such an absence is intrinsic to Badiou's position or whether it is instead determined by some avoidable properties that have been ascribed, perhaps unjustly, to 'anti-capitalist' politics.

We could legitimately begin this investigation by interrogating Badiou on the question of antagonism. This is, after all, the crucial instance around which the passage from his Maoist philosophy of destructive subjectivation to his later thinking of a subtractive 'politics without a party' was articulated, most explicitly in that brief but pivotal text which is *Can Politics Be Thought?* To comprehend the tortuous fate of the figure of antagonism in Badiou's thought, following its arresting apotheosis in *Theory of the Subject*, is perhaps to seize the conjunctural and theoretical necessity of the qualified break with the dialectical impetus that had driven Badiou's thought up to his 'destruction' of the political fictions behind much Marxist politics. Alas, this would be a gargantuan task, one that would need to track the many mutations in Badiou's thinking of subjectivation and face up to the successive formalisations that sustain them (vital indications in this direction have been made by Bruno Bosteels;[1] I have

---

1   See Bosteels 2001, 2002 and 2011.

attempted to track some of these transformations in terms of Badiou's visions of 'communism'[2]). To put it succinctly, what becomes of the metapolitical conception of capitalism when it is no longer linked to class struggle as the chief arena of political subjectivation?[3] Whilst I hope, in the final analysis, to have elucidated some of the motivations for such a suspension or transfiguration of antagonism, it will be only by a detour, one undertaken against the grain of the theory of the subject, that is, from the perspective of the structure of situations, or, to use the terminology of Badiou's sequel to *Being and Event*, from that of the 'logics of worlds'.[4] This detour will not be so subtle, however, beginning as it does with the rather vulgar question: What does Badiou's more recent (post-Maoist or post-dialectical) work have to say about capitalism? And what resources does his thought supply to come to terms with the intrusion of Capital into the field of philosophy?

Before we touch upon the explicit replies to this question, we must confront the resolute disdain for empiricism ubiquitously evinced by Badiou's thought. Both in his mathematised ontology and his theory of the subject – and *a fortiori*, in the delicate articulation of these two – Badiou's founding gesture is that of evacuating the phenomenal density and persistent enticement borne by the 'fact' that things are 'thus and so'. In the dimension of politics, this inaugural evacuation is accompanied by a sovereign disregard – when not indeed a full-blown contempt – for anything that smacks of socio-economic analysis.[5] What summons thought, whether it be the rigorous formalisation of the inconsistency of being-multiple or the infinite composition of a truth from the vanishing irruption of an event, as sustained by the fidelity of a subject, is beyond, or rather beneath, the realm of phenomena. In other words, it is impervious to any generally applicable regime of visibility, whether cognitive, sociological, or straightforwardly empirical.

Whilst it would be fundamentally unfaithful to attribute this stubborn anti-empiricism to any sort of Gnostic or negative-theological inclinations on Badiou's part, and though, as I hope to show, the configurations of factuality do play a role in his thinking, it is undeniable that a stark *disqualification* of reality (as opposed to the immanent exception of the Real) is what, for Badiou, defines thought as a separation, a distancing, or, more technically, a subtraction.[6] Philosophy (in its indifference to experience) and politics (in its scorn

---

2   See Chapter 1 in this volume.
3   As it remained in Badiou 1982, p. 44.
4   Badiou 2006b and 2008.
5   Hallward 2003, pp. 279–84.
6   Badiou 1992 and 2004a; Hallward 2003, pp. 161–3, and Chapter 1 in this volume.

for the administration of reality) bear a more than elective affinity. Abstraction and subjectivation, as moments when the 'human animal' lays claim to the status of 'Immortal',[7] precisely involve a disfiguration of the limits of possibility that define any reality principle. In this respect, for Badiou, politics and philosophy exist for the sake of affirming an impossible-Real *and to draw the consequences of this impossible-Real for 'reality' and 'possibility'.* This is something all-too easily forgotten by those among Badiou's critics who mistakenly view him as a thinker of the fulgurating, immaculate Act. As Badiou himself remarks: 'we must point out that in what concerns its material the event is not a miracle. What I mean is that what composes an event is always extracted from a situation, always related back to a singular multiplicity, to its state, to the language that is connected to it, etc. In fact, so as not to succumb to an obscurantist theory of creation *ex nihilo*, we must accept that an event is nothing but a part of a given situation, nothing but a *fragment of being*.'[8]

Furthermore, to the extent that in the last instance facticity can only be sustained by a dense network of placements, a network whose principle guarantees the localisation of every existential instance in an ordered and structured space of appearing, as well as a seemingly exception-less count, the political ontology at work in Badiou's writings is founded, as Peter Hallward has insistently indicated (and criticised), on a profound disregard for the primacy of relation.[9] Not only is there no natural or cosmic bond, no Aristotelian *telos* that would essentially bind a being to its *topos*, but the resources of set-theoretical ontology allegedly allow us to approach being qua being (i.e. the multiple) irrespective of any constitutive form of interaction, as well as independently of any concern for the supposedly relational character of processes of individuation. One of the fundamental categories of Badiou's politics, as well as of his ontology, is unbinding, *déliaison*. Being qua being, as axiomatically presented in mathematical ontology, and the generic being of the collective, as affirmed by a political truth procedure, are both unbound, that is infinite, non-denumerable and unrepresentable. It is at this crucial juncture that Capital enters the scene as a figure pregnant with ambivalence for a thinking of a radical, egalitarian and fully 'unbound' politics.

If we turn to the *Manifesto for Philosophy*, and specifically to the section entitled 'Nihilism?', we witness, *pace* Badiou's disdain for socio-economic facticity and regulation, a genuine paean to the equivocal grandeur of Capital, explicitly re-affirming, and indeed quoting, the epochal diagnosis of that other

---

7 Badiou 1993, p. 75.
8 Badiou 2004a, p. 43.
9 Hallward 2003, pp. 284–91.

manifesto, penned a century and a half earlier by Marx and Engels. In a few, rather lyrical, lines Badiou sketches a figure which, whilst it may be familiar to anyone reflecting upon the link between communism and modernism, is nevertheless a somewhat disruptive, if inevitable, intruder into the coherence of his own account of politics and of the metapolitical assumption of politics by philosophy.[10] Briefly, Badiou reiterates the image of Capital as the solvent of the natural, self-evident or revealed bond, whether this be social (the particular community) or religious (the *re-ligio*, literally the binding of the sense of the world to the reason and/or will of the creator). Yet what is at stake here is not the mere registering of the corrosive force borne by the 'roaming automatism' of Capital – to wit, the subjection of any available being to the inhuman imperative of surplus-value. Were that the case, Badiou's stance would be inconsequential, yet another reason for passivity, pessimism or idolatrous apologia. The claim is far deeper and more unsettling in what it bodes for thought in general. Capital is not simply the empirical effectuation of a ubiquitous unbinding, as determined by the measureless measure that is money as a general equivalent, and by the transcendental requirement of surplus value; rather, Capital is the 'historical medium' of a subtractive ontology, an ontology that would regard being qua being as inconsistent multiplicity woven out of the void. An ontology, moreover, which would serve as the background for the 'communist invariants' and 'communism of singularities' espoused by Badiou.[11] As Badiou writes in the *Manifesto*:

> That everything that is *bound up* proves that in terms of being it is unbound; that the reign of the multiple is the unfathomable depths of what is presented without exception; that the One is but the result of transitory operations – there lies the inescapable effect of the universal placing of the terms of our situation within the circulating movement of the general monetary equivalent. [...] Yet, for Marx, and for us, desacralisation is not in the least nihilistic insofar as 'nihilism' must signify that which declares that the access to being and truth is impossible. On the contrary, desacralisation is a *necessary condition* for the disclosing of such an approach to thought. It is obviously the only thing we can and must welcome within Capital: it exposes the pure multiple as the foundation of presentation; it denounces every effect of One as a simple, precarious configuration; it dismisses the symbolic representations in which the bond found a semb-

---

10   Badiou 1998.
11   Badiou 1991a and 2003b, pp. 126–40; see also Chapter 1 in this volume.

lance of being. That this destitution operates in the most complete barbarity must not conceal its properly *ontological* virtue.[12]

Adding, in a further variation on this text:

> The passage where Marx speaks of the desacralisation of all sacred bonds
> in the icy waters of capitalism has an enthusiastic tone; it is Marx's enthu-
> siasm for the dissolving power of Capital. The fact that Capital revealed
> itself to be the material power capable of disencumbering us of the 'super-
> ego' figures of the One and the sacred bonds that accompany it effect-
> ively represents its positively progressive character, and it is something
> that continues to unfold to the present day. Having said that, the gener-
> alised atomism, the recurrent individualism and, finally, the abasement
> of thought into mere practices of administration, of the government of
> things or of technical manipulation, could never satisfy me as a philo-
> sopher. I simply think that it is in the very element of desacralisation that
> we must reconnect to the vocation of thinking.[13]

Most readers will be familiar by now with one of the distinctive features of
Badiou's speculative proposal, that of putting philosophy under the condition of events that produce truths in immanent registers of thought, otherwise
known as the *conditions* of philosophy. In this regard, the seemingly subject-less
or impersonal operation of Capital seems as though it should be immediately,
if not intuitively, disqualified from any pretension to 'conditional' status. Its
'mediocrity', to use Badiou's own term, derives from its unthinking, asubjective
barbarity. Capitalism is the 'truth-less horror which exposes the material for a
possible truth', whose desert-like imperative we are summoned to 'displace'.[14] I
submit that there is perhaps more than meets the eye in Badiou's passing statement that Capital is 'certainly the only nihilistic potency of which men have
succeeded in being the inventors as well as the prey': statements such as this
could open up the field for a critical inquiry into how Capital 'itself' has been
successively subjectivated, in what sequences, with what effects ... As Domin-
iek Hoens has brought to my attention, we could even think of the IMF or the
WTO, or credit agencies like Moody's or Standard & Poor's, as faithful 'subjects'
of Capital, strenuously eliminating any obstacle in the path of the hegemony of
surplus-value. It's undeniable that names like 'Bretton Woods', 'Davos', the 'Fed',

---

12   Badiou 1999, pp. 55–6.
13   Badiou 1990a, p. 6.
14   Badiou 1992, p. 218.

and figures like Paul Volcker or Alan Greenspan have often generated, among our elites, political affects of considerable intensity; moreover, as some have pointed out, 'class consciousness' today is arguably a concept more suited to the Fortune 500 than the factory floor. As the billionaire Warren Buffett notoriously quipped: 'There's class warfare, all right, but it's my class, the rich class, that's making war, and we're winning.' All the more reason to note that Badiou himself has struggled for many years with the question of whether reactionary or non-egalitarian politics are to be envisaged as subjective. In *Theory of the Subject* he begins by ascribing subjectivity to the bourgeoisie[15] only to subsequently repeal it, whilst in his work on the axiomatic theory of the subject he seems to be returning to a notion of the possibility of a non-egalitarian subjectivity, through a schematisation of subjective space.[16]

Yet, though it is perhaps not a condition of philosophy in the strict sense, Capital does seem to present the occasioning or inaugural cause for a subtractive ontology of the multiple (such that we could even envisage it, following Deleuze and Guattari, as a meta- or hyper-condition of ontology[17]). This idea of a 'historical medium' cannot but strike us as a short-circuit of the strictly mathematical immanence of the ontological situation, as if Capital were the Christ – Badiou does, alas, speak of a 'revelation' – of the multiple, the *transcendental (or meta-) event* which doubles as the harbinger of the very conditions for eventality itself. Leaving aside for a moment the arduous question of how to integrate such an instance into the conceptual and formal frame of Badiou's system, we should reflect upon how Badiou himself qualifies this historical-transcendental status of Capital.

For Badiou, Capital is *by no means* the irruption of the multiple *as such* (which is, after all, what transits through the subjective production of truths); what guides the originary (*ursprüngliche*) accumulation whereby Capital disregards and disfigures all bonds – to wit, the 'algorithmic', recursive imperative of surplus value[18] – is also what requires it to perpetually reproduce figures of the bond, (ac)countable instances of relationality that can supply it with the materials from whence to extract surplus. Without the territorialisation of production, the myriad manners in which 'incorporeal' or fictitious capital constantly reconfigures its spatio-temporal parameters and the exploitable sources of surplus-value, capitalism would literally have no hold over social and economic being. Every extraction and forced integration – of labour-power,

---

15   Badiou 1982, p. 60. See Chapter 5 in this volume.
16   Hallward 2003, pp. 144–8.
17   See Brassier 2000 and 2004.
18   Brassier 2004.

intellectual property, biological material ... – into the cycles of accumulation represents by the same token a 'new enclosure'.[19] To borrow from the Marxist historical geographer David Harvey, there is no accumulation of capital and no global consolidation of capitalism as a hegemonic system of social interaction and reproduction without 'uneven geographical development'. As Harvey writes, capitalism's 'radical transformation' has been accompanied by

> physical transformations that are breathtaking in scope and radical in their implications. New productive forces have been produced and distributed across the face of the earth. Vast concentrations of capital and labour have come together in metropolitan areas of incredible complexity, while transport and communications systems, stretched in far-flung nets around the globe, permit information and ideas as well as material goods and even labour power to move around with relative ease. [...] [T]his physical transformation has not progressed evenly. Vast concentrations of productive power here contrast with relatively empty regions there. Tight concentrations of activity in one place contrast with sprawling far-flung development in another. All of this adds up to what we call the 'uneven geographical development' of capitalism.[20]

Without a determinate if fleeting anchor, without spatial and temporal organisation, the predatory excess of surplus value is entirely powerless – in other words, there is an *intrinsic* link between the ever more unbridled and unbound character of fictitious finance capital and the creation of new spaces of exploitation, such as the export-processing zones in the 'developing' world,[21] as well as the relentless attempts at producing 'spatial fixes' to perpetuate capital accumulation in the face of periodic crises.[22] In this light, we can regard Capital's disdain for any particularity *as such* (this or that source of surplus-value) as but the reverse of its need for *any* particularity as such (*a* source of surplus-value). Whence Badiou's claim that Capital is the 'singularity *that has no regard for any singularity as such*'.[23] To put it in different terms, Capital is *a pure operation and not a truth procedure*.[24] This constitutive ambivalence – grandeur and

---

19   Notes from Nowhere 2003, p. 27.

20   Harvey 1999, p. 373.

21   Klein 2000, pp. 204–29.

22   Harvey 1999.

23   Badiou 1997a, p. 10.

24   The repercussions of this claim for Badiou's notion of politics and of mathematics have been admirably dealt with in Brassier 2004.

mediocrity entwined – which Marxists have often sought to present as *the* contradiction in capitalism, as an index of imminent and immanent demise, might be the very force of capital, what may be defined as its full-fledged ontological *opportunism*.

Viewed at a sufficient level of abstraction or formalisation, the unbinding praised in our two manifestos – whilst it must be seconded by any philosophy that extricates itself from the pious glue of meaning and religion – is an *asubjective* consequence of the operations of surplus value, for which multiplicity, pliant and unfettered, is nothing but an object of exploitation. In this respect, surplus-value is nothing if not the figure of an 'excessive count', a count that draws, from the socio-economic materials that it indifferently affects, the means whereby to perpetually exceed itself (it is telling that in Badiou's brief presentation in the *Manifesto* the link between surplus-value and surplus-labour is ignored if not effaced, as are the 'workerist' themes of real subsumption, general intellect and social cooperation – this is the obverse, of course, of the return of 'worker' as a political or subjective name purged of systemic-dialectical rationality in the directives of L'Organisation politique, as discussed in our previous chapter).

A conclusion, albeit a tentative one, can now be drawn – to wit, that the ontological status of Capital differs from that of the State. When Badiou tells us that: 'No symbolic sanction of the bond is capable of resisting the abstract potency of Capital',[25] how can we not consider – especially on the grounds of the obscene evidence of contemporary national and geopolitical situations (from the sordid debates on 'national identity' to the sinister edicts of the Project for a New American Century in the 2000s and MAGA and related national-capitalisms in the 2010s and 2020s) – the extent to which all States do effectively resort to an often unspoken primal bond, at the very least in the shape of the fundamental biopolitical fantasy that links the contingency of a birth to the putative endowment of rights? Undoubtedly there is no unambiguous sense in which Capital *intends* the dissolution of the State bond, and it is certainly the case that the State provides what is perhaps an indispensable instance of reterritorialisation, a 'fix' that not only generates sufficiently stable parameters for the roaming accumulation of Capital, but also provides the most visible means for the required political and military control over the systematic, yet highly selective removal of the barriers to Capital's automatism. However, on the basis of Badiou's own pronouncements, it is clear enough that whilst the articulation may be necessary for one of our two partners (State and Capital) in the

---

25   Badiou 1999, p. 55.

seizure and control of singularity, what we are confronted with here is a difference in kind, the difference between two logics – along the lines of what
Giovanni Arrighi has identified as the territorial logic of (State) power and the
capitalist logic of power.[26] Indeed, the empirical resistances of actually existing States against moments of stark capitalist rationality are more numerous
than one may at first suspect – a case in point is represented by the *territorial*
measures against immigration into states whose welfare systems are presently
unsustainable, according to the *capitalist* logic imposed by fiscal exigencies and
debt crises.

Whilst it may be intuitively plausible to argue that Capital and State, though
perhaps *de facto* inextricable, are distinguished by a (logical) difference in kind,
it would be somewhat imprudent to base ourselves here on writings by Badiou
which are arguably in a 'peripheral' position vis-à-vis his doctrine (a 'manifesto' and the introduction to his *Saint Paul*). This is all the more imperative
to the extent that an intra-theoretical distinction between State and Capital is
not to be found in Badiou's own writings, and, in one instance at least, seems
to be altogether elided.[27] Now, if a collective politics of emancipation is to be
viewed, in line with Badiou, in the guise of an immanent and illegal excess,
bringing forth into presentation the void that the representation of a situation
is calculated to foreclose, then surely the qualification of *what* precisely this
politics exceeds – interrupting it with its void, engineering a systematic upsurge
of inconsistency – is a crucial matter. To put it more concisely, if State and
Capital are not isomorphic, then we should be able to assess, *from the point
of view of the subject of an event* (in this instance, an organised political collective), how a counter- or extra-State politics differs from an anti-capitalist
one.

To delineate this hypothesis, let us briefly recall the ontological determination of Badiou's concept of State. Distilling the matter to what is strictly essential for our present purposes, and admittedly blurring the distinction between
the political and ontological senses of the term, the State is the structure that
forecloses the danger posed by the errancy of the ontological void – an errancy
that would reveal the unfounded character of the political datum – by doubling the counting that a situation already effects with a count of the count,
in the guise of a counting (or 'partition') of all the parts of a situation (in
set-theoretical vocabulary, this entails a move from belonging to inclusion; in
philosophical terms from presentation to representation). This re-presentative

26   Harvey 2003, p. 27.
27   Badiou 1998, p. 164.

articulation of the State onto the situation is marked by an immeasurable excess, of the relationship of *inclusion* (the parts of a situation counted or represented by the State) over belonging (the elements of the situation counted by its 'native' structure). This excess, according to the Cohen-Easton theorem, is wholly erratic, cannot be fixed from within the situation and must be the object of an 'unfounded' decision. With the addition of Badiou's theorem of the point of excess this means that there is always something in the representative operation of the State that stands in a 'relation' of *excrescence* to the situation. This is what Badiou defines as the *impasse of being* and the sole point at which politics may be said to pass, by way of the formalisation of a rupture, a dysfunction, allowing the Real of inconsistency to affect a consistent reality.[28]

The excess of inclusion over belonging is the ontological inscription of a constitutive *domination*, a domination deriving from the intrinsic imperative of the State, which is that of foreclosing the errancy of the void by blocking the possibility that un-binding may present itself as such. The imperative is plain: nothing must be out of place, nothing unaccounted for. On this basis, Badiou concludes that the only politics of emancipation, the only politics that could strive to undo the partiality of representation founded on this excessive principle of domination, must base itself upon, or rather must *decide* for something that invisibly lies 'beneath' the law of the State, in the sense that the domination of the State is so absolute that this element, this fragment of the Real, is not even allowed to enter into representation.

From a certain vantage point, this political *singularity*, inscribed in an event-site that *belongs to* but is not *included by* the State, is utterly empty, devoid of content, and can only be retroactively attested by what it can force the State to include, thus terminating the given regime of its functioning. Politics invariably takes its departure from an excess – the hidden excess of a singularity subtracted from but absolutely dominated by the law of a situation – and is aimed at inhibiting or terminating another excess, the excess of domination, the excess of the State. It follows from this dialectic of two excesses – the infra-representative excess of singularity and the supra-representative one of the excrescent State – that *no politics of non-domination can be founded on the proposal of a new order with which to substitute the old*. Not the figure of a new bond, but the invention – extracted from the singularity of an event and directed at the structure of representation – of an experiment in political unbinding, is what, according to Badiou, the politics of non-domination requires. This definitional hostility to the very thematic of order and power signifies that a politics

---

28   Badiou 1988, pp. 109–28.

of the generic must take place at a distance from the State or, more precisely, that it must hold fast to the wager that such a distance is in fact possible.

Having inventoried these relatively minimal indications, let us turn once again to the question of Capital. Whilst politics may indeed be characterised in its subjective figure by a certain mode of self-presupposition – given that nothing in the State allows an instance of immanent and generic exception to appear, to be represented – and thus appear marked by its distance *vis-à-vis* the excrescence of State representation, it is not beside the point to consider what this distance may be *to*. The non-dialectical and anti-systemic principle of distance that defines real politics for Badiou, the principled intransitivity of politics to the laws that order social or economic situations – i.e. the outright denial of any *reformist* or *revisionist* image of politics – *does not* entail the ascription to politics of any sort of purity or autonomy. Whilst there is no politics without an initial disregard for the laws of representation or the rules of appearance – without a wager on the impossible linked to the singularity of an event – there is no fidelity to this event without an insistent and organised inquiry into the consequences to be drawn from the irruption of the singular into the ordered. Returning to the differential articulation of the logic of the State and the logic of Capital, let us pose the following question: are the distance and fidelity of politics, qua criteria for its integrity as the truth procedure of non-domination, affected, or even transformed, by the ubiquity of Capital as a mode of domination heterogeneous to, if articulated with, that of the State?

As we have already remarked, Capital as indifferent singularity and historical medium is related to the fundamental ontological unbinding in a manner that differs from the ordered and apparently exhaustive inclusion effected by the State. At a basic level, whilst 'the State is not founded on the social bond, which it would express, but on un-binding, which it prohibits',[29] Capital is instead, by Badiou's own definition, the most prominent historical *agent* of unbinding. Though in his *Saint Paul* Badiou may have termed it a singularity,[30] Capital is *not*, to remain within the doctrinal apparatus of *Being and Event*, a presented-without-representation. Indeed, whilst the representatives of Capital are legion (though they are never its representatives *sans phrase*, always of this or that corporation, this or that interest – pharmaceuticals vs. oil, Big Tech vs. manufacturing, Democrats vs. Republicans ...) as is its universal lieutenant, money, Capital 'itself' – conceived as the abstract principle of social transformation – is, alas, nowhere to be found. Conversely, it is not technically speaking

29   Badiou 1988, p. 125.
30   Badiou 1997a, p. 10.

an 'excrescence', in that whilst it counts and partitions with an abstract ferocity arguably unmatched, especially in its mobility and plasticity, by the representations of the State, it does this with lavish disregard for any stable figure or symbol of the count. As Deleuze presciently remarked in his 'Postscript on the Society of Control',[31] the object of Capital in the age of ubiquitous control is not the individual body of discipline, but a *dividual* material, an indifferent coded sequence (which can go above or beneath the threshold of individuality) from which surplus-value may be extracted.

Remaining at this level, that of the fugitive ontological composition of Capital, it is also worth considering Giorgio Agamben's remark, in his *Homo Sacer*, that a fourth ontological figure of the articulation of the State and its situation adds itself to the three outlined by Badiou (i.e. singularity, normality and excrescence). This figure, famously borrowed from the political theology of Carl Schmitt, is that of sovereignty as a state of exception. The exception, like Capital, is technically not a singularity: 'what defines it is precisely that it applies itself by dis-applying itself, that it includes what is outside of it. This is the figure in which singularity is represented as such, that is, as unrepresentable. What can in no case be included, is included under the form of exception'. Not only is this figure not singular, but it also provides a threshold of indiscernibility between singularity and excrescence, 'something like a paradoxical inclusion of belonging itself. It is what cannot be included in the whole to which it belongs and cannot belong to the set in which it is always included'.[32] Is this ambivalent topology of sovereign exception adequate to a thinking of Capital? In its favour it would have the capacity to acknowledge the 'unworldly' nature of our global predicament – a predicament that Badiou has defined as transitional or intervallic.[33] At the same time, it might go some way towards acknowledging the complex ontological effect of contemporary Capital on the logic of situations and the structure of the State.

And yet, I think that accepting this topology of exception or endowing Capital with the equivocal figure of the Schmittian sovereign would be tantamount to subjecting both thought and politics to an immeasurability so extreme that only a sort of poetic abeyance, if not outright abdication, would follow. The reason for this is that the state of exception remains prisoner to the discourse of representation (and to its Heideggerian critique), at the very moment that it provides us with what is perhaps both the most exquisite and the most stifling

31   Deleuze 1990.
32   Agamben 1995, pp. 29–30.
33   Badiou 2003d.

figure of representation's excess. Sovereignty extenuates the State by under-mining the clear-cut separation between presentation and representation (the 'vertical' topology of politics) and perpetuates it by making its immeasurable excess into the very space of politics. No surprise then that the paradigm (the abstract machine) of this figure is the camp, considered as the minutely struc-tured site of the presentation of the unpresentable, bare life exposed to a thor-oughgoing illegality indistinguishable from the most absolute law. This errant site of 'unrepresentation' makes any distance impossible, and ultimately forces politics to assume the obverse of sovereignty's dominion. Any coming politics is consequently bound to assume the exposition of this unrepresentable being, of 'bare life', to generalise and affirm, against the logic of the camp, the unworldly aspect of the 'state of exception', in such a way as to operate a kind of indistinc-tion between presentation and representation (the State and its biopolitical support), between 'life' and its 'forms'. As Agamben's provocative forays into political messianism reveal, such an attempt to suspend sovereignty, tied as it is to a truly epochal horizon, is incapable of providing a metapolitical capture of currently existing political sequences, and, in its resolutely all-encompassing, metaphysical scope, threatens to obfuscate what exactly the current visages of power and control might require of political invention, what strategies and tac-tics might be equal to our contemporary conjuncture.

Whilst this is not the place to erect an argument against the pertinence of Agamben's paradigm of exception, I do believe its value lies in suggesting a fig-ure of the possible and perhaps even actual suspension of the 'representative' State, and in warning us that the nature of domination may be far more difficult to master, the demand of pure presentation far more difficult to uphold, than the double articulation of State and situation may have us expect. If sovereignty presents the unpresentable, accesses it *as* void, *as* inconsistent, in other words, as 'bare', what resistance can politics provide? How will the uprising of the unrepresentable itself guarantee the possibility of a politics of non-domination if it is already dominated *as* unrepresentable? At the edges of representation, under the twofold sign of Capital and sovereignty, the material from which the force of political distance may be drawn appears here to have lost the force afforded it by its irruption into the order of the State.

Yet for all the impasses that the distance to representation presents to the definition and to the real capacity of a collective politics of emancipation, I believe that Badiou's thinking – in particular the reflections on the logic of appearance developed in *Logics of Worlds*[34] – still affords us the possibility of

---

34   Badiou 2006b and 2008. See also Badiou 2004a.

thinking the specificity of a politics that could come to terms with the constitutive excess of capitalist domination and accompany a philosophy finally equal to the ontological virtues of which the operations of Capital are both the vehicle and the primary obstacle. If Capital, in the principle of its operation, which is the abstract demand to dissolve the autonomy of bonds for the sake of the maximisation of surplus-value, is of a different order than the State, it is in great part because – whilst always coupled to those representations of identity and difference on the basis of which it can produce its excessive count – Capital does not 'itself' represent anything or anyone. Its relationship to the State is akin to that of a parasite to its host, though it may often – as is the case today with a fragile US hegemony over the global economy – assume the lineaments of a symbiont.

I would thus hazard the hypothesis, that, far from constituting a capitulation to the sophistries of signification or the comforts of phenomenology, the passage from the re/presentative articulation of State and situation to the formulation of the logic(s) of appearance might provide us with a way of thinking a politics that would both measure and 'distance' the domination of an entity (or operation) that does not itself fit into the schemas of representation. The key development in this regard is the 'substitution' of the category of 'world' for that of 'situation' (a fortiori displacing 'the state of the situation'). We may here have a means to bolster the theory of the subject with an account of the ordering principle of our political existence which is not indifferent to the vicissitudes of Capital (of credit systems, financial flows, interest-rates, etc.) and its role as an impersonal operator of acute transformations.

Broadly speaking, the shift from the concept of situation to that of world entails an increased concern with the ontological structuring of reality (of that very reality into which events, truths and subjects make their violent irruption). Moving beyond the founding insight concerning the 'excrescence' of representation, the concept of world tries to articulate what the parameters and modalities for the consistency of reality may be, how this consistency might find itself regulated and stabilised. Of course, this is with the sole speculative purpose of gaining a rational purchase on the subjective and effective consequences of an irruption of inconsistency. If 'the true problem is the question of the localization of being',[35] it is to the extent that, from the standpoint of the subject of an event (the only legitimate spur for either analysis or 'phenomenology' in Badiou) the intra-situational logic of placements – of identities and differences, of intensities and exclusion – requires

---

35   Badiou 2003b, p. 171.

a more exhaustive, if comparatively abstract, 'topological' account. In other words, whilst the 'concrete analysis of concrete situations', to cite Lenin, is *not* an ontological, philosophical or metapolitical object (since it must always operate from within a truth procedure or subjective sequence), the logics of worlds developed by Badiou signals the need for a more densely articulated framework for 'abstract analysis' than the one provided in *Being and Event* via the concept of State. Without delving too deeply into a complex and layered philosophical-mathematical argument,[36] I would simply like to consider how the aforementioned shift might relate to the differential articulation of State and Capital that I have already alluded to. In what can only be a blueprint for future inquiry, I would like to do this by considering four aspects of Badiou's argument: the theoretical innovations announced by the concept of *world(s)*; the possible resonance of Marx's notion of *real subsumption* to Badiou's thinking of political distance; the tenability of an idea of the *global* within Badiou's schema; the potential for an *anti-capitalist politics* within this framework.

Like *Being and Event*, *Logics of Worlds* affirms the non-totalisable plurality of consistent ontological set-ups, as well as the variability of their structuring principles. Against any philosophy of the One or of Totality (whether virtual or actual, real or negative) and in line with the advances in mathematical theory of Cantor, Russell, Gödel, and Cohen, Badiou affirms the impossibility of identifying any meta-consistency that would integrate the dissemination of ontological arrangements.[37] It is in these milestones of logic and mathematics that we are to find the source of Badiou's resolute acosmism, of his rationalist atheism. Where Badiou's later work goes further is in the postulate that every arrangement (read 'world') is endowed with one element (a multiple) that functions as its structuring principle, localising all other existent (or appearing) multiples and determining their degrees of existence (or appearance), in other words, their degrees of identity or difference from one another. This element is defined as the *transcendental* of the 'world' – it is, so to speak, what individuates the world, providing it with maximal and minimal degrees of appearance and intensity.[38]

Rather than relegating the structuring agency to the nebulous domain of a perennial and unquestionable law (a danger arguably incurred by the focus on the 'count' in *Being and Event*), Badiou's determination of the transcendental

---

36   See Hallward 2003, pp. 293–315.
37   Badiou 2004a and 2006b.
38   Badiou 2008; Rabouin et al. 2011; see also the remarks in Hallward 2003, pp. 299–300.

as a structured element (or multiple) *within* the situation itself heralds the possibility of a far more immanent, which is to say, of a substantially more *materialist*, consideration of order and placement than the one provided in *Being
and Event*. What we are given is not the ubiquitous pertinence of 'structure' *per
se*, but rather an abstract schema to consider how, rather than being shrouded
in ontological invisibility, the organisation of a particular ontological region is
determined by an identifiable element or complex. What is more, it is no longer
clear – despite the capital importance of the excess of the State for *Being and
Event* – whether we need any longer retain the hiatus between presentation
and representation. 'Worlds' are not presented and 'then' re-presented – rather,
a collection of multiples is articulated through the (transcendental) agency of
another multiple, such that we are no longer in obvious need of a supplementary dimension. The wager of the 'minimal phenomenology' that Badiou wishes
to construct around the concept of world (whose technical details I cannot
elaborate upon here) is that all the fundamental, abstract principles of localised
existence (or appearance) can be adequately dealt with by means of concepts
gleaned from the mathematical domains of the theories of categories and *topoi*,
namely *structure of order, minimal degree, conjunction, envelope, dependence,
reverse* and *maximal degree*.[39] Crucially, these abstract determinations of the
plurality of structures *do not* announce the deductive obsolescence of concrete
analyses.[40]

Now, we can consider the key tenets of Marx's socio-economic analysis and
critique as resulting precisely from an inquiry into the concrete and identifiable structuring principles of a particular world (in praising them as some
of the very few 'scientific' truths in the field of the 'human sciences', Badiou
seems to indicate as much himself[41]). Indeed, much of the unfortunate fate of
supposed Marxist science, from Engels's *Dialectics of Nature* onwards, can be
understood as a fallacious *generalisation* of a principle of localisation that is
itself localisable, that is to say, not simply global (an inconsistent adjective in
Badiou's framework). As a brand of 'transcendental materialism' – to borrow
from Deleuze and Guattari – Marx's thought, with Capital as its 'object', stands
somewhere between the general logic of appearance proposed by Badiou and
the kind of concrete analysis that can only be a tool and a consequence of specific political projects and sequences. As a particularly significant instance of
Marx's study of the transformation in the structuring principles of capitalism,
consider the distinction between real and formal subsumption, proposed in

39   Badiou 2004a, 2006b, 2008.
40   Badiou 2003b, p. 174.
41   See Badiou 2004b.

the 'Results of the Immediate Process of Production', the unpublished fragment from the notebooks for the first volume of *Capital*. With formal subsumption, writes Marx:

> There is no change as yet in the mode of production itself. *Technologic-ally speaking*, the *labour process* goes on as before, with the proviso that it is now *subordinated* to capital. Within the production process, however ... two developments emerge: (1) an *economic* relationship of supremacy and subordination, since the consumption of labour-power by the capit-alist is naturally supervised and directed by him; (2) labour becomes far more continuous and intensive ....[42]

On this basis, the jump to real subsumption signals a veritable event in or for the transcendental, a qualitative and systemic transformation in the ordering principle of the socio-economic situation. As Marx declares:

> With the real subsumption of labour under capital a complete (and con-stantly repeated) revolution takes place in the mode of production, in the productivity of the workers and in the relations between workers and cap-italists. With the real subsumption of labour under capital, all the changes in the labour process ... now become reality ... *capitalist production* now establishes itself as a mode of production *sui generis* and brings into being a new mode of material production.[43]

In other words, we move from an organising principle which, through exploit-ation and subordination, is grafted onto the logic of semi-autonomous worlds (formal subsumption) to one that itself becomes the principle to which all worlds of production, consumption and circulation are intrinsically indexed (real subsumption). To put it in slightly different terms, we move from logic of capture to a logic of immanence.[44] The strength of Badiou's turn to a phenom-eno-logic of appearance might then lie in allowing us to eschew the interpret-ation of real subsumption in terms of the dialectical movement of totality, in favour of a figure of Capital as an operationally ubiquitous transcendental instance that does not as such confer 'regional stability' upon a capitalist world. By abdicating the vision of Capital as totality, but maintaining its efficacy as a

---

42   Marx 1990, p. 1026.
43   Marx 1990, p. 1035.
44   Negri 1987. On formal and real subsumption, see the crucial analyses in Harootunian 2015.

structuring principle, we might eventually be able both to analyse the generative, organising force of the capitalist transcendental *and* to think the irruption of anti-capitalist subjectivity as a 'dysfunctional' movement *intransitive* to a systemic logic, as a *separation* not anticipated by the parameters of Capital.[45]

Much as I have tried to suggest that Badiou's *Logics of Worlds* could be employed to redress the ambivalent status ascribed to Capital in his *Manifesto* (as simultaneously constituting 'the' transcendental medium for the historical advent of unbinding and as representing a blind, mediocre empirical datum), it remains the case that Badiou's actual pronouncements on Capital and the contemporary world in no way presage such a transformation. The erratic status of Capital as a kind of anti-singular singularity implicitly returns in the talk 'The Caesura of Nihilism',[46] where Badiou makes the provocative claim that our times, in which the rule of Capital is seconded by the vacuous emblems of 'democracy', are *devoid of world* – that is, they deploy a protocol of exclusion but do not effect a transcendental distribution of existence. The implication here is that the hegemony of Capital, seconded by an unstable mix of 'humanitarian' oratory and brazenly imperial pronouncements, does not constitute a 'world' proper. The reasons for this, however, are problematic: the 'unworldly' nature of Capital is connected by Badiou to its evacuation of any *names* that could be the bearers of subjectivity (consider the way that, prior to what Badiou calls the Restoration that began in the 1980s,[47] we could encounter living, effective names such as 'proletariat', 'national liberation', 'black power', 'women's liberation', etc.). Such an account cannot but raise several questions.

If, ontologically speaking, *all* existence (presented, represented or 'worldly') is *consistent* (until the advent of an event and the generic inquiries that define truth procedures), how is it possible that an arguably non-evental predicament such as ours *manifest inconsistency*? Once again, we encounter, as we did with the *Saint Paul*, this uncanny figure, that of a non-subjective (and non-subjectivisable?) unbinding, or, alternatively, that of a non-evental inconsistency. (Incidentally, that is precisely what we are told by world-systems theory, which considers our unstable phase as the rare, epochal occasion of free political intervention on a global scale. In other words, *because the system is off the rails, we have the rare chance to take real, i.e. system-constituting, decisions.*[48]) The upshot of this non-evental inconsistency is that whilst in Badiou's theor-

---

45   See Chapter 1 in this volume.
46   Badiou 2003d.
47   Badiou 2005a.
48   See Wallerstein 2003.

etical writings on the appearance of worlds[49] he cogently argues that events engender the *dysfunction* of worlds and their transcendental regimes, in his 'ontology of the present' Badiou advocates the necessity, in our 'intervallic' or world-less times, of *constructing* a world, such that those now excluded can come to invent new names, names capable of sustaining new truth procedures. As he writes, 'I hold that we are at a very special moment, *a moment at which there is not any world*' (though their frameworks are hardly compatible, one can't help noting the strange convergence on this point with some of Immanuel Wallerstein's recent analyses on our transitional age). As a result: 'Philosophy has no other legitimate aim except to help find the new names that will bring into existence the unknown world that is only waiting for us because we are waiting for it'.[50] In a peculiar inversion of some of the key traits of his doctrine, it seems that Badiou is here advocating, to some extent, an 'ordering' task, one that will inevitably, if perhaps mistakenly, resonate for some with the slogan of the 'anti-globalisation' movement: 'Another World is Possible'.

And yet, unlike the avowed partisans of anti-capitalism, Badiou seems to refuse the status of 'world' (which, after all, is 'merely' a neutral phenomenological descriptive, not a qualitative term) to the system of global capitalism.[51] The way that he does this, however, seems to indicate that we still remain within the logic of re/presentation, not in the sense that the excluded need their 'identity' represented, but in the subjective sense that only new names will really make the excluded present. It is in light of this that Badiou enjoins us to struggle against the false names generated by today's imperial 'democracies', to hold true to those exceptions that attack the notion that today's parliamentary apparatuses and the rhetoric of human rights (or 'freedom') have effectively joined forces to saturate the field of politics. But what of the possibility that Capital may be untouched by the upsurge of new presentations and names? That it is perfectly capable, in line with what Agamben and Deleuze have argued, of directly accessing the 'unrepresented'? Arguably, Badiou's scepticism toward anti-capitalist politics derives from his crucial repudiation of any fully dialectical or transitive notion of political subjectivity[52] and his related critique of a notion of systemic totality. It is these arguments combined that explain his hostility to the proposals of Hardt and Negri, as well as of Deleuze and Agamben.[53]

---

49   Badiou 2004a and 2006b.
50   Badiou 2003d. See also the discussion of these themes in Badiou's seminars of the 2000s and 2010s, Badiou 2014a and 2017.
51   Though contrary indications seem to transpire from Badiou 1997a, p. 10.
52   Badiou 1985a; see Chapter 1 in this volume.
53   Badiou 2002a and 2003c.

Badiou has written that 'there is no Universe, only worlds. In each and every world, the immanent existence of a maximal value for the transcendental degrees signals that *this* world is never *the* world. The power of localisation held by the being of a world is determinate: if a being appears in this world, this appearance possesses an absolute degree; this degree marks, for a given world, the being of being-there'.[54] This undermines any ontological idolatry of Capital as *the* motor of production, *the* expression of the 'natural' logic of the Totality. It might even entail redefining 'globalisation' as a kind of transcendental regime devoid of totalisation, not a bounded world (not a world, in Badiou's technical vocabulary, provided with maxima and minima of appearance, with a transcendental 'envelope' and so on), but rather an operational principle which, whilst abstractly identifiable, resists localisation, relentlessly generating and exploiting worlds (worlds of labour, intellect, culture, matter, and so on). In other words, considering the operations of globalised capitalism, via the category (admittedly absent from Badiou's own work) of a *world-less transcendental*. Whilst they connect to entirely different figures of subjectivity, this potential consequence of Badiou's doctrine might not be entirely alien to Hardt and Negri's own definition of globalisation as 'a *regime* of production of identity and difference, or really of homogenization and heterogenization'.[55] The passage from formal subsumption to real subsumption would then signal the impossibility of basing a political antagonism to Capital on the 'local' resistance of some specified world, and, more importantly, the necessity to invent forms of distance and autonomy not directly deriving from any pre-existing localisation.

On these grounds, it is imperative from Badiou's perspective to subject the ambient concept of *diversity* to unsparing criticism, to reassert the force of a notion of generic equality *without identity*, a notion intransitive to, or at a distance from, available parameters of identification. Crucially, when the unbinding automatism of capital becomes ubiquitous (in real subsumption), such distance cannot depend on breaking through representational exclusions; rather, it must attack the very principle of organisation of Capital as *the* dominant transcendental regime (its dominance is testified by the fact that 'democratic' representation remains increasingly optional in today's world, whilst subtracting oneself from the logic of profit is simply not an option). In this respect, we disagree with Badiou's strong claim that 'today the enemy is not called Empire or Capital. It's called Democracy'.[56] This is emphatically not because we think

---

54   Badiou 2004a.
55   Hardt and Negri 2000, p. 45.
56   Badiou 2002a, p. 14.

that Badiou's attack on the fetishism of democracy is problematic, but rather because we contend that – despite chattering battalions of smug idolaters and renegade ideologues – Badiou overestimates the inhibiting force, as an 'ideological, or subjective, formalisation' of the liberal-democratic notion of equality. It is not the principle of democratic representation that hampers the political emancipation of subjects, but rather the deep-seated conviction that there is no alternative to the rule of profit. The cynicism of today's 'democratic' subjects, who know full well that they play a negligible role in the management of the commons and are entirely aware of the sham nature of the apparatuses of representation, is founded on the perceived inevitability of capitalism, not vice versa.

More importantly, against certain formulations of a 'politics of the multitude', we think that anti-capitalism need not be the expression of a creativity latent in the movement of Capital itself. In other words, it is vital to think simultaneously the *anti-singular* (or *indifferent*) *singularity* of Capital as the hegemonic principle of political regulation and partition *and* the necessity of a politics *intransitive* to the transcendental regime of Capital; to divert politics from a focus on demands for representation and to accept the lesson that there is no pre-existing subject that anticipates the invention of egalitarian political modes that might be capable of forcing the dysfunction of the transcendental rule of surplus-value. This is not to rule out a politics of prescriptive distance from the State, of the sort practiced by L'Organisation politique;[57] it is to affirm the necessity of a subjective traversal of both logics, 'territorial' and 'capitalist'. To think otherwise would be entirely to ignore the subjective significance of trans-national Capital (and *capitalists*) as a distributed but remarkably consistent source of brutally mobile partition and regulation, a recognition that has informed several among the political subjects which in the past few years have worked towards the dysfunction of the capitalist subsumption of worlds and names, subjects who have actively resisted their 'liberalisation' and in so doing sketched out new regimes of organisation, new forms of subjectivity at a distance from the accepted forms of mediated representation: the Ejército Zapatista de Liberación Nacional in Mexico, the Karnataka State Farmers' Association in India, the Assembly of the Poor in Thailand, the Movimento dos Trabalhadores Rurais Sem Terra in Brazil ....[58] It is from such instances of politics, from their practices and pronouncements, that we might begin to think beyond the intra-State logic of representation, the logic of claims and

---

57   Hallward 2003, pp. 226–7.
58   Notes from Nowhere 2003.

concessions, and towards ways of terminating the expanding sway of capitalist accumulation, doubling the logic of the place with the logic of its interruption.[59] The challenge, of course, is to do so whilst eschewing the increasingly desperate resuscitation of subterranean teleologies and latent subjects of history, experimenting instead with new configurations of equality, autonomy and distance.

---

59   Badiou 1982, p. 301.

CHAPTER 4

Can Violence Be Thought?

What is the relationship between the thinking of violence and the thinking of politics in Badiou's writings? The very text where he proposes – at the putative close of his own Maoist or Marxist-Leninist sequence of political militancy – the 'destruction' and 'recomposition' of Marxist politics, is entitled *Can Politics Be Thought?*[1] At the very outset of this short book, in amicable but firm polemic with the instigators of the seminars from which it is drawn – Jean-Luc Nancy and Philippe Lacoue-Labarthe (who had invited Badiou to present this work at their Centre de recherche philosophique sur le politique in 1983–84) – Badiou, intervening in a lexical controversy that has taken on multiple guises in several politico-philosophical settings, is adamant that his preoccupation is with *politics* (la *politique*) and not *the political* (le *politique*). The political, he stipulates, must be fixed in its status as a *fiction*, the fiction of the link between the social bond and its measure (or measurement). *The* political, in other words, is something like the transcendental illusion of relationality, of communal ties and a sovereign authority over the social. In this regard, the short-lived vogue for the 'retreat of the political'[2] is not to be read as the occasion for an endless melancholia over the vanished essence or empty place of the political, but rather to be welcomed and assumed as the opportunity to recover the independent force and determinacy of a thinking of *politics*, a thinking that Badiou locates between Machiavelli and Lenin, and whose philosophical capture he proposes to organise with the resources bequeathed by what he calls 'the four great French dialecticians': Pascal, Rousseau, Mallarmé, Lacan.[3] Without entering into the nature of the philosophical and metapolitical project initiated by *Can Politics Be Thought?*,[4] we can note that Badiou's immanent critique of his own earlier positions – his 'post-Leninism', to follow his own shorthand, or

---

1 Badiou 1985a. See Chapter 2 in this volume.
2 Lacoue-Labarthe and Nancy 1997.
3 See Badiou 1985a and Badiou 1983. In Badiou, this thinking of politics, or better, the idea that politics is itself a thought, is diametrically opposed to the practice and ideology of *political philosophy*, especially as formulated by the heirs to the thinking of Hannah Arendt. See Alain Badiou, 'Against "Political Philosophy"', in Badiou 2005c.
4 In this book, the key coordinates of an ontology of inconsistent multiplicity and of an event-bound theory of the subject – formalised and elaborated in the 1988 magnum opus *Being and Event* – are already sketched out.

'post-Maoism', to recall Bruno Bosteels's impressive study[5] – takes the form of declaring *the autonomy or separation of politics from the political*. As Badiou states: '*The political* has never been anything other than the fiction which is punctured by *politics* as the hole of the event'.[6]

Why focus on the theme of violence in Badiou? The stakes are twofold. First, I wish to bring my ongoing research on Badiou's contorted relationship with Marxism into dialogue with the debates elicited by Étienne Balibar's work on the historical-materialist coordinates and aporias that inhere in the notion of *Gewalt*.[7] Indeed, as I will suggest by way of conclusion, thinking in terms of *Gewalt*, rather than mere *violence*, might open up the possibility of considerably complicating Badiou's relationship to Marxism and his proposal of an autonomy of politics. Second, because it is through the immanent critique of the broadly Leninist political experience of struggle, organisation, conflict and (State) power – as well as of the (often parasitical) reactionary condemnations thereof – that the issue of violence has played a key role in various attempts, progressive and regressive, to evaluate the vitality and possibility of a Marxist politics.

A third and final remark is perhaps required, concerning the role of such reflections in the context of the ongoing reception of Badiou's writings. In brief, attention to Badiou's political thought in the Anglophone arena began, especially in the pioneering work of Peter Hallward, with a focus on the uncompromising *sui generis* 'axiomatic' egalitarianism and, so to speak, 'decisionism' seemingly manifested by his 'mature' works – with a specific attention to the novelty of a non- or even anti-social treatment of political action and innovation. Further investigation of the full scope of his work has led to more sustained considerations of his relation to Marxism and, of course, to Maoism. This has allowed for a more 'continuationist' position, persuasively promoted by Bosteels in commentaries that home in on Badiou's 'post-Maoism', disinterring his tracts on the cultural revolution and the militant and theoretical texts penned as one of the leaders of the small French Maoist grouping, the UCFML.[8] I have tried to contribute to this debate with a couple of articles and presentations, the principal one entitled 'Communism as Separation'.[9] In that

5 Bosteels 2005a and 2011.
6 Badiou 1985a, p. 12.
7 Balibar 2001; Balibar 2009.
8 See Bosteels 2005a and 2011, for the details of Badiou's political engagement and for a theoretical analysis of its grounds and repercussions. It is worth noting that Bosteels's continuationist hypothesis has affected Badiou himself, who has put his work once again under the aegis of materialist dialectics, see Badiou 2005d, 2006b and 2008.
9 Chapter 1 in this volume.

text, which was cogently if not (in my inevitably biased view) definitively criticised by Bosteels for its excessive zeal in positing a kind of 'metapolitical break' around 1985 (the year of publication of *Can Politics Be Thought?*), I proposed a sort of periodisation of Badiou's thought in terms of its relation to communism. Badiou himself is, among other things, a remarkable and under-appreciated theorist of periodisation.[10] Following him, I would like to think periodisation as anything but a simple question of segmenting time and thought, but rather as a 'spiralling' movement conditioned by all sorts of forceful anticipations, retractions and reversals, not to mention returns (not least the return, in *Logics of Worlds*, the sequel to *Being and Event*, of the materialist dialectic). Slightly revising the dating proposed in Chapters 1 and 2, we could sketch the phases of Badiou's work as follows:

- *Pre-1968*: Badiou's 'apprenticeship' with Sartre, followed by a participation – at a slight distance – in the Althusserian school during what Gregory Elliot calls its 'high' period.[11] Given Badiou's ensuing self-criticisms we could call this the stage of *theoretical communism*.
- *1968–1977*: After his 'Road to Damascus' moment[12] and the passage from his dissidence within the PSU (Parti socialiste unifié) to the leadership of the UCFML (Groupe pour la formation de l'Union des communistes de France, marxiste-leniniste), Badiou and his comrades formulate what they term a *communism of production*.[13]
- *1977–1982*: In the ebb of the Maoist sequence, Badiou recapitulates the theory of force and destruction sketched out in *Theory of Contradiction*,[14] detaching it more and more from any reference to the production process and

---

10 Badiou 1982, pp. 62–5, with reference to Marx's and Lenin's distinct estimations of the Paris Commune. As far as Badiou's periodisation of the shifting context for his own political militancy and (meta)political theory, I refer the reader to the 'Preface to the English Edition', in Badiou 2005c, pp. xxxiv–xxxv, as well as to his political memoir, Badiou 2023. For Badiou's thinking on history, historicity and periodisation, see Chapter 6 in this volume.

11 The key publications in this phase are the following: Badiou 1966, 1967 and 1969. The second of these pieces, a review of *Pour Marx, Lire le capital* and a further pamphlet by Althusser on the dialectic, already lays out the groundwork for a synthesis of Sartre and Althusser and prefigures Badiou's mathematical predilections in terms of its concluding suggestions regarding a theory of historical sets. The often-unexpected links between Sartre and Badiou on the relationship between politics and mathematics have been impressively investigated by Stathis Kouvelakis in his article on Badiou and Sartre, Kouvelakis 2005. Badiou's relationship to Sartre is explored in Badiou 1980 and 1990b.

12 For statements on his experience of '68, see Badiou 2005a, p. 178, and Bosteels 2005c, pp. 237–8. See also Bensaïd 2004.

13 See Chapter 1 in this book.

14 Badiou 1975.

the role of the masses qua producing classes. The subject (i.e. the party) takes centre stage in a formidable and forbidding dialectical construction, anchored around what I have chosen to call a *communism of destruction*. *Theory of the Subject*,[15] which recapitulates and extends a series of seminars given during this period, is the key text for this 'destructive' paradigm.

– *1982-present?* Badiou declares the end of the three great references of historical communism: the 'statist' referent, i.e. the existence of political actualisations of the communist project that can carry the theme of *victory*; the martial referent, i.e. the wars of national liberation that witness 'the invention, under the direction of modern parties, of a new form of war, a dissymmetrical war, rooted in the countryside, organising the peasantry, and deploying itself in a prolonged manner, in stages';[16] the subjective or class referent, i.e. the subjective presence of the workers' movement itself. The so-called 'crisis of Marxism' is seen as the progressive collapse of this system of references. Whilst maintaining the conviction that a true politics can only be a radically egalitarian and in some sense *communist* politics – so that he will write of an eternity of communism qua 'eternity of the equal'[17] – Badiou operates a de-historicisation and de-statification of communism in the *ontological* conviction that beneath the fiction of the social and political bond there lies the reality, or rather the Real, of unbinding, of an inconsistency and multiplicity that is only fictionally counted and represented by the State. Suspending any transitivity between the subject of politics and the situation in which it arises (rarity and discontinuity becoming paramount), Badiou proposes, through the category of the *generic*, the criterion of what might be regarded as a non-Marxist communism. This is thought in terms of a local and discontinuous production of Sameness, in a stage that I characterised in Chapter 1 in terms of the *production of communism*.[18] Of course, with the later Badiou's turn towards a 'materialist dialectic' we may wonder whether a recidivist Maoist spirit has not given the spiral yet another twist ...

---

15   Badiou 1982.
16   Badiou 1985a, p. 28.
17   Badiou 1991a, p. 15.
18   This evaluation of Badiou's work has been strongly countered by Bruno Bosteels in Bosteels 2005b and 2011. Despite its persuasive depiction of Badiou's resolute opposition, throughout his political and philosophical development, to rightist structuralist dogmatism and leftist spontaneist decisionism, for the sake of a dialectic of scission (a theme also expanded upon in his article on 'Post-Maoism', Bosteels 2005a), Bosteels fails in my view to contend with the problematic erasure of the critique of political economy from the field of Badiou's thinking, and seems to propose that Marxism can continue in the absence of such a reference. It is a fallacy, I believe, to argue that a rigorous aversion to leftism (which

But how does this periodisation and Badiou's idiosyncratic trajectory within the theoretical topology of Marxism relate to the question of violence, and even of *Gewalt*? Schematically, my argument is as follows: in the wake of his Damascene conversion to Maoist militancy, Badiou produced one of the most steadfast, lucid and unsettling accounts of the fundamentally violent character of the Marxist dialectic, as filtered through Leninist and Maoist political thought and practice. To be more precise, Badiou linked his Marxist-Leninist concern with *truth, justice* and the *new* to the immanent requirement of a destructive antagonism, an argument that is most exhaustively laid out in his meticulous and insistent exegesis of the Maoist watchword: 'It is right to rebel against the reactionaries'.[19] The possibility of revolutionary novelty is intimately linked here to the organised, systematic and, importantly, *inegalitarian* destruction of the reactionary adversary. The movement away from this dialectic of destruction (peaking philosophically in *Theory of the Subject*, but probably politically exhausted some years earlier) takes the guise of a subordination of the theme of antagonism to that of an independent political *capacity* and the 'forms of conscience' of an egalitarian collective subject.[20] Indeed, as the retrospective if elliptical self-analysis constituted by *The Century* suggests,[21] Badiou's rethinking functions by splitting the very concept of antagonism into a destructive and what he calls a *subtractive* variant, in an explicit reminiscence of Mao's distinction between antagonistic contradictions and contradictions among the people. This passage – to which I will return in the conclusion of this chapter – is marked, especially in later texts, by an implicit critique of political violence as a sign of the organisational weakness and metaphysical corruption of emancipatory thought in its 'metaphysical' guise as Marxism-Leninism.[22] In other words, rather than an inherent condition of egalitarian novelty, *destruction* is seen retrospectively as a doomed attempt to dominate a fundamental unbinding (*déliaison*) and to do so through the lethal fiction of the bond provided by

---

is definitely present in Badiou's work, and which Bosteels presents brilliantly) suffices to retain the reference to Marxism. Having said that, Badiou does seem to propose a kind of *minimal* Marxism, articulated around the concept of the factory as event site, in a chapter excised from the final publication of *Being and Event*, which I discuss in Chapter 2. See Badiou 1986.

19   Badiou 2005e.
20   Sandevince 1984b.
21   Badiou 2005a.
22   In a kind of Heideggerian *scherzo*, Badiou writes of 'the extreme political weakness of an entire epoch, the Marxist-Leninist or Stalinist epoch, which with respect to what is required in order to unearth the being of politics, would appear to have been equivalent to the strictly metaphysical epoch of this lost ontology'. Badiou 2005c, pp. 69–70.

State, nation, party and/or class as agents of a real equality whose proof can only be given in the destruction of the old. This centrality of destruction was arguably at the speculative heart of Badiou's own Maoist phase.

In 1975, in the UCFML's 'Yenan' imprint at the Éditions Maspero (a series he co-directed with Sylvain Lazarus), Badiou published the first of what were intended to be a series of pamphlets on dialectical materialism, *Theory of Contradiction*, to be followed by *On Ideology* the following year.[23] In these texts Badiou set down, in painstaking detail, the philosophical groundwork of a Marxist-Leninist theory of revolt (or rebellion). The primacy of revolt – that is, the primacy of *practice* – is in fact the militant *leitmotiv* of Badiou's writings in the seventies. This is especially true of *Theory of Contradiction*, a terse speculative commentary upon Mao's dictum 'it is always right to rebel against the reactionaries'.[24] In it, we read the following: 'Rebellion does not wait for its reason, rebellion is what is always already there, for any possible reason whatever. Marxism simply says: rebellion is reason, rebellion is subject. Marxism is the recapitulation of the wisdom of rebellion.'[25] Basing himself on this equation between political practice and antagonism, Badiou can write: 'The real is not what brings together, but what separates. What happens is what disjoins'.[26]

Here we must hear the materialist thesis that the *factum* of revolt – or, in Badiou's more recent discourse, the irruption of the event or dysfunction of a transcendental regime – comes first, subjectivation second. Moreover, to the extent that any structure of placements, any represented situation, is in a sense the fallout from, or recuperation of, its forceful dislocation by a subject, resistance, as Badiou puts it, is the secret of domination. Badiou comes closest to a dualistic matrix of the political – such as the one propounded by the heretical post-Maoist *nouveaux philosophes* Christian Jambet and Guy Lardreau in their book *The Angel*[27] – when he states that the *reason of revolt* (or rebellion) is an

---

23 Badiou 1975; Badiou and Balmès 1976. As Bosteels notes in his 'Post-Maoism' (Bosteels 2005a, p. 596), the third volume of these didactic texts in Maoist theory, to be entitled *Antagonisme et non-antagonisme. Les différents types de contradiction* [Antagonism and Non-Antagonism: The Different Types of Contradiction], was never published.

24 We should perhaps complement this maxim with the saying of Lin Piao, quoted by Badiou in his contribution to Peter Hallward's collection of critical articles: 'the essence of revisionism is the fear of death'. Badiou 2004b, p. 237.

25 Badiou 2005e, p. 673.

26 'Le réel n'est pas ce qui rassemble, mais ce qui sépare. Ce qui advient est ce qui disjoint.' Badiou 1975.

27 Lardreau and Jambet 1975. For an extended reflection on the relation between the works of Jambet and Lardreau on revolt and mastery and Badiou's philosophy, see Toscano 2011. See also Bosteels 2005a, pp. 612–17.

invariant, 'deep and inextricable'; that the refusal of mastery – as the mastery of authority and of knowledge – constitutes a subjective given that *precedes* Marxism and any causal or structural analysis that a critique of political economy may be capable of providing. This suggests an ontological anteriority of revolt, an autonomous power of egalitarian opposition that operates like a trans-historical constant.

Following the Maoist thesis that division is the very essence of dialectics ('One divides into two'), Badiou's theory of contradiction is founded on the asymmetry of the terms of the contradiction, purifying *force*, on the one hand, the system of *places*, on the other. But, and here lies the key point, no angelic purity is given beforehand and neither can we put our hopes in a simple epiphany spontaneously emerging from the ruins of the old. As Bosteels persuasively argues, 'speculative leftism' remains one of Badiou's nemeses (all the more virulently attacked, one might argue, to the extent that it is an intimate possibility of his thinking of the subject, once it has detached itself from any straightforward systemic transitivity). As Badiou writes in the *Theory of the Subject*: 'in every contradiction, force manifests its impurity through the aleatory process of its purification'. In the *Theory of Contradiction*, the thesis of the rightness of rebellion (or of the justice of the new) is linked by Badiou to a whole partisan theory of consciousness and truth, whereby both Marxism as a science of social formations and the objective historical reality of revolts are doubled by, and indeed find their reason in, the conscious assumption of the tasks of revolt in organisation and directive, in short, in a *party*. Marxist truth, Badiou starkly states, 'is that wherein rebellion finds its reason in order to demolish the enemy' and, in a tone seemingly absent from his latest works, declares that it repudiates all equality before truth.[28]

In Badiou's work of the 1970s, but also in his later production, 'subject' names precisely that point through which what is impossible in a given situation is forced into possibility: 'A subject is a point of conversion of the impossible into the possible. The fundamental operation of a subject is to be at the point where some impossible is converted into possibility'.[29] The crucial question, if we wish to engage in a philosophical reflection on the role of violence in Badiou, is whether this point of conversion demands destructive antagonism as a precondition, or whether, as some of his later writings suggest, destruction and even

---

28 Echoes of the theory of partisan truth do remain. See 'Against "Political Philosophy"', in Badiou 2005c, p. 23, where he writes, apropos of the concept of consensus: 'An event is never shared, even if the truth we gather from it is universal, because its recognition *as event* is simply at one with the political decision'.

29 Badiou 1996–97, p. 8. See also Book I in Badiou 2008.

terror might be the (contingent) consequence of an event-bound capacity to independently affirm the existence and effects of a political subject.

In Badiou's *Theory of Contradiction* there is no mistaking the fact that the view of revolt as an affirmation of being is intimately bound to the possibility of a radical destruction, an abolition by the force of an insurgent subject, of certain places and positions within the structures of representation and domination.[30] Or, to quote one of Badiou's more lyrical passages: 'To the nothing new under the sun the thinking of revolt opposes the ever new insurgent red sun, under the emblem of which the unlimited affirmative hope of rebellious producers engenders ruptures'. Having done with the 'nothing new under the sun' entails the possibility of a total death, a death without *Aufhebung* and without mourning. Such, for instance – in one of Badiou's most pertinent examples – is the way in which colonialism should die, consigned to eternal forgetting. This is not to be understood in the impoverished sense of a disavowal or repression, but rather as the effective destruction of all traces of colonial domination. 'Cultural revolution' is thereby affirmed as anti-memory. The paradox openly assumed by Badiou, in which I think is encapsulated what I have called his communism of separation, is that the destruction of inequality, the obliteration of mastery, has a dualistic asymmetry as its condition.

The political conundrum is therefore that of the necessity to master (control, direct and violently lead) the path to masterlessness, to dominate domination in order for non-domination to arise. This is the paradox that in the history of Leninism takes the name of the dictatorship of the proletariat. But what then, we may ask, of Jambet's sober observation, aimed in part at Badiou himself, that the theme of anti-memory, of the Year Zero so famously linked to the killing fields of Cambodia, depends on the most radical hypostasis of Mastery, on a discourse reduced to the inscrutable secrecy of an unknowing command to work and submit to anonymity, coupled, inevitably perhaps, with the most pointless and exorbitant practices of confession – witness the destructive ferocity of the S-21 prison in Phnom Penh?[31] In response to such objections, we could recall

---

30   Here are a set of relevant citations from Badiou 1975: 'There are radical novelties because there are corpses that no trumpet of Judgment will ever reawaken'; 'To resolve is to reject. History has worked best when its dustbins have been better filled'; 'The field of Marxist knowledge is always in ruins – all truth is essentially destruction'; 'There is no veritable revolutionary thought but for the one that takes the recognition of the new all the way to its unavoidable obverse, the old must die. ... Not just death but the scattering of the ashes'. Unless otherwise noted, further quotes are from the French edition of this text.

31   See Christian Jambet's chapter in Jambet and Lardreau 1978. The reality of the Khmer Rouge's paranoid politics of purification has been registered by the documentary *S21: The Khmer Rouge Killing Machine* (2002), dir. Rithy Panh.

that one of the key theses in Badiou, stemming from his readings of Mao, is that it is not from the primary contradiction, the one between exploiters and exploited, that novelty emerges, but rather from a 'secondary' contradiction, from a separation or division within the camp of the primary contradiction itself – from the partisan truth of a faction, for instance, which separates itself in order to separate out (or subtract) a real that is denied by the state of the situation, by its dominant and dominating representation. It is transforming this secondary contradiction into a primary one that constitutes the formal- isation proper to the act of revolt. In other words, division and separation – and not just pure destructive antagonism – are conditions of possibility for the engendering of a generic equality.

In these early writings, Badiou can be found arguing that the presence of subjectivity changes the nature of violence itself. Inasmuch as the dialectics of a real revolt introduces qualitative novelty into a situation – such that the 'State, which is to say the concentrated form of all phenomena of domination, no longer even has the same name' – it divides death itself, into what is incorpor- ated and metamorphosed under a new law (or symbolically reinscribed, if we wish to adopt a Lacanian framework) and what is simply abrogated. In purely structural phenomena devoid of novelty, in which it is only a quantitative shift of places that is at stake, be it colonialism or World War 1, the drive to conserve and continue is accompanied for Badiou by enormous violence. In his stark words: 'When nothing changes, men die.' It is precisely the lack of asymmetry, the ultimately non-antagonistic basis of the massive antagonisms that appear to deploy themselves on the battlefield which mean that such '"structural" ant- agonisms depend on pure quantitative triumph, and are thus cumulative, non- creative, interminable, bloody and sterile.' In brief, then, against the opposition of resistance and power, Badiou proposes a dialectics of (materialist) structure and (subjective) tendency. Without the 'violent' inscription into the situation of a subjective tendency or force of transformation, which is itself the product of internal divisions and separations, we are left only with the dumb brutality of structural violence.

It is not possible in these brief considerations to track the political and philo- sophical reasons for Badiou's dislocation of the destructive thematic and his move towards a new, mathematically founded dialectic of inconsistency that undermines the concept of totality and takes its distance from many of the principal referents of the Marxist or historical materialist tradition. However, we could say that the questions that arise from Badiou's thematisation of viol- ence and from his political critique of terror (a critique that he vehemently counterposes to what he regards as the capitalo-parliamentarian and anti- totalitarian critique, such as we may find in François Furet's writings on the

French Revolution) might also be questions on the basis of which to reassess Badiou's complicated and incomplete relationship to Marxism, all claims to the latter's non-existence aside ...[32] A preliminary conclusion, or perhaps a simple intuition, is that the theme of *Gewalt*, of a tension and dialectic between power and violence – and of an emancipatory attempt to break the solidarity between all these meanings – might constitute a kind of blind spot in Badiou's thinking. Before concluding, and in order to simply lay the signposts for future research, let me enumerate five key points that any further investigation of the theme of violence in Badiou's thinking will need to touch upon:

1. *Marxism, Leninism and militarism.* Many of Badiou's attempts to formulate a post-Leninist 'politics without a party' rest on the thesis that egalitarian politics was fundamentally corrupted, through a kind of historical inertia, by the military or martial referent. It is important to note here that Badiou, following Mao's military essays, initially defends and praises the specificity of the Maoist contribution to the uneven and combined development of dialectical thought and its halting periodisation precisely in terms of the martial innovations made by Mao against the Leninist-Stalinist model. It is also worth indicating the disparate, ambiguous and uncertain status of the quasi-references that populate Badiou's attempt to think towards a demilitarised, post-Leninist politics: the Polish trade-union movement Solidarność, the Iranian revolution, the experience of the *sans papiers* movement in France and the Zapatista insurgency in Mexico.

2. *The distance from the State.* This is where we could argue Badiou *evades* the dialectics of *Gewalt* and equivocates in his fidelity to the inevitable and salutary call for a destruction *of* violence or a destruction of domination. Diagnosing the state either as the capture and co-optation of the force of subjectivity or as its perversion in a murderous spiral of suspicion (explicitly following Hegel's classic analysis of the terror in the *Phenomenology of Spirit*), and judging contagion with its subject-less mechanisms to be fatal to the autonomous capacities of egalitarian thought and practice, the thesis of politics at a distance from the State – a politics of prescription rather than demand or attack – has become central to Badiou's formulations. Even this evasion of an assumption of *Gewalt* on the part of the political subject is nevertheless based on a mathematical formalisation

---

32   'I believe, to put it quite bluntly, that *Marxism doesn't exist.* ... "Marxism" [is] the (void) name of an absolutely inconsistent set, once it is referred back, as it must be, to the history of political singularities'. Badiou 2005c, p. 58.

of the problem of *Gewalt* in terms of the crucial and intuitively attractive thesis of incalculable *excess* of the power-set of a situation (the State)
over that situation itself. In other words, of the excess of representation
over presentation, inclusion over belonging.[33] The upshot of this is that
the crux of politics for Badiou lies in its capacity to *measure* and arrest this
excess of the State, but from an extrinsic position, through a political and
organisational capacity that does not translate into a legal, bureaucratic
or military *power*.

3. *The force of the subject.* To remain within the semantic field of *Gewalt*,
    we should note that the anchors of Badiou's materialist dialectic are,
    for the period that I have called that of the communism of production
    and destruction, the notion of *force*, and, in *Being and Event* and sub-
    sequent writings (following the mathematician Paul Cohen), that of *for-
    cing*. In both cases we have concepts resonating with the notion of *Gewalt*
    that qualify the relation between a (political) subject and the creation of
    novelty, equality and justice – or indeed, to use, the central category of
    Badiou's later philosophy, *truth*. The first (force) is linked to the notion of
    destruction, the second (forcing) to one of subtraction, and both circulate
    around the subject's capacity to *intervene* in a situation at specific points
    so as to elicit or follow the dysfunction of a system of domination, a sys-
    tem that Badiou persistently depicts as a system of placement, identity,
    counting.[34] It is from the comparison between the function and possibil-
    ities inherent in these two terms that we might also begin to reconsider
    another constant in Badiou's thought, which has also been emphasised
    by Slavoj Žižek, among others, that of *partisan truth*.

4. *Terror and terrorism.* Though Badiou has tried to recuperate the notion
    of Terror as a necessary, if not founding, moment in political subjectiva-
    tion,[35] a critique of the terroristic temptation is a mainstay in his 'post-
    Maoist' work.[36] However – and this is what fundamentally separates
    Badiou from every stripe of revisionist, moralist and guilt-monger – the
    underlying argument is that only an immanent and determinate subtrac-

---

33 See Badiou 2006a, pp. 93–111.

34 It is worth noting that this conception of power and domination clashes on several points
    with other estimations of the nature of contemporary forms of coercion, for instance
    Gilles Deleuze's seminal annotations on the 'society of control' or Hardt and Negri's reflec-
    tions on the immeasurable character of imperial sovereignty.

35 Badiou 2008, pp. 81–87, with reference to ... Pierre Boulez.

36 Above all in Badiou 2001, p. 77, where terror is however explicitly distinguished from *Jac-
    obin* terror, the unilateral affirmation of radical discontinuity which Badiou deems insep-
    arable from the trajectory of a truth.

tion from the destructive innovations of politics, only the critique of terror *from the side of emancipation*, could herald a new thinking of politics at a distance from the State. Badiou also perspicuously links the virulence of twentieth-century century violence not just to its dark foundations in the colonial hecatombs but to the 'emancipatory' idea – in many respects born of the barbarous nightmare of World War 1 – of a violence to end all violences, a war against all wars (a theme also present in Mao). Moving to the more immediate conjuncture of the late 1970s and early 1980s, Badiou sees the emergence of 'red' terrorism in terms of a political weakness, and moreover, of a fallacious relation between movement, organisation and State.[37] In a text published in the *Le Perroquet*, he meditated on the disastrous combination – in the absence of an organised politics within the factory – of a 'democratic movement' with military clandestineness, of the kind that had briefly affected the ex-Gauche Prolétarienne, and which was later to lead to bloody impasse in the Brigate Rosse, the Rote Armee Fraktion and Action Directe.[38] Badiou, writing under the pseudonym Georges Peyrol, noted the following: 'To liquidate the terrorist temptation, the terrorist retreat, is a political criterion that demands to be invented. The upshot of such a criterion is that politics is superior to antagonism. Of course, revolution always comes down to changing a hostile real, made up of oppression and division. But the values of unity, from which it proceeds, and which are linked to forms of conscience, have value in and of themselves, and not just as instruments of violence'. Manipulating the hatred or fear of the other as a unifying factor is instead a pernicious phenomenon of what Sartre had called 'terror-fraternity'. The antidote is expressed as follows: 'we must establish at the heart of the people a principle of political unity whose reference is less the adversary than the real which must be changed. For terrorism the only real is the enemy. Politics begins perhaps when one subordinates the image of the adversary to the transformation of the real which the adversary wishes to impede. The object of terrorism is the obstacle to the real and not the real itself'. We can register here the influence of Badiou's heterodox reading of the politics of Solidarność, especially in terms of the idea of a primacy of popular unity over antagonism, and the connected thesis that the essence of politics is not war. Terrorism, and here Badiou concurs with the later Debord of the *Comments on the Society of the Spectacle* – a text also concerned with

---

37   For a convergent analysis of terrorism as a product of subjective political weakness, see
      Massari 1993.
38   All quotes in this section are from Peyrol 1982, pp. 6–7.

the phenomenon of the Red Brigades and akin groups – is simply a capitulation to the power of symbols and media, a spectacle. Both terrorism and the State feed on the absence of politics, of a determinate and independent political capacity that does not simply allow itself to be absorbed by the ruses of power and its forms of violence. Whence the key thesis that 'everything depends on the existence, or even the simple project of existence, of a politics that is excessive with regard to the State. In other words, which does not define itself by the capture of the State, or even its destruction'. An egalitarian politics that can circumvent terror (or at least terrorism) constitutes the horizon of Badiou's post-Maoist project, but the point, once again, is that it is from the perspective of an autonomous politics of emancipation, and not on the basis of any *raison d'État*, that one should subject the mistakes of that politics to scrutiny.[39] This is the sense in which Badiou's metapolitics could be defined, in terms of the conjuncture within which it emerged, as anti-anti-totalitarian.[40]

5. *Antagonism.* If dialectics and political practice are demilitarised, wrested from the State and stripped of their historical references, what remains the role of antagonism, or of what Badiou, in a Platonic vein, often calls the Two? To put it otherwise, can there be contradictions among the people without the preliminary confrontation with antagonistic or drastically polemical contradictions? In *The Century*, Badiou has written of an 'anti-dialectical Two' at the heart of the twentieth century's political experimentation, and of two ways of arranging the confrontation between a 'we', a fraternity, and its outside: 'Either one sees it as a polymorphous formlessness – a disordered reality – or else one sees it as *an other we*, an external and consequently antagonistic subject.' In the first instance, the task, to use a key signifier in Badiou, is 'formalisation', a protocol for producing the forms that will rally the not-we to the we. Formalisation requires incorporating the apparent alterity of what is outside the militant subject into its autonomous capacity, into what, in *Logics of Worlds*, Badiou calls a 'subject-body' (*corps-sujet*).[41] Where formalisation is weak or inexistent, we witness the rise of a frontal concept of antagonism, the veritable face-off between two substantial, pre-constituted subjects. This second conception of the relationship between the we and the not-we is *intrinsically* violent, and its violence is not simply that of

---

39   See Badiou 1985b.
40   See my review of Michael Scott Christofferson's *French Intellectuals Against the Left: The Antitotalitarian Moment of the 1970s*, Toscano 2006a.
41   'Book VII: What is a Body?' in Badiou 2008, pp. 449–503.

formalist 'conversion', but rather that of a frontal struggle, its objective 'is the destruction of the other'. It is in the context of the 'dialectics of the non-dialectical', of the confrontation between two modes of confrontation that Badiou returns, provocatively, to one of his abiding sources of metapolitical inspiration: 'Mao's essential directive is never to treat the "contradictions at the heart of the people" in an antagonistic manner, *to resolve the conflict between formalisation and destruction by means of formalisation.* This is perhaps one of the most profound lessons, but also one of the most difficult, that the century has bequeathed to us.'[42]

The development of Badiou's political thought – within, without, and at a distance from Marxist thought, or from the incompossible singularities of 'Marxist' politics – can also be read, especially in the light of his reflections on the twentieth century, as a subterranean confrontation with the seemingly immemorial entanglement of politics and violence. The movement that I have elsewhere sought to discern in Badiou's work from a communism of destruction to a communism of separation[43] is also – as some of the above notes on force, antagonism and terror might suggest – a movement from a conception of violence as *intrinsic* to the constitution of political subjectivity[44] to a vision of violence as a factor which, whilst perhaps an inevitable consequence of political militancy in certain situations, must never be conceived as *constitutive* of a political subject. It is in this light that we can understand Badiou's comments on the corrupting effects of the violence of the civil war on Bolshevik politics: 'In some cases violence is a necessity; everyone knows that. That is not the problem. The problem is that violence is also a subjective corruption. That is the great political problem. The constant use of violence is a subjective corruption and so we have to measure violence, something like moderation of violence as much as possible. Certainly, the rule is: when we can solve a problem without violence, it is better'.[45]

Beneath these seemingly anodyne remarks, we can discern that much of the motivation behind Badiou's communism of separation, his politics at a

---

42   Badiou 2005a, p. 158.

43   See Chapter 1 in this volume.

44   It is worth noting that in this regard Žižek, in formulating a theory of the radical subjective act, is far more sanguine about the need for violence (whether physical, symbolic, or, most likely both), for instance, when he writes of 'the violent act of actually changing the basic coordinates of a situation'. Žižek 2006, p. 381. One could compare the respective thinking of violence in Badiou and Žižek in terms of the difference between a thinking of the subject in a truth *procedure*, on the one hand, and a Lacanian thinking of the *act*, on the other.

45   Badiou 2005f.

distance from the State, consists in keeping this corruptive threat of a constitutive violence at bay from the political subject. Badiou's nuanced sublations
and revisions of a materialist dialectic can also be fruitfully grasped in terms
of an attempt to have done with what Balibar refers to as 'the theological and
philosophical schema of the conversion of violence into justice'.[46] The extern-
alisation of the 'agent' of conversion into the event and the constitution of an
autonomous subjective capacity that is not defined by a dialectic of destruction
appear as means for relegating violence to a subordinate role in what remains a
politics of radical and egalitarian transformation. And yet, in light of Balibar's
outstanding survey – which takes its cue from the intrinsic ambiguity of the
German term *Gewalt* – we may wonder whether in establishing the political
subject as that which follows upon a measurement or 'prescription'[47] regarding
the excess, or super-power, of the State (or, more problematically, of Capital[48]),
Badiou is not evading what Balibar defines as the tragic inner bond between
politics and violence. In other words, isn't the price to be paid for subtracting political capacity from the amorphous pull of political violence – whether
structural, opaque or purificatory – that of not having the means of thinking
the violence internal to the subject? To be more precise, and without delving
into all the problems that are rife in the idea of 'changing the world without
taking power', we may ask whether the formulation of a politics at a distance
from violence doesn't freeze the problem of State *Gewalt* into a kind of structural invariant which is simply external to (egalitarian) politics proper whilst
simultaneously depriving us of the means to think – beyond the destructive
paradigm – how power and violence may function *within* the constitution of a
political subject.

To reintroduce the theme of terror as that of a necessary, if limited, moment
of outright confrontation, as Badiou seems to have suggested in *Logics of
Worlds*, does not suffice, since it still bypasses the problem of power as something that may characterise the subjective procedure itself. Badiou's wish to
surpass the paradigm of constitutive violence is commendable and remains a
challenge worth pursuing. However, it is not clear how a politics of prescrip-

---

46   Balibar 2001; Balibar 2009.
47   'When the political procedure exists, such that it manages a prescription vis-à-vis the
     State, then and only then can the logic of the same, or the egalitarian maxim proper to
     every politics of emancipation, be set out. ... It is not the simple power of the state of
     the situation that prohibits egalitarian politics. It is the obscurity and measurelessness in
     which this power is enveloped. If the political event allows for a clarification, a fixation, an
     exhibition of this power, then the egalitarian maxim is at least locally practicable'. Badiou
     2005c, pp. 148–50.
48   See Chapter 3 in this volume.

tion[49] that seeks to measure and halt the obscure super-power, the immeasurable excess of what Badiou calls the State of a situation can do without the 'tragic' task of assuming some of that power, and some of that violence, into its own transformative trajectory. Perhaps we could give the following as a provisional indication for future research: any political subject driven to truly transform a situation cannot but risk the corruption of violence; it cannot simply maintain its political capacity (which is after all another way of saying its *power*) pure from the temptations and necessities of *Gewalt*. Having said that, what every political subject must establish is a kind of *internal* distance from violence, a way of thinking it and 'measuring' it as a potential consequence of its founding tenets or axioms – without ever making it either constitutive (or worse, the Real) of its identity or seeing in it the extorted evidence that it has indeed changed the world.

---

49   Hallward 2005.

The Bourgeois and the Islamist, or, the Other Subjects of Politics

1 Subjects of Untruth

Among the less fortunate by-products of the resurgence in emancipatory theories of political subjectivity is the tendency to depict the subject in an exclusively militant or, at the very least, 'progressive' light. Bracketing the contradictions of social class, or the pathologies of ideology, the political subject seems endowed, by fiat, with the steadfast virtues of universalism. Though when confronted with a proliferation of noxious political 'agents' and ideas such a stance may possess an attractive if minimalist rectitude, reserving the term 'subject' solely for the kind of collective egalitarian figure that could divert our baleful course might mean depriving ourselves of a potent instrument to intervene in the present. If we relegate the reactionary, or at best ambiguous, figures that loom large on our political horizon to the rank of structural epiphenomena, fleeting phantoms or mindless tendencies, we run the risk of producing political theories that differ little from wishful thinking or self-satisfied sectarianism. Even within the generally optimistic politico-philosophical paradigm which, by way of shorthand, we could call 'the theory of the multitude', some have begun to foreground the deep *ambivalence* of contemporary forms of political subjectivity.[1] But can there be any concessions to such an ambiguity, to the presence of 'untruthful' subjects, in Badiou's affirmative, and avowedly 'Promethean' theory of the subject?

Badiou's decades-long preoccupation with political subjectivity does indeed seem marked by an increasingly trenchant and 'internalist' treatment of the subject as both rare and aloof from the vicissitudes of social mediation. What's more, Badiou makes 'subject' inseparable from the novelty of an exception and the arduous trajectory of a truth which is always in the world, but in many ways not of it (or rather, a truth which, by forcefully including itself in the world, makes sure that the world will never be the same). He does this by advocating a strenuously 'post-Cartesian' thinking of the subject in which the latter is only figured as an *effect*, an aleatory trajectory or point of arrival, and not

---

1 Virno 2004.

as a pre-existing source. After Marx and Freud, the subject is not a starting point, it must be 'found'.[2] All signs point to a stance that is wholly refractory to any analysis of the subject's particularistic attachments, violent and violating impulses, repressive desires, and so on. Badiou's explicit decision not to treat the subject by way of a theory of ideology, and – despite his grounding allegiance to Lacan – not to delve into its Freudian unconscious, also militate for a purified, formal theory that would shun the subject's unsavoury, pathological side. And yet, as I would like to explore in this chapter, within the strictures of an asocial, non-ideological and uncompromisingly universalistic theory of the subject, Badiou has proposed a number of ways to think and formalise the existence of other subjects, ones which are not the bearers but the enemies or obfuscators of truth.

2   Ambivalence of the Bourgeoisie

Given Badiou's roots in revolutionary theory one cannot but expect some traces in his work of the numerous contributions to the theory of anti- or semi-universalist subjectivity within Marxism – from Marx's own paean to bourgeois destruction in *The Communist Manifesto*, to the wrestling with the rise of fascist politics in the writings of Trotsky and many others. It is evident, for instance, that a reckoning with the figure of *reaction* has been a constant in Badiou's work. But perhaps one of the more interesting points of entry into Badiou's theory of 'untrue' subjects concerns the status of the bourgeoisie. To begin with, Badiou intends to dislocate the apparently frontal confrontation, the class struggle, between proletariat and bourgeoisie. For the proletariat as a *force* (a crucial concept in Badiou's dialectical writings of the 1970s and early 1980s) does not seem to be pitted against the bourgeoisie as another force. In some of the early seminars that make up Badiou's *Theory of the Subject*, the bourgeoisie is depicted as a mere agent of a system of places, of a Whole which the proletariat seeks to destroy by what Badiou calls a 'torsion', whereby an included but suppressed element comes to limit, then destroy, the totality of which it is a part: 'To say proletariat and bourgeoisie is to remain with the Hegelian artifice: something and something else. And why? Because the project of the proletariat, its internal being, is not to contradict the bourgeoisie, or to cut its legs off. Its project is communism, and nothing else. That is to say, the abolition of

---

2 Badiou 1982, p. 295.

any place wherein something like a proletariat could be situated'.[3] And, *a for-tiori*, anything like a bourgeoisie. In this sense, whilst the confrontation with the bourgeoisie might be the 'motor' of history, the proletariat's target is really the social Whole, i.e. 'imperialist society'.

However, advancing through the series of seminars that make up Badiou's first major theoretical work, we encounter, in the course of an analysis of the subjective weakness of May '68, a portrait of the bourgeois as subject and force. Indeed, Badiou stresses that revolutionaries have always made the mistake of thinking themselves to be 'the only subject and represent the antagonistic class to themselves as an objective mechanism of oppression led by a handful of profiteers'. On the contrary, one of the lessons of the Chinese Cultural Revolu-tion, according to Badiou, is that the bourgeoisie too engages in politics, and not simply by means of exploitation or coercion. Asking himself *where* this polit-ics takes place, Badiou answers, with atypical Gramscian overtones: 'Exactly as with the proletariat: in the people, working class included, and I would even say, since we're dealing with the new bureaucratic State bourgeoisie, working class *especially* included'. The reason for thus foregrounding the 'subjective force of the adversary' is to counter the feeble-minded and objectivist 'anti-repressive logorrhoea', for which the only enemy would be a Moloch-like State. Contrary to this anarchistic 'leftism', Badiou proposes the following assertion: 'Of course, they are a handful, the bourgeois imperialists, but the subjective effect of their force lies in the divided people. There is not just the law of Capital, or the cops. To miss this is not to see the unity of the space of placements [*esplace*], its con-sistency'. The suggestion here is that the social space wherein the latent force of the proletariat is captured, placed and instrumentalised cannot be envisaged in a purely structural manner, as an impersonal given, but must instead be con-ceived in terms of that counter-revolutionary or reactionary subjectivity that carries its own project into the pre-subjective mass of the people. Or, as Badiou summarises in a Hegelian pastiche: 'We must conceive of imperialist society not only as substance, but also as subject'.[4] This, at least, is the position put for-ward in the seminar dated '15 April 1975', which appears to rectify the earlier understanding of the proletariat as the sole political and subjective force.

In the seminar dated '14 February 1977', Badiou approaches the question of the proletariat/bourgeoisie relation from a topological angle. If we follow an economistic tradition, which sunders Marx's *Capital* from the concrete (stra-tegic) analysis of concrete (socio-political) situations, bourgeoisie and prolet-

---

3   Badiou 1982, p. 25.
4   Badiou 1982, p. 60.

ariat appear topologically exterior to one another – the first defined in terms
of its ownership of the means of production, the second in terms of its separation (alienation) from them. The result of this purely external topology is
paradoxically to render the proletariat functionally interior or immanent to
the bourgeoisie. Reduced to alienated labour-power, the proletariat is nothing
but a piece in the apparatus of exploitation, whose identity is entirely heteronomous, dictated by the laws of capital. Briefly, 'capital is the place of the
proletariat'. Badiou deduces from this the possibility of Soviet state-capitalism,
since it is perfectly possible, given this arrangement, to 'suppress capitalists,
all the while maintaining the law of capital'. To depart from the compulsion to
repeat and the allergy to novelty that characterise the economistic framework,
Badiou enjoins us to think the 'interiority of the bourgeoisie to the working
class'.[5]

Citing Marx's analyses of the series of uprisings ('social hysterias' in Badiou's
Lacanian phrasing) of the 1830s, 40s and 50s, Badiou sees the emergence of a
proletarian figure not as a functional cog in the machinery of capital, but as
an internal 'torsion', an 'exceptional disorder' within the political trajectory of
the democratic bourgeois movement. The proletarian subject is born out of its
bourgeois impurity, its being indexed to a heteronomous capitalist order, and
only emerges by the 'expulsion, the purging ... of the internal infection that, to
begin with, constitutes it'. The proletariat is thus depicted, through these somewhat unsettling medical metaphors, as perpetually in the process of healing
from the malady of the bourgeoisie. Insisting with the topological vocabulary,
Badiou writes that 'the politics of the proletariat is in a situation of internal
exclusion with regard to bourgeois politics, that is, with regard to its object'. The
proletariat is thus both within and against the bourgeoisie, constantly 'purging'
its intimate bourgeois determination. Its 'topology of destruction' means that
it is enduringly engaged in an effort to dislocate and ultimately destroy the site
of its existence (without this destruction, it might just be a mask or ruse of the
bourgeoisie, as Badiou deems to be the case for the USSR); but it can only do
so, because of its originary impurity, in an immanent, dialectical combat with
the bourgeoisie that internally excludes it. This topological vision transforms
the standing of the bourgeoisie within Badiou's theory of the subject yet again:

> Does the bourgeoisie make a subject [*fait sujet*]? I said so in this very
> place, in April 1975. Let us contradict ourselves, it is just a trick of semb-
> lance [*par-être*]. The bourgeois has not made a subject for a long while,

---

5   Badiou 1982, p. 147.

it makes a place [*lieu*]. There is only one political subject, for a given his-toricisation. This is a very important remark. To ignore it is to become confused by a vision of politics as a subjective duel, which it is not. There is one place and one subject. The dissymmetry is structural.[6]

Class struggle, if the term still applies, is thus not between two separate *forces*, two subjects indexed to different places within the apparatus of capital. It is an effect of the proletariat (that 'surviving body, born from the rot') expelling itself from bourgeois politics, and thus gaining its existence through that very pro-cess of organised destruction. The theory of subjectivation as destruction thus appears to require the exclusivity of the term 'subject', and the relegation of the bourgeoisie, and any subjects other than the proletariat, to a phantasmagorical structural semblance.

This oscillation in the appraisal of the bourgeoisie, and the dialectical argu-ments that motivate it, indicate the thorny problem posed to Badiou's project by the existence of other, non-emancipatory subjects: if the bourgeoisie is not a subject, the theory of the proletariat risks a 'leftist' solution, a repressive hypo-thesis that singles out an impersonal state or capital as its only enemy; if the bourgeoisie is a subject, antagonism seems to absorb Badiou's theory of torsion-destruction, and the historicity of politics seems doomed to ambivalence with the introduction of multiple forms of universality into the situation. As we will see further on, this antinomy of the other subject continues to haunt Badiou's work.

3   Justice and Terror, Nihilists and Renegades

Abiding within the rich confines of *Theory of the Subject*, we witness the return, in a very different guise, of the problem of the 'other subject' in Badiou's attempt to formulate an *ethics*. Insisting with the metaphors of location and the topological arsenal that dominates the recasting of dialectics in *Theory*, Badiou proposes to rethink the question of ethics in terms of a 'topics' [*topique*]: 'There is no major Marxist text that is not driven by the question: Where is the pro-letariat? That is why politics is the unity of opposites of a topics (the current situation) and an ethics (our tasks)'.[7] But this topics also acquires a more pre-cise meaning, referring to the affective figures that the subject (viewed as an

---

6   Badiou 1982, p. 148.
7   Badiou 1982, p. 297. The philosophical notion of a 'Topics', concerned with the *topoi*, the places or locations of discourse, derives from Aristotle's eponymous treatise.

unstable mix of destructive 'subjectivation', and restorative 'subjective processes') moves across. This ethics is thus, first and foremost, immanent to the becoming of a subject – so how might it allow us to deepen our investigation of other, non-emancipatory subjects?

Given the centrality of radical novelty to Badiou's investigation, and what he has already indicated regarding the proletariat, born of a rotting bourgeoisie amid an upsurge of social hysteria, the starting point for an ethics of subjectivity can only be *disorder*. What *affects* are borne by a subject that might try, by bringing itself into the world, to draw novelty out of this disorder? To begin with, a methodological proviso is required: like his theory of the subject, Badiou's theory of affect is also post-Cartesian, which is to say it treats the subject as a formalisation and an aleatory trajectory, meaning that 'affect' does not refer to an experience, a capacity, a spiritual or mental disposition. This ethics of affects, which principally concerns the subject's stance vis-à-vis the law of the world that is being destroyed, circulates through four concepts: anxiety, superego, courage and justice. 'These are categories of the subject-effect. What they allow us to know is a specific material region, at the basis [*principe*] of every destruction of what sustains it'. How these concepts are articulated to one another by the subject will determine its disposition with regard to the situation and its aptitude for the tasks of innovation.

Anxiety (*angoisse*) treats the given order as *dead*. It does not foresee the splitting and re-composition of the symbolic around a new law, but the simple 'killing' of the symbolic by the real. The consequence of this non-dialectical treatment of destruction as chaos and paralysis, abrogation of sense, is that 'the law, always undivided, glimmers in the distance of what it no longer supports'.[8] The excess over the law has no other symbols than those of its death, and remains in a sense hysterical, 'a question without an answer'.

The intervention of the *superego* is thus depicted as a response to the morbid paralysis of anxiety: 'as a figure of consistency, [superego] puts excess back in place *by distributing it over all the places*. The superego is the structural aspect of excess. Through it the algebraization of the topological is effected, as if, filled with subjectivating anxiety, the place recomposed itself upon itself in the terrorizing prescription of placement. ... The superego is the subjective process of terror'.[9] The model here is provided by one of the crucial sources for Badiou's treatment of the dark side of subjectivity, Hegel's diagnosis of the French revolutionary Terror. Where anxiety signalled the chaos of a world

---

8 Badiou 1982, p. 307.
9 Badiou 1982, p. 308.

without law, the superego determines a fixing of excess (and of death); a piti-
less control of the situation by the forcible introduction of a new law, which, as
Hegel shows, takes the shape of a purely negative and persecutory universality. But, foreshadowing the use of the same passages from Hegel in his lectures
on the twentieth century, for Badiou the superego-Terror 'is a phenomenon
of the subject, and not of the state ... terror is a modality of politics and not
the mechanical product of the modern state'.[10] What does it mean to think
terror as internal to the subject? For Badiou it means that the criminal ravages of terror (e.g. the gulag) cannot be the object of an anti-statist moral
critique but must be rethought from within a (Marxist) politics that compre-
hends the superego as an internal, dialectical and 'restorative' figure. If terror is
subjective, it is only by understanding the ethical trajectory of subjects from
within that it may be parried or limited. External critique, which excises or
ignores the subjective element, merely prepares the return or repetition of terror.

The third ethical figure, *courage*, presents an important alternative to the
subjectivity of terror qua antidote to the ravages of anxiety – where anxiety was a 'question without an answer', courage is presented as 'an answer
without a question'. As an affect, courage qualifies the kind of subject capable
of facing disorder and the anxiety that issues from it, without demanding the
immediate restoration of the law. What is more, courage subtends the capacity to act, to traverse the chaos of anxiety, without the coordinates provided
by the law. When gnawed at by anxiety – so goes Badiou's recommendation –
to act with courage is to do that very thing you think impossible, or before
which you anxiously recoil. Or, as his motto has it: 'Find your indecency of the
moment'.[11]

Possibly the most interesting ethical concept proposed in this 'topics' is that
of *justice*, which is presented as basically the opposite of terror in its relationship to the law. While – to the extent that its terroristic implementation
is self-justifying – the superego absolutises law, justice relativises it, working
by the criterion that the more Real and the less law, the better. But for this
very reason, justice is a deeply unsettling affect, generating ever further anxiety as it casts doubt on the viability of rules for dealing with disorder. Insisting
with a dialectical approach, this is why the institutive character of justice can
never be wholly sundered from the restorative procedure of the superego, and

---

10   Badiou 1982, p. 309. See also Badiou 2007, especially Chapter 5: 'The passion for the real
      and the montage of semblance', where Hegel features as the principal philosophical ref-
      erence for a reckoning with the molten core of the twentieth century.
11   Badiou 1982, p. 310.

why justice calls forth two stances that deny its autonomy: *dogmatism*, which demands the untrammelled supremacy of the superego over courage; and *scepticism*, in which the non-law of justice does not open up to the institution of new laws, but is merely the stand-in for the undecidability of law, which is to say, for anxiety. 'Justice is the *flux* [*flou*] *of places*, the opposite, therefore, of the right place [*la juste place*]'.[12]

What are the consequences of this quadripartite schema for a thinking of other subjects? I would like to focus on two. The first concerns the ideologisation of subjects, the second Badiou's typology of ethical discourses.

Besides serving as a psychoanalytic clue to the functioning of Hegelian terror, the superego is also employed by Badiou to account for the immanent production of ideology out of the travails of subjectivation. Following a general methodological principle, which is that of following the vicissitudes of the subject without immediately imposing upon it the marks of structure, Badiou here proposes to see ideology as a product of something like an ethical failing within the subject itself. While 'true' subjectivation involves the real piercing into the symbolic, and the hazardous effort to recompose a new order after the destruction of the system of places, ideology is a question of the imaginary. Holding to the dialectical demand that organises his ethics of the subject – the idea that faithful subjectivity must topologically adhere to its other – Badiou sees subjectivation and ideology as facets of the same process. He illustrates this with an example from an event, the German Peasants' War of 1525, which he had already touched upon in his earlier collaborative work on ideology: 'When Thomas Müntzer sets the German countryside aflame with an egalitarian communist aim, he subjectivates courageously, on a background of death, and calls for justice. When he names his courage on the basis of the absolute conviction that Christ wants the realisation of this project, he imaginarily articulates the rebellious bravura on the superego whose allegory is the "kingdom of God"'.[13] The same lesson can be drawn from the Cultural Revolution: it is the incapacity of the Red Guards to sustain their egalitarian programme, with courage and justice, that calls forth the imaginary and ideological guarantee, the ethical stop-gap provided by the superego-cult of Mao. The anxiety produced by egalitarian disorder is thus assuaged, not just through the idolatry of a new, if under-defined law (Mao-Tse-Tung-thought), but, following Hegel, through the persecution it gives rise to: the superego's manner of 'saturating places', which can only be occupied, without ambiguity, by revolutionaries or enemies.

---

12   Badiou 1982, p. 312.
13   Badiou 1982, p. 314. See also Badiou and Balmès 1976.

The imaginary dimension thus arises as a way of comforting the anxious subject, unable to sustain the uncertain discipline of courage and the undecidable measure of justice.

The terror exercised by the superego thus represents a weakness of the subject. But this does not exhaust the content of ethics. If ethics 'makes discourse of what cannot wait or be delayed', if it 'makes do with what there is', then its key problem, as Badiou explicitly draws from Lacan, is that 'the world only ever proposes the temptation to give up', 'to inexist in the service of goods'.[14] What an 'ethics of Marxism' would therefore need to confront are the various ways in which the temptation to give up on the labour of subjectivation, the labour of destruction, manifests itself. If 'subjectivation' names the destructive process whereby the subject subordinates place to excess, while 'subjective process' defines the contrary, conservative tendency, then the character of defeatism or even reaction involves giving up on subjectivation for the sake of an older subjective process. The source for this remains internal to the subject itself, in the failure of 'confidence' (*confiance*) ('the fundamental concept of the ethics of Marxism'). If the ethical subject is identified with the party pure and simple, then the ethical nemesis is surely the renegade, the traitor to be liquidated (thereby returning us to superego-Terror). But if we rein back this ferocious form of placement, what light can ethics shed on the existence of other subjects?

While Badiou had abandoned the idea of plural subjects when wrestling with the conundrum of the bourgeoisie, the issue seems to return once he declares ethics to be 'a naming of the subject as historically effectuated in the form of discourse'. For there is not just one, but *four* discourses of the subject for Badiou and thus, in a complex and problematic sense, if not four separate subjects, at least four tendencies within subjectivation and subjective processes. These four discourses are the discourse of praise, that of resignation, that of discordance, and the 'Promethean' discourse. Their fundamental affective tonalities are belief, fatalism, nihilism and confidence. Now, without delving into the detail of how these positions are derived from the prior distinction between superego, anxiety, courage and justice, it is important to note that the ethical subjects indexed to these discourses are intrinsically relational. In other words, they only exist by designating their others and the discourses of these others.

The discourse of praise and the Promethean discourse are the two that in a sense lie beyond anxiety. But they are diametrically opposed in their rela-

---

14   Badiou 1982, pp. 325, 328, 334.

tions to the Whole (or space of placements, *esplace*) and the force of novelty (or the out of place, *horlieu*). It is a matter of belief (or confidence in the space of placements) versus confidence (or belief in the out-of-place). While belief opens up the possibility of salvation, and the potential eternity of the subject in a finally realised space of placements (without lack but determined by law), confidence, instead, works with fidelity to the innovative decision (courage), and a more porous recomposition of the real, less open to the law (justice). The subject of praise can here be recast in terms of something like the subject of the system itself, the believer and defender of its righteousness, a truly *conservative* subject. But the Promethean subject of destruction and recomposition, the universalist (proletarian) subject, has two other counterparts, mired in different forms of anxiety. These are the resigned fatalist and the nihilist. The resigned fatalist is most likely the one who has succumbed to the service of goods, who, though not beyond the pale, is in a sense a *passive* nihilist and something like an after-subject. It is the real nihilist instead who, plunged into the discordance of an anxious world, but without the safety of knowing scepticism, is the subject whom the Promethean discourse wishes to capture and persuade. For the nihilist is indeed imbued with a certain form of courage (the passion for the act, for excess) but is incapable of justice, of the right measurement of the relationship between the real and the law. He lacks the confidence which alone allows the organisation and endurance of both courage and justice in a universal figure.

Thus, despite his arguments to the contrary when addressing the possibility of a bourgeois subject, Badiou already recognises, in *Theory of the Subject*, the need to think different subjective configurations, not all of which can be regarded as the ethical bearers of novelty and universality. Though his later writing on ethics has been far more widely discussed than the earlier foray into an ethical 'topics', we can identify some manifest continuities, which bridge the theoretical caesura triggered by the introduction of the theory of the event and its meta-ontological, set-theoretical armature. In the first place, there is the idea that a subject is ethically defined by the manner in which it relates to other subjects within the space created by its confidence, or fidelity: 'Every fidelity to an authentic event names the adversaries of its perseverance'.[15] This *agonistic* dimension of subjectivation clearly relates to the relational character of the theory of ethical discourses (e.g. there is no Promethean subject without 'its' nihilist). Secondly, there is the idea that one can only rescind one's incorporation into a subject by *betrayal*. This theory of betrayal is in

---

15   Badiou 2001, p. 75.

some respects akin to the discourse of resignation in *Theory of the Subject*. The (ex-)subject of betrayal in fact *denies* having been seized by a truth, drowning his previous courage in deep scepticism and bowing to the imperative according to which we must avert the risks imposed by any truth procedure. Thirdly, there is the key tenet that the pathologies of subjectivity – more particularly the emergence of 'false' subjects that trade in *simulacra* of truth (e.g. Nazism) and the *terror* that exerts a full sovereignty of truth over all places – can only be understood from out of the possible impasses of a subject of truth.

The last is a persistent conviction underlying Badiou's treatment of what, for lack of better terms, we could refer to as 'non-universal' subjects. In other words, it is the irruption of a subject of truth that serves as the aleatory condition of possibility for the formation of other subjects. In the case of Nazism, for instance, '[s]uch a simulacrum is only possible thanks to the success of political revolutions that were genuinely evental (and thus universally addressed)'. This is why it is only from the standpoint of fidelity to events that are bearers of a universal address – 'the truth-processes whose simulacra they manipulate' – that these other, non- or anti-universal subjects become intelligible.[16] Or, in Badiou's more classical terms, why Evil can only be understood from the standpoint of the Good.

4   Struggles over Subjective Space

The foregoing discussion suggests that the problem of other subjects – in its ethico-political, rather than epistemological sense – has been an abiding preoccupation and a thorny challenge for Badiou's thinking ever since the mid-1970s. In this regard, the treatment of the theory of the subject in *Being and Event*, wholly concerned with the subject of truth, seems to hark back to one of Badiou's theoretical tendencies, already encountered in the *Theory of the Subject* – the one which contends that, for a given situation (or space of placements) and for a given historical sequence, *there is only one subject*. As we observed with reference to the concept of the bourgeoisie, there is something structural about this oscillation in the work of Badiou. Are there one or many subjects? Prior to the publication of the *Logics of Worlds*, Peter Hallward already indicated, in his indispensable and lucid summary of Badiou's 1996–97 lectures on the axiomatic theory of the subject, that Badiou has found

---

16   Badiou 2001, p. 77.

it necessary to introduce a modicum of mediation[17] and plurality into his account of the subject. As Hallward puts it, 'Badiou realizes that an event can evoke a range of subjective responses. ... He now sees each effect of truth as raising the possibility of a countereffect, no longer considered as simply external to the process of subjectivation, but as internal to subjective space itself'.[18]

As I have already suggested, however, this realisation should not be seen as a sudden innovation in Badiou's thinking, but as the recovery of a problem intrinsic to his theory of the subject ever since his seminars of the 1970s. Besides the abiding preoccupation with the lessons of Hegel's phenomenology of terror, and the attempt to flesh out a theory of subjective betrayal, Badiou has demonstrated an abiding concern with the possible existence of subjects who veer from, react to or occlude the struggle for transformative universality. In this respect, the *topique* presented in his ethics of Marxism, with its nihilists, fatalists and believers, is a clear precursor of the theory of subjective space sketched out in his 1990s lectures and, with some amendments, introduced in his 'meta-physics' of the subject in the *Logics of Worlds*.[19] In other words, I think it is useful, especially in order to survey the gamut of subjective possibilities investigated by Badiou's thought, to recognise that it is not just in the past few years that he has come to consider 'the subjective realm precisely as a *space* – as something that no one figure can fully occupy and determine, as something that every subject must traverse'.[20]

Given Hallward's exhaustive treatment of the earlier and unpublished sketch of the theory of subjective space, I will focus here solely on the shape that this notion of subjective space takes on in Book I of *Logics of Worlds*.

To begin with it is necessary briefly to outline the parameters of Badiou's more recent finessing of his formal theory of the subject. Pitted against hermeneutic, moral, and ideological models of subjectivity, it is worth reiterating that Badiou's theory is not interested in the *experience* of subjectivity, but simply in its *form*. Nor is Badiou particularly concerned with the subject as a source of statements, a subject of enunciation capable of saying 'I' or 'we'. Rather, the subject is depicted as what *exceeds* the normal disposition and

---

17   'To lend the event an implicative dimension is already to submit the process of its affirmation to a kind of logical mediation, as distinct from the immediacy of a pure nomination'. Hallward 2003, p. 145.

18   Hallward 2003, pp. 144–5.

19   Among the differences between the two is that what appears as the 'faithful subject' in *Logics of Worlds* was split into two figures, the hysteric and the master, in the lectures discussed by Hallward.

20   Hallward 2003, p. 145.

knowledge of 'bodies and languages' – the exclusive focus upon which defines Badiou's ideological nemesis in *Logics of Worlds*, what he calls 'democratic materialism'.[21] While the theory of the subject as a whole certainly tackles the 'subject-bodies' (political parties, scientific communities, artistic configurations ...) that support truth procedures, the formal theory as such limits itself to the various formalisations of the effects of the 'body' of the subject. The theory propounded in Book I of *Logics* brackets the body (which is why Badiou dubs it a 'meta-physics'), providing the general parameters for thinking how subjects exceed the situations whence they arise. The notion of subject therefore 'imposes the legibility of a unified orientation onto the multiplicity of bodies'.[22] This means that it also suspends a consideration of the specific historicity of a process of subjectivation, the manner in which the body of a subject is composed by incorporating certain elements of the situation and disqualifying others. The subject is thus viewed as an 'active and identifiable form of the production of truths'. The emphasis, evidently, is on 'form'.

But does this entail that the only subjects deserving of our theoretical attention are subjects of truth, of the *one* truth that may affect and dislocate any given situation? The particular inflection that Badiou gives to his definition tells us otherwise: 'Saying "subject" or saying "subject with regard to truth" is redundant. For there is a subject only as the subject of a truth, at the service of this truth, of its denial or of its occultation'.[23] This 'with regard to' already indicates that there are indeed, as Hallward suggests, different subjective positions or comportments, determined by a subject's stance towards the irruption of the event and the truths that may follow from it. Badiou himself presents this theory as a self-criticism of sorts, arguing that his earlier work (he is thinking of *Theory of the Subject* in particular) stipulated an all too firm and drastic opposition between the new and the old. In this new formal theory, he wishes instead to confront the existence, amongst others, of what he calls '*reactionary novelties*'.[24] To resist the new, to deny it, one still requires arguments and subjective forms. In other words, the theory of the subject needs to countenance the fact that reactionary forms of subjectivation exist – which for Badiou unsurprisingly take the shape of the anti-communist anti-totalitarianism which spurred the backlash of revisionist historians (François Furet) and the renegade *nouveaux philosophes* (André Glucksmann) to the emancipatory innovations arising in the wake of May '68.

---

21   Badiou 2005d. This is an excerpt from the preface to Badiou 2008.
22   Badiou 2008, pp. 46–7.
23   Badiou 2008, p. 50.
24   Badiou 2008, pp. 54–8.

Now, as I suggested above, it is not entirely true that *Theory of the Subject* foreclosed the possibility of reactionary novelties. The briefly explored possibility of a bourgeois subject (not just in the French 'new bourgeoisie', but in the Soviet bureaucratic caste) depended on that subjct's ability to generate some kind of novelty, however abject or corrupt. Similarly, the subjectivity of betrayal and resignation, or even that of active nihilism, as explored in Badiou's early 'ethics of Marxism', depend on the particular manner whereby they avoid or repress the courageous subjectivity and the just praxis of a revolutionary proletariat. They too are new by dint of how they respond (or better, *react*) to the disturbing irruption of that subjective figure. The fact that this formal theory of the subject comes after Badiou's formulation of a theory of evental subjectivity (first sketched in *Can Politics Be Thought?*) does make a difference to the account of 'other', non- or anti-universal subjects. For one, as we already intimated in our discussion of the *Ethics*, the dependency of subjectivation on the event permits Badiou to propose a philosophical argument as to why 'other' subjects are radically dependent on a subject of truth. As he writes: 'From a subjective point of view, it is not because there is reaction that there is revolution, it is because there is revolution that there is reaction'.[25] This Maoist thesis of the primacy of revolt, which Badiou had already formulated as early as his 1975 *Theory of Contradiction*, is now philosophically articulated in terms of the key 'temporal' category of Badiou's theory of the subject, that of the *present*. In responding to the *trace* of a supernumerary, illegal event, and in constructing the *body* that can bring the implications of this event to bear on a given world, a faithful subject is involved in the production of a present. Indeed, the only subjective temporality, which is to say the only historicity, envisaged in Badiou's system derives from such an irruption of generic universality into the status quo.

But if the present, as a kind of rigorous and continued sequence of novelties (a permanent revolution ...), belongs to the subject of truth, how can 'other subjects' partake in it? Badiou's contention is that they do so in a strictly derivative and parasitic (albeit by no means passive) manner. As he puts it, subjective 'destinations proceed in a certain order (production → denial → occultation), for reasons that formalism makes altogether clear: the denial of the present supposes its production, and its occultation supposes a formula of denial'.[26]

---

25   Badiou 2008, p. 62. This means, incidentally, that Badiou reiterates his intolerance for those, generally 'leftist' positions which base their notion of revolt on the prior reality of oppression, and for whom the political subject par excellence is therefore the oppressed.

26   Badiou 2008, pp. 62–3.

Given the arduous and ongoing production of a truth, *reactionary* subjects seek to deny the event that called it into being, and to disaggregate the body which is supposed to carry the truth of that event. It is for this reason that reaction, according to Badiou, involves the production of another, 'extinguished' present. The thesis of reaction, at bottom, is that all the 'results' of a truth procedure (e.g. political equality in the French Revolution) could be attained without the terroristic penchant of the faithful subject, and without the affirmation of a radically novel event. As Badiou recognises, this constitutes an *active* denial of truth, which demands the creation of reactionary statements and indeed of what we could call reactionary anti-bodies. Think, for instance, of the elaborate strategies of cultural organisation with which the CIA and its proxies sought to incorporate some of the innovations of aesthetic radicalism in order to deny their link with communist politics, invariably borrowing many formal traits and discursive dispositions from their nemeses.[27] Or consider the emergence, among what some referred to as the 'pro-war left' in the context of the US invasions of Iraq and Afghanistan, of reactionary subjectivities. The resilience of such subjectivities was convincingly mapped by Georg Simmel when he set forth his portrait of the 'renegade'. Due to the drastic violence of his conversion, the renegade, according to Simmel, is in a sense a far more steadfast and loyal subject than a militant or partisan who, for whatever reason, might not have adhered to his camp with the same conscious resolve. As Simmel writes:

> The special loyalty of the renegade seems to me to rest on the fact that the circumstances, under which he enters the new relationship, have a longer and more enduring effect than if he had naïvely grown into it, so to speak, without breaking a previous one. ... It is as if he were repelled by the old relationship and pushed into the new one, over and over again. Renegade loyalty is so strong because it includes what loyalty in general can dispense with, namely, the conscious continuance of the motives of the relationship.[28]

While the reactionary – and the renegade as one of its sub-species – suspends or attenuates the present produced by an event, denying its novelty but absorbing many of its traits, the second type of 'unfaithful' subject, what Badiou calls the *obscure* subject, entertains a far more severe relation to the new present that the faithful subject had given rise to. Rather than *denying* its novelty,

---

27   See Saunders 2000.
28   Simmel 1964, pp. 385–6.

the obscure subject is focussed on actually *negating* the very existence of this new present. The obscure subject, in order to occult novelty, 'systematically resorts to the invocation of a full and pure transcendent Body, an ahistorical or anti-evental body (City, God, Race ...) from which it follows that the trace will be denied (here, the labour of the reactive subject is useful to the obscure subject) and, as a consequence, the real body, the divided body, will also be suppressed'.[29] The obscure 'anti-body' is thus very different than the reactive one. While the latter may be repressive, it is also aimed at persuading the faithful that 'it's just not worth it', that they should resign themselves to a 'lesser present' and enjoy its diminished but secure rewards. The transcendent body conjured up by the obscure subject is instead a kind of 'atemporal fetish', writes Badiou, under whose weight novelty must be thoroughly crushed and silenced.

Persisting with a conviction that dominates both the *topiques* of *Theory of the Subject* and the account of evil in the *Ethics*, Badiou suggests that the faithful subject, the subject that produces a new present by drawing the worldly consequences of an event, must entertain a differentiated relationship to the other figures who inhabit the new subjective space that his fidelity has opened up. Compared to the treatment of the fatalist and the nihilist in *Theory*, in *Logics*, Badiou strikes a more cautious note. I will take the liberty of quoting at length the passage where he compares the two figures of the reactionary and the obscurantist, in part because of the literary flair with which he gives flesh to these formal figures:

> The crucial thing here is to gauge the gap between reactive formalism and obscure formalism. As violent as it may be, reaction conserves the form of the faithful subject as its articulated unconscious. It does not propose to abolish the present, only to show that the faithful break (which it calls 'violence' or 'terrorism') is useless for engendering a moderate, that is to say extinguished present (a present that reaction calls 'modern'). Moreover, this instance of the subject is itself borne by the debris of bodies: frightened and deserting slaves, renegades of revolutionary groups, avant-garde artists recycled into academicism, old scientists now blind to the movements of their science, lovers suffocated by conjugal routine. Things stand differently for the obscure subject. That is because it is the present which is directly its unconscious, its lethal disturbance, while

---

29   Badiou 2008, pp. 59–60. Badiou links the theory of 'obscure' fascism to the 'production of imaginary macroscopic entities' and 'passive bodies of subjectivation' in Badiou 2007, Chapter 9.

it de-articulates in appearing the formal data of fidelity. The monstrous full Body to which it gives fictional shape is the atemporal filling of the abolished present. Thus, what bears this body is directly linked to the past, even if the becoming of the obscure subject also crushes this past in the name of the sacrifice of the present: veterans of lost wars, failed artists, intellectuals perverted by bitterness, dried-up matrons, illiterate musclebound youths, shopkeepers ruined by Capital, desperate unemployed workers, rancid couples, bachelor informants, academicians envious of the success of poets, atrabilious professors, xenophobes of all stripes, Mafiosi greedy for decorations, vicious priests and cuckolded husbands. To this hodgepodge of ordinary existence the obscure subject offers the chance of a new destiny, under the incomprehensible but salvific sign of an absolute body, whose only demand is that one serves it by nurturing everywhere and at all times the hatred of every living thought, every transparent language and every uncertain becoming.[30]

While the reactive or reactionary subject incorporates the form of faithfulness, the obscure subject seems to be defined by the twofold movement of laying waste to the immanent production of the new and generating a transcendent, monolithic novelty, essentially indistinguishable from the most archaic past. Leaving aside the return of faithfulness in the fourth subjective figure, that of *resurrection*,[31] what changes does this theory of subjective space bring to the earlier theorisation of non-universalist subjects, and what prospects for formal analysis does it harbour?

Most importantly, the theory of subjective space appears designed to resolve the conundrum about other subjects which, in the earlier work, had been most acute in the figure of the bourgeoisie. In a sense, the new formal theory allows Badiou to affirm the relative autonomy of non- or anti-universalist subjects, whilst holding true, in his account of the sequence of subjects, to the primacy of revolt, in other words, to the primacy of the universalist subject. The new theory can thus be seen as a return, with the aid of a different formalism, of the 'topical' theory provided by *Theory of the Subject*, though now instead of a discontinuous field of subjective affects we are presented with more clearly distinct subjects (faithful, reactive, obscure, resurrected). The relative exteri-

---

30   Badiou 2008, p. 61.
31   For some interesting comments on the figure of resurrection, and its introduction into
      Badiou's thought of a complex link between novelty and repetition, see Žižek 2007.

ority of these figures to one another is also explained by the forsaking of the destructive-dialectical schema which, in *Theory of the Subject,* had portrayed the proletariat as an immanent purification of bourgeois space, a subjective torsion whose aim was to destroy the space of placements constituted by imperialist capitalism.

5   The Obscure Subject of Current Affairs

What purchase can such a formal theory have on the identification and examination of contemporary political subjects? In his philosophical considerations on the facts of 11 September 2001, Badiou opted for the notion of 'nihilism' to capture the specular relationship between the 'infinite justice' of Bush's God-bothering 'capitalist-parliamentarian' regime and Bin Laden's pyrotechnic theological terror. The current situation would thus be framed by the 'disjunctive synthesis of two nihilisms'.[32] These nihilisms, unlike the youthful discordant nihilism courted by Badiou in *Theory of the Subject,* are clearly not subjectively recoverable. What's more, it is rather opaque what relation, if any, they might entertain with faithful political subjects. So, it is once again to *Logics of Worlds* that we turn for some clarification.

One of the more striking features of this sequel to *Being and Event* for our aims is that, despite its formality, the meta-physics of the subject it deploys is marked by some extremely concrete examples. The most striking of these concerns Badiou's treatment of 'Islamism' as the present-day incarnation of the obscure subject:

> it is futile to try to genealogically elucidate contemporary political Islamism. This is particularly true of its ultrareactionary variants, which rival Westerners for the fruits of the oil map through unprecedented criminal means. This political Islamism represents a new instrumentalization of religion – from which it does not derive by any natural (or 'rational') lineage – with the purpose of occulting the postsocialist present and countering the fragmentary attempts through which emancipation is being reinvented by means of a full Tradition or Law. From this point of view, political Islamism is absolutely contemporary, both to the faithful subjects that produce the present of political experimentation and to the reactive subjects that busy themselves with denying that ruptures are

---

32   Badiou 2003b, p. 143.

necessary in order to invent a humanity worthy of the name – reactive subjects that parade the established order as the miraculous bearer of an uninterrupted emancipation. Political Islamism is simply one of the sub-jectivated names of today's obscurantism.[33]

Following the foundational thesis of the primacy of revolt (or primacy of the universal) Badiou is obliged to argue that if there is indeed an Islamist sub-ject, then this subject is derivative (by way of occultation) of a faithful subject. Rather than a regurgitation of the past, Islamism is the contemporary of a politics of emancipation (which is why it is useless to engage in 'genealogical' explanations). Possibly the most important, and disputable, aspect of this argu-ment is that the *purpose* (whether conscious or otherwise) of contemporary Islamism is 'occulting the post-socialist present'. Osama bin Laden's jihadist piety is precisely depicted as a kind of sinister fetishism: 'the sole function of the God of conspiratorial Islamism is to occult the present of the rational polit-ics of emancipation among people, by dislocating the unity of their statements and their militant bodies'.[34] In what follows, I will briefly survey some of the debates about the nature of Islamism's relation to the politics of emancipa-tion. For the moment, I want to indicate one of the most problematic aspects of Badiou's account, which inserts it directly into some bitter and vociferous recent debates. This has to do with the equation between Islamism and fas-cism.

In his response to the attacks on the Twin Towers and the Pentagon, Badiou had in fact already characterised those acts as 'conjuring up the fascist concept of action' and thus as 'formally fascistic'.[35] Moreover, the Islamist use of reli-gion was judged to be akin to that of 'anti-capitalism' by the populist fascism of the thirties, a mere demagogic vocabulary cloaking in Bin Laden's thirst for oil and political supremacy. At bottom then, the 2001 attacks signal the presence, under the instrumental facade of 'Islam' of 'a type of fascistic nihilism' typi-fied by the 'sacralization of death; the absolute indifference to the victims; the transformation of oneself and others into instruments'.[36] In *Logics*, this verdict is corroborated by the inclusion of Islamism under the rubric of obscure sub-jectivity, which is by definition 'fascist'. Thus, according to Badiou's definition: 'The obscure subject engineers the destruction of the body: the appropriate word is *fascism*, in a broader sense than the fascism of the thirties. One will

---

33   Badiou 2008, p. 59.
34   Badiou 2008, p. 60.
35   Badiou 2003b, p. 143.
36   Badiou 2003b, p. 160.

speak of generic fascism to describe the destruction of the organized body through which the construction of the present (of the sequence) had previously passed'.[37]

Besides the all too hurried identification of Bin Laden with Islamism (when many commentators indeed see him as a phenomenon which is subsequent to, and incompatible with, 'political Islam' proper), one cannot but register the unexpected convergence of this formal theory with one of the theses that permitted the convergence between American neo-conservatives and left renegades, to wit, the existence of something like 'Islamic fascism' or 'Islamofascism' as the archenemy of today's democrats and progressives – a notion promoted by the likes of Christopher Hitchens, and publicised, in some particularly incoherent speeches, by Bush himself. Leaving aside the dubious invocation of crimes of association, what is interesting about this congruence lies in its preconditions. It is indeed the short-circuit between a notion of 'generic fascism' (or of Ur-fascism)[38] and the specific subjective history of anti-fascist politics that allowed members of the so-called left to sign up to the propaganda wing of the 'war on terror' as if they were joining the International Brigades. It is important to note in this respect that the historical and sociological debate on fascism has long been dominated by polemics regarding its specificity and extension, both historical and geographical. So, it is rather peculiar to see Badiou, so adamant about thinking the subjective singularity of particular political sequences (e.g. Nazism in *The Century*), sign up to a thesis, that of 'generic fascism', which, in its formality, seems to forestall an inquiry into that very singularity. By way of contrast, we can note that one of the more exhaustive recent studies of fascism, starting from the methodological imperative to, as it were, 'take the fascists at their word' (to treat their political thought and practice as a subjective form), concludes with a nuanced repudiation of the notion of 'Islamic fascism'.[39]

---

37   Badiou 2008, p. 72.

38   For a treatment of (and intervention in) the scholarly debate on 'generic fascism', see Griffin 1993 and 2003. On 'Ur-fascism' or 'eternal fascism', see Eco 1995. It is worth noting that while those who advocate the concept of generic fascism tend to stress the modern and modernising character of fascism, Eco regards the 'rejection of modernism' as a key feature of fascism. Badiou's formal notion of 'generic fascism' seems far more ample than either Griffin or Eco's proposals. See also my Toscano 2023b.

39   According to Michael Mann, in none of the disparate, and often incompatible, instances of political Islam do we find 'the complete fascist package'. Rather, 'the term "Islamic fascism" is really just a particular instance of the word "Fascist!" – a term of abuse for our enemies … the most powerful term of abuse in our world today'. As for Islamism and Hindu nationalism, he makes the following judgement: 'They most resemble fascism in deploying the means of moral murder, but the transcendence, the state, the nation, and the new man

But, as we have already intimated, at the core of Badiou's vision of the obscure subject as generically fascist there lies not a political taxonomy of the elements necessary for a fascist politics, but a formal evaluation of how this type of subjectivity relates to the subject which, by definition, opens the subjective space: the universalist subject of emancipation, the faithful subject, the communist subject. For Badiou's theory of the obscure subject to find its exemplification in Islamism it must be possible to argue that, in some sense or another, the relationship between Islamist obscurantism and the politics of emancipation is one where the purpose of the former is absolutely to neg-ate the latter, through the production of a full subjective body and an archaic future. Now, in the case of Bin Laden, while it may be disputed whether the portrait of a cynical oil-fiend can withstand much scrutiny, it is indeed correct that, ideologically forged in the fight against the Soviet Satan, his relationship to communism bears all the hallmarks of the obscure subject. Consider this declaration, from Bin Laden's first public statement, addressed to religious jur-isprudents and spurred by the Saudi royals' support for the south Yemenis in the 1994 civil war:

It is ludicrous to suggest that Communists are Muslims whose blood should be spared. Since when were they Muslims? Wasn't it you who pre-viously issued a juridical decree calling them apostates and making it a duty to fight them in Afghanistan, or is there a difference between Yemeni Communists and Afghan Communists? Have doctrinal concepts and the meaning of God's unity become so confused? The regime is still sheltering some of these leaders of unbelief in a number of cities in the country, and yet we have heard no disapproval from you. The Prophet said, as related by Muslim, 'God cursed him who accommodates an innovator'.[40]

---

they seek are not this-worldly'. See Mann 2005, p. 374. While the polemical character of the appellation is obvious, and the point about the categorical differences well taken, I think it can be argued that most of the aims of Islamist politics, whether economic, legal or political, are incontrovertibly 'this-worldly'. It is also worth noting that Badiou himself, contradicting his use of it in *Logics of Worlds*, has even disputed the political value of the term 'Islamism'. As he declared in a 2004 interview, 'words like "terrorism", "Islamism" and "crimes against humanity" are only destined to confuse situations and to create a kind of international political stupidity'. Badiou 2004c.

40   Osama Bin Laden, 'The Betrayal of Palestine' (29 December 1994), in Lawrence 2005, p. 8. Badiou's portrait, according to which Bin Laden's 'point of departure is a series of extraordinary complex manoeuvres in relation to the manna of oilfields in Saudi Arabia and that the character is, after all, a good American: someone for whom what matters is wealth and power, and for whom the means are of less concern' (Badiou 2003b, pp. 149–50), seems to underestimate the sinister sincerity of his conviction, and indeed the fact

This ferocious hatred of innovation, of non-submissive secular equality, and of 'this torrential current of global unbelief',[41] seems to single out Bin Laden and his cohorts as sterling examples of Badiou's figure of the obscure subject.

But if we leave aside the not exactly representative figure of Bin Laden, with his propaganda of the deed and kitsch fantasies of the caliphate, the relation between Islamism and emancipatory politics appears far more ambiguous. Taking the paradigmatic case of 'political Islam', the post-revolutionary Islamic Republic of Iran, we can see that the theocratic forces did not engage in a straightforward reaction to the mass revolts against the Shah – in which they, alongside the various groups of the radical left, instead played a mobilising role – or in a simple occultation. It is certainly true that – as Badiou himself already noted in *Theory of the Subject* – the Islamist superego in the figure of Khomeini played a role akin to that of the Mao, and the archaic and transcendent reference prepared the brutal occlusion of emancipatory trajectories. But the suppression of the left by theocratic forces worked, in the ideological arena, primarily by *borrowing* the left's prescriptions and 'Islamicising' them, leaving the left with the abject alternative of either abetting its own suppression or becoming traitor to the revolution. as Val Moghadam noted, in an incisive appraisal of the strategic and discursive failures of the Iranian left:

> The shared language of opposition had a further negative effect in that it obfuscated very real differences between the socio-political projects of the Left and the Religious Right ('national-popular government' versus political Islam/ theocratic rule). moreover, most of the Left seemed unaware in the 1970s that the religious forces were weaving a radical – populist Islamic discourse that would prove very compelling – a discourse which appropriated some concepts from the Left (exploitation, imperialism, world capitalism), made use of Third Worldist categories (dependency, the people) and populist terms (the toiling masses), and imbued certain religious concepts with new and radical meaning. For instance, *mostazafin* – meaning the wretched or dispossessed – now connoted and privileged the urban poor in much the same way that libera-

---

that, were wealth and power the objective, Bin Laden could have attained them with far greater ease without undertaking his peculiar brand of 'obscure' militancy.

41   Osama Bin Laden, 'Under Mullah Omar' (9 April 2001), in Lawrence 2005, p. 98. It is worth noting that an 'obscure' notion of equality, the kind of equality by divine submission also favoured by Qutb, is part of Bin Laden's doctrinal arsenal. Thus, he writes in his declaration 'To the Americans' (6 October 2002) that Islam 'is the religion of unity and agreement on the obedience to god, and total equality between all people, without regard to their colour, sex, or language' (Lawrence 2005, p. 166).

tion theology refers to the poor. But in an original departure, the authors of the revolutionary Islamic texts, and especially Ayatollah Khomeini, declaimed that the *mostazafin* would rise against their oppressors and, led by the *ulama* or religious leaders, would establish the *umma* (community of believers) founded on *tauhid* (the profession of divine unity) and Islamic justice.[42]

Even if we accept that the 'purpose' of Iranian Islamism lay in the occultation (and indeed, the persecution and often slaughter) of any body that carried a promise of immanent universality – in what Gilbert Achcar calls 'a permanent revolution in reverse' and a 'reactionary retrogression'[43] – it cannot be argued that it simply foreclosed the statements and organs of emancipatory politics. Rather, in a far more insidious and powerful move, it *incorporated* them, transcendentalising, for instance, the concept of anti-imperialism into a religious duty bound to the defence of the *umma* rather than the creation of a truly generic humanity. Still remaining with the Iranian case, we can see that Islamism even produced a kind of revolutionary populism, in the figure of Ali Shari'ati, which, though posthumously manipulated by the clergy and its militias for their own rightist ends, is difficult to class simply as either reactive or obscure.

In Shari'ati we find an uneasy combination of the popular principle of rebellion, on the one hand, and an organicist vision of religious society, on the other. Via the likes of Fanon and Sartre, he incorporates an emancipatory drive into his political theology. For instance, he declares that 'Islam is the first school of social thought that recognizes the masses as the basis, the fundamental and conscious factor in determining history and society';[44] that history is a struggle between the pole of Cain (of power, coercion, or imperialism) and the pole of Abel (a religiously oriented primitive communism); that 'it is the responsibility of every individual in every age to determine his stance in the constant struggle between the two wings we have described, and not to remain a spectator'.[45] But the very principles of the emancipatory politics that provides the obvious matrix for Shari'ati's thought (primitive communism, the classless society, rebellion ...) are hypostasised into spiritual notions which, to use the language that *Theory of the Subject* applied to the religious politics of the German Peasants' War, take equality into the *imaginary* domain of cosmopolitical unity, in the form of the opposition between unity (*tauhid*) and discordance or contra-

---

42   Moghadam 1987, p. 14.
43   Achcar 2004, p. 57.
44   Shari'ati 1979, p. 49.
45   Shari'ati 1979, p. 109.

diction (*shirk*),[46] together with a radical reading of the notion of *umma* that nonetheless sees it, against the supposed shortcomings of socialism, as 'the divine destiny of man in the plan of creation'.[47]

A related 'translation' of emancipatory themes can be found in the earlier and much more evidently revolutionary-conservative writings of Sayyid Qutb, whose sombre anti-philosophy,[48] organicist vision of society, and definition of 'equality and freedom as common submission before God'[49] captured an authentic demand for justice and twisted it into an archaic and transcendent vision of a society finally free, not just of imperialism, but of the discordance and anxiety of modernity.

According to the group of theorists and activists RETORT, this dialectic of appropriation is also present in the most recent incarnations of 'revolutionary Islam'. This movement is characterised, in its diffuse and networked 'body' by a remarkable degree of organisational, theological and technological 'democratization', the invention of a new, post-Leninist (or post-anarchist[50]) articulation of vanguard and violence, and what they appositely refer to as 'a new, and malignant, universalism'.[51] While they too note the gestation of contemporary Islamism in the writings Qutb, and some of the 'proto-fascist' (but also 'crypto-communist') organisational models at the origins of the Muslim Brotherhood, they regard its causes as originating in 'the *crisis of secular nationalist development* – abetted by a specific (and poisonous) political-economic conjuncture whose vectors were oil, primitive accumulation, and Cold War geopolitics'.[52] A similar judgement was put forward in the wake of the Iranian Revolution by Gilbert Achcar. His theses on Islamic fundamentalism, which provide a classical analysis of the petty-bourgeois roots of the Islamist phenomenon, echo the analysis of fascism – such as when he writes that 'the violence and rage of the petit bourgeois in distress are unparalleled'. Indeed, Achcar sees the bourgeoisie's relationship to the phenomenon of Islamism (particularly in Egypt) as typical of its customary stance towards far right movements and fascism in gen-

---

46   Shari'ati 1979, p. 82.

47   Shari'ati 1979, p. 120. It is worth noting that this umma is distinguished by Shari'ati in terms of its 'purity of leadership', which he explicitly juxtaposes to the 'fascist' purity of the leader, obviously sensitive to the potential confusion.

48   On Qutb's relationship to philosophy and modernity, see Euben 1999, p. 69.

49   RETORT (Iain Boal, T.J. Clark, Joseph Matthews, Michael Watts) 2005, p. 146. See also Euben 1999, pp. 62–3.

50   'For jihadist, read anarchist', *The Economist*, 18 August 2005, available at http://www .economist.com/node/4292760.

51   RETORT, p. 153.

52   RETORT, p. 162.

eral – in other words, to borrow Badiou's terminology, reactionaries are always happy to use obscurantists against progressives, especially if the obscurantists can 'outbid the Left on the Left's two favourite issues: the national question and the social question; any gains made by Islamic reaction on these two issues mean equivalent losses for the left'. Islamic fundamentalism in this sense represents 'an *auxiliary for the reactionary bourgeoisie*'.[53] But for Achcar this emergence of a petty bourgeois reaction is only possible because of the feebleness of the revolutionary proletariat and the incapacity or unwillingness of the bourgeoisie to take on the aims of a national and democratic revolution.[54]

In this sense, the emergence of Islamism as a political subject does not necessarily represent an express reaction to emancipatory politics, but may rather constitute a capitalisation on its absence, on the temporary incapacity of progressives to actually produce a present. Unlike Badiou, whose view of political subjectivation seems to preclude notions such as alliance or hegemony, Achcar does consider the possibility, which was of course the reality in

---

53 Achcar 2004, p. 56.

54 This position is corroborated by one of the most in-depth, revealing and sympathetic treatments of the subjective trajectories and resources of Islamism, Burgat 2003. Burgat, while discounting the kind of socio-economic analysis favoured by Achcar and other Marxist analysts of West Asian politics, and refusing its characterisation as *primarily* reactionary, violent or anti-democratic, places Islamism firmly in the history of emancipation from imperialism and colonialism: 'At first political, then economic, the distancing of the former colonizer through the rhetoric of oppositional Islam becomes ideological, symbolic and more broadly cultural, on the terrain where the shock of colonization has been most traumatic. In addition to its own language, local culture and history endow the dynamic of independence with something that has been missing for a long time: the precious attributes of a sort of ideological "autonomy" which perfects it, the right of those who propagate it to regain universality, without denouncing the structural elements of their "specificity" ... it is essentially in the old dynamic of decolonization that Islamism has taken root' (p. 49). While Burgat's sociological and anthropological focus on identity is at odds with Badiou's theory of the subject, it is worth remarking the interest in this interpretation of Islamism as a tool for attaining a kind of universalising autonomy. Without seconding Burgat's sympathies, it is important to note that such a demand for autochthonous universality is a sign of the failure of classical emancipatory discourses within the Muslim world to attain a truly 'generic' status and not be perceived as alien or imperial implantations. Moreover, Burgat's work is almost alone in providing detailed accounts, using numerous interviews and autobiographical texts, of the life-paths of north African Islamists – paths which, it should be noted, passed not only through Arab nationalism, but through Marxism too. For an attempt to delve into the subjectivity of extremist and terrorist variants of Islamism, see Juan Cole's intriguing study of the 'spiritual' documents left behind by the perpetrators of the attacks on the wtc and the Pentagon, Cole 2003. Cole's text provides a useful sketch of what a situated phenomenology of the obscure subject might look like.

Iran (his main point of reference in these reflections), that the proletarian sub-ject might be obliged to struggle alongside Islamism against a common enemy, imperialism, and for 'national, democratic, and social issues'. And yet, this does not by any means constitute a real alliance, since 'the duty of revolutionary socialists is to fight intransigently against the spell [Islamic fundamentalism] casts on the struggling masses'.[55] The least that can be said then, is that even from this classical Marxist position, the problem of other subjects – of how to confront reactionaries and obscurantists whilst producing an emancipatory political present – appears as both urgent and inescapable.

6   Conclusion

So how does Badiou's theorisation of 'untrue' subjects fare in the face of Islam-ism? The few cases and figures we have looked at point to the difficulties in formalising most politics that may be identified as 'Islamist' in terms of Badiou's theory of subjective space. Even if we accept the thesis of the primacy of the universal – the idea that 'other' subjects only arise in the wake of the emer-gence of a faithful egalitarian subject and of the present it strives to produce – it is the specific relationship between the faithful subject and its two counter-parts, reactive and obscure, that remains problematic.

First, the obscure subject – the subject that submits its action and state-ments to a transcendent, full body – does not necessarily have the occultation of the faithful subject as its express purpose. One of the difficult lessons of the present conjuncture might be that – having vanquished the semblance or placeholder of communist politics – reactionaries and obscurantists are facing one another without necessarily passing through a direct opposition to faith-ful subjectivity. Or rather – at least at the spectacular level – what we are faced with is the struggle between slogans, be it 'freedom and democracy', or myth-ical and theological corruptions of anti-imperialism, which, whilst bearing the traces of emancipatory subjectivities, do not refer to them directly.

When its genesis was coeval with that of progressive subject, the obscure subject of Islamism did indeed eventually crush anything that could have given body to a generic emancipatory subject, but it did not, contrary to what Badiou seems to intimate, erase all traces of the founding tenets of emancipatory polit-ics. On the contrary, its tactic, largely effective against a left deluded by its own populism and strategic ineptitude, was to adopt and hypostasise the key prin-

---

55   Achcar 2004, p. 59.

ciples of emancipation, making out as if their secular, communist version was merely a degenerate form of an archaic and eternal Islamic politics, with a submissive vision of organicist egalitarianism. In this sense, the obscure subject is more a thief of the present than simply its destroyer.

When instead, as is mostly the case nowadays, Islamism is not in direct contact with figures of emancipation, it seems to operate with the epigones of capitalist reaction (Cold Warriors like Rumsfeld and Wolfowitz) as its counterparts, and entertains no univocal relationship to a politics of emancipation (aside from gloating at the defeat of its Soviet simulacrum, peddling theological variants of anti-imperialism and egalitarianism, or even, in today's Lebanon and Egypt, making tactical alliances with socialist and communist groups). In a sense, this goes to corroborate Badiou's sequence, which moves from the production of the present, to its denial, to its occultation. But, for reasons very much having to do with the concrete strategic history of these movements, the phantasmagorical anti-bodies of Islamism (e.g. the Caliphate) are more to be understood as the mythical filling-in of a political void produced by reaction than as a direct occultation of a subjectivised universal body. This is not to say that Islamism cannot be obscurantist, and indeed openly and virulently anti-communist (recall Bin Laden's exterminationist rhetoric), but to note that our subjective space is currently dominated by struggles between non-universalist subjects far more than it is by their struggle against intelligible forms of 'post-socialist' subjectivity.

Having said that, the presence of a *gigantomachia*, a bloody and disjunctive synthesis, between reactionaries and obscurantists does not as such occlude the emergence of 'true' subjects. Which is why, in this grim interregnum, it is not a bad idea, not only to maintain open the possibility of universalist courage and justice, but to build on Badiou's several attempts to develop a theory of the subjects of contemporary untruths and half-truths.

CHAPTER 6

Emblems and Cuts: Philosophy in and against History

In his 1997 novel, *Calme bloc ici-bas*, Alain Badiou tells the story of Julien Olde-nay, professor of the philosophy of history in the imagined country of Pré-montré – a country set apart from that of the reader not simply by fictive space but by its time and calendars, born of founding, constitutive events and therefore incommensurable with our own. The tale is one of 44 that make up approximately half of the novel, all of them beginning with classic incipits such as '*C'est l'histoire de ...*', '*Je conte de ...*', '*Ce conte est ...*' and in this case a simple 'Once upon a time ...', '*Il était une fois ...*'. The irreverent portrayal of Oldenay is indicative of Badiou's philosophical instincts when it comes to history, as both concept and discipline. Aside from his unkempt appearance, Oldenay is portrayed as combining a certain degree of self-satisfaction with a 'chronic intellectual hesitation', as well as a rhetoric marked by nuance, retraction and interminable self-criticism. Lecturing on the history of Prémontré, Oldenay hesitantly declares:

> ... this History, if we provisionally accept that the word 'History' is legit-imate, which would require elaborate argumentation, I would say, with all the precautions that this concept demands of us, that it is very clearly dia-lectical. Of course, 'very clearly' is a manner of speech, since the History of Prémontré is anything but clear. And as I have already said, 'dialectical' is also a manner of speech, until we have distinguished between the seven possible senses of the word ...

Oldenay perseveres in these comedic, scholastic convolutions. But among Oldenay's students, there is one, David Monvoisin, who intends to put a twist in this infinitely qualified and typologically differentiated dialectic: 'It seemed to him', writes Badiou, 'that one could "cut" through the conceptual uncertain-ties of his professor by mentioning some symbolic events, on the basis of which one could then reconstruct, without looking for a continuous characterisation, the general sense of Prémontré. He fixes his grey gaze, his thin athlete's beauty, on Julien Oldenay, and all of a sudden asks him if "dialectics" should not be understood in terms of the contrast of violent cuts, or emblems'.[1] Monvoisin

---

1 Badiou 1997b, pp. 302–5, 'Un professeur scrupuleux'.

then draws such punctual emblems from the history of Prémontré, in the form of a series of events and dates, which are then followed by the consternation of the other students and Oldenay's own stringently inconclusive reply, which slowly lulls our young, radical dialectician to sleep.

In more than one respect, this vignette dramatises one of the central stakes in Alain Badiou's decades-long confrontation with the concept of history. Mediated by the heterodox allegiance to Marxism that still defines much of his thought, this is of course the problem of *dialectics* – to be understood, at least in a first moment, as a dialectic of the break and the period, of continuity and discontinuity.[2] But, of course, it can never suffice to juxtapose the cautious professor's dialectics of continuity and hesitation to the impetuous student's dialectics of emblematic violence. Even if we opt for the latter, it behoves us to ask what new notions of continuity and periodisation are generated by an emphasis on the break, what are the internal criteria of these 'cuts' that Badiou-Monvoisin speaks of, and indeed what concept (if any) of history may be reconstructed in their wake.

To begin with, we need to interrogate how historicity and temporality have been affected by Badiou's recastings of the dialectic – a question that cannot avoid some assessment of the legacy of Hegelianism within Badiou's philosophy. Secondly, the issue of a dialectics of *periodisation*, which emerges out of Badiou's confrontation with Hegel in his 1982 *Theory of the Subject*, should be contrasted both with Badiou's stance vis-à-vis the existence or otherwise of 'objective' historical periods (ages, centuries, or even meta-historical categories such as 'modernity') and his thinking regarding the periodisation immanent to the trajectory of a subject. Third, and following on from this issue of periodisation, the conflictual articulation and scission of politics and history needs to be considered, together with the diverging status of history as viewed from the vantage points of philosophy and of politics (or other truth procedures). Fourth, we must address the question of how Badiou's struggle with the question of history is affected by his demarcations (which are often also appropriations) from his intellectual forebears and contemporaries, namely Sartre, Althusser and Foucault.

I'd like to take this last question first by exploring Badiou's stance vis-à-vis accounts of historical ruptures that do not identify the bearers of such ruptures (or of their systematic consequences) as *subjects*, namely positions that

---

2   Jameson 2002, p. 23. The choice between the break and the period, discontinuity or continuity marks, according to Jameson, 'an absolute historiographic beginning, that cannot be justified by the nature of the historical material or evidence, since it organises all such material or evidence in the first place'.

adopt the theme of transcendental transformations but avoid the formalism of decision and militancy. This is a matter tackled by Badiou in a paper on Foucault, tellingly subtitled 'continuity / discontinuity'. In dealing with Foucault's own archaeological treatment of epistemic discontinuities, Badiou qualifies such a thinking of history as fundamentally non-philosophical.[3] Why? To begin with, because of Foucault's disdain for great names and great inventions – his construction of refined archival periodisations in which Descartes features as a footnote and Marx as a minor Ricardian economist. Alluding to the figure of the eighteenth century emerging from Foucault's *The Order of Things*, Badiou starkly proposes that such a history is unacceptable for a philosophy which, by his definition, is concerned with the eternity and transmissibility of revolutionary truths. One of the insistent themes of Badiou's thinking – most prevalent perhaps in the first lesson from his book *The Century* – is that historical time (in the guise of periods, epochs, ages, or indeed events) only exists for philosophy to the extent that it presents singular but immortal (atemporal) truths, moments of subjective exception that explode their spatio-temporal particularity and are available for universalisation. Indeed, philosophy itself is defined as the exercise of sheltering the heterogeneous truths of a given 'time', rendering these plural and singular truths *compossible*. Thus, it is in a sense up to philosophy to produce a time, to give rise to the concept of a period in which certain truths are contemporaneous to one another, in a kind of localised network of universalities (of the kind that might conjoin Einstein, Cantor, Lenin, Picasso and Freud, for instance). Thus, an eighteenth century filled with minor but momentous scientists, infamous men and imperceptible, clandestine transformations, but deprived of Lavoisier or Lagrange, Rousseau or Goethe, is simply in Badiou's eyes a non-philosophical century. It is worth noting here the preponderance in Badiou's concept of history not just of the emblematic dates so dear to his character Monvoisin, but of proper names. Much could indeed be said, especially at the level of the thinking of eventality delineated in *Being and Event*, of the periodising function of proper names (and of their necessary duality: Freud/Lacan; Marx/Lenin; or even Plato/Badiou ...) as representatives of the unrepresentable, opaque markers of the transcendental transformations that so preoccupy Badiou. But if, as Jacques Rancière noted, 'the revolution in historical science [carried out by the likes of Marc Bloch, Lucien Febvre and Fernand Braudel] wanted precisely to revoke the primacy of events and proper names for the sake of long durations and the

---

3   Badiou 2004d. Quoted from the original manuscript.

life of the anonymous',[4] then Badiou's operation, within the field of philosophy, constitutes a kind of partial counter-revolution, albeit one that retains a considerable dose of anonymity within the constitution of the subject and also strives to eschew talk of motives and intentions. Having said that, it is worth keeping in mind the extent to which Badiou's attachment to names and events obliges him into certain narrative gestures seemingly alien to his overall formalising drive. This might indicate the degree to which his thinking too is determined by the poetics of history, understood as, to quote Rancière once more, the 'power of articulation of names and events which is linked to the ontological indeterminacy of the story [*récit*]'.[5]

But, possibly because of the impact of the likes of Braudel,[6] and, even more strongly, of his own past, but never repudiated, Marxist allegiances, it does not seem that for Badiou history as a discipline could be conceived in terms of the *singularity* of the articulation between names and events. This is why he thinks that Foucault, as a non-philosophical thinker of singularities, in the end cannot be co-opted by what Badiou sardonically refers to as the 'terrible union of historians', *le terrible syndicat des historiens*. For history appears to Badiou first and foremost as a search for regularities, which, incorporating a reflection on time (versus Foucault's immersion of temporal forms into the 'spaces' of discourse) has as its 'central formal object ... the State/society couple' (where Foucault's guiding couple is instead the transversal articulation of power/knowledge).[7] Inasmuch as Badiou links the very concept of the State to the fundamentally conservative logic of knowledge and representation – such that the State is a domain for him devoid of truth or subjectivity – this appears at first as a kind of indictment, a drastic (and we might even say *idealist*) separation between history, on the one hand, and philosophy and subjectivity, on the other.

In his assessment of Foucault's *Society Must Be Defended*, Badiou salutes Foucault's attempt to move beyond the epistemic discontinuities set out in *The Order of Things*, and to introduce, in the wake of the events of '68, an element of genealogical continuity predicated on the notion of subjective struggles. According to Badiou, Foucault's later texts can be read in terms of the desire to think politics and history together, and to explore their bond without subsuming it under the classical categories of sovereignty or the Marxist critique of political economy. Badiou's negative judgement on this attempt, however, is based on the idea that in the last instance Foucault cannot surpass the horizon

---

4   Rancière 1992, p. 7.
5   Rancière 1992, p. 18.
6   Badiou 2004b.
7   Badiou 2004d.

that subordinates both politics and history – or, more precisely, the historicity of politics – to the paradigm of the State. Foucault's turn to *strategy* as the binding concept between politics and history – founded, in the narrative of *Society Must Be Defended*, on the convergence of historical narratives of struggle and the biopolitical transformation of the State into an agency for the government and management of life (a convergence which is in turn anchored in the concept of 'race') – fails, according to Badiou, to fulfil Foucault's own philosophical desideratum, which consists in being able to think the very activity of politics from a subjective point of view. In other words, Foucault's two equations, according to which politics = the State = power, and history = war, end up, in Badiou's estimation, subordinating the invention of political forms to the train of historical becoming. Badiou's indictment – which resonates with a very significant bone of contention within the Marxist tradition[8] – is that Foucault collapses into *historicism*. The consequence of such a historicism is that, having stuck politics in the narrow space between 'the theory of powers and the tactics of struggles', Foucault is incapable of producing 'an affirmative theory of politics' – of politics defined by Badiou as an 'irreducible thought/practice'.[9]

This theme of anti-historicism, echoing in part Althusser's famous critique of Gramsci in *Reading Capital*, is one that has marked much of Badiou's thinking of politics. In his very sympathetic treatment, in *Metapolitics*, of *Anthropology of the Name*, a book by his erstwhile political comrade Sylvain Lazarus, Badiou is most explicit in linking the aim of thinking the affirmative and irreducible singularity of politics (or more precisely, of a political *sequence*) to a critique of historicism and indeed a separation from history itself, of the kind that might indeed warrant Hallward's estimation that Badiou's philosophy is grounded in 'the radical subtraction of politics from history altogether'.[10] According to Lazarus then, 'it is only possible to think the singularity of a thought by *evacuating time*'.[11] The reason for this stark verdict is that predicating the singularity of thought and politics on time introduces a dimension of heteronomy, such that politics is constantly obliged to refer to something (a context, a base, a motor) beyond itself, leading to a capture or reduction of that very dimension of singularity that was sought in the first place. This politics of singularity is not simply pitted against the recuperative dialectics of totality proper to a Hegelian lineage, but also repudiates historical-materialist critique, which, according to Lazarus, undermines Hegelian absolute-subjective time

8   See Jameson 1988.
9   Badiou 2004d.
10   Hallward 2003, p. 43.
11   Badiou 2005c, p. 35.

by making it circulate between two heterogeneous realms (objective-material and ideological-subjective), and is therefore incapable of thinking singularity. The temporal substance of historical change is thus replaced with a primacy of names (such as 'worker') which define the singularity of a politics. As Badiou puts it, in Lazarus there is an 'abolition of time by the name'. And yet, as Rancière suggests, the names of politics cannot simply be sundered from their articulation with events, and therefore from their affinity with some notion and experience of time. Hence the prominence in the thinking of both Lazarus and Badiou of the notion of a *sequence*, to be understood in the first place as a temporality immanent to the singularity of a politics. As Lazarus himself puts it, 'the work of identification [of a singular political thought] is carried out through the delimitation of a sequence and its dating'.[12] Whence a certain calendrical obsession that almost replaces the traditional concern with political history and returns us to the 'emblematic' thinking (or 'monumental' history, to use a Nietzschean term) dramatised in the tale from *Calme bloc ici-bas.*

This problem of the linkage between history and politics, and of the capacity for the latter to achieve genuine autonomy as a truth procedure, is also the guiding idea in Badiou's reckoning with Althusser, whose seminal attack on historicism does not suffice, in Badiou's eyes, to provide him with the means to develop a thought of insurrectionary and emancipatory subjectivity, which is to say a thinking of politics. Whence Badiou's question: 'how are we to distinguish politics from the science of processes without a subject, that is to say, from the science of history, in the form of historical materialism? How do we distinguish politics from (the) science (of historical materialism) without, quite obviously, reducing it to ideology?'[13] For Badiou, Althusser's solution is dependent on a certain understanding of philosophy which, as an agent of demarcation, is aimed at indicating the space of politics (the space of the subject, of militancy, contingency and antagonism) without allowing it to be fully colonised by the theory of science or the logic of ideology: 'Philosophy is guarded from the danger of confusing history and politics (therefore science and politics) on account of itself lacking history. Philosophy authorises a non-historicist perception of political events'.[14] This last sentence encapsulates an important aspect of Badiou's own research programme. Significantly, Badiou's own attempt at generating an anti-humanist theory of the subject was first announced in his 1967 review of *For Marx* and *Reading Capital*, which ended on

---

12   Quoted in Badiou 2005c, p. 38.
13   Badiou 2005c, p. 60.
14   Badiou 2005, p. 62.

the promissory note of complementing the Althusserian grasp of the epistemological break constituted by Marx's discovery of the continent of history, with a
militant and subjective focus on a Sartrean 'theory of historical sets'.[15] However,
though Badiou commends Sartre for holding fast to the question of the subject
in the face of structuralist 'objectivism', and for providing guidance on how to
think a radical upsurge of emancipatory novelty, he cannot ignore Sartre's own
historicism, which is to say, his temporalised thinking of social totality. Thus, in
the pamphlet he wrote on the occasion of Sartre's death in 1980, Badiou looks
back on his old mentor, and more specifically on the project outlined in the
massive *Critique of Dialectical Reason*, in the following terms:

> But in the end we can say the following: the Subject, which is necessar-
> ily in question today is not the subject of History. The idea of a historical
> totalisation is not admissible. It is the political subject, an altogether par-
> ticular subject, which is in question. So, Sartre's question is not exactly
> the right one. ... But Sartre remains an awakener of Marxism. He precisely
> invites us to reflect on politics and on History, because he has taken to its
> limit a purely historical and revolutionary conception of Marxism.[16]

In the work produced following the high period of his 'militant' philosophical
production, Badiou appears to radicalise the Althusserian attack on historicism
and theories of expressive totality and to jettison the very notion of historical
totality altogether, severing him from much of what would pass for Western
Marxism. In *Theory of the Subject*, this de-totalisation is extracted from a heterodox or anti-synthetic reading of Hegel, as well as from Lacan's theses on the Real
as the impasse of the symbolic. In later work, it will depend more heavily on
mathematical logic and the set-theoretical axiomatic, though Hegelianism will
remain both the target and touchstone of Badiou's thinking.[17] In a painstaking
endeavour to disarticulate the circularities and redundancies of the Hegelian
dialectic, Badiou seeks to generate a materialist dialectic that would be capable
of including the unpredictable irruptions and interventions of organised subjects, to affirm radical novelty at the very point where the Hegelian dialectic
maintained not just a structure of expression but one of recollection, such that
any novelty is always-already a kind of unfolding, if not a mere return. It is this
attempt to force political novelty into the dialectic that obliges Badiou to face
the question of periodisation, of the time, and indeed the *timing* of politics. The

---

15   Badiou 1967, pp. 466–7.
16   Badiou 1980, pp. 8, 16.
17   Alain Badiou, 'Hegel and the Whole', in Badiou 2004a, pp. 227–38.

paradox that dominates this theoretical moment, and to some extent his later work as well, can perhaps be formulated as follows: in order to avert the absorption of politics by History, Badiou must think through the historicity proper to politics.

Ontologically speaking, the requirement of a periodising dialectic is founded on the statement that 'history does not exist' for it would otherwise be a 'figure of the whole'.[18] The whole is here seen by Badiou, already a thinker of the radicality of transformation, as synonymous with a ban on the new. Moreover, such a detotalisation is explicitly concerned with the issue of communism, which as we have seen, dominates, at least in a first phase, Badiou's thinking on history. The inexistence of history-qua-totality is explicitly linked to a Maoist conception of communism that refuses to consider it as a domain of the pure and simple realisation of equality, as an end of history – and which thus opens onto the ineluctability of periodisation and the need to think the trajectories of the subject (what Badiou refers to, following Lacan, as the subject's 'topology'). The lesson that Badiou draws from this militant critique of totality is summed up in the words: 'Periodise, and move beyond'.[19] From success to failure to new success to new failure, the political subject journeys through linked but discontinuous conjunctures, every one of which is relative to the sequence in question, such that the subject is not permitted any horizon of final victory. Making show of a kind of Beckettian communism, Badiou thus declares: 'Every victory is the beginning of a new type of failure'.[20] Struggles may be final, but final relative to the sequence, and this finality is the internal mode of historicisation or temporalisation proper to a given sequence, what Badiou calls its 'saturation'.[21] This is the sense in which the theory of the subject as a theory of Marxist politics (as opposed to historical materialism) depends for Badiou on overturning the traditional image according to which Marxism depends on a thinking of capitalist society as a *totality*. If history as totality – as the history of the totality and the totality of history – does not exist, what is the element in which the subject traces the arduous path of its novelties (and its destructions)? For Badiou only historical epochs, or better 'historicisations' are given, not History.

The subject of these historicisations, wrested from the repetition that governs any order, is identified by Badiou with novelty, with the struggle between the old and the new. This constitutes what we could call the heroic frame under-

18   Badiou 1982, p. 110.
19   Ibid.
20   Ibid.
21   See the interview in Badiou 2006c.

lying much of his thought. As Badiou emblematically declares: 'every right-ness (*justesse*) and every justice are in principle novelties, and everything that repeats itself is unjust and inexact'.[22] Such a novelty can only be attested by its *consequences*, and these consequences can only be gauged in terms of how a novelty traverses and transforms (or destroys) the situation or world whence it arose. Looking beyond the dates that punctuate a sequence, there is thus a need to think the historicity internal to a truth procedure or a process of sub-jectivation. In the earlier works, this can be found in the theme of *purification*, such that 'in every contradiction, force manifests its impurity by the aleatory process of its purification'.[23] In the more recent writings, this temporality or historicity is provided by the extraction of a generic set which is impervious to (or technically speaking, 'indiscernible') to the knowledge of the situation, and which generates a truth of the situation in what Badiou refers to as a 'future perfect' (*futur antérieur*).

Though the temporality or historicity immanent to a subjective sequence has perhaps not received sufficient attention in Badiou's work – excepting perhaps his treatments of the Paris Commune and the Cultural Revolution collected in *Polemics* – as I've noted already his thinking has struggled quite consistently with the issue of periodisation. Indeed, in *Theory of the Subject* the very task of history is defined as that of finding 'the right period'. Badiou thus presents periodisation in *Theory of the Subject* as a dialectical alternative to the Hegelian absolute, understood as a thinking that closes the dialectical process. According to Badiou, the Hegelian notion of the absolute depends on the idea that a 'dialectical sequence approaches its closure when the practical process carries the theory of its own trajectory [*sillage*]'.[24] But it is vis-à-vis this question of closure that dialectics splits into two. The Hegelian option is that of 'theological circularity, which, presupposing the absolute in the germs of the beginning, leads us back to this very beginning once all the stages of its effectuation, exit-from-itself, or alienation have been deployed'. It is a *theo-logical* circularity, which finds its explicit model in the relationship between God and his Son, such that the sundering of the divine is ultimately evidence and guarantee of its eternal unity and totality. The path of periodisation is instead marked by the violence of discontinuity, by a 'pure passage from one sequence to the other, in an irreconcilable and unsuturable lag, in which the True of the first stage is only given as a condition of the *fact* of the second, and

---

22   Badiou 1982, p. 57.
23   Badiou 1982, p. 56.
24   Badiou 1982, p. 37.

leads to nothing but the deployment of this fact. ... The second sequence gets into gear when the condition for the theoretical balance-sheet of the first are ready.'[25]

Albeit enriched by his attempt to recast the Hegelian dialectic as a dialectic of irreducible division, Badiou's model of periodisation here is explicitly political. It is a matter of grasping, from within the Marxism's militant history, how revolutionary politics is itself periodised by the non-expressive relation between sequences. This discontinuity marks the fact that we are not dealing with a seamless and cumulative tradition, where later sequences would simply learn from the lessons of the old, but with the notion that it is in the impasses and impossibilities of a previous sequence, a first moment, that a second sequence intervenes, generating the kind of novelty that doesn't simply solve the problems of the first but generates an entirely new evaluation of the requirements of novelty and emancipation. It is this creative retroaction, according to Badiou, which permits us to periodise, and to understand the act of periodisation as immanent to the deployment of a subject (and thus incommensurable with any objective chronology). The dialectic of cumulative completion and resolution is thus replaced by a dialectic of failure and innovation, where what stood as an impasse and remained unthinkable in a previous sequence is not the germ but merely the *site* for the inventions of a later one. It is thus that 'Lenin's Bolshevik party is the active bearer of the failures of the Paris Commune. This is what Lenin marks by dancing on the snow when power has been held in Moscow in 1917 for one more day [73] than in Paris in 1871. It is the break of October that periodises the Paris Commune, turning a page in the history of the world'.[26] This periodisation, made up 'deferred and differing retroactions', whereby nothing can be deduced in the passage from the first sequence to the second, is at the heart of Badiou's attempt to recast dialectics in *Theory of the Subject*. Against the single time of the Hegelian dialectic, Badiou, by taking the evaluations of the Commune by Marx and Lenin respectively as his material, points us to the splits internal to the very notion of periodisation, and *a fortiori*, to that of novelty:

> Every periodisation must embrace its dialectical double time, to contain, for instance, October '17 as the second, and provisionally final, scansion of the balance-sheet [of the Paris Commune]. Whence the embarrassment

---

25   Badiou 1982, p. 38.
26   Ibid. See also the appraisal in 'The Paris Commune: A Political Declaration on Politics', in Badiou 2006d.

of historians: according to the relation between force and place, the Commune is new (Marx). According to the relation between the objective and the subjective, it is instead October that is new, and the Commune is that *edge of the old* whose practical perception, by purifying force, partakes in the engendering of its novelty.[27]

In other words, the dialectical criteria of periodisation are themselves split (at least) into two, thus demonstrating the complexities of subjective periodisation – which here depends on the retroactive intervention of the Bolshevik sequence (a thinking of the party and of the subjective 'art of insurrection') – and its irreducibility to any criteria of objective chronology.

Though, as I've noted, the problem of periodisation, and of the articulation between politics and history, is one that has remained with Badiou, his later work, with its attempt to bolster a theory of the subject with a set-theoretical ontological infrastructure, has found itself obliged to grapple with, and substantially reinvent, the demarcation between nature and history. Without delving overmuch into the technical details, 'nature' in *Being and Event* is understood as the form of homogeneity of the (structured) multiple, or multiple-in-situation. 'History' is instead recast by Badiou as a meta-ontological category; it enters the fray with the issue of 'what-is-not-being-qua-being', with the interruption of the natural order, or the excess vis-à-vis the normalcy of nature. In other words, where his earlier *Theory of the Subject* found it necessary to declare the inexistence of history to make room for the discontinuous historicity of periodisations, in *Being and Event*, history stands for the untotalisable and the singular. As Badiou writes:

> The *place* of thought of that-which-is-not-being is the non-natural; that which is presented *other* than natural or stable or normal multiplicities. The place of the other-than-being is the abnormal, the unstable, the anti-natural. I will term *historical* what is thus determined as the opposite of nature.[28]

Moreover, whereas even in texts like his talk on Foucault, history is equated with a thinking of the State, in *Being and Event*, the category of 'history' is used to very different ends, to indicate those multiplicities that are *singular*, in other words multiples one of whose terms is presented in a situation but not repres-

---

27   Badiou 1982, pp. 64–5.
28   Badiou 2006a, pp. 173–4.

ented by the State (Badiou's example is that of a 'singular' family, one of whose members – a clandestine lodger, for instance – cannot be counted or recognised by the state, understood as the agent of re-presentation). A situation is defined as historical then, when it includes not just singular multiples but what Badiou calls an 'evental site', to wit a multiple none of whose parts is accounted for in representation.

We might wonder what is the strategy or reasoning behind this equation of history with singularity – especially if we take into account the de-totalising character of the dialectic as presented in *Theory of the Subject*. To an extent this strategy is dictated by the parameters of *Being and Event* as a historically specific philosophical intervention. Writing in the mid 1980s, and no longer preoccupied directly with salvaging a kernel of dialectic novelty from Marxism and Hegelianism, Badiou was really trying with the aid of his formidable meta-ontological capture of set theory, to seize the ontological mantle from Heidegger. Hence the new formalisation of the notion of 'historicity': 'The multiple-form of historicity is what lies entirely within the instability of the singular; it is that upon which the state's metastructure has no hold. It is a point of subtraction from the state's re-securing of the count'.[29] Where historicity is linked to singularity, 'history', as a non-totalisable domain, is related to the idea of the *entirely abnormal multiple*, the evental site – a concept that Badiou had coined in order to maintain the idea of a rational grasp of the sources of emancipatory politics, drawn from the Marxist notion of the proletariat, whilst abdicating any notion of historical totality or direction.[30]

The void of the proletariat as a historical exception is now transferred onto a void in the situation, and history – inasmuch as it is linked to multiples whose elements are unrepresented, excluded – is always in a sense a history of, or from, the void (whilst, if we remain within the situation as it is ordinarily represented, all we have is knowledge and its repetition). In Badiou's definition, a 'historical situation is therefore, in at least one of its points, on the edge of the void. Historicity is thus presentation at the punctual limits of its being'.[31] History and historicity are thereby withdrawn from the domain of meaning and totality, and rendered over to an interventionist notion of singularity, whereby subjectivity is that which forces the unrepresented, what is foreclosed from the situation, into appearance. In other words, the subject is that which gives body and voice to what was, viewed from the standpoint of the state of the situation, a nullity. This also means that the Hegelian notion of the absolute in history, of

29   Ibid.
30   See Chapter 2 in this volume.
31   Badiou 2006a, p. 177.

an absolute history – already attacked by the earlier theory of periodisation – is further distanced. As Badiou writes, in his most succinct definition of the nature/history dichotomy:

> Nature is absolute, historicity relative. One of the profound characterist-ics of singularities is that they can always be *normalized*: as is shown, moreover, by socio-political History; any evental site can, in the end, undergo a state normalization. However, it is impossible to singularize natural normality. If one admits that for there to be historicity evental sites are necessary, then the following observation can be made: history can be naturalized, but nature cannot be historicized. There is a strik-ing dissymmetry here, which prohibits – outside the framework of the ontological thought of the pure multiple – any unity between nature and history.[32]

But this very notion of the relativity of history is what allows Badiou to incor-porate, into the speculative fabric of *Being and Event*, the declaration of *The-ory of the Subject*, according to which 'history does not exist'. For in this new schema, there is no such thing as History conceived as a trans-situational site for the emergence of the new, a global context of subjectivation. As argued above, historicity can only be defined situationally, never intrinsically (unlike nature): 'there are situated evental sites, but there is no evental situation'.[33] This is why the criterion for defining a historical situation is always 'local' according to Badiou.[34] In other words, the idea of an absolute or total domain of history is chimerical, since it would be the idea, in Badiou's terms, of a domain, a region of absolute abnormality. That is why he can declare: 'We can think the *histor-icity* of certain multiples, but we cannot think *a* History'.[35] This thesis is then at the heart of Badiou's distancing from what he now regards as the largely *ima-ginary* idea of *revolution* – as the 'idea of an overturning whose origin would be a state of the totality' – and the obverse move to what he calls a 'differential topology of action' in which every 'radical transformational action originates *in a point*, which, inside a situation, is an evental site'.[36] Though this seems to radically limit the purview of history, there is a sense in which Badiou seems to be recovering a notion of history as revelation, a notion that is far more imme-

---

32   Badiou 2006a, p. 176.
33   Ibid.
34   Badiou 2006a, p. 511.
35   Badiou 2006a, p. 176.
36   Ibid.

diate than Hegel's expressive dialectic of historical revelation. As Badiou writes in *Being and Event*, inasmuch as history and historicity are linked to the pivotal notion of the evental site, it is 'solely in the point of history, the representative precariousness of evental sites, that it will be revealed, via the chance of a supplement, that being-multiple inconsists'.[37] In other words, it is only in 'history' that the inconsistency which Badiou argues is at the heart of being makes itself felt through the irruption of novelty and the construction of the generic by a subject. But this means that history is once again – albeit outside of any figure of totality, as a kind of flash and aftershock – the arena for the *revelation* of being (inasmuch as what is not being qua being, the illegality of the event, is the only thing that allows the thinking of being qua being, i.e. inconsistency).

Finally, and to complicate even further the history of Badiou's relation to history – which as we've seen is also full of anticipations, retractions, and impasses, which is to say of *periodisations* – we must note that ontology itself (which is to say *mathematics*) is itself open to historicity, in a way which we could provocatively say turns Badiou into something like an *absolute historicist*. As he writes in *Being and Event*: 'Our goal is to establish the meta-ontological thesis that mathematics is the historicity of the discourse on being qua being'.[38] In other words, far from being a static eternal formalisation of abstract being, ontology (mathematics) is itself structured by radical events. Indeed, it was one of these events, the invention of irrational numbers against the background of Pythagorean mathematics, that in Badiou's *Being and Event* served as the paragon of subjectivation, understood as that which forces an impossible into the field of the possible, and draws the consequences of this new inclusion. As he wrote:

> The real is the impossible, to wit the resistance of the in-numerable, of *what is not* a natural number. The subject presents, in the failure of the imaginary [the philosophical wish for the simple order of natural numbers], the numerable to the innumerable: it effectuates itself as the mathematical desire to number the innumerable, to legalise the impossible.[39]

Badiou's own thinking of periodisation, not just of mathematics, but of politics, is explicitly founded on this model, on this gesture of historicising mathematics and mathematising history, in order to retain both the absoluteness of truth and the contingency of its emergence.

---

37   Badiou 2006a, p. 177.
38   Badiou 2006a, p. 13.
39   Badiou 1982, p. 219.

I want to allude to at least one of the problems opened up by such a powerful gesture, when its own criteria are dialectically applied to itself. In a superb commentary on some of the possible impasses and paradoxes generated by such a historicisation of ontology via mathematics, Quentin Meillassoux, author of *After Finitude*, defines the fundamental tenets of Badiou's philosophy in terms of two statements, to wit that 'mathematics is ontology' and that 'every truth is post-evental'. The consequence of the first statement, as noted, is rather momentous for what concerns the relation between philosophy and history:

> To assert that mathematics is ontology comes down to attributing to ontology a *history*, and a history which is moreover *independent of any philosophical postulation*. This history is the history of mathematics, which no one can anticipate, which makes ontological novelties *to come* into essentially unpredictable emergences.[40]

But according to the second statement, since all truths are post-evental, the very structure of the historicity of mathematics will remain faithful to the schema of evental truth – as laid out by Badiou's philosophy. However, Meillassoux argues, the tension between the two statements – born of the fact, confronted by Badiou himself, that not all mathematical ontologies are compatible with his thinking of truth – results in the subordination, in Badiou's work, of the first to the second. In other words, the philosophy of the event filters mathematics, and legislates in a way over how the history of ontology may 'turn out'. Meillassoux instead proposes to invert the subordination and – by affirming the tendency in Badiou's work to absolutising the *history* of ontology – to problematise the very thinking of history borne by Badiou's later intellectual production. The option proposed by Meillassoux consists in saying that 'since nothing can be anticipated about the becoming of ontology – including its future compatibility with the philosophy of the event – the evental status of truths itself *must be able to* succumb under the weight of a new ontology' (which is to say that ontological novelties might no longer be truths).[41] This possibility, of a novelty that dislocates Badiou's own concept of novelty (qua post-evental subjectivation and construction of a generic truth) is a risk that a philosophy which began by breaking open the Hegelian circle for the sake of an unpredictable spiral of periodisations cannot avoid. It is perhaps in this sense that Badiou's philosophy, by holding fast to its anti-historicist impetus

---

40   Meillassoux 2002, p. 39.
41   Meillassoux 2002, p. 42.

in order to save the singularity of the event and the emancipatory potentials of novelty, cannot help but confronting the challenge and the threat that an absolute historicism poses to the concept of truth.[42]

---

42   In Jameson's terms, this designates the Marxian scandal of 'the conjunction between an absolute scientific truth and its enabling situation in contingent, empirical history'. Jameson 1988, p. 164.

CHAPTER 7

Politics in Pre-political Times

The philosophical injunction to grasp one's time in thought is beset today by an oscillation between disorienting anxiety and a renascent enthusiasm.

The anxiety is determined by the objective temporality of crisis, understood, in keeping with the medical derivation of the term from Hippocratic medicine, as that phase 'in which a decision is due but has not yet been rendered';[1] when, so to speak, decisions are looking for their subjects. It is an anxiety that is also shadowed by a catastrophic tonality, inasmuch as, without heralding sublime images of final collapse, there is a deep-seated sense that social stagnation or regression are the only figures that any 'recovery' will take, and that the only events punctuating an otherwise featureless future will be profoundly negative.

The enthusiasm is that of a spectating consciousness once again solicited to express a collective, universalisable and impassioned judgement about political action. Provisionally taking the public celebrations of the French Revolution in Kant's Königsberg, and his transcendental capture of that moment, as a kind of 'primal scene' of philosophy's ambivalent relation to revolution, we could say that we are faced today with pre-historical signs. That is, not the historical signs whose anchoring in a regulative history of the species could be problematically judged bearers of progress, bracketing out the Terror and instrumentality that conditioned them, but signs that politics and history could again be objects of both collective and philosophical affirmation – which is also to say that the post-historical, or post-modern interpretation of political judgement would be suspended or terminated.

These signs are 'pre-historical' also to the extent that the 2011 uprisings in Tunisia and Egypt put the name of revolution back into global circulation, but that a concept and a practice of revolution proper to our time remain to be developed. Folding these affective registers into one, we could say that something like an anxious enthusiasm has marked recent thinking of emancipation (needless to say, another term of our modern political lexicon standing-in as a problem and a demand, in wait of its concept and its practice). At a merely intra-philosophical level, it seems evident that a certain widely shared, politically over-determined, if often implicit 'common sense' of the radical thinking of the past forty years is in question today.

---

1 Koselleck 2006, p. 361.

Having assumed the obsolescence of narratives of inexorable emancipation and global revolution – often by contrast with a two-dimensional effigy
of historical materialism – such radical thinking tried to remain faithful to the
emancipatory negation of the status quo by elaborating figures of political discontinuity such as event, act or dissensus. Schematically, we could say that
the emergence of the notion of the 'event' in the 1970s and 1980s as a pole
of attraction for 'Continental' philosophical and political thought goes hand
in hand with the loss or the critique of a totalising horizon that would justify
the use of the category of revolution, as the name for a global change, a world-
transformation. Indeed, to offset a despairing estimation of the social resources
of political subjectivity, or the absence of a class subject, there has been a
tendency to maintain the possibility of an emancipatory break at the price of
curtailing its comprehensiveness, and making agency the result of discontinuity, rather than vice versa. In other words, the decision now comes before the
decider, and the latter is no longer the overt bearer of a global project of change.

That said, the breaks and discontinuities that have so exercised radical
thought over the past three decades or so are at the very least implicitly subjective; though the social existence of a collective agent may be uncertain, the only
real interruptions and dysfunctions of the ruling order are ones borne, however
precariously, by a subject. In this regard, for all of their avowed anti-economism
and anti-determinism, most variants of post-Marxist radical thought arguably
flirt with the error, criticised by Antonio Gramsci under the rubric of 'historical mysticism', of treating rupture as both a necessary and sufficient cause of
subjectivation, and neglecting Gramsci's suggestion that only the preliminary
construction of a collective agent can prepare for, intervene in, and if needs be
accelerate the crisis of a social and economic order.[2]

---

2   'The immediate economic element (crises, etc.) is seen as the field artillery which in war
    opens a breach in the enemy's defences – a breach sufficient for one's own troops to rush
    in and obtain a definitive (strategic) victory, or at least an important victory in the context
    of the strategic line. Naturally the effects of immediate economic factors in historical science
    are held to be far more complex than the effects of heavy artillery in a war of manoeuvre,
    since they are conceived of as having a double effect: 1. they breach the enemy's defences,
    after throwing him into disarray and causing him to lose faith in himself, his forces, and his
    future; 2. in a flash they organise one's own troops and create the necessary cadres – or at
    least in a flash they put the existing cadres (formed, until that moment, by the general histor-
    ical process) in positions which enable them to encadre one's scattered forces; 3. in a flash
    they bring about the necessary ideological concentration on the common objective to be
    achieved. This view was a form of iron economic determinism, with the aggravating factor
    that it was conceived of as operating with lightning speed in time and in space. It was thus
    out and out historical mysticism, the awaiting of a sort of miraculous illumination.' Gramsci
    1998, p. 487.

But what is precisely in question today is whether, as was more or less explicit in the turn in the 1970s and 1980s away from Marxism conceived as a political metaphysics, a ontology and teleology of emancipation, the idea of a politics of the event (or act or dissensus) is the correlate of a saturation and obsolescence of the idea of revolution. The displacement of revolution by event as the name of emancipatory, anti-systemic discontinuity has been deeply entwined with the attack on the metaphysical inconsistency of categories of totality and totalisation.

Badiou's philosophy, metapolitics and political commentary is a unique bearer and barometer of these questions. The play between the inscriptions of politics and philosophical creation that marks out his work also registers, especially in its gestures of periodisation – the opening of phases or the closing of sequences – shifts in the very notion of what it might mean for philosophy to grasp its time in thought. Whether that time is a purely political time, born of a subject of exception, or whether it can also be totalised, represented, 'idealised' as History, is one of the critical questions instigated by his thought, which I want to explore here in terms of the resilience – however tenuous, however obscure – of a revolutionary horizon in our thinking of emancipation. In partial testament to the daunting character of accounting for the dyad event/revolution in anything but an extremely cursory way, I want to do this by a detour through a category present in the two books that, perhaps optimistically, could be said to bookend Badiou's attempt to reinvent the concept of a politics of non-domination under conditions of reaction and restoration – *Can Politics Be Thought?* (delivered as seminars in 1983 and 1984, and published in 1985) and 2011 *The Rebirth of History* (*Le réveil de l'histoire*), the sixth entry in Badiou's *Circonstances* series of polemical essays and political interventions. The category, which resonates so well with the anxious enthusiasm I've spoken about, is that of the *pre-political*.

Now, the link between the pre-political and a politics of revolt, riot, uprising defined by a lack or deficit of revolutionary consciousness and orientation (or of an Idea of communism) is of course not specific to Badiou. It defines the various attempts by historical materialism, ever since Engels's *The Peasant War in Germany*, to draw – along the axes of temporality, subjectivity and (capitalist) totality – the border between revolt and revolution. When the British Marxist historian Eric Hobsbawm, in *Primitive Rebels*, sought to apply Engels's schema to the study of modern millenarian movements among the peasantry in the impoverished and peripheral areas of European countries suffering the dispossessions and upheavals of capitalist modernisation (Sicily in Italy, Andalusia in Spain), it was the category of the pre-political that in many ways organised his research.

In this framework, millenarianism emerges as a reaction-formation whose 'primitive' character is to be understood in political terms: the peasants who respond to the capitalist cataclysm by mobilising on millenarian grounds are not yet capable of attaining the organisational solidity and political impact that qualify mature varieties of anti-capitalism – namely, the labour movement – which have grown in the belly of the capitalist beast. Noting that they still make up the numerical majority of the world's masses, Hobsbawm famously refers to the objects of his book as *pre-political* people who have not yet found, or only begun to find, a specific language in which to express their aspirations about the world'.[3] The 'pre' is determined by a spatial exteriority or peripherality that translates on the temporal axis into backwardness, in terms of both political mentality and organisational capacity. Hobsbawm prefaces his study of modern millenarian movements with this instructive statement:

> The men and women with whom this book is concerned differ from Englishmen in that they have not been born into the world of capitalism as a Tyneside engineer, with four generations of trade unionism at his back, has been born into it. They come into it as first-generation immigrants, or what is even more catastrophic, it comes to them from outside, insidiously by the operation of economic forces which they do not understand and over which they have no control, or brazenly by conquest, revolutions and fundamental changes of law whose consequences they may not understand, even when they have helped to bring them about. They do not as yet grow with or into modern society: they are broken into it, or more rarely ... they break into it. Their problem is how to adapt themselves to its life and struggles, and the subject of this book is the process of adaptation (or failure to adapt) as expressed in their archaic social movements.[4]

Millenarian movements respond to this problem of adaptation in what is, at least initially, a purely negative form. Insofar as they are driven by 'a profound and total rejection of the present, evil world, and a passionate longing for another and better one', failure to adapt seems to be their *raison d'être*. Suffused with apocalyptic ideology, drawn from a pre-existing canon or syncretically

---

3 Hobsbawm 1965, p. 2. For a further discussion of Marxist theories of millenarianism, and of the relation between Engels and Hobsbawm's accounts of peasant revolt, see Toscano 2017.

4 Hobsbawm 1965, p. 3.

fashioned, they are also, because of their hostility to the political world as it stands, affected by a 'fundamental vagueness about the actual way in which the new society will be brought about'.[5]

If politics entails an organisation of means in view of calculable ends (Hobsbawm's classically 'programmatic' premise) then these movements are indeed pre-political – though perhaps this should be understood in the sense of proto-political, of harbouring a radical potentiality to which alliances and struggles can accord real political valence. Hobsbawm's compelling thesis is that it is precisely the all-encompassing negativity and 'impossibilist' desire for a wholly new world of millenarian movements that makes them – unlike other forms of pre-political mobilisation, such as social banditry – politically modernisable. Paradoxically, the very fanaticism that makes it difficult to identify their 'rational political core' is, in the last instance, their rational political core.

Millenarian utopianism is a *sui generis* political realism. It is 'probably a necessary device for generating the superhuman efforts without which no major revolution is achieved'; what is more, these movements prove to both activists and observers that the world can indeed be utterly changed, to begin with by utterly transforming previously depoliticised masses into political subjects.[6] Conversely, revolutionism translates into doomed revolt if it is unable to find organisational forms that can actually gain traction on the very capitalist system that triggered the cultural crisis in the first place. Hobsbawm's own politics are manifest here, as he negatively compares Andalusia's conjunction of peasant millenarianism and anarchist agitation with the sublation of the Sicilian *fasci* into the socialist labour movement, the former coded in terms of the recurrent defeat of heroic revolts, the latter as incorporation into a revolutionary politics capable of wresting real reforms from capitalism.[7]

The critique of Hobsbawm's political model of millenarianism played an important role in the genesis of subaltern studies in India. For Ranajit Guha, the very notion of the 'pre-political' occludes the logic of peasant revolts in the subcontinent, but more importantly it takes their practical consciousness and political subjectivity – *negative* consciousness and *negative* subjectivity – away from those who time and again rose up against the domination of the British Empire. For Guha, this logic and this consciousness are based on a politics that systematically negates the radical distance and oppression that characterises the subaltern's relation to the imperial authorities, as testified to

---

5   Hobsbawm 1965, pp. 57–8.
6   Hobsbawm 1965, pp. 60–1.
7   See Löwy 2000 for some perspicuous criticism of Hobsbawm's evaluation on Spanish anarchism.

in the types of violence employed by the peasant rebels. As he writes, 'once the glare of burning mansions died down and the eye got used to the facts of an uprising, one could see how far from haphazard it had been'.[8] For him, the idea of 'pre-political people' suggests forms of blind spontaneity or false consciousness that do not do justice to the distinctive features (the 'elementary aspects') that can be gleaned from more than a century of peasant insurgencies. What's more, since economic exploitation took place in late eighteenth and nineteenth-century India through the application of direct force, 'there was nothing in the militant movements of the rural masses that was not political'.[9]

The formulation and formalisation of the pre-political in Badiou's *Can Politics Be Thought?* prolongs, in an arguably more dialectical vein, his own articulation of Engels's treatment of the 1525 revolution of the common man in terms of the theory of 'communist invariants', in *On Ideology*. What is at stake in the 1985 text, with its schematic division into the *destruction* and *recomposition* of Marxist politics is at one and the same time the abandonment of a totalising, transitive, programmatic and/or expressive conception of revolutionary politics *and* the refutation of the 'idealism' that would – as in much post-Marxism – vouch for the potential upsurge of politics from any point whatsoever within the landscape of subjection and domination.[10] Abandoning the canonical temporal and subjective understanding of pre-politics in the likes of Hobsbawm – where it would come *before* real revolutionary politics on a developmental line, and would somehow stand *beneath* the attainment of full political consciousness – Badiou compellingly presents the pre-political as the problematic field and material of a politics of non-domination, of communism. What are pre-political are situations, not people.

As Badiou writes in *Can Politics Be Thought?*: 'I call *pre-political situation* a complex of facts and statements such that worker and popular singularities find themselves collectively engaged within it, and such that a failure of the regime of the One is discernible in it. Thus, an irreducible "there is (some) Two". Or: an unrepresentable point. Or: an empty set'.[11] Pre-politics is itself an eventual effect, to the extent that it already defines a situation in which the closure of action within the bounds of the law and language of a situation has been undermined. The pre-political in this respect is not a kind of social latency, but already a political effect. But politics, that is organised, transform-

---

8   Guha 1999, p. 20.
9   Guha 1999, p. 6.
10   See Chapter 2 in this volume.
11   Badiou 1985a, p. 76.

ative politics, does not involve the mere recognition or assumption of this new alteration and duality, this dysfunction in the One, but its extension, through a series of consequential inquiries and decisions, beyond the original situation. Whence the definition: 'I call *politics* what establishes the consistency of the event within the regime of intervention and propagates it beyond the pre-political situation. This propagation is never a repetition. It is a subject-effect, a consistency'.[12]

Yet this propagation does not take the shape of a strategy that would invest pre-identified levers of power and transformation. It intervenes *in* the world, but is not *of* the world, to the extent that it has already broken with its para-meters of possibility. Hence, in arresting counterpoint to the idea of philosophy as a grasp of one's time in thought, the notion of a 'deafness to one's time', to everything within it which 'impossibilises' politics. As Badiou declares, in homage to Rousseau: 'It is important to put all the facts aside, so that the event may come'. Even more starkly, perhaps, Badiou argues that the wager-intervention which defines his conception of the politics of non-domination is always *beyond analysis*: 'An intra-political defeat is for me the intervention-ist incapacity to disjoin politics from analysis. To fail is not to interrupt a given state of certainty'.[13]

The pre-political is here created, and it is created by that deafness, that laying aside of the material rationality and immanent law of a given state of affairs.

> The historically assigned essence of the impossible is thus to be deaf to the voice of time. A pre-political situation is thus created, whose prin-ciple, it is clear, is interruption. Interruption of ordinary social listening, the putting aside of the facts. That is why the police arrives, which is always the police of the facts, the police against the deaf. 'Are you deaf?', says the cop. He's right. The police is nothing but the amplifier of already established facts, their maximum noise, addressed to all those whose speech and action attests, because it is historically impossible, that they are hard of hearing.[14]

The pertinence of this *détournement* of the Althusserian scene of interpella-tion to our present day is considerable, both in terms of an increasing refusal to tolerate the injunctions to listen to social and economic reason, and with respect to the repressive repercussions meted against this strategic, liberating,

---

12   Badiou 1985a, p. 77.
13   Badiou 1985a, p. 104.
14   Badiou 1985a, p. 96.

pre-political deafness. And it is in separation from the pervasive, persistent demand to bow down to the way of the real world, that collective subjectivity finds its resources, as Badiou encapsulates in a striking definition: 'The organised collective body is above all a constructed deafness to the injunction of established facts'.[15]

To follow the threads tying this formalisation of the pre-political to the development of the theory of the subject and to a politics of the event would transcend the purposes of this chapter. But I think we can identify several crucial questions bequeathed by *Can Politics Be Thought?* to contemporary reflection on the problem of the pre-political, which are differently, at times contrastingly, articulated in *The Rebirth of History*,[16] a book whose sustained reflection on this problem would almost warrant subtitling it, *Can Pre-Politics Be Thought?*

First, the problem of revolution. In the conclusion of *Can Politics Be Thought?*, with reference to the workers' movements in Poland that had defined for him what he elsewhere called 'the expatriation of Marxism', Badiou writes:

> That the infinite is the evental consistency propagated by the risk of intervention makes it so that this infinite is never presentable. Inadmissible at its source, politics is unpresentable in its procedure. In this way it is both radical and interminable. Since there is no halting point nor symbol of its infinity, politics must give up the sublime. This is doubtless why, in subjective terms, it distances itself so strongly from the revolutionary representation. As one sees in Kant, the sublime indexing of revolutionary historicity is present from the origin. But let us be attentive to that which is perhaps the deepest characteristic of the Polish movement, which is the constant internal struggle against the sublime of action.[17]

The Polish reference alerts us to an interesting change in the periodisation and judgement of political sequences. What in *Can Politics Be Thought?* had appeared as an inaugural precursor of a workers' politics beyond an expressive teleological theory of working-class revolution, is re-read in *The Rebirth of History*, alongside the Iranian revolution, as signalling the end of the 'clear period of revolutions'. Along with this periodising shift, comes a considerable alteration in philosophy's prescriptions. Not only does *Rebirth* propose what could,

---

15 Badiou 1985a, p. 110.
16 Badiou 2011a. All translations in this essay, written prior to the publication of the English translation (Badiou 2012a), are my own.
17 Badiou 1985a, p. 115. See also Chapter 2 in this volume.

by provocative contrast with Badiou's philosophical tenets, be termed a total-ising representation of History as emancipation, but it also shifts registers, as Badiou's texts on the idea of communism already had, from restricted action to a much more global horizon of opposition.

The tonal shift is thus also the index of a conceptual rearrangement. In what I don't think is a merely terminological question, the abandonment of the 'revolutionary representation' has morphed into the demand for its rein-vention. If the 'the present moment is in fact that of the very beginning of a popular global uprising against this [capitalist] regression', as Badiou declares in *Rebirth*, then we could say the problem has been reversed: no longer strug-gling against the sublime of action, but against its self-imposed restrictions, its false modesty. When, in *Rebirth*, he notes that 'an open, shared, and univer-sally practicable figure of emancipation is lacking', is Badiou not saying that what we most lack is ... a revolutionary representation? A totalisation? If find-ing a political *form* means drawing force from a *shared* Idea, can we really say we've left the politics of representation behind? Is there not a recogni-tion in the very formulation of the idea of communism by Badiou, and others, that there is an unsurpassable need for 'ideology', which is to say for a repres-entation that would both orient and mobilise? That 'affirmative singularities', to establish a kind of duration, are obliged to establish a fiction of consist-ency?

This question of representation is the second problem opened by inquiring into the standing of the pre-political across these two books, which can serve as theoretical and periodising markers both for Badiou's thought and for the thinking of politics (of the nexus of revolution, democracy and philosophy) more broadly. I would hazard that some of the oppositions that sustained Badiou's thought, along with that of other thinkers and currents, through what he calls the 'Restoration', have lost their metapolitical pertinence, if not necessarily their intra-philosophical coherence. Along with the displacement of revolution by event, and the repudiation of totality through multiplicity, I think there is something increasingly problematic – as indexed by Badiou's own turning to a discussion of communism in terms of the idea, the symbol or even the fiction – about the equation between emancipatory and non- or anti-representational thought (an equation often undergirded by a facile slip-page between epistemic representation and parliamentary representation).

In *Can Politics Be Thought?*, Badiou had recast the dialectic, in keeping with a *sui generis* French genealogy, as an anti-representational thought. This is dia-lectics as a thought-practice of the wager and the exception. 'One will recognise a dialectical form of thought', writes Badiou 'by its conflict with representa-tion. Such a thought stalks in its field the unrepresentable point, which testifies that one is touching on the real'.[18] And: 'Thought, which does not represent, produces effects, through the interruption of a chain of representations. Every dialectical thought is therefore above all an interpretation-cut'[19] – the refusal or break with representation is articulated with a hypothesis about a capacity for truth, the existence of a procedure in which truth circulates without being represented.

There is a certain irony then, in contrasting such formulations – which I believe still deeply determine Badiou's thought – with the nonchalant way in which Badiou treats the existence of capital as totality and argues for the necessity for a totalising representation of revolutionary or emancipatory politics in *Rebirth* and other recent texts. A politics of the event is predicated on the inconsistency of structure and the inexistence of totality, but inasmuch as both of these are thought as partisan, contradictory and processual, surely a certain notion of the event *is* compatible with a *dialectical* conception of totality. The irony then is that in *Rebirth* Badiou seems to propose a representation of contemporary capitalism – as oligarchy, banditry and regression to the age of Empire – much more seamless and non-contradictory than any which a Marxian theory of value or crisis could ever allow itself.

Conversely, the discussion of the Idea seems to put far more store and emphasis on representation than a relatively orthodox Marxism ever did. Marx's conception of a communist movement as a form of negative praxis may suffer from an ideological and motivational deficit, but it is telling that he rarely conceived the deficit of political agency principally in terms of a lack of ideational coherence. As he noted in the *Economic and Philosophical Manuscripts of 1844*: 'In order to supersede the idea of private property, the idea of communism is enough. In order to supersede private property as it actually exists, real communist activity is necessary'.[20]

In *Rebirth*, Badiou establishes a suggestive progressive phenomenology of our contemporary pre-political forms of antagonism, identifying the peculiarities of and relays between immediate, latent and historical riots (*émeutes*). The categories of the pre-political and the event are accordingly recast:

> A pre-political *event*, a historical riot, is produced once an intensive over-existence, articulated with an extensive contraction, defines a place in which the situation as a whole is refracted in a universally addressed visibility. You can identify an evental situation at a glance: because it is

---

18   Badiou 1985a, p. 86.
19   Badiou 1985a, p. 88.
20   Marx 1992, p. 365.

universally addressed, you are gripped, like everybody else, by this universality of its visibility. You *know* that the being of an inexistent has just appeared in a place that is proper to it. This is indeed why, as we've said, no one can deny it publicly.[21]

In this conceptually compressed passage, Badiou is in a sense both reviving the Kantian theory of the historical sign, of a presentation of the universal and of its publicity, and undoing it – tellingly, by explicitly presenting the subjective localisation of the break with the One of the situation, in phenomena like the popular occupation of Tahrir Square in Cairo, as a 'representation of the whole by contraction'.[22] The whole is here the People, again a category that seems inseparable from a problematic of representation, and from its familiar impasses, namely the internal division of the people between *sujet de l'énonciation* (subject of the enunciation) and *sujet de l'énoncé* (subject of the statement).[23]

If representation can be reprised in terms of the revolutionary idea and the revolutionary subject, I think it should also be revisited in terms of the question of capitalism. In staging his engagement with this question via a polemic with the post-workerist theme of capitalism as creative, cognitive and postmodern, I think that Badiou, in *Rebirth*, has eluded a more interesting political and philosophical problem, which is that of the relation between crisis and event, capital and its negation. Though this is a vast topic, especially in what concerns the articulations and disjunctions between capital and the state, the political and the economic, I would simply indicate that if we think through the problem of crisis and that of the limits to capital – as what Marx called an 'automatic subject' and a social form, rather than merely as an organisation of banditry by the 1%, which it *also* is – we may want to dissent with the idea that 'it is certainly not capitalism and its political servants that reawaken History, if we understand by "reawakening" the upsurge of a capacity which is both destructive and creative and whose aim is to really exit the established order'.[24]

Though it would be 'historical mysticism' to think of 'the' crisis as a unified phenomenon, one cannot gainsay its capacity to *negatively totalise* movements that are otherwise disparate, and which now are *not* united by a project, programme or Idea, but by their opposition to what Badiou rightly presents as an intolerable regression. In that regard any idea of communism will also need to contend with the malevolent objective spirit of the crisis, with 'the bad new',

---

21   Badiou 2011a, pp. 104–5.
22   Badiou 2011a, p. 97.
23   See http://cahiers.kingston.ac.uk/concepts/subject-of-the-statement-enunciation.html
24   Badiou 2011a, p. 26.

as what is in fact impelling – without in any way determining or automatically generating – the propagation of a global pre-political situation across sites that have no pre-given ideological or subjective commonalities.

Dialectics, historical materialism, and communism can in many respects be defined by their relationship to the pre-political. Is the latter a latency, a potential, a presupposition, a teleologically-oriented movement? In times of riots, which are also times of anxious enthusiasm, Badiou's thinking of the pre-political is a critical testing-ground or interlocutor for anyone concerned with rethinking the articulation between philosophy, revolution and politics today. To his formalisation and phenomenology of a time of riots,[25] I would wish to add the need to move beyond the oligarchic image of capital, so pertinent but also so misleading today, to really think the political valences of an ongoing crisis, the differential specificity of the pre-political in crisis, which is also to say the unpredictable but non-arbitrary intertwining of political sequences and capitalist temporality. Not to do so treats the pervasive form of social organisation and over-determination of politics, starkly present today in terms of the increasingly open 'dictatorship of the bourgeoisie' (where dictatorship should be understood not just as domination but as a logic of permanent emergency powers), as a kind of backdrop, or a purely subjective figure of enmity (oligarchs, bandits, the 1% ...), rather than as a crucial condition for social and political movements – movements which, to the extent that they tackle the brutality of capital's abstract domination, and its concrete personifications, cannot but engage in a practical critique of political economy.

-----

25   Toscano 2016b and 2021.

A Spectre is Not Haunting Europe

What does it mean to talk of communism today? In Europe? A quick survey of our dispiriting political landscape might suggest that communism is only a horizon in the sense of an infinitely receding orientation, unable even to cohere into a determinate regulative idea. Taking the writings of Badiou as occasion, provocation and prism, I want to suggest that, theoretically speaking, our predicament owes much to the aporia of the state within communist thought. To that end, I want to approach Badiou's concept of the state by way of a twofold detour, taking up, first, what I would like to call the *desire for the state* in contemporary movements for systemic reform in Europe, and second, the effort to think communism outside the state in the midst of the last period of concerted and consequential discussion of the 'idea of communism' in Europe, the late 1970s debate over the 'crisis of Marxism' orbiting around the interventions of Louis Althusser.

1   The Desire for the State

What do I mean then by the *desire for the state*? When Badiou – along with many others, albeit with different vocabularies and positions – greeted the surge of 'historical riots' around 2011, he noted a significant pattern: the tendency of these mass occupations of 'public' space to establish themselves at a distance from the representational apparatuses of government and legislation (notably in the ban on party presence within popular assemblies) and to prefigure or embody alternative ways of organizing everyday life. With commendable Leninist sobriety, he also indicated that the limit of this 'movement communism' lay in its unpreparedness for tackling the day after, its misprision about the relation between the uprising and the future of politics. As he writes in *The Rebirth of History*: 'riots do not possess all the keys – far from it – to the nature and extent of the change to which they expose the state. What is going to happen in the state is in no wise prefigured by a riot. ... a historical riot does not by itself offer any alternative to the power it intends to overthrow'.[1] This, for Badiou, is also the source for the Marxian articulation between internal egalit-

---

1   Badiou 2012a, pp. 45–6.

arian democracy and external popular dictatorship thrown up by communist movements, as well as for the entire problematic of the withering away of the state.

In Europe, or rather in the two main fulcrums of agitation over the political sequence that followed in the wake of the global financial crisis and the hard turn to austerity (Greece and Spain), the seeds of movement of communism were replanted, so to speak, on the terrain of the state, with at best ambivalent results (in the shape of Syriza and Podemos). Now, we could present this, in Badiou's wake, as the inevitable product of the incapacity to produce a political practice of a new type, extrinsic to the state, a kind of deficit of courage, capacity and invention. While not discounting this line of inquiry, I would suggest a different tack, one that demands we confront our collective *desire for the state*. To do so requires not only thinking of the state as an agency of representation (in a quotidian but also a philosophical sense, to which I'll return presently) but as a material apparatus of social reproduction. In its bare coordinates, social mobilisation after the 2007–8 crisis articulated the idea that 'they do not represent us' with the quotidian experience of a crisis of social reproduction (especially in health, housing and education), whose cause was to be sought in the collusion between financial oligarchies and state-party elites (whence the renewed fortunes of the theme of *corruption*). Now, though the practical forms of mobilisation (direct democracy, collective organisation of everyday life, generic indifferentiation of social differences) may have been tendentially communist, it seems evident that this moment was marked by the ideology of 'public service' that Althusser anatomised in his critique of Eurocommunism in 'Marx in His Limits'.[2] This is so much the case that the political translation of the 15M mobilisation in Spain, Podemos, explicitly re-signified patriotism and sovereignty as drawing their entire content from the notion of the state as guarantor of an egalitarian access to public goods and institutions. In the words of its onetime secretary general, Pablo Iglesias, 'being a patriot is defending the [collective] right to decide about everything and defending public services'.

Thus, rather than laying bare – except in a kind of symbolic performance – the superfluity of the state, I would argue that contemporary social and political movements ultimately reveal the extent to which the state permeates everyday life and is experienced as a vital presupposition of material existence, while degradation or collapse looms up as a catalyst for social anxiety and, at its worst, for 'a flight forward into the imaginary of the absolute community'.[3] In

---

2   Althusser 2006.
3   Balibar 1992b, p. 235.

this regard, I think Étienne Balibar's suggestion that Marxism has not grasped the ambivalence of mass ideology during conjunctures of crisis has considerable merit, especially as it stresses the effect on both emancipatory resistance and reactionary modalities of neo-racism of the form of the state as a 'national and social state', in which racism operates in 'a conflictual relationship to the state, which is "lived" in a diffracted way, "projected" as a relationship to the Other'.[4] Some of Balibar's writings from the 1980s and 1990s can help us further in grasping the place of 'Europe' in contemporary movements and their limits, especially with regard to the problem of the state.

Given the hegemonic form of the state as 'national and social', which is to say a state that is both identitarian in its creation of 'fictive ethnicities' undergirding the 'privileges' of citizenship and *reproductive*, the 'European construction', especially in its current 'austerian' figure, is a powerful contributor to a conjuncture of crisis. In a powerful 1991 essay significantly entitled *'Es gibt keinen Staat in Europa*: Racism and Politics in Europe Today', Balibar noted how the European 'state' is neither national nor supranational, marked as it is by redundancy and competition between multiple institutions with overlapping jurisdictions, contributing to a decomposition or deficit of state capacities, and fundamentally enacting a 'privatisation of the state' – in which the latter's function, in keeping with age-old (neo-)liberal utopias, was to institute a market. 'The upshot that we see all around us', Balibar concludes, 'is what might be called the reign of statism without a true state. If we understand by statism a combination of administrative/repressive practices and contingent arbitration of particular interests, including those of each nation or the dominant classes of each nation, then that is what is taking the place of the state, while giving the impression of a proliferation of the state'.[5] Following German social theorist Wolfgang Streeck, this statism without the state could be further specified in terms of a secular implosion of capitalist democracy, giving way to a 'Hayekian' international consolidation state aimed at fiscal discipline, in which the European Union and the Economic and Monetary Union represent a liberalising machine whose purpose is to bind national politics to the dictatorship of economic reason.[6] This is the array of institutional powers against which the likes of Syriza and Podemos tried (and largely failed) to erect a bulwark whose affective and symbolic component, crystallised around a left renascence of the syntagm 'national sovereignty', can be linked to a *desire for the state*.

---

4   Balibar 1992b, p. 184.
5   Balibar 1991, p. 17.
6   Streeck 2014.

2   *Imperium*, or, the Circle of the State

Some critical theorists, such as Frédéric Lordon in his *Imperium*, have even
tried to counter the prescriptive 'Europeanism' that still clouds the thinking
of much of the European left, by trying provisionally to recuperate the 'stato-
national paradigm' for emancipatory uses, identifying the prohibitions on left
articulations of 'nation', 'identity', and 'sovereignty' as reasons for the weakness
of the contemporary discourse on communism.[7] The constructive complement
to Lordon's polemic against the political and anthropological wishful thinking
of today's 'communists' involves enlisting Spinoza's political theory of affects,
as developed in the *Ethics* and the *Political Treatise*, to produce a general theory of the 'state' (or a theory of the general state) grounded in a sociologically
and economically informed political anthropology. Building on Lordon's prior
efforts to generate Spinozist theories of capital and the social, *Imperium* proposes that a critical anthropological realism concerning the state can instruct
left-wing thought in the weakness of a 'rationalist' (Badiou) or 'vitalist' (Invisible Committee) optimism that would ignore the lessons of Spinozism as it
envisages a communism beyond our 'passionate servitude'. For Lordon, such a
servitude to our affects, and their contingent worldly causes, is what subtends
the inescapable production of state-like institutions, which are both immanent
(there are no other-worldly or immaterial sources for them beyond the multitude itself) *and* transcendent (they exceed, capture and alienate the powers
of that multitude). This chimes with the definition of *imperium* as the 'right
that defines the power of the multitude', an ineluctable dimension of vertic-
ality that no anarchism, communism or insurrectionism can ultimately circumvent. *Imperium* is an 'extremely general mechanism, at work in all finite
human groups, the mechanism of immanent transcendence ... the power that
the multitude has to auto-affect'; the 'matrix of all powers in the social world'.[8]
The antagonistic potential of our *conatus* and the affects that guide it also dic-
tates that any belonging, any identity, will always imply an exclusion. To ignore
these minimal and general traits of political anthropology is to succumb to
political illusion. A Spinozist materialism, on the contrary, in a definition from
Louis Althusser that Lordon likes to recall, means at the very least 'not telling
ourselves stories'.

   It is at times uncanny, if perhaps misleading, to note how much in the current debate echoes the conjuncture of the late 1970s – not least in the spectre
of *euro*-communism that seems to be haunting contemporary left movements,

---

7   Lordon 2015 and 2022. See also Toscano 2016a and 2022, and my foreword to Lordon 2022.
8   Lordon 2015, p. 117.

with their talk of 'the sense of the state'. Balibar's trajectory since that moment is largely a product of a break with a French Communist Party (PCF) whose claims that the crisis was *above all national* embodied an incapacity to think critically about what communist action in a 'national and social state' meant, ultimately colluding in the racism of 'national preference' which has today brought the Front National/Rassemblement National to the threshold of state power. This was also the period of Louis Althusser's final political interventions on the 'crisis of Marxism' – which also triggered Balibar's first marked distancing from Althusser's positions, precisely around the question of the state. Of course, these debates only appear as analogous to our present concerns, as they were debates about mass communist *parties*. And yet, Althusser's demand that Marxism required a *critique of politics* to match its critique of political economy, a manner of thinking itself out of the *bourgeois forms of politics* towards another practice of proletarian politics, remains suggestive. As he declared in an important article on 'Marxism as a "Finite" Theory', which triggered an entire debate on Italian left: 'the fact that (bourgeois or proletarian) class struggle *has as its stakes* (hic et nunc) *the state does not actually mean it must define itself in relation to the state*'.[9] This statist circumscription of the political was linked by Althusser to what he called the 'juridical illusion of politics' (an illusion which, we should note, is alive and healthy today). The party-form had to be disarticulated from the state-form, but also entirely rethought in its relation to communist movements of liberation outside the workers' movement *sensu stricto*. As a 'matter of principle', the communist party had to reinvent itself *on the margins* of the state.

Shortly after Althusser made these pronouncements, Balibar, who would later summarise his own criticisms in terms of his opposition to the 'theoretical anarchism' plaguing Marxist theories of the state (whence their blindspot especially on citizenship and the *politics* of human rights), argued against this 'communism outside the state' that neither the masses nor the workers' movement had ever been truly *outside* the state, that the latter's separation was always at best partial and qualified, and that rather than a topology of outside and inside, communism should be thought through the internal, immanent contradictions of a system of state relations.[10] The irony of this criticism – for all of its applicability to other forms of communist thought – is that Althusser himself had strongly stressed how deeply the state penetrated into 'civil society', and indeed how one of the limits of Marxism (in the sense, as he ironically

---

9   Althusser 1978, p. 10.
10   Balibar 1979.

put it, of those signs indicating 'your ticket is not valid beyond this limit') was thinking that communism could mean an overcoming of ideology and social relations.[11] His critique of the (Eurocommunist) ideology of 'public service' in 'Marx in His Limits' (roughly contemporaneous with 'Marxism as a "Finite" Theory') puts the question in terms that remain extremely suggestive. I would like to quote it at some length, so as then to turn to the question of a 'communism outside the state' in the work of Badiou:

> there is no breaking out of *the circle of the state, which has nothing of a vicious circle about it, because it simply reflects the fact that the reproduction of the material and social conditions* encompasses, and implies the reproduction of, the state and its forms *as well*, while the state and its forms contribute, but in a 'special' war, to ensuring the reproduction of existing class society. [It is] the circle of the reproduction of the state in its functions as an instrument for the reproduction of the conditions of production, hence of exploitation, hence of the conditions of existence of the domination of the exploiting class which constitutes, in and of itself, the supreme objective mystification.[12]

Or, in the striking expression that Althusser uses to encapsulate this state-fetishism, *ça ment tout seul* (it lies on its own).

3   Thinking Communism outside the State

Badiou's metapolitics is arguably the most concerted contemporary philosophical effort to think communism outside the state. What is its concept of the state, and how might this antagonistic nexus of communism and state speak to our current European conjuncture?

The state, or more specifically the state of the situation, is a central concept or operator in *Being and Event*. I will not attempt here to revisit the articulation of Badiou's meta-ontology and of his socio-historical exemplification, but rather home in on the way in which his theory is oriented toward the issue of 'communism outside the state'. The theory of the state put forth in Meditation 9 of *Being and Event* is above all a theory of the state's *separation* and of its excessive or super-power over the situation it is re-presenting. Its replication of

---

11   Althusser 1978.
12   Althusser 2006, p. 125.

a classical Marxism is evident in its refusal of a theory of the state as expressive of the social bond, in favour of the notion that the state is to be related to
unbinding (*la déliaison*), to an effort to fix the void that threatens its underlying structure. In this regard, the state is fundamentally Hobbesian, a machine to
prevent *stásis*, tumult, chaos, plague, to snuff out the rioting crowd invariably
viewed as an 'emblem of inconsistency'. Illegitimately compressing a meticulous deduction, we can note that as the pre-emption of the void, the state
is concerned for Badiou not with terms, individuals, or multiples *as such* but
with collective subsets, striving to stabilise the relation between inclusion and
belonging. What the State does is to re-present what has already been presented. This requires structuring the structure of presentation, counting the count.
The state makes a One out of the parts of the situation (note that Badiou will
argue that one-ness in the 'immediacy' of the social is provided by non-state
structures, hinting at the social reproduction underlying political representation). The result of this is that the state will generate 'excrescent' multiples,
which are re-presented or included but not presented (which do not 'belong'
to the situation), and will only deal with individuals as 'singletons', not as multiples but as sub-sets (the voter, for instance). Whence its indifference to the
lives of the putatively 'represented'. The state's identification and homogenisation of multiples is for Badiou its 'elementary coercion', its 'atom of constraint'.
In *The Rebirth of History* this elementary coercion of 'inclusive' or 'representational' identity will be redoubled by the exclusivity of an identitarian operation
that manufactures the inexistence of certain multiples, or terroristically stig-
matises them, by creating fictions of identity – like the incoherent but dominating normative or average conception of the French citizen, 'F', an identitarian
operation that functions through 'separating names' (immigrant, Muslim, etc.).
As Badiou observes: 'The fictional F, measure of normality and matrix of suspicion, or its stand-in in any state structure, is always identitarian'.[13]

But *Being and Event*, like Althusser's writings of the late 1970s, also indicates
the 'limits' of Marxism in its theorising of the state. For Badiou, these limits
have to do with the notion that the state *itself* (rather than the multiples it
produces) is an *excrescence*, which could thus *wither away*, and in the related
axiom that politics is first and foremost *an assault on the state*. For Badiou, such
a horizon of the abolition of the state ignores its meta-ontological ineluctability: while the unpresentable errancy of the void and the excess of inclusion
over belonging, may, in the rarity of evental truth procedures, give rise to dysfunctions, transformations and subtractions from the state, this cannot *abol-*

---

13   Badiou 2012b, p. 76.

ish the state meta-ontologically (which is to say meta-historically and meta-politically) conceived. Recognition of this, combined with a steadfast commitment to the separation of egalitarian political capacities from the operations of the state – in other words the conviction that political truths are never, as such, a matter of representation – requires a very different image of 'communism outside the state' than the one provided by 'classical' communism. Abolition is accordingly rethought as distance, separation, subtraction, and, more affirmatively speaking, prescription. The militant can no longer be, in Badiou's poetic gloss, a watchman beneath the walls of the State but needs to transform herself into a patient tracker and stalker of the void and its irruptions. Accordingly, 'even if the route of political change – ... the route of the radical dispensation of justice – is always bordered by the State, it cannot in any way let itself be guided by the latter, for the State is precisely non-political, insofar as it cannot change, save hands, and it is well known that there is little strategic signification in such a change'.[14] The persistence of this perspective on the state is evident in the positions of *The Rebirth of History*, where we read that since 'the radicalized generic is incompatible with the state, which lives exclusively off identitarian fictions, any political truth presents itself as a restriction of the power of the State', meaning that the communist militants of the generic must 'decide what the State must do and find means of forcing it to', from the outside.[15]

Returning to Balibar's objections to the kind of 'theoretical anarchism' that would all-too-easily dispense with the state, it is evident that Badiou, meta-ontologically speaking, is *not* a thinker of the abolition of the state (whether his communism envisages state forms that are not bourgeois, national, or iden-titarian, is a different matter, requiring us to think the difference between the withering away of the state *as such*, versus, in Althusser's terms, the 'reorganization, restructuring and revolutionization of an existing apparatus').[16] Yet Badiou remains a thinker of 'communism outside the state'. But is the model of distance and prescription an adequate one to reinvigorate the communist hypothesis? There is little doubt that classic reformist and revolutionary hypotheses, viewing the state as the object and element of political action, are deeply damaged today, and that attempts at countering 'statism without a state' through an expansive conception of national and popular sovereignty are uncertain at best. That said, two reasons militate against the notion of a communism at a distance from the state. The first is already evident in Balibar's characterisation of the European non-state (which is the very opposite of the

---

14   Badiou 2006a, p. 110.
15   Badiou 2006a, p. 81.
16   Althusser 1977, p. 17.

communising 'barred state' of which Badiou tantalisingly speaks in 'Our Contemporary Impotence'[17]), but also in Badiou's understanding of contemporary imperialist power as a practice of *zoning* that practically deconstructs states.[18] Such zoning suggests that some of the characteristics of the meta-ontological and meta-political conception of the State from *Being and Event* no longer map so neatly onto our own present. Contemporary state or para-state power, including the agencies of a predatory capital, is an active *producer* and not just pre-emptor of 'unbinding'. Whence the 'conservative' or 'defensive' character of a contemporary politics objectively tied to the reaffirmation of the national and social state with all of its aporias and ideologies (not least that of Public Service). Whence our *desire for the state*, our 'statism without a state', to twist Balibar's formulation. But a communism of distance is also complicated by the fact that the state – in its materiality – is not a mere matter of representation, but, perhaps above all, one of reproduction. That, as Althusser suggested, is the objective mystification, the *circle of the state*, that any 'communism outside the state' still needs to confront. Distance implies too much innocence, and any communist must be first and foremost his or her own enemy, realising that the transcendence of the state is materially, affectively permeated with immanence, with our needs and desires. La Boétie's questions still haunts us:

> Where has he acquired enough eyes to spy upon you, if you do not provide them yourselves? How can he have so many arms to beat you with, if he does not borrow them from you? The feet that trample down your cities, where does he get them if they are not your own? How does he have any power over you except through you? How would he dare assail you if he had no cooperation from you? What could he do to you if you yourselves did not connive with the thief who plunders you, if you were not accomplices of the murderer who kills you, if you were not traitors to yourselves?[19]

Pace Nietzsche, perhaps we should start reckoning with the fact that the State is the *warmest* of all monsters.

---

17   Badiou 2013.
18   Badiou 2004e and 2014a.
19   La Boétie 2015, p. 48.

Communism and the Absolute

Can communism be thought?[1] And can it be thought in the element of the absolute? My starting point for this intervention is a strong interpretive hypothesis, namely that the principal stakes of Badiou's great speculative triptych, and especially its third 'panel', *The Immanence of Truths*, is a systematic redefinition of the *philosophical* problem of communism. As I hope to suggest, this largely implicit labour on the conceptual components of communism can be distinguished from the more directly political, metapolitical, and – in an entirely non-pejorative sense of the term – *ideological* arguments that Badiou has deployed around the idea of communism.

Following this line of questioning, I think it telling that the 'philosophical saga' of *Being and Event*, which comes to a close in a speculative immersion into political materials extracted from the Russian and Chinese revolutions – as well as with a return to Marx's *Manifesto* as defining 'the general conditions of existence of a political work, and therefore of a political truth' – was inaugurated by a *subtraction* of communism, to wit by the removal from the original design of the 1988 volume of a formidable meditation on 'The Factory as Event-Site', cut from the body of the book and published in the journal *Le Perroquet*. I have already commented on this crucial text,[2] where the defining objectives of Badiou's political reflections of the 1980s – to have done with the metaphysical epoch of Marxism-Leninism, with its faith in the proletariat as the subject and substance of a dialectical History – translates into a precarious albeit intransigent articulation of the site 'factory' with the subject-name 'worker'. One could interpret this subtraction not as the wish to hide the principal model and motor for Badiou's ontological labours, but as a way of forestalling the temptation to suture the speculative trajectory to a political desideratum, and to avoid the immediate ideological flattening of the articulation between the-

---

1 This talk was originally delivered on 1 October 2018, in the context of the study days on *L'immanence des vérités*, the third volume of Alain Badiou's *Being and Event* trilogy, organised at Théâtre de la Commune in Aubervillers, Paris. I take the opportunity to thank Badiou for interpellating me into this series of what he'd chosen to call 'declarations' about *The Immanence of Truths* (Q&As, dialogue or debate were studiously dispensed with in the *journées d'étude*). Badiou's interpellation cannot but recall Lucky's own, in *Waiting for Godot*: 'Think, pig!' – the comical and violent synthesis of the relation between subject of truth and human animal.

2 See Chapter 2 in this volume.

ory of subject-truth and set-theoretical ontology onto a Marxist problematic which in the mid 1980s seemed tainted by the signs of obsolescence. While a 'distant reading', to borrow the language of contemporary literary studies, only registers three instances of the word 'communism' (or the adjective 'communist') in *Being and Event* '1' – by contrast with the proliferation of the word (and the concept) in *Logics of Worlds* and *Immanence* – one may identify in the invention of the fundamental concept of the 'generic' – understood as the disjunctive synthesis of the ontology of sets and a reference, as crucial as it is discrete, to the *Gattungswesen* of Marx's Parisian manuscripts – the lever for the new philosophical articulation of communism that traverses Badiou's 'saga'.

To move, all too quickly, to a metapolitical consideration of *Immanence*, I think it is possible to discern, in the happy short-circuit engineered by Badiou between Paul Cohen's set-theoretical vocabulary and the language of Karl Marx, two fundamental operations. First, the displacement of what could be called the capacity (or power) of communism from the ambit of an anthropology of labour towards a formalised relation between universality and subject (i.e. truth) in which both universality and subject are to be conceived as *results* not *presuppositions*. Second, the felicitous hypostasis of a category of communist practice, namely the *inquiry*, to the status of model for the trajectory whereby the subject comes to extract from the oppressive finitude of the situation (to speak the language of *Immanence*) an integrally shareable political truth. This evacuation of Marxian philosophical anthropology for the sake of a (redoubtably complex) formal translation of the communist image of a new militant knowledge provides a powerful clue about the political foundations of the problem of the immanence of truths – the immanence of a generic procedure and not the immanence of a bio-political virtuality possessed by the human being.

We may note in passing that the thoroughgoing anti-humanism of the conceptual apparatus of *Being and Event* (and of its implicit redefinition of the communist problematic, in continuity and rupture with Marx), is in tension with Badiou's tendency, in his political-ideological interventions, to place his philosophy under the banner of what we could term an ultra-humanism. Consider for instance his remarks in *Petrograd, Shanghai* on the communism to come as 'a second revolution after the Neolithic revolution'[3] – a revolution defined by its reunification of humanity, that is, by the politicisation and realisation of an essence of the species, by contrast with its contemporary inegalitarian destiny. I would like to briefly return in what follows to this major

---

3   Badiou 2018a, p. 23.

problematic nexus, namely to the necessity or otherwise of a philosophical anthropology for a theory of communism. My intuition here is that the systematic and stratified solution of the question of the immanence of truths – a solution that traverses the philosophical saga in the guise of the *generic* subtraction from the encyclopaedia of knowledges (*Being and Event*), the *singular* surfacing of an intensity of existence in the appearance of a world (*Logics of Worlds*), and the embedding (*plongement*) of the *absolute* in works that attest the infinity of a truth (*Immanence of Truths*) – blocks the path to an ontological (i.e. mathematical) translation of the notion of humanity, a notion that is and must remain emphatically and affirmatively *ideological*. Or, to employ the terminology of *Immanence*: any and every distinction, any and every passage, between humanity as a distillate of finitude and humanity as the synonym of the infinite cannot be philosophically decided. I do not think that what Badiou calls 'the theoretical and practical conviction of an essential unity of humanity'[4] can be philosophically founded. Though there may be a non-humanist conceptualisation of communism (as I hope to sketch here) or a communist image of anthropology, *there is no communist philosophical anthropology* – if we remain within Badiou's materialist dialectic and refuse the entreaties of a democratic materialism oriented towards communism for which *the only truths are truths of bodies and languages*.

After these preliminary remarks, I'd like to sketch a way into *The Immanence of Truths* through the angle of the problem of communism (for reasons that may become clearer as I proceed, I think that *problem* is more adequate to the philosophical status of communism than *idea*). In order to do this, I'd like to isolate two themes that structure the classical textual locus in the modern history of communism where the *truth* of a society beyond classes and the value-form is thought in its *immanence* to capitalism, to wit Karl Marx's famous critique of the so-called 1875 'Gotha programme' of German Social Democracy (referred to in German as his *Randglossen zum Programm der deutschen Arbeiterpartei*, Marginal Notes on the Programme of the German Workers' Party). These two themes are *equality* and *transition*. The hypothesis, the hyperbolic fiction, governing my reflections here is that we could treat *The Immanence of Truths* as a vast commentary in the margins of Marx's *Randglossen*.

In a long endnote to *Logics of Worlds* concerning Plato, Badiou declares the communist destination of philosophy as such, defining communism as the political name of the *egalitarian* discipline of truths.[5] The operative link

4   Badiou 2018b, p. 546.
5   Badiou 2008, p. 557.

here is between philosophy, on the one hand, and a metapolitical translation of communism, on the other, and not between philosophy and a singular
instance of political thought-practice – which would instead signal the fall
into the *suture* between truths and philosophy, a suture that Badiou's entire
theory of *conditions* strives to prevent. But if communist equality conditions
our image of philosophy, what can be said about the philosophical determination of a concept of equality that might be compatible with the renewal of
a politics worthy of the name communist? Before exploring how *The Immanence of Truths* can orient us towards a reinvention of the concept of equality, it
seems necessary to recall that the centrality of the abolition of class inequalities, power hierarchies and differences of domination in any communist politics
does not signify, conversely, that communism may be simply defined as the
politics of equality. We may observe that the parliamentary-capitalist or liberal
saturation of the concept of equality is so powerful as to pose an enormous
danger of capture and neutralisation to any emancipatory politics. This risk is
perhaps the central theme in Marx's critique of the social-democratic followers
of Ferdinand Lassalle. It is also a critical concern for Engels who, in the same
year as the *Randglossen*, and after having himself proposed in a communist
horizon the substitution of the false idea of a 'free people's state' with *Gemein-
wesen* or *commune*, tells his correspondent August Bebel:

> The concept of a socialist society as a realm of *equality* is a one-sided
> French concept deriving from the old 'liberty, equality, fraternity', a con-
> cept which was justified in that, in its own time and place, it signified
> a *phase of development*, but which, like all the one-sided ideas of earlier
> socialist schools, ought now to be superseded, since they produce nothing
> but mental confusion, and more accurate ways of presenting the matter
> have been discovered.[6]

The fundamental thesis of the *Critique of the Gotha Programme* is that the
equality waved like a banner by the social democrats subsumes the image of
communism to a conception of work that is in the final analysis immanent not
just to the ideology of bourgeois society, but to the functioning and material
reproduction of capital, a reproduction in its turn sustained by a juridical ideology.

In this perspective every 'equality', not least the one imagined in the social
democrats' programme as the equitable distribution of the product of labour,

---

6   Friedrich Engels to August Bebel, 18–28 March 1875, in Marx and Engels 1991, p. 64.

remains prisoner *both* of a neglect of the difference between labour and labour-power *and* of an image of justice that ignores that profound solidarity between the inegalitarian laws of capitalist exploitation and the egalitarian ideology of right. The equality of 'equal rights' to which social democracy refers is an equality in *measurement*. As Marx has it in the *Randglossen*, 'the equality consists in the fact that measurement is made with an *equal standard*, labour'.[7] Consequently, 'this *equal* right is an unequal right for unequal labour'. *'It is, therefore, a right of inequality, in its content, like every right'*, since right 'by its nature can exist only as the application of an equal standard'.[8] This knot that binds together right, equality, measurement and labour means that every hope that one can found a non-capitalist measurement directly in right, equality *or* labour is revealed to be false, fatally haunted by its immanence to the extant mode of production. In Badiou's vocabulary, we must choose here between a constructible socialism and an inconstructible communism – one that is incommensurable to the rearrangement, however creative and 'progressive', of the elements of the present.

This is why Marx, and Lenin after him (in *State and Revolution*), were impelled to mark their difference from the social-democratic mainstream and to think communism not as the liberation of a fundamental equality but as the invention of a non-dominating way of experiencing and composing inequalities – inequalities which, when considered beyond their measurement, beyond the homogeneous standard of an 'equal right', will perhaps be no more, and no less, than *differences*. If every equality is an equality of measurement – a measurement originating in labour, money, the juridical status of the person or right and law in general – perhaps we will need to cease imagining communism as a politics of equality. This was the view of Althusser, for instance, who, in his self-interview, *The Black Cows*, warns that the 'demand for egalitarianism is historically an impasse and a trap', and who says, with reference both to Marx's marginal notes and Lenin's gloss on the same, that 'for unequal rights to cease, right itself must cease, and the real inequality of individuals among themselves must emerge' – a real inequality, or difference, we might add, that we struggle to think or practice enmeshed as we are in the ideological and material apparatuses of capitalist right, and which will only surface in that singular process that Althusser himself calls *the formal subsumption of capitalism by communism*.

To what end this doctrinal detour? Hopefully to remind us, first, that the identity between communism and equality is anything but obvious, and second, that every philosophical (or metapolitical) reinvention of equality must

---

7   Marx and Engels 1989, p. 86.
8   Ibid.

overcome its ideological and material saturation by the 'equal standards' of capitalism and of its democracy. While its transcoding into a political register perhaps suffers from the shortcomings of analogy, or homonymy,[9] equality as it appears in *The Immanence of Truths* is strongly demarcated from any measurement whatever, and especially the measurements of right (or law) and the state. This can be verified in the passage that examines the quasi-ontological antagonism between the infinite of the state and the infinity of a political truth-procedure. It would be interesting to explore the lags and displacements between this embryo of a theory of the state and the treatment of the latter in the eighth meditation of *Being and Event*.[10] Briefly, we could say that the place of juridical ideology shifts between the first and third 'panel' of Badiou's speculative triptych. In the 1988 book, it is lodged in a state apparatus of representation that captures social multiplicities in the 'singleton' of a juridical ideology. In *The Immanence of Truths* the critique of politics and its juridical ideology remains unshaken but its fundamental figure, to wit the *citizen*, is a residue or waste product (*déchet*) of a conflict between two infinites, in which the infinity of the state is no longer defined by its combination of immeasurable super-power and implacable measurement (as it was in *Being and Event*), but by its vertical and apparently external management of differences. As Badiou writes:

> The State is in effect an infinite of resistance to the partitions it induces: it is the Same at the heart of the irreducible alterities whose finicky manager it also proves to be. The infinite of the State escapes, at least apparently, the partitions of the human collective, partitions that it does not stop inducing, maintaining, codifying ... the infinite of the State belongs to a type of infinite whose singular property is its resistance to the divisions that it nevertheless produces and manages. We will call it, as mathematicians do, a 'compact cardinal'. The prohibited infinite is then the one that would result from an immanence of compactness: the infinite possibility of always wanting, in situation, the infinite of non-separation. Revolutionary politics has proposed no shortage of names for this type of infinity. ... The name that sums them all up is the name 'equality'. We can speak of an infinite of equality that resist partitions; not, like the State, by

---

9   As was forcefully suggested in Jacques Rancière's incisive 'declaration' ('Homonymes, synonymes, et équivalents') in the same study days in which this chapter was originally presented. See the video recording of his session at: https://www.youtube.com/watch?v=CzARgGCDktc.

10   See also Chapters 3 and 8 in this volume.

organising and protecting them but, like communism, by declaring their nullity and tearing up their roots (nations, divided labour, private property ...). In actual fact, contrary to what it claims, the modern State should be defined, not as a transcendence with regard to differences – when it is in fact their organiser and guarantor – but as the (sometimes violent) resistance to the infinite of equality, the bad infinite, the one about which one must confess, like the sinner does with regard to human pride, that it is impossible, and therefore prohibited.[11]

Modern political equality is therefore embedded by Badiou in the oppressive dialectic between an infinite egalitarian upsurge (non-separation) and an infinity of domination, the infinity of the state as guarantor and instrument of separation. The 'citizen' is here the basic by-product of this dialectic, the political residue or waste product (*déchet*) *par excellence*:

> The subjective product of the repression of immanent compactness (equality) by oppressive compactness (the State) has a name, which was once, briefly, a glorious name – during the birth of the modern republican State; it is the only name fully adapted to the deployment of Capital, but which is now nothing but the tired and rhetorical name of powerlessness. This name is 'citizen'. The citizen is with regard to the State what the true believer was with regard to the Church, namely a sinner confessing his sin ... what is, with reference to this example, the Subject that makes immanent (*immanentise*), against the State, the infinite compactness of equality? The response is beyond doubt, it is the communist militant, in the generic sense of the term. In other words the one who, in situation and independently, has as the norm of their action, at whatever scale it takes place, the broadest possible organisation of equality. And the intimate enemy of the militant, the enemy it often encounters in him or herself, is therefore the good citizen of the State of laws (*l'État de droit*). For the temptation to shelter oneself in the passive finitude of the residue (*déchet*) is that against which the militant work (*oeuvre*) must fight, both within and without.[12]

It is evident that communism as a politics of equality has, as a precondition, its separation from juridical separation, a separation identified by Badiou –

---

11 Badiou 2018b, pp. 79–80.
12 Badiou 2018b, p. 80.

in what we could call a metahistorical register – with the saturation and capture of equality by citizenship. We could wonder, in passing, whether the brief and glorious time of which Badiou speaks means that the citizen was once a true name (for instance in the Haitian Constitution of 1805, which operates the revolutionary transfiguration of race by citizenship in its Article 14: 'Haitians [a category that, in keeping with Art. 13, incorporated naturalised white women, Poles and Germans] will henceforth be known by the generic denomination of blacks') and 'became' a residue, or waste product, of the dialectic of emancipation. Or perhaps the process that Badiou terms, in his mathematical lexicon, 'recuperation' or 'recovery' (*recouvrement*) is also the production of simulacra, homonymous phantoms of the names of suppressed truths. What strikes me especially in this staged confrontation between the militant and the citizen is that it is a kind of inner conflict, as testified by the idea of an intimate enemy (an enemy who perhaps can never, or should never, be simply vanquished).

Hegel, in his early theological writings, spoke of tragedy as the form that allows us to grasp, through the notion of fate, the 'consciousness of oneself, yet as something hostile'.[13] I want to return to this 'tragic' side of political truth and political works, a tragedy that concerns the twisted dialectic of the finite and the infinite or, to employ the language of Badiou's *Ethics*, the 'consistency' between (militant) subject and individual (citizen), with particular reference to the communist problematic of transition. But first I want to bring to a close these remarks on equality by suggesting that we can perhaps perceive in *The Immanence of Truths* a unique effort to produce a philosophical concept of equality that breaks with the juridical idea of a measurable person and makes intelligible equality as an infinite process that traverses inequalities and differences by transfiguring them (a little like Saint Paul's 'universalism' may have done in Badiou's own rendering). Equality (and thus communism) in *The Immanence of Truths* must therefore be a concept incommensurable with the 'separating' concepts of measurement, identification, representation, and so on. It is notable in this regard that the ontological passage through the theory of 'great cardinals' associated equality no longer to a relation (between individuals) or to an order, but to a *power*. As Badiou declares:

> Infinite is the generic name of what institutes, in a point of a situation – in fact, in a post-evental point – a power that is simultaneously egalitarian and at the level of (*à la hauteur de*) the situation in its entirety. ... It is fundamental to think the necessary link between equality – the general

---

13   Quoted in Szondi 2002, p. 17. On Badiou, Hegel and tragedy, see Toscano 2015.

maxim, in all domains, of creations of thought with universal value – and the infinite. ... We have here the dialectical inversion of the most important oppressive thesis, the one that goes: since we are naturally finite, we are unequal by nature. To think the infinite is the ineluctable ontological condition for a thinking of equality.[14]

I think it is important to underscore here that this inversion must be *dialectical* – the refutation in communist practice of natural inequality is *not* natural equality (a thesis that, as we know, is easily compatible with a philosophy of domination, as shown most influentially by Hobbes's *Leviathan*), but another use, another experience of differences, of *ex*-inequalities. Here one could also reflect on how the most important 'works' (to use one of Badiou's categories in *Immanence*) of communist politics do not take the form of declarations, of texts anchored in indexical names, but are embodied and embedded in the invention of new *measures* capable of welcoming and enacting the infinite of equality, measures hostile to the unitary reduction to *the* person or *the* citizen operated by state representation.

Such a thought of communism as the creation of new measures that break with and depart from the measurements of state law, and thus leave behind the modern idea of political equality is the enigmatic, problematic legacy of those marginal glosses through which Marx (and after him, Lenin) sought to evade the capture of communism by the legal standards of capitalist democracy. It no doubt requires 'the invention of new forms able to dispossess the [withering] State of its transformed functions'.[15]

Now, while Badiou, from *Can Politics Be Thought?* onwards, may have broken with any Marxism of *transition*, perceived as irrevocably contaminated by a metaphysics of the State and History, I think that at a philosophical level, and especially in terms of a thinking of the infinite of equality and its truths or works, we are not done with transition, that Marxian name for the immanence (to capitalism) of communist truths. Badiou speaks to us of a 'materialism of the Idea, which is that the process of its existence is immanent to the world'.[16] In his *Critique of the Gotha Programme*, Marx declares: 'What we are dealing with here is a communist society, not as it has developed on its own foundations, but on the contrary, just as it emerges from capitalist society, which is thus in every respect, economically, morally and intellectually, still stamped with the birth-

---

14   Badiou 2018b, pp. 347–8.
15   Althusser 2016, p. 241.
16   Badiou 2018b, p. 350.

marks of the old society from whose womb it emerges.'[17] Or, to translate this into the language of the *Immanence of Truths*, every communist work is composed almost entirely of residua, of waste products (*déchets*), and, what's more, of constitutively oppressive waste products (the state apparatus, the organisation of labour, the function of intellectuals, etc.). This is why political truths in their unfolding are always *tragic* truths – not in the sense accorded to this term by liberal doxa, which admonishes us that every effort to realise equality throws us back, through inevitable disaster and untold suffering, onto our ineluctable finitude – but in a sense immanent to these truths themselves. This is the sense in which in 1920 Trotsky (but we could also cite Lenin, Bukharin, or others) declared that 'our position is in the highest degree tragic',[18] to the extent that the political novelty of the revolution passes through a destructive catastrophe, or in that of Andrei Platonov's notes on 'the first socialist tragedy'.[19] But we can also refer to the narration of the reversals and heterogeneses that accompany the trajectory of the Haitian revolution in C.L.R. James's *The Black Jacobins*, not least the reimposition of a plantation system for the sake of national-economic survival in the liberated Saint Domingue. In all these cases, and many others, we are confronted with the fact that a political truth is not only the effort to escape the operations of finitude, but that in emancipating oneself from the waste of the past it produces its own, new residua, in what we could see as a dialectic whose most efficacious and suggestive formulation perhaps remains the idea of the practico-inert and of matter as anti-praxis in Sartre's *Critique of Dialectical Reason*.

To conclude: *The Immanence of Truths* culminates in the definition of the task of philosophy as the affirmation, armed with a formidable mathematical rationality and a polymorphous circulation among diverse truth-procedures, that *the true life is possible* (or, more precisely, that philosophy must 'create, in the conditions of its own time, *the knowledge of the existential possibility of the true*'). In the iron cage of our corrupt present, we may be tempted to respond with the Adorno of *Minima Moralia* 'no true life in the false'. But this pessimism of reason *and* will is not obligatory, if we treat tragedy, waste and finitude as immanent and dialecticisable elements of a communist procedure. Then we may be able to repeat, with a great Italian communist critic and poet, the maxim of an affirmatively, infinitely tragic communism: 'no true life *except* in the false'.[20]

---

17   Marx and Engels 1989, p. 85.
18   See Lih 2007.
19   Platonov 2011.
20   Fortini 1971, p. 113.

PART 2

Toni Negri, or, the Communist Tendency

∴

CHAPTER 10

Chronicles of Insurrection: *Operaismo* and the Subject of Antagonism

> One time I went to May Day. I had never got May Day – *la festa del lavoro*: what a joke, the festival of work. The workers' festival, the workers who celebrate a festival. I didn't get what the festival of workers, or the festival of work, meant. I didn't get why work should be celebrated. It's like, when I didn't work, I didn't know what the fuck to do, because I was a worker, that is, someone who spent the greater part of his day in the factory, and with what was left all I could do was rest up for the next day. But that holiday I went to May Day on a whim, to listen to a rally speech by I don't know who.
>
> NANNI BALESTRINI, *We Want Everything*

• • •

> Force ... is itself an economic power.
>
> KARL MARX, *Capital, Vol. 1*

∵

1   Before Empire, behind the Multitude

Though much work has been carried out to rectify, whether critically or affirmatively, a dehistoricised understanding of the political content of the theses forwarded in books like *Empire* and *Multitude*, there remains a strong tendency – at times enabled by their own rhetoric of rupture and transformation – to treat the works of Hardt and Negri as a kind of theoretical UFO, or better a time-machine emancipated of all nation and class coordinates, visiting us from a vibrant future that the authors insist in describing as our present. Behind the figures of Empire and the multitude lies a long, punctuated history of theoretical work and political practice aimed at testing the validity of Marxist categories in light of empirical transformations in modes of production and reproduction, tendencies in class composition and shifts

in the forms of capitalist domination, driven by political struggles and economic reconfigurations in post-war Italy.[1] Behind the non-dialectical pairing of
Empire and multitude, one needs to discern the figures of a far more classical
albeit 'mutant' antagonism between capital and labour, of the kind formulated in what can loosely be defined as the 'workerist' (*operaista*) and 'post-
workerist' (*post-operaista*) development of critical Marxism beginning with
the work of Raniero Panzieri and the *Quaderni Rossi* journal, and then gaining greater prominence chiefly in the writings of Mario Tronti and Antonio
Negri, whose intellectual production of the sixties and seventies will concern
me here.

My aim in this chapter is to explore the following question: What drives the
move from the 'workerist' dialectic of antagonism and its capture, through the
insurrectionary unilaterality of worker's autonomy, all the way to later theories
of exodus? In order to sketch an answer to this question, we need to investigate
the juncture between the political-economic logic of capital and the revolutionary logic of separation – of *communism as separation*.[2] In the epoch of what
Marx referred to as 'real subsumption', wherein all labour and production processes take place within the ambit of capitalist relations, it is only an organised
act of antagonistic separation that, from the vantage point of *operaismo*, can
elicit the emergence of living labour as a collective subject capable of appropriating a production process founded on the exploitation of its capacities. As
Negri remarks, capitalist 'totality is a texture in which we find ourselves and
in which we must separate ourselves in order to exist – but it is the intensity of
the separation, the force with which antagonism is recognised, that constitutes
us as singularities – as subjects'.[3] The open paradox of the workerist 'tradition'
(to adopt a term whose intensely problematic character has been highlighted
by Sergio Bologna) and of the political philosophy of the multitudes that has
followed in its wake – which is of course a paradox faithful to some of the
key insights of Marx – is precisely the twin affirmation of an integral *immanence* of capitalist relations to the social (of a thoroughgoing *socialisation* of
production) and of the radicalisation of the antagonism between capital and
labour. Subsumption, precisely to the extent that it is real, manifests itself as an
irrational form of command and heralds the possibility of a communist appropriation of production. In a nutshell, the problem is that of the realisation of
communism in a situation of advanced and dynamic capitalism, wherein political crisis and antagonism are by no means necessarily accompanied by scarcity

---

1   Wright 2002 and 2006; Borio et al. 2005.
2   See Chapter 1 in this volume.
3   Negri 1987, p. 224.

or stagnation (witness the fact that the golden age of FIAT in Italy was con-
current with fierce struggles that invested the factories themselves, whilst the
relative social peace of the 80s and 90s saw its progressive enfeeblement and
eventual collapse).

2   Tendency and Communism

Such a perspective rests on the conviction that the rule of capital has been
divested of any possibility for mediation, dialectics or measure. It posits the
rupture, catalysed by worker's struggles, of any social-democratic, Roosevel-
tian, or Keynesian project. However, and this point is paramount if workerism is
to include its own 'refutation of idealism', the putative collapse of measure and
mediation must itself be the outcome of a historical process. In other words,
it must be the product of a dialectic – albeit a dialectic that seems to signal
the impossibility of further dialectical mediation. In Negri, it is the concept of
tendency that provides this historical determinacy, rather than that of a closed
and endogenously developing dialectical totality. Negri defines it as follows:

> The tendency gives us a forecast that is determinate, specified by a mater-
> ialist dialectic which is developed by the factors comprising it. The tend-
> ency is the practical/theoretical process whereby the working-class point
> of view becomes explicit in its application to a determinate historical
> epoch. This means that to pose the tendency, to describe it and to define
> its contradictions is a far cry from economic determinism. Quite the
> opposite: to pose the tendency is to work up from the simple to the com-
> plex, from the concrete to the abstract, in order to achieve an adequate
> overall theoretical perspective within which the specificity and concrete-
> ness of the elements which were our initial starting point may then
> acquire meaning. ... [It is] reason's adventure as it comes to encounter
> the complexities of reality.[4]

Without such a concrete tendency, communism would be reduced to the unilateral purity and impotence of a terroristic decisionism incapable of intervening in the real articulations of systemic social processes. Viewed in this
light, workerism, as the militant combination of political-economic forecast
and organised intervention, can serve as a useful corrective to the dominant

---

4   Negri 1988, p. 125.

perception of Marxism as first and foremost a theory of systemic transformation, one that necessitates supplementing by specifically 'political' theories of
antagonism, hegemony and subjectivation. The workerist gambit – later radicalised in the theories of proletarian autonomy and self-valorisation – lay in
arguing that one can move beyond a treatment of the dynamic of capitalism
solely in terms of exploitation and the vampire-like 'absorption' of living labour
as variable capital into the process of production, towards a consideration of
the decisive importance of the subjectivity and organisation of the working
class, shifting analyses of the transformations of capitalism firmly onto the level
of a materially and temporally determinate antagonism. In other words, workerism revitalises the Marxian thesis whereby the parameters of the capitalist
domination and exploitation of labour-power and the extraction of surplus-
value are political through and through. As we shall see, this is not simply a
theoretical posit but is accompanied by an analysis of the politico-economic
conjuncture via the prism of the tendency. From this perspective, according to
Negri, the complex mediations of the law of value that had played such a dominant role in the American New Deal, in the fortunes of Keynesianism and in
the entire tradition of social democracy become increasingly obsolescent, as
capital manifests itself increasingly as a form of political command demanding ever greater autonomy from, and ever-diminishing concessions to, living
labour-power.

The thesis of Negri and his comrades in 'red decade' and its aftermath was
that such an 'autonomisation' of capital – marked by an increasing reliance on
monetary, fiscal, and financial policies to the detriment of social planning, as
well as by the concomitant forms of enforcement, control and organised state
and para-state violence – can be regarded as the *effect* of an ever-greater claim
to autonomy and self-determination exerted by working-class struggles striving to appropriate a domain of production and reproduction which, far from
being relegated to the factory alone, now covers the entirety of the social fabric.
Though the concepts of 'class composition' first and of 'organised autonomy'
later mark the sensitivity of this approach to the complexity and power dynamics of antagonism, we could still say of 'antagonism in general' what Marx says
of 'production in general'; to wit, that it is 'an abstraction, but a rational abstraction insofar as it really brings out and fixes the common element and thus saves
us repetition'.[5]

The question of workerism – and then of autonomism and post-workerism
broadly construed – was that of how to perpetuate, at the level of political

---

5   Marx 1973, p. 85.

strategy and organisation, the idea of communism as the suppression of work. In other words, how to enact a practical transition to communism in the conditions of a highly socialised economy but also one characterised by a high quantum of political repression. It is in this sense that we should grasp the three theses that Negri posits as crucial to his politics of antagonism: 'All Marxist categories are categories of communism';[6] 'Communism has the form of subjectivity, communism is a constituting praxis';[7] 'communism is in no way a product of capitalist development, it is its radical inversion'.[8] Evidently, the principal theoretical enemy here is any variety of (parliamentary) socialism or social democracy, to wit any attempt to think the suspension of capitalist relations as a possible result of a mediation organic to the capitalist mode of production – be it as a 'natural' outcome, as the progressive accumulation of victorious reforms, or as the gradual effect of the shows of force of the working class and its party leadership. Against any such faith in mediation, Negri wishes to affirm the 'antagonistic nature of Marxist logic'. As he writes: 'The antagonism must become social, *global revolutionary power must become a revolutionary class* against capitalist development'.[9] Such affirmations cannot fail to trail a whole set of thorny questions in their wake. To begin with: What is the nature of the purported independence of the proletariat? Does it possess a kind of social latency or is it a product of political will and organisation, *ex nihilo*? How can we think the political and programmatic autonomy of the exploited, as well as the full immanence of the antagonistic class within capital? In other words: What is an immanent antagonism, a separation in and against real subsumption? It is only by confronting these questions that I think light can be shed on the practical-historical shortcomings and theoretical potential of workerism and autonomism, as well as upon the antagonistic theses that determine both *Empire* and much of the theoretical discourse of contemporary post-socialist anti-capitalism.

3   Tronti's Copernican Revolution

The source for this turn to an explicitly and systemically antagonistic brand of Marxism is twofold. Historically speaking, it was born of the resurgence – outside of the direct sway of the PCI (Italian Communist Party) and official trade

---

6   Negri 1989, p. 161.
7   Negri 1989, p. 163.
8   Negri 1989, p. 165.
9   Negri 1989, p. 168.

unions – of fierce workers' struggles in the late 1950s and 1960s, where what was at stake was no longer the participation in the nationalist and productivist agenda of progress and negotiation, but rather the unilateral demand for the *immediate* satisfaction of workers' needs outside of any rationale that would see these needs as predicated upon the buoyancy of the economy, the continuation of high levels of investment, and a general increase in production and profitability. Theoretically speaking, this wave of openly 'egotistical' struggles, marked by the refusal of any socialist idolatry of work as the essence of the human as well as by disdain for the reformist impetus behind economic plans, was eminently registered in the Mario Tronti's epoch-making *Operai e capitale* (*Workers and Capital*).[10] This work, together with the analyses and theoretical proposals of some of Tronti's comrades in the journal *Quaderni Rossi*, tried to operate a radical reversal of the theoretical standpoint that regarded labour-power as a *factor* within the cycles of production and their political rationalisation. This was a view of living labour-power as at best delegating political command over itself to the party as class representative, but which, until the attainment of the receding threshold of communism, would remain fettered by the demanding discipline of the essentially capitalist relations obtaining in the factory and beyond.

Against this ideology of productivism, economic planning and worker sacrifice, Tronti attempted to translate the antagonistic demands for appropriation that had marked a decade of workers' struggles into an adequate theoretical framework. Contrary to the view whereby it was possible interminably to engage capital in reformist political mediations safeguarding the livelihood (if not the desires) of the working class, Tronti argued for the illusory character of this position, on the basis of the following thesis, which becomes more persuasive by the day: The political history of capital is *the history of the successive attempts of the capitalist class to emancipate itself from the working class.* The strategic ambivalence of the working class as a subject of exploitation was framed by Tronti in the following characteristically lapidary lines:

> The working class *does* what it *is*. But it is, at one and the same time, the *articulation* of capital, and its *dissolution*. Capitalist power seeks to use the workers' antagonistic will-to-struggle as a motor of its own development. The workers' party must take this same real mediation by the workers of capital's interests and organise it in an antagonistic form, as the tactical terrain of struggle and as a strategic potential for destruction.[11]

---

10   See Tronti 1971.
11   Tronti 1980a, p. 29.

What we have here is neither an organic dialectic nor a Manichean theory of pure antagonism. Rather, we are introduced to the idea that capital is concerned with a *dialectical use of antagonism*, whose ultimate if utopian horizon is the withering away of the working class and the untrammelled self-valorisation of capital; whilst the working class and its political vanguard aim at an *antagonistic use of antagonism*, which refuses precisely the capitalisation of antagonism whereby, for example, the flight from the factory is turned into an opportunity for profitable technological leaps and the exploitation of a de-unionised 'flexible' work force. In Harry Cleaver's useful gloss, this means that 'capital seeks to incorporate the working class within itself simply as labour-power, whereas the working class affirms itself as an independent class-for-itself only through struggles which rupture capital's self-reproduction'.[12] Communist politics is thus aimed at exploiting the inner tensions of a capitalism whose 'strength' lies in the 'production of ever-renewed antagonism',[13] and which depends on 'breaking the autonomy of labour-power without destroying its antagonistic character'.[14]

In a sense, the exasperation of capital's bid for freedom, which became more obvious in the 1960s in the transformation of the organic composition of capital (the ratio of constant to variable capital, specifically involving an increase in controllable technologies and the marginalisation of uncontrollable workers for the sake of increased productivity) did nothing but reveal that process, indicated by Marx in the *Results of the Immediate Process of Production*, whereby the working class (*qua* living labour) confronts the seemingly monolithic character of capital's command over the production process.[15] Here then lies the vampirism of capital, whose only fluidity is offered by the process of absorption of living labour. As Bruno Maffi, editor of the *Results* in Italian, noted: 'Capital is truly *capital* only if it becomes "value in process"; only if, *within* the process of production, the magic touch of human labour transforms it from a constant to a variable magnitude'.[16]

This dual phenomenology of the production process, split between the immediate point of view of production and that of capital's self-valorisation is the object of Tronti's attempt at forcing a political assumption of this antagonism, in the here and now, which would not subordinate itself to economic rationalisation (which is always the prelude of capital's emancipation from the

---

12   Cleaver 2000, p. 66.
13   Tronti 1980b, p. 58.
14   Tronti 1980a, p. 217.
15   Marx 1990, pp. 987–8.
16   Marx 2002, p. xi.

working class). By facing the totality of the conditions of labour as capital, alongside the increasingly intimate bond between these conditions and a practice of command and discipline (such that exploitation is sedimented by and articulated through objective technologies of discipline in production), we can, according to Tronti, begin to project the political constitution, through antagonism, of an explicitly militant and anti-systemic working class. On the terrain of the command over production, what serves as a structural or phenomenological antagonism must be assumed, doubled and reinforced (to the point of crisis) by a *political* antagonism that directly targets the capitalistic process of self-valorisation, and tends towards a self-valorisation of the working class, which is to say, towards a destabilisation and de-structuring of capitalist command. The entire issue, both strategically and tactically (and the deep cause of numerous splits on the Italian left), concerned the means of moving from certain practices of autonomy that characterised workers' struggles to the political formation of what Tronti refers to as a *class against capital*. From insurrection to organisation, and back again.

This is Tronti's 'Copernican revolution', whereby 'the economic laws of the movement of capitalist society must be newly discovered as the political laws of the movement of the working class', and '*bent* with subjective force of organisation brutally to serve the objective revolutionary needs of antagonism and struggle'.[17] Capital, through this openly political torsion, becomes a function of the working class, in a situation wherein politics 'precedes' science. As Cristina Corradi has duly noted in her history of Italian Marxism, if we wish to stick with the scientific analogy, this Copernican revolution is really a 'post-Copernican', or Einsteinian one. Tronti's vision of a new politicised antagonistic science of capital is not that of a 'general methodology and universal science' but of a '*partial, subjective, unilateral science, in the ambit of a system marked by a high degree of indeterminacy*. The Marxist inquiry is compared to the discovery of non-Euclidean geometries, just as the spirit of the October revolution is argued to have an affinity with the break represented by Einstein's theory of relativity'.[18] This idea of a partisan science of capital, which dominates Tronti's work and is also present, in a different guise, in Negri, has a number of significant consequences, two of which I want to mention. First, it entails that there is no scientific theory from which one could simply deduce political action. Rather, theory, as an attempt to grasp the objective tendencies of accumulation and the class struggles interleaved with them, is always in a relation of disjunctive

17   Tronti 1971, p. 224.
18   Corradi 2005, p. 169.

synthesis to politics as the 'global refusal of objectivity', the attempt to vanquish the tendency. In other words: 'Theory is anticipation. Politics is intervention'.[19] Furthermore, it means that the link between politics as a science of intervention and Marxism as a science of anticipation must always be conquered in and against changing conjunctures: 'Science as struggle is an ephemeral knowledge. It lasts as long as it's useful. ... This is a happy condition of thinking: when you know that there is one part, and one part only, of the world that asks you a question. A state of exception in which thinking is the force that decides'.[20] And contrary to any facile determinisms, as Tronti argues, 'to predict the development of capital does not mean subjecting oneself to its iron laws: it means forcing it to take a path, waiting for it at some juncture with weapons stronger than iron, attacking and breaking it at that point'.[21] Crucially, this link between tendency and initiative in 'brief political moments' can mean that certain opportunities for ambushing capital can be irretrievably lost, that defeat is a real possibility. As Tronti warns in *Operai e capitale*, 'we don't have much time'.[22]

Tronti's work does not simply represent a voluntaristic adjunct to the critique of political economy but wishes to recast capitalist society and its forms of domination as *reactive formations*, something recognised by Marx himself in his accounts of the theft of workers' knowledge and ensuing structural adjustments in the process of production. As Marx once remarked, capital (with all its technological prostheses) chases strikes. The key axiom here, which shaped Negri's own work throughout the 1970s, and which remains embedded in later analyses of the 'multitude' is the following: there is a primacy of resistance over exploitation and domination. The corollary of this axiom is that 'capital is a consequence of worker's labour'. In Tronti's own words: 'it is the specific moments of the class struggle which have determined every technological change in the mechanisms of industry'.[23] Contrary to Tronti's later stance, which would see the possibility, heralded by the 'political centrality of the working class', of a communist use of 'the provisional autonomy of state manoeuvres from capitalist interest'[24] (echoing the PCI's view of itself as a superior organiser of capitalist production), his writings of the early and mid-1960s exude a combative *irresponsibility* on the part of the working class within

19   Tronti 1971, p. 258.
20   Tronti 2001, p. 19.
21   Tronti 1971, p. 17 and 1980b, p. 64.
22   Tronti 1971, p. 21.
23   Tronti 1980a, p. 30.
24   Tronti 1980b, p. 64.

a society riven by antagonism: 'It is not up to the workers to resolve the conjunctures of capitalism. Let the bosses do it, on their own. It is their system: let
them sort it out. It is here that a strategy of the total refusal of capitalist society
must find the positive tactical forms for the most effective aggression against
the concrete power of capitalists'.[25] Against the neutrality of technology, its
manipulation and 'evolution', and against any productivist compact between
big government, big business, big unions and a big party, this position argues
for the use of the political antagonism of labour and capital as a prism for com-
prehending the dynamics of social transformations in terms of the subjection
and absorption of living labour by dead capital, foregrounding the subjectivity
of the working class, which is both the presupposition and the principal threat
to capitalist reproduction.

It is on this basis that Tronti articulates the paradoxical situation of workers labouring under capitalist command: 'the only thing which does not come
from the workers is, precisely, [the conditions of] labour'.[26] That is, it is the
overtly political framework of command, discipline and rationalisation of the
labour process that serves to shackle living labour to the demands of capital,
such that the 'ontological' primacy and ineluctability of living labour is subjected to a thoroughgoing instrumentalisation. As Marx himself had acerbically
indicated: 'It is not the worker who buys the means of production and subsistence, but the means of subsistence that buy the worker to incorporate him
into the means of production'.[27] But for Tronti, Negri and their comrades, in
the phase of 'high' workerism, these mechanisms of coercion that situate the
bearer of labour-power within the system of production, circulation and distribution mask the very real *dependency* of capital, which cannot be simply dispelled by means of changes in the organic composition of capital. Capitalism is
both thoroughly dependent on the capacity, relative docility and availability of
the working class and constantly dreams of (often brutally destructive) ways
of escaping this dependency, of evading the moment of labour in the cycles
of accumulation. As Tronti writes: 'Exploitation is born, historically, from the
necessity for capital to escape from its *de facto* subordination to the class of
worker-producers'.[28]

Thus, it can be argued that capital is in a double bind, which demands
from it both a ruthless command and minimisation of workers' demands (or
at least of any of those demands that would interfere with capitalist valor-

---

25   Tronti 1971, p. 98.
26   Tronti 1980a, pp. 30–1.
27   Marx 1990, p. 1004.
28   Tronti 1980a, p. 31.

isation) *and* a capacity to absorb not simply living labour-power in terms of the physical expenditure of the worker, but a whole host of skills, knowledges and capacities for cooperation that are inseparable from workers' struggles for an emancipation *from* and not *of* work. The problem of capitalist command becomes that of a parasitic capture of the political vitality of the working class joined to a neutralisation of its deeply menacing nature. This is where Tronti points to the role of 'organic forms of political dictatorship' in the history of capitalism, and we may consider today the twin phenomena of the *grand ren-fermement* of the American 'underclass' – racialised mass incarceration – and the punitive and selective measures aimed at migrants in Europe and else-where in this light.[29] The paramount function, within social conflict, of the state *of* capitalism means that the antagonism at the heart of the process of production can only manifest itself as an attack on the state, what Negri would call a destabilisation and a de-structuring. Tronti's *Operai e capitale* outlines the tendency towards the ever more explicit face-off between two separate but reciprocal processes of subjectivation: the subject of capitalist command and the subject of communist insurrection. Here Tronti introduces the specific *political difference* of labour and capital: the first does not need institutions, but only organisation, while the second must be institutionally articulated. As he writes:

> From the very beginning, the proletariat is nothing more than the imme-diate *political interest* in the abolition of every aspect of the existing order. As far as its internal development is concerned, it has no need of 'institu-tions' in order to bring to life what it is, since what it is is nothing other

---

29 The continuing vitality of the partisan methodology of workerism – linking the study of class composition, the primacy of struggle and the forms of capitalist dictatorship – is evident in the work of a generation of researchers who have combined its prescriptions with the tools of other radical theoretical traditions (from the Foucauldian and Deleuzian study of societies of discipline and societies of control, to notions of subjectivation ori-ginating in subaltern studies and postcolonial theory). Alessandro De Giorgi's studies of post-Fordist regimes of penality (2000 and 2002) and Sandro Mezzadra's *Diritto di fuga* (2006), with its thesis on the 'autonomy of migration', are of great significance in this regard. For an insightful post-workerist attempt to think struggle, discipline and control in terms of the transformations and uses of money, see the collective volume *La mon-eta nell'Impero* (Fumagalli et al. 2002), especially Andrea Fumagalli's 'Moneta e potere: controllo e disciplina sociale'. It is on the subjective side, which is to say vis-à-vis the articu-lation between class and organization, that these texts show the contemporary difficulties facing a workerist legacy. In this respect, the concept of 'multitude' appears to function more as a placeholder than a solution when it comes to the present impasses of a politics of working-class insurrection.

than the *life-force* of that immediate destruction. It doesn't need *institutions*, but it does need *organisation*. ... *The concept of the revolution and the reality of the working class are one and the same.*[30]

Against a social-democratic politics of mediation, Tronti argues that the strategic setbacks of the working class movement have always been based on seeking to transfer the model of the bourgeois revolution to the communist revolution – to wit, of imagining a slow takeover of economic power, followed by the reversal of political control.[31] In other words, the perpetual delay of a full assumption of antagonism and autonomy on the part of working-class movements has meant that:

> Basically, all the communist movement has done has been to break and overturn, in some aspects of its practice, the social democratic logic of what has been its own theory ... here we see the working class articulation of political development: at first as an initiative that is positive for the functioning of the system, an initiative that only needs to be organised via institutions; in the second instance, as a 'No', a refusal to manage the mechanism of society as it stands, merely to improve it – a 'No' which is repressed by pure violence. This is the difference of content which can exist – even within one and the same set of working class demands – between *trade union demands* and *political refusal.*[32]

4   Fantasy Wears Boots

Whilst Tronti – convinced that the workers' movement could only be articulated through a mass party – returned to the PCI and tried to formulate the idea of an 'autonomy of the political' as a way of achieving working class hegemony over economic planning and rationalisation (as part of a theoretical shift skilfully tracked by Matteo Mandarini),[33] Negri's entire political and theoretical development is founded on the non-dialectical intensification of antagonism.

---

30   Tronti 1980a, p. 34.
31   In his later, more melancholic reflections on the closure of twentieth-century political subjectivity, Tronti will note that it is the very illusion of social-democracy that it can subsist without the fire of insurrection: 'No reformist practice can advance if it is not accompanied, fuelled, and given substance by a thinking of revolution' (Tronti 1998, p. 52).
32   Tronti 1980a, p. 34.
33   Mandarini 2009.

His aim was to find an insurrectional and organisational outlet for Tronti's exhortation: 'As a matter of urgency we must get hold of, and start circulating, a photograph of the worker-proletariat that shows him as he really is – "proud and menacing".[34] Negri's turn to an expanded reproduction of antagonism throughout the social sphere, beyond the factory and the mass party, depended once again on a certain assessment of the tendency at work within late capitalism, a tendency characterised by an ever-increasing exercise of command, crisis and control on the side of capital, aimed at the subjection of workers, the decomposition of any possible form of class unity and an extraction of surplus-value that tries to emancipate itself from any dialectic or negotiation with the bearers of labour-power.

In this phenomenon of tendency – which included the grim blackmail of austerity policies, the Cold War's nuclear emergencies, and the ever-increasing role of monetary policies after the oil crisis of 1973 – Negri registers a swelling violence and irrationality on the part of capital. This violence ultimately lies in trying to maintain the *measure* and *command* of salary relations in a situation where social cooperation and technological advance are at such a level that the continuation of exploitative relations becomes ever more irrational. The 'crisis politics' and 'strategy of tension' that characterised the Italian state, but also the violent class de-composition that marked the onslaught against organised labour by Thatcherism and Reaganism, making way for a neoliberal regime of predatory flexibility, are emblems of the necessary vertical force required to reproduce capitalist social relations. As Negri remarks:

> My denunciation is not therefore directed against the normality of violence, but against the fact that in the enterprise form of capitalist domination, violence has lost all intrinsic, 'natural' rationale ('naturalness' being always a product of historic forces), and all relation with any project that could be deemed progressive. If anything, the enterprise form of violence is precisely the opposite: it is an irrational form within which exchange value is imposed on social relations in which the conditions of the exchange relation no longer exist. It is the intelligent form of this irrationality, simultaneously desperate in its content and rational in its effectiveness.[35]

In these passages, albeit in a far less morbid and claustrophobic vein, Negri anticipates the analysis of post-historical character of state violence forward

---

34   Tronti 1980a, p. 31.
35   Negri 1988, p. 131.

by Debord in his *Comments on the Society of the Spectacle*, and later seconded by Giorgio Agamben, who writes of how in 1970s Italy, 'the governments and servants of the entire world had observed then with attentive participation ... the way that a well-aimed politics of terrorism could possibly function as the mechanism of relegitimation of a discredited system'.[36] But for Negri the collapse of the dialectics of value and measure still has its source in the subjective pressure of antagonism, and indeed of constituent power. This means that the capitalist use of crisis and emergency, or rather the emergence of a 'crisis state', cannot be metaphysically and trans-historically sublimated into a view, such as Agamben's, for which '*the state of exception is the rule*' and 'naked life ... is today abandoned to a kind of violence that is all the more effective for being anonymous and quotidian'.[37] Contra Agamben, for Negri (as his critiques of the thesis of bare life make evident) this violence is always a determinately *capitalist* violence, that is to say a violence that *reacts* against a primary resistance, or better a prior antagonistic production of subjectivity.

Thus, the tendency to an integral *socialisation* of capitalism (following Marx's *Grundrisse*, the 'Bible' of *operaismo*), spreading far beyond the factory gates and encompassing all facets of social reproduction within the extraction of surplus value,[38] comes into conflict with the endurance, enforced by exquisitely political means, of the measurability of production in the form of the wage. Arguing from the loss of any proportionality or translatability between a production now entirely socialised (the thesis of real subsumption) and its measure in labour-power or wage, Negri, beginning in the 1970s, identifies the tendency as the site of a *communist transition*. This transition, however, does not take the form of a plan or programme, but of an outright refusal of capitalist command and a consequent reappropriation of workers' experience and productivity grounded on an analysis of class composition, that is, of the power-relations and differentiations within the working class itself. The self-valorisation of capital through command is thus confronted by the self-valorisation of the working class via practices of autonomy aimed at destabilising and de-structuring the political conditions for the perpetuation of capitalism. The programme is thus that of 'the direct social appropriation of produced social wealth'.

---

36   Agamben 2000, p. 127.
37   Agamben 2000, p. 113.
38   Negri would later connect this nexus of real subsumption and social reproduction to the Foucauldian theme of biopolitics, see my exposition and critique of this stance in 'Always Already Only Now'.

It is here that the concrete practices of the movements gathered under the banner of *Autonomia organizzata* – agitating in Rome, Padua, Milan and other urban areas in the 1970s, and supported by publications such as *Rosso* – find their theoretical legitimacy. The practice of mass illegality (unilateral reduction of bills, house occupations, and so on), sabotage and violent assertions of the material reality of worker independence, all of which characterised the 'autonomist' movement, are thus conceptualised as an attempt to force the structural antagonism and its tendency towards an ever-greater arbitrariness of command. As I explore in the next chapter, this strategy, not just of refusal but of the conquest of metropolitan 'red bases' and the irrecuperable intensification of antagonism, was aimed at preparing a generalised insurrectionary situation. The assumption of autonomy was thought to function directly as means of destabilising and destructuring, recomposing class unity and countering the neutralisation of resistance that the capitalist state effects through means both punitive (repressions and redundancies) and programmatic (the decomposition of a factory-based working class and creation of a precarious and flexible class of 'immaterial' workers: a situation that backfired in 1977, when the micropolitical strategies of the crisis-State – dispersion of workers, flexibilisation – led to mass uprisings of unemployed and often highly educated urban youth).

This insurrectionary programme is based on the analysis of a twofold tendency. On the one hand, we have the increasingly brutal attempt on the part of capital to emancipate itself from workers and workers' struggles, its 'dream of self-sufficiency'. On the other, we confront the increasing socialisation of value, such that processes of production and reproduction, as well as circulation and distribution, become increasingly integrated and less and less linked to the mediating space of the factory and the official working-class movement. The antagonism is therefore posited as an extreme contest between, on the one side, a capital hell-bent on the absoluteness of its own command and the fragmentation of any class initiative; and, on the other, a class of social workers (*operai sociali*, the mutant descendants of the Fordist mass worker) to attain a direct appropriation of the social production that finds its source in their own living labour as well as their everyday practices and desires (chiefly in the domain of a consumption that is 'put to work'). The subjectivation, singularisation and socialisation of living labour is thus the aim of a movement that seeks to force the separation from capitalist command.

But this is a subjectivation that, as we move into the 1970s and the further decomposition of the factory, is obliged to spread itself across the entire social field. This is where the concept of class composition and the analysis of power-relations are so crucial, as without them only an entirely indeterminate dualism of class against state – ripe for a vanguardist and terrorist takeover *à la* Red Brigades – can take place. Here is where we encounter the fundamental non-homogeneity of class composition, the emergence of a *disseminated* figure of the worker and the need to generate novel organisations of class struggle on a new terrain. In this context, the politicisation of marginal labour-power into the working class is never given (in the factory, in the 'movement') but must be conquered explicitly. This is where the notion of the 'refusal of work' – to be understood as the refusal of the reproduction of capitalist wage-relations for the sake of an emancipation of social production, or of what Negri calls the 'force of invention' – takes root and acquires a pivotal role. Refusal of work, articulated outside the factory, is aimed both at class unity (crystallisation of a new class composition beyond the factory) and geared toward destroying capitalist relations by means of the unconditional demand for a *right to income*, a *political wage* entirely detached if not wholly destructive of the conditions for the reproduction of capitalist cycles of profit and investment (this proposal returns in a somewhat different guise in both *Empire* and *Multitude*).

Ultimately, the very terms of the antagonism, of the 'method of tendency' espoused by Negri, demand the confrontation – determined by the particularities of class composition, organic composition and capital's strategies of restructuring and command, but neither mediated nor dialogical – between the violence of a command that tries to maintain the wage-relation and the measure of labour-power, on the one hand, and the creative violence of a self-valorising working class, on the other. We could thus say that both the force and the shortcomings of Negri's stnce lie in his determination to sap any possibility of institutional compromise, and his insistence in addressing the question of *power* in its two senses of power over the state (of capital) and of power-relations within classes themselves (class composition). To use the Spinozist distinction so dear to him, we behold here the face-off between the *potentia* of the working class and the *potestas* of a state dominated by the logic of the enterprise, the firm. If the confrontation cannot be avoided, whatever its forms, it is because the very analysis of the tendency means that a counter-autonomy or counter-self-valorisation – in brief, insurrection – is the only countervailing force against the violence of capitalist command over the socialisation of production. As Negri says, in discord with some of his later pronouncements about the exodus of the multitude: 'The *jouissance* that the working class seeks is the *jouissance* of power, not the tickle of illusions'. This theme returns in other texts from his 1970s Feltrinelli pamphlets, confiscated and incinerated by the very state whose violence they dissected: 'Fantasy wears boots, desire is violent, invention is organised.' And further: 'The party is the army that defends the borders of proletarian independence'. But this counter-violence against the state, which is the violence of a sabotage aimed both at the defence of workers' needs and experiences, and at the destruction of capitalist relations, was forced by its objective weakness and disadvantage into a strategy that could easily be portrayed as one provocation; a strategy which, at least in the Italian case, proved that, alas, in Negri's own words: 'Crisis is a risk taken by the working class and the proletariat. Communism is not inevitable'.[39]

Where the insurrectionary *élan* of *operaismo* for a time promised a refusal and a separation from a position of strength (in the conviction that the primacy of resistance heralded the eventual obsolescence of capitalist command), a post-Fordist or neo-liberal conjuncture – witness the 'post-workerist' writings of Marazzi, De Giorgi, Fumagalli, Vercellone and several others – led to an inevitable preoccupation not so much with separation or autonomy, as with the identification of subjective and material levers to disarticulate forms of command and compulsion that have grown more recondite and redoubtable since the 1970s. The challenge today is to think an antagonism whose autonomy would not entail a doomed attempt at separation, an antagonism that would not be entirely detached from the conditions of production and reproduction of contemporary capitalism. The mere positing of a duality, say between Empire and multitude, without the conflictual *composition* that can provide this duality with a certain degree of determinateness, may be seen to generate a seemingly heroic, but ultimately ineffectual horizon for theoretical analysis and political militancy. In political-historical figures such as those of the 'immaterial labourer', a certain post-workerism glimpsed not just the end of the measured dialectic of capital and labour, but the overcoming of the need politically to confront the violence of capitalist command. Negri himself viewed his later work as leading to the 'theoretical observation that the social transformation of class relations is definitively over. Today, *against* capital, rises up the social figure of immaterial labour'.[40]

In this regard, any perspective that seeks to reinject the workerist method of antagonism into the current composition of social relations, into the uneven and combined development of capitalist command and political struggles, will be obliged to tackle two questions: How do we confront a situation in which capitalism's vicious rounds of accumulation by dispossession point to its continued and virulent, if contradictory, desire to emancipate itself from the working class, if not from humanity as a whole? And what does it mean to revive or

---

39   Negri 2006a.
40   Negri 2006a, p. 16.

prolong the methodologies and political gestures of workerism and autonomy
at a time when – in many of the core capitalist economies that were always
the privileged terrain of workerism – we are confronted by 'a depoliticisation
of society that reinforces the power of dominant forces'?[41]

41   Tronti 1992, p. 13.

CHAPTER 11

Factory, Territory, Metropolis, Empire

New figures, or larval forms, of political organisation and often opaque redistributions of geopolitical power, coupled with a welter of communicative, technological, and economic mutations, gave rise at the millennium's end to what some dubbed a 'spatial turn' in the social sciences.[1] The unrelenting and often inconsistent proliferation of discourses on so-called globalisation, accompanied by a host of descriptive enquiries into the changing patterns of contemporary life, displayed a marked obsession with all things spatial; a relentless, if often monotonous, usage of topographic metaphors and topological concepts. Theoretical discourse is still saturated with diagrams, cartographies, networks, dwellings, frontiers, and so forth. The sources for this trend are very heterogeneous, but they do appear to derive, whether sociologically, philosophically or politically, from a repudiation of progressive philosophies of history, as well from a suspicion of models of modernity that couple the lucid rationality and imposing will of a sovereign ego with a *res extensa* reduced to an indifferent, objective domain of coordination, calculation and control, itself directed by the temporal dimension of a project. Whether we are dealing with debates over the 'global' or with the turn to Heidegger's nostalgic ontology of habitation, spatial specificity is often enlisted to inhibit or undermine the pretensions of the kind of universal theory or politics that would smooth over the folds of particularity.[2]

When a commitment to such a universal account remains, spatial differentiation schematises the general theory into a particular conjuncture.[3] Whilst work of this kind maintains a commendable balance between scientific ambition and a non-reductionist attention to the different logics at work in the spatial reality of politics, it arguably suffers from a propensity to envelop spatial differentiation within systemic logics that elide the generative role of political subjectivity, and social antagonism. This is not at all to say that such approaches need to be supplemented with a kind of phenomenology of resistance or, worse

---

1 See, for instance, Kumar 1995, pp. 146–8, where he cites Foucault's characterisation of the twentieth century as 'the epoch of space'.

2 On all these debates see the insightful mapping in Marramao 2003.

3 This is the case, in some respects, in David Harvey's historical geographical materialism, and its theorisation of uneven development and the 'spatial fixes' that capitalism produces to tame its internal contradictions. See Harvey 1999, pp. 431–45.

still, with an anti-universalist discourse of spatio-cultural particularity or difference. The point instead is that the 'spatial turn' has often been marked by what could be termed a deficit of praxis, of a materialist concern with the effects of collective political action, subjectivity and organisation on the composition of the social and the functions of command.[4] If the vast and multifarious interrogation of the multiple spaces of contemporary social experience is not to turn into a more or less reactionary, anti-modernist nostalgia, a parochial theory of cultural differences or a fatalistic logic of systemic transformation; if it is to enter into some sort of dialogue with the resurgence of interest, practical and philosophical, for notions of militancy and organisation, then it is imperative to begin formulating a truly political topology, one that binds together the subjective forms of political action and the shifting configurations of space. What is required is a thinking of the antagonistic, or, at the very least, agonistic production of space, not just an account of the heterotopias of resistance or the creative destruction of space that accompanies capitalist accumulation.

As a kind of prolegomenon to such an enterprise, and for the sake of a coherent localisation of this political topology itself,[5] I would like briefly to interrogate, both theoretically and historically, a very definite political sequence which, I will argue, bears some important lessons for a political thinking of space that seeks to eschew the many pitfalls of the spatial turn, from romantic nostalgia to systemic fatalism, from the naturalisation of the social to an exoticist condescension to cultural difference. This sequence is the one that goes by the somewhat imprecise name of Italian *workerist* or *autonomist Marxism* (*operaismo*), emerging in conjunction with the factory struggles of the 1960s through the journal *Quaderni rossi*, branching into a number of distinct political and intellectual projects, reaching its point of organisational crisis in the late 1970s, and spreading its theoretical influence through a number of antagonistic social

---

4   Though methodologically Harvey maintains a classical Marxist perspective somewhat at odds with the theses of workerism, he has undertaken some important inquiries into the construction of spaces and places from below; see 'Body Politics and the Struggle for a Living Wage' in Harvey 2000, pp. 117–30. In 'The Geography of Class Power' in Harvey 2002, p. 381, he tellingly speaks of 'the non-neutrality of spatial organization in the dynamics of class struggle.'

5   It almost goes without saying that such a political topology would require to be complemented by an account of the temporalising character of political subjectivity, coupling the dislocation of the place of production and the 'biopolitical' extension of labour time. As Bologna writes in 'La percezione dello spazio e del tempo nel lavoro indipendente': 'The labour time of the waged worker is a regulated time, the time of the independent worker is a labour time without rules, and therefore without limits.' Bologna 1997.

movements (*Tute bianche, Disobbedienti*) and, most prominently, in the theoretical production of one of its originators, the philosopher Antonio Negri.[6]

The choice of workerism as the object of a preliminary enquiry into political topology is motivated principally by two factors. First, the nexus of theoretical production and political militancy represented by this 'tradition', for want of a better word,[7] is particularly rich, spanning a period of considerable social tumult and transformation and intense political conflict. What is of particular interest is how theorists of workerism, whose aims where more often than not explicitly political, tried to anticipate material transformations and spur political strategies – as well as how they were also forced to reckon with changes in the political terrain they had not entirely fathomed. Furthermore, *operaismo*'s combination of critical fidelity to Marxism as a theory of social transformation and political practice, coupled with its emphasis on organisational experimentation, make of it a privileged instance for trying to glean how we may begin to think spatiality or placement in terms of the two interlinked facets of materialism: a theory of praxis or subjectivation, on the one hand, and a theory of historical change, on the other. Second, the persistence of the workerist inspiration in the work of Negri and Hardt – in how they describe the production of a smooth space of capital regulated by a placeless imperial sovereignty as the product of the militancy and desires of the multitude – warrants renewed examination of its political and theoretical sources, both to veer away from the more simplistic criticisms of *Empire* and to really grasp the sources, the archaeology as it were, of a prominent contribution to the formulation of a contemporary political topology.

I would like to take my cue from a very simple question, albeit one that has gained a certain urgency in the wake of the widespread, if contradictory, attempts to fashion new forms of political militancy adequate to current

---

6 By far the most thorough and insightful treatment of workerism is to be found in Wright 2002; a bold attempt to update some of the tradition's theses, accompanied by an impressive CD-ROM archive of interviews with its political and theoretical protagonists, is available in the Italian volume by Borio et al. 2004; aside from Negri's work, the anglophone reader can refer to the excellent collection by Lotringer and Marazzi (1980) or, for a more philosophical take, to Virno and Hardt's volume (1996).

7 In his review of Wright's *Storming Heaven*, Sergio Bologna pointedly asks: 'Is it possible to apply the category of continuity to this movement? Doesn't continuity belong to the traditional methods of writing history? Is it not proper to the histories of dynasties and parties? Those who, from the beginning, positioned themselves outside of a party perspective, who regarded the revolution as a lifeblood rather than an event, do they have a right to continuity, do they have to be subject to it?' Bologna 2003, p. 105. As far as this chapter is concerned, the only continuity we have availed ourselves of is the continuity of a problematic, with all the internal ruptures and displacements that entails.

dynamics of accumulation and command: how might the localisation of political action, the kinds of places in which it is anchored or dimensions it traverses, affect its claims and its consequences? Or – to apply the key workerist
thesis of the primacy of labour over capital, of resistance over power – how does
political antagonism around the loci of production and accumulation give rise,
in the processes of conflict, negotiation, and compromise, to different spatial
configurations? Flashing forward, what is the effect of the dislocation of the
intimate bearer of antagonism within the capitalist system, when any 'proletariat' or 'multitude' can no longer be found anchored and included in a specific
locus, both material and symbolic, of society? Vice versa, does the differential
localisation of a fragmented labour-power, in the absence of a real subjective
unification, of a paradigmatic figure (the working class organised in the party)
and a proper place (the factory, or the assembly) allow anything like the self-
destitution that is the hallmark of any theory of the proletariat as the instance
of a generic emancipation? More concretely: where does militancy take place?
What, to borrow from Sylvain Lazarus,[8] are the 'places of politics'? In what
sense do they overlap with the places of the economy, the sites of capitalist
exploitation and accumulation or those of spatiotemporal 'fixes' led by processes of what Harvey has dubbed, with reference to the occupation of Iraq,
'accumulation by dispossession'?[9] Should our understandings of space be in a
dialectical relationship to how we figure political antagonism? Indeed, one of
the questions that needs to be addressed by any political topology that wishes
to incorporate into itself a discourse on subjectivity is whether political organisation is necessarily bound to some sort of spatial composition, be it in the
sense of following the configuration of social space or of eliciting its transformation. In other words, what is the precise nature of the correlation between the
objective political space of the factory and the subjective form of the party or
the union, or between the 'delirious' metropolis and autonomous instances of
appropriation and occupation, or, more recently, between the political constitution of Empire and the movement of social forums? And, in all these cases,
is economics what 'sutures' politics to place, in the guise of the anchoring of
a labouring subjectivity to the material locus of a given mode of production?
Or is our task instead, as authors such as Lazarus and Badiou contend, to think
the places of politics, the topologies of militancy and subjectivity, without a
reliance on their localisation within a system of economic accumulation, circulation and reproduction?

---

8 See Lazarus 1996, pp. 166–76, where he discusses the factory as a multiple and non-dialectical
   place of politics.
9 Harvey 2003, pp. 137–82.

The Marxist and Leninist legacy that still influences much radical politics, for good or ill, crucially depends on the postulation of a critical point, a localisation of antagonism within the social totality of capitalism, a 'weakest link' in the capitalist chain or, in its workerist guise, 'the material lever of the dissolution of capital planted in the decisive point of its system': can any such point, or points, be identified today?[10] Inasmuch as we recognise that he debates that roiled the revolutionary left from the 1960s onward were accompanied by shifts in political topology, is it possible to understand the practical and theoretical disputes over issues such as organisation and strategy as either the products or the instigators of spatial displacements in the sites of antagonism and militancy? Traversing the phases of development of the workerist tradition from the centrality of the factory to the nonplace of contemporary capitalism in its imperial figure is perhaps not the worst place to start to gain some analytical purchase on the tasks of a political topology. For one, it allows us to bridge the gap between the debates in the 2000s over the tactics and strategies of a 'Global Justice Movement' converging on 'World Social Forums', and the long tradition of theoretical insights and organisational forms bequeathed by the workers' movement and the Marxist tradition from the nineteenth century onward. Arguably poised at the tumultuous twilight of what we might see as the 'classical' form of the political topology of antagonism, workerism, with its sensitivity to the crises that beset orthodox models of the relation between politics and space, and with its concern with anticipating (in order to deflect or transform) new regimes of spatialisation, accumulation and command, remains a rich source for a sustained interrogation of current spatial forms and practices.

Throughout the discontinuous and contested history of workerism there is arguably a constant tension, perspicuously emphasised by Steve Wright, between, on the one hand, the explanation of the tendencies guiding the transformation of capitalism and its state form, and, on the other, the militant assumption and contestation of these changes in political action. The question turns out to be exquisitely spatial, and relates to whether the extension of what Tronti influentially called the 'social factory' (*fabbrica società*) – the

---

10   Tronti 1971, p. 39. Apropos of Lenin, Tronti proposes the 'neo-Leninist principle': '*the chain will break not where capitalism is weakest, but where the working class is strongest.*' In the introduction to *Operai e capitale*, Tronti makes this point very forcefully: 'We will never tire of repeating that predicting the development of capital does not mean subjecting ourselves to its iron laws: it means forcing it into a certain path, waiting for it with weapons stronger than steel, and there assaulting it and breaking it'. Tronti 1971, p. 21. See also Negri 2003a, p. 176.

consequence of the 'real subsumption'[11] of all labour and all social relations to the requirements of capitalist accumulation – still demands the identification of the factory and the wage as the key sites of struggle; or whether, on the contrary, the increasing diffusion and decentralisation of production and antagonism, marked by the explosive growth of the service sector and diminution of manufacturing and labour-intensive heavy industry, leads to acknowledging the necessity for different forms of struggle, other figures of organisation and subjectivity – perhaps ones that evade the dialectical articulation that had been afforded by the centrality of the factory.

In the specific case of workerism, the analysis of the problem of the place of politics was filtered throughout by its signal conceptual contribution to the intellectual arsenal of Marxism: the notion of class composition. Like most of the concepts gleaned by Tronti, Negri and others from Marx (such as 'social worker', 'general intellect', 'tendency', 'real subsumption'), class composition was formulated on the basis of the urgent necessity to anticipate the transformations and command strategies of capital, on the one hand, and to contribute to the consolidation of an organised proletarian subject, on the other. Negri defines class composition as

> the combination of political and material characteristics – both historical and physical – which makes up: (a) on the one hand, the historically given structure of labour-power, in all its manifestations, as produced by a given level of productive forces and relations; and (b) on the other hand, the working class as a determinate level of solidification of needs and desires, as a dynamic subject, an antagonistic force, tending towards its own independent identity in historical-political terms. All concepts that define the working class must be framed in terms of the *historical transformability of the composition of class*. This is to be understood in the general sense of its ever wider and more refined productive capacity, the ever greater abstraction and socialisation of its nature, and the ever greater intensity and weight of the political challenge it presents to capital. In other words, the *re-making of the working class!*[12]

---

11   On the concept of real subsumption see Negri 1987, pp. 9–25, 75–80; see also Harootunian 2015. The principal source is the unpublished Book VI of chapter I of *Das Kapital*, 'Results of the Immediate Process of Production', now in Marx 1990, pp. 1023–5 and 1034–8. A later formulation of real subsumption as socialisation, but in the absence of the centrality of the factory, is the following: 'production and living in society have become elements in one whole, and the consequent social productivity (generalized and without the factory) is captured by the company'. Negri 2001b, p. 198.

12   'Archaeology and Project: From the Mass Worker to the Social Worker' (1982) in Negri 1988, p. 209.

As I shall argue, the question that persistently preoccupied the various theories of workerism – how to combine the structural vicissitudes of labour-power with the organised politicisation of the needs and desires of the working class – was always spatially articulated or indexed, and inevitably so, one might add, such that the crisis of the large factory as the privileged place of politics was of momentous importance to both the theory and the practice of workerism. What is more, with the diffusion of production and the dissemination of labour-power occurring in the 1970s – diagnosed by workerists as a political response on the part of the state to the manifestations of workers' autonomy – one might even argue that the Leninist focus on the critical point, the lever of revolution, lost its own index, left to float, diaphanous, over a highly differentiated, inhomogeneous social terrain, or forced into life via the violent confrontation with the state, a confrontation which, having lost or abandoned the centrality of the factory, was placed beyond the dialectics of recuperation. Negri's *remaking of the working class* here manifests all of its problematicity, since the subjective recomposition of the class was, especially as the decade of the 1970s wore on, an explicit response to the effects of capitalist restructuring, effects among which the tendential disappearance of a central place of labour was first and foremost. In light of the internal debates and destiny of workerism, we could even hazard the hypothesis that in the articulation of the two dimensions of class composition highlighted by Negri – 'technical' and 'political' composition[13] – the question of the *spatial composition of class* becomes of paramount importance, dictating both the political strategies of workerism and its theoretical valence. In this regard, its experience of the collapse of the factory as the site of the dialectical articulation of the structural and militant dimensions of class, and of their overall placement with a social totality, rendered *operaismo* sensitive to the potentially *disjunctive* character of social spaces, divided between production and politics with no a priori fit on the horizon.

It might be useful at this point to spare a couple of words about the question of method. Most, if not all, the authors working in the orbit of workerism share two broad theoretical commitments. The first is to the aforementioned notion of 'class composition', the gist of which is that any militant Marxism must concern itself not just with the objective analysis of the relation of labour to the means of production and capital's command functions but also with the dynamics of internal differentiation of the working class and their impact on its capacities for organisation and antagonism. The second, which relies on this preoccupation with the antagonistic motor of the process of capitalist accumu-

13   Wright 2002, p. 3.

lation, is an interpretation of the transformations in the political configuration of capitalism and its means of domination from the angle of its most advanced, and in a certain sense 'revolutionary', sectors: a method of *tendency*, as Negri referred to it, in which the movement toward an ever more intense socialisation of capital and 'real subsumption' of society by capital is taken as the analytical key through which to grasp, anticipate and intervene in concrete political conjunctures. The theory is thus itself shot through with a kind of insurgent subjectivity, with an overt partisan hostility to detached contemplation (which it deems anchored in the denial of division) and scientific disinterest (whose systemic complicities it finds it easy to unveil, namely in the class composition of the figure of the expert or technician), thereby foregrounding its specific temporal regime: a partisan theory that fuels a recomposition of class and a political strategy of organisation by anticipating the future moves of capitalist command, through an analysis of the tendencies at work in the management and localisation of production.

The accelerated modernisation undergone by Italy in the post-war period, with its massive internal migrations (from the agricultural South to the industrial North) and rapid urbanisation had a profound impact on the theoretical tendencies and political tactics of the dissident left of the Italian Communist Party (PCI) and Italian Socialist Party (PSI) and in particular of extra-parliamentary groups that formed in the wake of the strikes and mobilisation of the so-called 'hot autumn' of 1969. The 1950s and 1960s witnessed a thorough rearrangement of the relation between class composition and the political cartography of production, consumption and circulation, such that the Italian cities that Sartre had singled out in *Search for a Method* for their evasion of a classist topography, of the kind instead visible in Paris, were now far more 'striated' by the cycle of production.[14] As Balestrini and Moroni note, this was a period when the streets 'became the assembly chains of the work force'.[15] In this regard, the importance of migration and the overwhelming transformation of Northern industrial cities under the guidance of capitalist planning cannot be underestimated – especially for the manner in which it spurred the theoretical and political work of Italian Marxists. This is not just in terms of dislocation and the uprooting, if not obliteration, of spatially entrenched existential patterns, the cultural dispossession and destruction that has notoriously accompanied capitalism ever since its inception.[16]

---

14   Sartre 1968, p. 81.
15   Balestrini and Moroni 1997, p. 46.
16   The phenomenon of migration was, of course, twofold, both to the north of Italy and giant factory complexes such as Fiat in Turin or the Petrolchimico in Marghera, near Venice, and

It also entails a deeply ambivalent phenomenon: on the one hand, the radical disruption of the political memory sedimented in certain experiences of
social space (say, the experience of the artisan or professional worker as compared to that of the displaced and 'disqualified' mass worker), on the other, the
emancipation from political inhibitions and irrational allegiances that comes
with the evacuation of cultural and territorial ties. Danilo Montaldi, a path-
breaking and unorthodox socialist thinker, one of the forebears of workerism,
made the following observations about the new face of the industrial metropolis:

> In Milan, 'time' and 'space' have different meanings than those of the
> humanism whose passing is lamented in our universities. Neither time
> nor space must remain 'empty'. ... The owner of a condominium had
> placed in six apartments, of three rooms each, eighteen families: one
> family per room, with shared amenities. ... From the digs and galleries
> of the metro rise up all the dialects of Italy ... . It is especially in com-
> mon dives and commuter trains that one can still hear talk of politics
> in terms of wages and work hours. The silence that elsewhere dominates
> the mass constitutes, for the sake of the continuity of the City's rhythms,
> an even stronger armature than the newly restored buildings. ... The City,
> expanding the frontiers of the public until the farthest moral peripheries,
> multiplies within the reaches of its horizons, the attacks on habits and
> traditions.[17]

The effects of this massive dislocation of the social geography of Italy – aesthetically encapsulated by the passage from the neo-realist city of the immediate post-war period (*The Bicycle Thief*) to the alienated urban landscapes of

---

spreading out to the burgeoning industrial centres of Europe: 'This new figure of the proletarian is the one that, emigrating from southern Italy, has made capitalist development
throughout Europe: from Fiat to Volkswagen to Renault, from the mines of Belgium to the
Ruhr. Who has made the great worker struggles of the last few years. Who has smashed
everything, who has thrown Italy into crisis. Who determines today the desperate response
of capital, at the level of both the factory and the institutions. Who today forces the own-
ers to use the extreme weapon, the weapon of crisis. [...] This enemy is the proletarian
from the South: with a thousand trades because he has none, "uprooted, unemployed
[...] this mobile, disposable, interchangeable labour-power" [...]. Who cannot find work
in the South and therefore looks for it in Turin, in Milan, in Switzerland, in Germany, anywhere in Europe.' Nanni Balestrini, *Vogliamo tutto*, quoted in Balestrini and Moroni 1997,
pp. 281–2.

17   'La migrazione' in Balestrini and Moroni 1997, pp. 48–9.

Michelangelo Antonioni (*La Notte*) – arguably lay the perilous foundations for a later phase that saw the unfurling of Lotta Continua's 1970 congress slogan *Prendiamoci la città* (Let's Take the City) and the theorisation by Potere Operaio of the appropriation of autonomous spaces, or *basi rosse* (red bases),[18] not to mention an extension of social conflict outside of the factory gates and into the metropolitan arena.

The drastic transformation testified by Balestrini and Montaldi, with all its subjective and cultural effects, was openly promoted by what Negri would refer to as the 'planner-state' and focused on the factory as both physical and symbolic space. The theorists working in *Quaderni rossi* thus turned to enquiries into the changed experience of class composition, to a kind of militant sociology concerned, for instance, with the particular subjectivity of the new workers from the South, but also to a renewal of Marxist theory on the basis of this Italian experience.[19] It is thus that the theoretical thrust of workerism, whilst elicited by such phenomena of modernisation and dislocation, came to be fashioned, first of all, in a radical reflection on the antagonism between labour and capital as localised in the factory – conceived as the critical point of articulation of the capitalist system of exploitation and the subjective, organisational resources of the working class.

In its inaugural formulation, as set forth in Tronti's seminal *Operai e capitale*, the factory is a strategically and 'genetically' totalising particularity within the system of production, the privileged site of a partisan comprehension of the whole from the part upon which the whole depends. In Tronti's early work this objective and subjective centrality of the factory is characteristically dissimulated by the fetishistic logic of capital, it *appears* as a mere moment, at the very point where capitalism is moving toward real subsumption and the factory is de facto the material and spatial schema of all social existence.

As Tronti writes:

> The more capitalist production penetrates in depth and invades in extension the totality of social relations, the more society appears as a *totality* with respect to production and production as a *particularity* with respect to society. When the particular is generalised, is universalised, it *appears* as represented in the general, the universal. In the capitalist social relation of production, the generalisation of production is expressed as the

---

18   It is worth noting that in a later article, 'La moltitudine e la metropoli', Negri says that these 'often were not places, but urban spaces, sites of public opinion.' Negri 2002b.

19   Whilst I shall not be able to do justice to the sociological (or historiographic) contributions of workerism, these are dealt with admirably in Wright 2002, Chapters 2 and 8.

hypostasis of society. When *specifically* capitalist production has woven the entire net of social relations, it itself now appears as a *generic* social relation.[20]

The political use of the factory as a site for political mobilisation, organisation and conflict thus depends on an organised subjective reversal which takes cognisance of the extension of the factory as a political and economic reality onto the whole social terrain. Focusing the antagonistic efforts of the working class on using the factory as a lever for attacking capital means both recognising the *tendency* of the political logic of production to produce a *social factory* and anticipating or counter-actualising this tendency by turning the factory into the destructive part at the centre of the social whole:

> The more capitalist development advances, that is, the more it penetrates and extends the production of relative surplus value, the more the production-distribution-exchange-consumption cycle tightens, the more, that is, the relation between capitalist production and bourgeois society, factory and society, society and State becomes organic.[21]

What must be avoided at all costs is accepting the appearance, arising from the boundless extension of *capitalist* relations, that society is no longer moved and riven by the antagonistic structure of production. Beneath the organic semblance that makes of the factory a mere moment, the militant task is, in the same gesture, to exacerbate the 'anorganic' antagonism of the working class and to affirm the factory as the matrix of this society, not just a mere moment. As Luciano Ferrari Bravo perspicuously notes, the seeming pacification brought about by the dissolution of the factory itself as a site of antagonism, when viewed from the angle of the theory of the social factory, reveals itself as built on an armature of command, a structure of power that extends domination farther and farther into the social fabric rather than dissipating it in a set of local negotiations:

> Social factory, capitalist *social plan*: within the first historical realisation of this movement is born the optic that sees the 'extinction' of the exponential agglomerate of social violence. One is not able immediately to see that the social diffusion domination, the apparent 'appeasement' of 'polit-

---

20   Tronti 1971, p. 49.
21   Tronti 1971, p. 51.

ics' and 'economics' necessarily harbours within itself the concentration of factory despotism on the whole of society.[22]

Needless to say, the question of revealing the factory as a 'critical' locus, a socio-political matrix, is an eminently practical one, since it involves the organised affirmation of labour as the exploited *power* cloaked by the seeming rationality of the social organisation of production.

This political reaffirmation of the centrality of the factory, however, cannot be simply deduced from the thesis of the social factory. In his judicious assessment of the various impasses, at once political and theoretical, of workerism, Wright directs our attention to the strategic ambivalence arising from this thesis. If we do not entirely endorse the dialectical matrix of Tronti's argument, which identifies the factory, qua site of the immediate process of production, as the privileged site for forcing antagonism into the apparent social peace planned by the state, then it becomes difficult to adjudicate theoretically whether the notion of the social factory is to be read as a call to remain with the factory and the political forms it has traditionally given rise to, anchored as they are to particular types of struggle (strike, sabotage, demonstration, negotiation) and centred on the (Leninist or social-democratic) party, or, alternatively, whether the task is that of inventing new modes of political behaviour capable of assuming the qualitative jump generated by the extension of the social factory – such that the anti-capitalist 'lever' might lie elsewhere (or nowhere in particular ...).[23] On one level, we could argue, in favour of Tronti, that the creeping generalisation of the factory, of 'industrial production', to cover the whole of 'social production' (or rather, to make the social itself a matter of production in the capitalist sense), does not obviate the privileged localisation of the factory – inasmuch as the latter is the one site where the reality behind the seeming pacification of the social factory can appear for what it is, and where the class struggle can be made explicit, organised and intensified. There is here also the realisation, on Tronti's part, that this is a moment to be seized, a *kairòs* for political action which, once the conjuncture has been well and truly worked over by capitalist socialisation, may never return. On another level, it is difficult to shake off the impression, corroborated by Wright, of a tension between Tronti's brilliant updating of Marx to the Italian situation and the more rigid localisation of his extremely antagonistic dialectics in the factory. The latter suggests that

---

22   Ferrari Bravo 2000, p. 66. 'Appeasement' is in English in the original.
23   Wright 2002, pp. 40–1.

his political topology might depend, if not on a teleology – of the kind that elsewhere heralded the onset of a dedifferentiated world market – at least on a determinate law-like tendency, without which nothing would guarantee the role of this place, the industrial factory. In Tronti's seminal work this law is, of course, not the objective law of transition between modes of production, but the far more subjective 'laws of motion' of the working class and its class composition. At the heart of this whole debate is, of course, the oscillation, elicited by the term 'social factory', between the actual factory (say, the Fiat Mirafiori plant novelised in Balestrini's *We Want Everything*) and the factory as a conceptual, rather than material, site, a kind of capitalist diagram.[24]

It was to be a few years until the contradiction that Wright discerns in the political assumption of the thesis of the social factory was to be made painfully urgent by the capitalist strategies of restructuring that invested the factory in reaction to the virulent struggles of 1968–69 and were in turn militantly interpreted by groups such as Potere Operaio as a signal to move beyond the factory gates. By any standard, the 1970s in Italy saw a veritable spatial attack on the social hegemony of the working class, which had manifested itself, beyond the factory dialectic of the unions, in the political form of autonomy.[25] This forced dislocation was not simply a creative destruction, or dispossession, for the sake of profitability, but involved a political confrontation over the control and experience of space. For Sergio Bologna, this was accompanied by the insurgent left's incapacity to make a durable political link between the factory proper and the social factory (which included the movements of the unemployed, of women, of students) and by a peculiarly Italian co-opting of the independent organisation of the working class in the factories by the party system – via a corruption of what had been the system of delegates and workers' councils. Bologna thus deemed the 'retreat from the factories' (and from the framework of class composition) as 'suicidal'. In his sights, among others, was the 1971 'turn' by the extra-parliamentary grouping Potere Operaio, led, among others, by Negri.

We encounter here a very complex knot of themes, many of which were vigorously, even violently, debated at the time: the question of mobility, both in the sense of migration into the factories and flight (whether forced or inten-

---

24 The question is whether the factory is to be defined as a specific place, the industrial establishment, or rather more generally as 'the place (whether tangible or not) of the organisation of the process of production'. Borio et al. 2004, p. 19. See also Wright 2007.

25 'The Tribe of Moles' (1977) in Lotringer and Marazzi 1980, p. 40.

tional) from them;[26] the tactical and strategic role of the factory; the relation between class composition, militancy and the shifting spaces of production. A Potere Operaio pamphlet from 1971 gives a sense of this debate:

> The new task proposed by the crisis: a new strategic level of the struggle. Some do not understand that in the crisis the following fact must be reckoned with: factory struggles as such, the terrain of demands, no longer dig the owner's grave ... if the task of revolutionaries in the phase of capitalist development is to promote autonomy, to organize struggles and strikes, halts in production, grassroots committees – today, of course, all of this needs to be carried out, it needs to be accomplished wherever possible; but today, in the crisis, it is also a matter of setting out and realizing, within the time imposed by the crisis, a jump in the level of the political struggle, of the revolutionary struggle.[27]

Not just workerist theory, but the fate of political action motivated by that theory, can thus be seen closely to relate to assessment of the factory as the fulcrum of antagonism. The militant expressions of the workerist tendency can be placed on an arc that moves from the work within and against the factory, whether by workers themselves or by strenuous mobilisation at the factory gates, to an attempt to invest the entire 'productive fabric of the metropolis'[28] – reformulating, in the industrial setting of Northern Italy, the theory of 'red bases' originating in Mao's revolutionary agitation in the 1920s; promoting the direct appropriation of commodities and auto-reduction of services (transport, utilities) on the basis of the needs and desires of the metropolitan proletariat. This move out of the factory thus entails a much greater emphasis on the subjective, or political, aspect of composition. As we read in a Potere Operaio pamphlet from 1972:

26　It is in these experiences, as well as in a provocative reading of Marx's writings, that authors from the workerist tradition draw the resources for a theory of 'exodus'. See Hardt and Negri 2000, but especially Virno 2002a, pp. 179–84.

27　As demonstrated by 'Lotta sociale e organizzazione nella metropoli', a text dated January 1970 from the Collettivo Politico Metropolitano – a group that was shortly thereafter to morph into Red Brigades – a particular take on the collapse of the factory as the site of a spatial dialectic between, on the one hand, accumulation and command, and, on the other, workers' needs and autonomy, could also be at the source of a turn to clandestine violence and armed struggle, a direct confrontation with a supposedly monolithic state in the absence of any social dialectic.

28　Negri 1988, p. 210.

The new political composition of the class, the connotation of the majority of employed labour as proletarian, is not given in the objectivity of the production process [...]. No, the political figure of the reunified proletariat is given only as estrangement, as antagonism, as struggle against the capitalist system, as will of destruction and as Communist programme.[29]

Amid the oscillations between a revamped Leninism and a dissolution of militancy into a radical politics of the everyday what emerged from this turn was a key shift in emphasis from the dialectical, if extreme, antagonism situated in the factory to an almost entirely unilateral politics of autonomy, based on notions such as *need* and *desire* (somewhat reductively treated as a politics of consumption by certain critics), and spread over the metropolis and the territory at large.[30] At the level of the theory of class composition this was signalled by the pivotal passage from the *mass worker* that accompanied the centrality of the factory to the *social worker*, marked by a greater degree of socialisation and the spatial diffusion of production.[31] The theoretical question, which arguably continued to determine Negri's later work, is the following: can need (or desire) localise antagonism? If power is no longer indexed to the immediate process of production, is the new site of antagonism to be identified in the multiplicity of needs that try to counter the mechanisms of accumulation and command? In this regard, while there remains a fundamental conviction in the dualist matrix of class struggle, we can no longer speak of *a* site, be it in the sense of a matrix or paradigm, but rather must speak of sites, themselves generated by subjective needs. As Negri and his comrades wrote in 1983:

The autonomous movement [...] sought to go beyond the previous 'workerist factory' perspective and to understand the changes in the labour process which were taking place. But above all, it expressed the new subjectivity of the movement, the richness of its multiple differences, its rejection of formal politics and the mechanisms of representation. It did not seek a 'political outlet' or 'solution'. It embodied an immediate exer-

---

29   'Proletari, è guerra di classe', *Potere Operaio* 47–48, quoted in Wright 2002, p. 138.

30   On the variety of these post-factory practices of autonomy, see the collective, retrospective text 'Do You Remember Revolution?' (1983) in Negri 1988, pp. 237–8, and Eddi Cherki and Michel Wievorka, 'Autoreduction Movements in Turin' in Lotringer and Marazzi 1980, pp. 72–9.

31   See especially 'Archaeology and Project: The Mass Worker and the Social Worker' in Negri 1988, pp. 203–28.

cise of power within society. In this sense, localism and pluralism are a defining characteristic of the experience of autonomy.[32]

These new subjectivities are therefore not predetermined by a place that would already be given as the site of an articulation of politics and production.[33] What is more, they inflect the relation between space and power, force and place. Retrospectively, the concept of *power* in classic Marxism and earlier phases of workerism is criticised for obliterating the space of needs under the weight of a particular temporality, for being a 'projection into the future, rather than a lived experience within the liberated spaces of the present'.[34]

The problem of power over space, thus linked to the subjectivity of need and political organisation, is one of the key contributions of workerism. As Harvey writes: 'Whoever controls space can always control the politics of place even if – and this is an important aspect – one must first control some specific space'.[35] The shifts from the factory to the metropolis and to the overall territory as a complex, differentiated fabric of productive needs could also be considered as a privileged prism for understanding the problem of violence, namely the manner in which the latter is linked to determinate forms of spatial expression (think of the difference between the occupation of a neighbourhood and the occupation of a factory, for instance). The passage from workerism proper to autonomy can thus be understood in terms of the drive to conquer and control one's own everyday spaces. But it is also connected to the importance of the

---

32 'Do You Remember Revolution?' in Negri 1988, pp. 236–7. This move out of the factory was also an exquisitely tactical question: 'the extension of the struggles to the entire social sphere at a territorial level and the building of forms of counter-power were seen as necessary steps against the blackmail of economic crisis' (p. 232).

33 By subjectivities I am not simply referring to a dimension of militancy and political organisation, but also to the more widespread effects of these spatial dislocations of production on the 'phenomenology' of work and the worker. We are dealing with 'a historical phase in which the organisation of space moulded by Taylorism, both in the factory and in offices, was being destructured. The perception of space of the waged worker was referred to clearly distinct "place", two separate systems of culture and rules, the house and the factory, the flat and the office, the place of private life, of the family, of affections, on the one hand, and the place of work, on the other. ... Whilst the "alienation" of waged work divided the individual into two socio-affective cycles, the cycle of private life and the cycle of working life, the (apparent) non-alienation of independent work reduces existence to a single socio-affective cycle, that of private life. ... Whatever return to the Taylorist organisation of space we might imagine, it will no longer be possible to delete the new mental disposition of autonomous work, born of the superimposition of the socio-affective domestic sphere and the sphere of work'. See Bologna 1997.

34 'The Tribe of Moles' (1977) in Lotringer and Marazzi 1980, p. 56.

35 Quoted in Krasivyj 1994.

overall sphere of reproduction outside the immediate process of production, as emphasised by feminists developing an immanent critique of workerism.[36] No longer intrinsically tied to the capitalist regime of antagonism via the factory, politics now emphasised the distance of its insurgent power (*potentia*) from commanding power (*potestas*). As Negri and his comrades remarked, what really defined the movement that peaked in 1977 was its being 'asymmetrical in its relation to power': an asymmetry that showed 'the authentic basis of the social processes that underlay it' and evaded 'frontal counterposition'.[37] From within the political topology of this sequence of Italian politics we can thus witness the division of antagonism into the dialectical antagonism of the factory struggle, on the one hand, and the capillary, self-organised antagonism of metropolitan needs, on the other.

A move toward the latter did not necessarily mean abandoning the question of political composition, the 'objective' side of political topology. Whence the attempt, prolonged in the theoretical and sociological research of workerism's heirs, to formulate a theory of the *diffuse factory*, linked to a figure of *diffuse labour*,[38] which could take many forms: the marginal or peripheral work of illegal labour, the invisible gendered work of reproduction and domestic labour, the sometimes creative, sometimes self-exploitative forms of autonomous labour. This research also had a privileged locus, the Italian Northeast, what Bologna called 'a prime laboratory of the new system of flexible accumulation'.[39] The attempt to understand the passage from waged factory workers to 'autonomous workers' and the formation of highly technological industrial districts in that region, thereto relatively poor and agriculturally driven, can thus be seen as the Italian counterpart to the anglophone debate over post-Fordism and flexible accumulation, namely by the 'New Times' theorists of *Marxism Today* – but a counterpart which is singularised by its focus on antagonism and class composition as the motor of the political and spatial transformation of production.[40]

---

36 Fortunati 1981.
37 'Do You Remember Revolution', in Negri 1988, p. 237.
38 Negri 1988, p. 214.
39 Bologna, 'Prefazione' in Ferrari Bravo 2000, p. 25.
40 An 'industrial district' was defined at the beginning of the century by Alfred Marshall, writing about areas such as Manchester, as a 'factory without walls'. This theory, whose modern counterpart is the network *intra muros* – which emerges once the reticular structure of the industrial district is grasped as a model for the internal space of the factory and the company itself – was revived by those trying to think the social reality of the Italian Northeast after the demise of the centrality of the large factory. In a more optimistic vein, the industrial district was viewed as a more positive terrain of struggle than the factory

Negri himself, presenting his collective sociological work on new forms of 'post-Fordist' production emerging in the 1980s and 1990s, asks: 'Why has my research moved from the big factory to the territorial diffusion of production?'[41] His own thinking started from an experience of Fordist militancy, under the banner of Potere Operaio, at Porto Marghera, the massive petrochemical plant near Venice.[42] After the relative collapse of factory work, Negri experienced firsthand the phenomenon of unemployed workers building forms of autonomy and counter-power in the territory surrounding the plant, using their lay-off payments (*Cassa integrazione*) as a basis for entrepreneurship, 'operations of decentering', drawing on the experiential density and localised geography of factory antagonism and its relation to the efficacy and productivity of capital. It is crucial to the maintenance of the workerist thesis of the primacy of struggle that this phenomenon be thought not just a result of the unilateral impetus of capital but also as a product of antagonistic subjectivity – of the desire to spread cooperation over the territory and flee factory discipline. In this regard, Negri emphasises the role of the *political entrepreneur*, 'the autonomous agent of an ever more cooperative social work on the territories of production', the weaver of the objective, institutional and subjective networks that made 'industrial districts' possible, of the kind capitalised on by Benetton, 'a multinational of the informal organization of diffuse production'.[43]

The various concepts and periodisations put forth by workerism with respect to the question of political spatialisation – from the social factory to the diffuse factory, from the productive territory to the insurgent, post-Fordist metropolis – present us with a rich resource for the development of a political topology for our time. What emerges from this materialist lineage, through its political initiatives and crises, and the manner in which the latter inflected the

---

with its *rigidity* and its limits as a site for mobilisation, especially to the extent it could incorporate the role of extra-economic variables in the functioning of networked 'territorialised' industries, and brought about new forms of class composition in networks of interaction combining competition, imitation and cooperation. See Grassi, 'Distretti industriali' in Zanini and Fadini 2001, pp. 94–100. For a powerful critique of 'New Times', see Sivanandan 1989.

41   Negri 1996, p. 67. The research Negri is referring to is contained in Negri et al. 1993.

42   On the militant history of *operaismo* in Porto Marghera, with important reflections on working-class environmentalism, see Sacchetto and Sbrogiò 2009 and Feltrin and Sacchetto 2021.

43   Negri 1996, p. 73. For Negri, this sequence did peak around the years 1977–83, in the phenomenon of small to medium enterprises and was swallowed up again, after 1983, by the return of the large company hoarding information and services with the aid of state policies.

development and construction of its theoretical apparatus, is not a single transcendental aesthetic for the phenomenology of labour-power and antagonism,
but a series of spatio-temporal dynamisms, dramatisations of class struggles in
different sites, marked by a variety of tactics.

Yet we may ask whether, with the full deployment of real subsumption and
its correlate of non-dialectical antagonism, as developed by Negri from his writings on the social worker to his research with Hardt, we have not just left behind
the spatial anchoring of a social dialectics in the factory, but any localisation of
social analysis and political project. I am thinking especially of the kind of localisation afforded by the part/whole relationship of the working-class to the
capitalist system of production which, in the theory of Empire, is abandoned
for the sake of an unlocalisable, immeasurable interplay between a parasitical regime of command and accumulation, on the one hand, and a seemingly
smooth space of cooperating subjectivities, on the other.

From the vantage point of *Empire*, and its assumption of the Deleuzo-
Guattarian distinction between smooth and striated space, it is possible retrospectively to elucidate the strong spatial content of Negri's reading of the Marxist notion of real subsumption such that the latter, by extending the social factory beyond any possible measure (of time and value) and beyond any univocal
indexing of production – any privileged point for the dialectical articulation
of capital, labour, and insurgency – necessitates a renewed effort to abandon
the 'transcendental aesthetic' of traditional radical politics and to think both
production and subversion in terms of divergent constructions of space (and
time). Turned 'right side up' and viewed from the autonomous standpoint of a
cooperative class of exploited producers (proletariat, social worker, multitude)
socialised within capital, the thematic of real subsumption has led Negri to a
notion of space as 'constitutive of the common', whereby 'co-operation is the
space constituted by the common and so is multiplied in its productivity'.[44]

Whilst globality and locality are not generated or accounted for by a dialectical matrix, Negri does maintain the line, which he regards as being of the
utmost tactical importance, that locality is not given but produced (whether
as discrete, commanded or common is a matter for struggle). This interpretive line is based on a fundamentally antagonistic understanding of the relation between smooth (or molar) and striated (or molecular) space. Indeed, we
could hazard the observation that Negri's work in this direction, in collaboration with Hardt and on his own, rests in great part on reading *A Thousand
Plateaus* through the lenses of class struggle (and vice versa). When he writes

---

44   Negri 2003c, pp. 212–13.

that 'the global world is a striated world', this should therefore be understood in the sense that the deterritorialising logic of capitalist accumulation and the common spaces of cooperation are crosscut by territorial logics of power. Conversely, if the territorial striations of the world system may lead us to acknowledge the endurance of the nation-state, 'from a molecular perspective', that is, from the standpoint of the productive and antagonistic dynamics behind social transformation, for example, 'we can see the period of the Cold War as one in which there was *a transformation in the effective form of sovereignty*', whose outcome was '*a sovereignty with no outside*, or rather one that does not recognize the distinction between inside and outside'.[45] Crucially, this abolition of the outside, whose Marxist analysis 'classical' workerism had inaugurated via the notions of the 'social factory' and 'real subsumption', also rescinds the more or less dialectical articulation of (welfare or planner) state, bourgeoisie, and working class as principally mediated via the locus, both physical and formal, of the factory. Reading antagonism via Deleuze and Guattari's onto-ethology of difference, Negri can thus state that '*Molecular civil war* is characterized by overlapping structures that fight one another in a common space, along multiple variable fronts'.[46] Notice the shift here from the frontal confrontation, which 'classical' workerism endeavoured to intensify, between (the state of) capital and (the party of) labour, to a refracted and non-synthesisable multitude of struggles which, though they may be theoretically identified with the vestigial antagonism of the exploiters and the exploited, nevertheless do not converge on a privileged site of antagonism, on a critical point that would be like the historical a priori for any insurgency, any anti-systemic movement. Notice, too, that instead of seeking out tactics for the recomposition of class as the prelude to a confrontation – whether this be organising at the factory gates or constructing 'red bases' throughout the metropolis – the emphasis on the ontological notion of 'a common space' both makes any a priori placement of antagonism ineffective and, by the same token, tends to make the struggle more virulent. After all, a molar, factory-centred class struggle certainly seems more recuperable than a 'molecular civil war'!

This is not to say, however, that the problem of localisation has been simply passed over by Negri. Indeed, his account of the 'crisis of political space' is closely wedded to the thinking of non-dialectical forms of territorialisation that would eschew the traditional relationships between modes of accumulation and figures of sovereignty, that 'machine of authority which traverses

---

45   Negri 2003a, pp. 58–9.
46   Negri 2003a, p. 63.

and structures the territory'.[47] In contradistinction to a dialectical schema that would deduce the site of antagonism and the critical point or lever of insurrection, within a social totality oriented by a more or less irreversible temporal motor, Negri's later work is very sensitive to the undecidability of the place of politics. Whilst general regimes of spatial production may be identified, for instance in line with the intuitions of Harvey's Marxist geography, they do not as such amount to the deployment of a veritable political topology. For the latter, bereft of the transcendental aesthetic that would link the sovereign space of the nation, the productive place of the factory and the time of development and crisis, must now turn its attention to the evental, non-totalisable nature of antagonism and try to glean the spatio-temporal dynamisms that would permit such events to individuate themselves in political bodies capable of struggle and antagonism, of exodus and separation. Having acknowledged 'the difficulty of recognizing the spatial dimension of a new Leninist project', in this absence of an a priori spatio-temporal determination of politics, Negri's neo-Leninism, very much unlike that of Tronti's in *Operai e capitale*, is predicated upon the reciprocal determination of the event and the place of resistance, and the concomitant thesis that the production of subjectivity depends on a body that is 'always localized and is always in *that time*'. In a certain respect, the dislocation of the industrial link between the sites of production and the places of politics, which workerism had experienced *in practice* ever since the setbacks in the factory struggles of 1971 and the consequent determination to 'take over the city', serves only to intensify the imperative to think the fugitive schemata and urgent tactics of localisation.

As an aside, we might here ask whether in the final analysis there isn't an irreparable disjunction between the conceptualisation of molecular antagonism and the idea that such an antagonism is localised in a *body*. How symptomatic of a theoretical shortcoming is Negri's oscillation between the molecular and the incarnate? Not only are the body and the flesh constantly attacked by Deleuze and Guattari for their incircumventable ties to phenomenological humanism, but, as Badiou has noted in *The Century*, isn't the most problematic and potentially disastrous localisation of politics the one that saw the call for revolution linked to the creation of 'passive bodies of subjectivation', monumental reifications of subjectivity that shifted the attention from the concrete and diversified places of politics to its transcendental place and agency? Negri contends that the tactical point and event of revolution depends on the

---

47   'La crisi dello spazio politico' [The Crisis of Political Space] in Negri 2003b, p. 20. This is a
      crucial essay for capturing the role of political topology in the work of Negri.

strength of the cooperative subject or multitude, but that the latter cannot be linked to a pregiven space or a 'date with history': 'the theme of the space for the party is thus subordinated to a specific *kairòs*, to the untimely power of an event'.[48] The real question here is whether the non-dialectical articulation of subject and event takes the common space as a product or as a presupposition and, more specifically, whether such a space is to be understood as the space of flows of real subsumption or in terms of the loci of insurgent political subjectivity.

The difficulty is compounded by the fact that the thinking of Empire, whilst hostile to Hegelian dialectics or to cybernetically enhanced systemic logics *à la* Luhmann, retains a preoccupation with totality, with capitalism as totality, as a system that is both deprived of an outside and endowed with a kind of parasitical transcendence (Empire's sovereignty). To understand the maintenance of a kind of totality (be it of an open or a virtual sort) in conjunction with the abandonment of a dialectical articulation of production and politics, of the two halves of class composition, is perhaps the key to assessing Negri's relation to the Marxist tradition. What must be kept in mind, in light of the narrative we have outlined here, is the fact that the termination of the dialectical schema is for Negri a *concrete and localised historical event*, itself determined by the transformations in the regime of accumulation and political forms of capitalism – not a capricious metaphysical preference. More specifically, it is the collapse of the factory as the nexus of anti-capitalist struggle, not just as a concrete site with bodies, protests, machines, but as a paradigmatic function within the capitalist system, that makes the dialectical comprehension of politics anachronistic. Negri's concern with totality, and especially with the 'totalisation' of space as a smooth space traversed by vectors of accumulation and subjectivity, or by molecular civil wars, is not, however, aimed at the identification of a point of negative critique or a consciousness that could extricate itself from the nets of real subsumption. Rather, it promises a renewal of materialism founded on the articulation of political subjectivity, in its various states and figures of composition and organisation, with the concrete transformations in the forms taken by capitalist accumulation and command. It is in this respect that the work of Hardt and Negri remains tied by a red thread to the earlier 'thought of class composition' which, Balestrini and Moroni argue:

> radically contests the possibility of grounding consciousness in the 'idealist nostalgia' of the human and formulates the conception according to

---

48   Negri 2003a, pp. 175–6.

which the revolutionary process is born from the social and material dynamic (without a presupposition of any originary ideality or alienated authenticity): the dynamic that finds its motor in the sphere of work, and more precisely in the workers' refusal of work (in the refusal to give one's time to activity that is expropriated and commanded by capital). ... The reading of the *Grundrisse* ... makes possible a new notion of totality, understood as a totality in situation (from the point of view of work and struggle) and at the same time as the subsumption of the singular within the ... process of capital. ... We must therefore consider two distinct aspects: on the one hand, totalisation is a process indiscernible from subjectivity, from historical, social and militant partiality ('the whole can be understood only by the part', writes Mario Tronti); on the other, however, capitalist subjectivity constitutes a process of totalisation ... articulated as subsumption, as the despotic assumption of real existences within its functioning. This is Marx's reign of abstract labour.[49]

Whilst Negri maintains his corrosive scepticism vis-à-vis any figure of 'national' politics, something that has led to sometimes myopic denunciations by more orthodox Marxist or political theorists, this does not mean that, as a reading of *Empire* might plausibly suggest, he has dissolved the problem of the politics of place in the non-place of imperial command. The metaphysical focus on the construction of a common space as constitutive of the antagonistic subjectivity of the multitude has been accompanied by a renewed interest in the theme of the metropolis as a potential site for the production of subjectivity and the confrontation with the mechanisms of command and accumulation dictated by the logic of capital. To dispel the impression of a clear and linear historical sequence that might have been elicited by the title of this chapter, and to try to problematise simplistic understandings of the legacy of workerism, it might be of interest to conclude with some of Negri's later reflections on the political topology of the metropolis.

Writing about architecture, Manfredo Tafuri declares: 'The construction of a physical space is certainly the site of a "battle": a proper urban analysis demonstrates this clearly. That such a battle is not totalizing, that it leaves borders, remains, residues, is also an indisputable fact'.[50] It is to this view of the met-

---

49   Balestrini and Moroni 1997, pp. 276–7.
50   Tafuri 1987, p. 8. Tafuri collaborated with Massimo Cacciari, Asor Rosa, and Negri (who would stay only for the first issue) on *Contropiano* – a journal close to the workerist tendency. It was in the first issue of this journal that he published his pioneering study of the relation between architectural theory and the critique of ideology, 'Per una critica

ropolis as a site of contestation and counter-power that Negri has turned, attempting to think of it as a possible localisation of struggle in the epoch of Empire, which would not petrify the antagonistic singularities that comprise the multitude. Against the 'industrialist' or 'factoryist' bias that beset much historical communism and even some of the early formulations of workerism, Negri's conviction, arising from the experiences of autonomy in the mid-1970s, is that

> the revolutionary decision today must base itself on another constituent schema: it no longer poses as preliminary to an industrial and/or developmental axis but, through that multitude in which mass intellectuality configures itself, it will forward the programme of a freed city in which industry will be bent to the urgencies of life, society to science, work to the multitude.[51]

Negri asks himself whether the metropolis plays the same political-topological role for the multitude as the factory did for the working class. Can the 'social worker' (*operaio sociale*) overturn productive subordination and the violence of exploitation within metropolitan space? But what kind of political space is the metropolis? What Negri called the crisis of the planner-state[52] could also be linked to the crisis of the planned city, of those projects of organic rationalisation that wished to tie the urban fabric to the teleology of production, to create an urban factory (and its associated forms of leisure and social reproduction) within the social factory. Even, or especially, in their social-democratic guise, these projects foundered when confronted with the irreducibility of the metropolis to a univocal organisation. Writing about the failure of such architectural visions of the metropolis as a regulated space of production and circulation, and even emancipation, Tafuri – that great critic of 'Red Vienna' and other endeavours in the socialist planning of built space – writes:

> Extending its manner of existence to the entire region, the metropolis gave rise to the spiraling problem of development-disequilibrium. And indeed, the planning theories based on the hypothesis of a reestablishment of equilibrium – and first among them, those of the Soviet Union –

---

dell'ideologia archittetonica', later incorporated in the book *Progetto e utopia*, translated into English as *Architecture and Utopia*, Tafuri 1976.

51   Negri 2003a, pp. 175–6.

52   'Crisis of the Planner-State: Communism and Revolutionary Organisation' in Negri 1988, pp. 97–148.

were destined to be revolutionized after the great crisis of 1929. Improbability, multifunctionality, multiplicity, and lack of organic structure – in short, all the contradictory aspects assumed by the modern metropolis – are thus seen to have remained outside the attempts at a rationalization pursued by central European architecture.[53]

But what becomes of the metropolis in the era of the crisis-state and later of an imperial capitalism driven by financialised capital?

For an anticipation of the spatial phenomenology of this 'imperial' metropolis, Negri chooses to turn to Rem Koolhaas and his 1978 book *Delirious New York*. Beyond the greater or lesser coherence of various forms of planning, Koolhaas, according to Negri, shows how the city was always traversed by 'dynamics, conflicts and powerful superimpositions of cultural strata, forms and styles of life, a multiplicity of ideas and projects about the future'. In other words, Koolhaas allows us to grasp the passage from the frontal counterposition of plan and working class to the metropolis as a 'molecular' space of antagonism which, moving beyond the 'prescriptions of power and utopias of opposition' revives the thinking of political spaces of autonomy that was the hallmark of the autonomist movement. Beyond project and utopia, Koolhas's work heralded, for Negri, a microphysical analysis of the metropolis which, against the macrophysical analysis of urban planning, could reveal a 'common world', the metropolis as 'the product of all – not general will but common aleatory space'.[54]

Negri's working hypothesis is that a renewed focus on the metropolis as a space of subjectivation, in which antagonism is inseparable from collective practices of construction and experimental forms of life, permits the dislocation of politics from the factory-(nation-)state axis. The metropolis is thus grasped not only as a 'hybrid and internally antagonistic aggregate', a 'beehive',[55] but, in its strategic location vis-à-vis financial and informational flows, not to mention flows of people, it is, following the work of Saskia Sassen, 'a homologous figure of the general structure that capitalism has assumed in its imperial phase'.[56] Does this mean that we have returned to the implicit dialectic governing the relation between factory and social factory, with metropolis and Empire as the two poles of our political topology? Not really. While such an analysis of

---

53   Tafuri 1976, p. 124.

54   Negri 2002b.

55   In Negri 2001b, p. 198, Negri speaks of an *alveare metropolitano* [urban beehive] to describe a formidable mobility of the spaces of production and a mixed site in which 'are combined new productive places and new activities without place'.

56   Negri 2002b.

the metropolis, by delineating the points of conflict between needs and commands, construction and exploitation, permits a localisation of antagonism which the theory of Empire might have appeared to evade, that antagonism is not itself directly reducible to a single, 'frontal' figure. Unlike the factory, the metropolis is a hybrid space, which in a sense demands further emphasis on political over technical composition. And, showing that the intellectual tools of workerism have not been jettisoned, Negri even explicitly revives the categories of classical workerist analysis: 'The capitalist recomposition of the metropolis constructs traces of recomposition for the multitude'.[57] Labour-power becomes multitude in the metropolis inasmuch as it weaves 'internal' relations of cooperation, which, while not directly mediated by the spatial organisation of production (factory), are the object of the extraction of surplus value. It is in this respect that the multitude, and the metropolis with it, is always a deeply ambivalent phenomenon, a multiplicity that can be decomposed into a social material functional to accumulation or recomposed into various foci of antagonism. As always, the workerist emphasis on anticipation and intervention asks how theory might work to identify differential and antagonistic tendencies, in this case within the fabric of the city, for the sake of the recomposition and construction of common, but not homogeneous, spaces that would not be subjected to the measure of capital.

Finally, what sets these latest hypotheses at a remove from the sequence of dislocations we have tracked up to this point is the fact that the socialisation of production is no longer simply thought in terms of a diffusion of the factory, but rather in view of the increasing importance of 'immaterial labour',[58] of the subjective, affective, volitional aspects of production and reproduction that tend to become the main targets for the extraction of surplus value. Inasmuch as we exit the dialectic of the factory, this extraction – relying on the *autonomous* existence of (metropolitan) cooperation between subjectivities – becomes ever more parasitic, often engaging in a mere capture of creativity that contributes little by way of fixed capital, or real investment, turning more and more into sheer command (as in the 'new enclosures' that permit drawing surplus value from such 'parasitic' activities as patenting and copyright, in a reinvention of the rentier as a key avatar of capital). The spatial dislocation out of the factory is thus accompanied by the formation of distributed sites of immaterial cooperation (the metropolis), in which exploitation is no longer accompanied by the dialectical measure of labour-time, but rather extends over the entirety

---

57   Ibid.
58   See Maurizio Lazzarato's key essay 'Immaterial Labor' in Virno and Hardt 1996.

of social existence – whence Negri's insistent focus on the theme of *biopolitics*, the theme of our next chapter. It is in this respect that, rather than defusing antagonism, the multiplicitous character of metropolitan life and production can be seen, in Negri's schema, to exacerbate it. Inasmuch as in today's 'immaterial' society (and in the political topology that accompanies it) there is no longer any objective measure of productive value: '*The new standard of measurement can only be a standard of power*. ... Measure thus becomes the measure of control, the measure of the capitalist capacity to develop production in the absence of any objective criterion of measurement and in the presence of relations of force that require domination'.[59] On this basis, the research programme laid out by Negri is quite unique, in so far as it points us to a dimension outside (or beside) the classical sites of political topology, to spaces of conflict and subjectivation that are no longer determinate, in the manner of the factory, but lie in the borderland, hinterland or no man's land (Negri writes of *terreni di mezzo*) between the immaterial and ideal interactions of what Marx called the general intellect and the concrete sites of contemporary material production.[60]

---

59   Negri 2001b, p. 201. Whence Negri's focus on the increasing role within 'imperial' capitalism of non-dialectical spatial strategies of policing, exclusion, war. In this respect his reference to the works of Mike Davis on the militarisation of Los Angeles is instructive.

60   It is as an interface between immaterial cooperation and material productivity that the school as a locus of *formation*, that is, of subjectivation, receives special attention in Negri 2001b.

CHAPTER 12

Always Already Only Now: Limits of the Biopolitical

1   Questions of Method

The turn of the millennium witnessed the constitution of a veritable biopolitical field in the domain of radical thought. I say field and not camp, not simply because of the loaded echoes of the latter term, but because the appropriations of the notion of biopolitics (and related terms such as biopower, or, more recently, bioeconomics) have been numerous and disparate, even antagonistic. What is Negri's position within this field? How has the concept of biopolitics affected his intellectual trajectory, and how, vice versa, has the concept been inflected, transformed by its inclusion within Negri's philosophical machinery? To answer these questions, in order hopefully to generate some new (and rather less pedantic) ones out of them, I'd like to begin by tackling the most obvious 'genealogical' issue, that of Negri's indebtedness to Foucault.

Foucault is at the fulcrum of the debate on biopolitics. Despite the fact that he did not coin the term – which had appeared in various iterations ever since it was introduced in 1911 by the Swedish political scientist Rudolf Kjellén[1] – it is Foucault's formulation of biopolitics in the first volume of the *History of Sexuality*, and his subsequent elaborations of it in the late 1970s (particularly in the Collège de France lectures of 1976 to 1979) which serve as the touchstone for contemporary debates. Though it exceeds the remit of this chapter to establish this point, I think it may be suggested that the vibrancy as well as the frequent vagueness and imprecision of the current use of the concept of biopolitics derive from some crucial features of Foucault's method. The dominant tendency among those with a predilection for this concept, Negri included, is to treat biopolitics as a kind of 'epochal' category, such that we may speak of an age of biopolitics, a biopolitical condition, biopolitical capitalism, and so on. Of course, though he subtracts historical and discursive periodisation from any kind of cunning of reason, consigning them to the impersonal conjunctions of archive and event, Foucault's own introduc-

---

1   Esposito 2004, pp. 3–16.

tion of the term is not devoid of an 'epochalising' impulse, in line with the epistemic dislocations traced in *The Order of Things* and *Discipline and Punish*.

And yet Foucault's methodology, especially as concerns biopolitics, is also polemically positioned against the totalising and universalising approaches that he deems common to both traditional political theory and Marxism. As he announces, at the very outset of his series of lectures on the 'birth of biopolitics' (which will turn out to concern mainly the excavation of neoliberal discourse): 'choosing to speak of, or to start from, governmental practice, is also an entirely explicit way of putting aside – as a first, primitive, pre-constituted object – a whole set of notion such as, for example, the sovereign, sovereignty, the people, subjects, the State, civil society: all these universals which sociological analysis, as well as historical analysis and the analysis of political philosophy, utilise effectively to account for governmental practice'.[2] Foucault continues by distinguishing his method from that of historicism:

> Historicism starts from the universal and passes it, as it were, through the sieve of history. My problem is precisely the inverse one. I start from the decision, both theoretical and methodological, which consists in saying: let us suppose that universals do not exist. And I pose at that point the question to history and historians: how can you write history if you do not assume a priori that something like the State, society, the sovereign, or subjects exist? ... So, not to interrogate universals by utilising history as a critical method, but, starting from the decision of the inexistence of universals, to ask what history one can make.[3]

Such pronouncements have prompted Ian Hacking to observe that 'Foucault's dynamic nominalism is a historicized nominalism'.[4] How is this methodological nominalism reflected in the introduction of the theory of biopolitics? In the first place, we can see it at work in the way Foucault poses the problem of biopolitics, namely by asking: how did a domain of 'social life' come to be constituted as an object for knowledge and as a correlate of certain regulatory practices of power? How did an entity both epistemic and material, such as the 'population' – possibly the pivotal category of biopolitics – emerge at the intersection of statistical knowledge and epidemiological power? Note that Foucault's nominalism precludes him from positing the pre-existence of the

---

2   Foucault 2004, p. 4.
3   Foucault 2004, p. 5.
4   Hacking 2002, p. 49; also Balibar 1992a.

population, just as it makes him sensitive enough to its material constitution to forsake mere ideological critique of the term's misuses and instrumentalisations. Furthermore, biopolitics is approached through the discontinuous genealogy of discourses around the 'art of governing' and is thus envisaged through the lenses of political rationality.

What Foucault called 'the biopolitics of the population', which, together with the 'anatomo-politics' of discipline makes up the protean 'bipolar technology'[5] of 'biopower', is thus included within the problematic of 'government', understood as that which 'enables a problem to be addressed and offers certain strategies for solving/handling the problem [and] also structures specific forms of *intervention*'.[6] Given the plurality of mechanisms (or *dispositifs*), agents, and points of application of this biopolitics, we arguably encounter here a 'strategic logic of heterogeneity' whereby Foucault 'substitutes the proliferation of devices that constitute substantial unities, as much as degrees of unities contingent in each instance, for the totalising principle of the economy or the political'. Despite its capacity to delineate a major shift in the practices of power, the biopolitics of the population, which envisages 'the management of power as a management of multiplicity',[7] thereby appears as a category with a localised operation, aimed at describing a specific rationality, with all of its proper technologies and sui generis material effects, but *not* as a new universal to replace notions like State or civil society. On the contrary, biopolitics is configured by Foucault as an 'anti-universal' concept.

2   Mediation Is Dead, Long Live Biopolitics

Now, even a cursory glance at Negri's later writings will reveal that his use of the term biopolitics is anything but an analytically restricted one. Indeed, not only does the notion of the biopolitical permit Negri to give a common framework to theoretical affirmations of an ontological, political, social, economic and historical character, it often appears, building on his distinctive use of the Marxian concept of 'real subsumption', as the master-term to identify a situation of full social and productive immanence. Or rather, according to Hardt and Negri, Foucault, along with authors such as Deleuze and Guattari 'has prepared the terrain ... for an investigation of the material functioning of imper-

---

5   Rabinow and Rose 2003, p. 2.
6   Lemke 2001, p. 191.
7   Lazzarato 2005.

ial rule',[8] inasmuch as his conceptualisation of power and social reproduction allows us to wrest the notion of a real subsumption of society under capital away from 'the linear and totalitarian figure of capitalist development',[9] lending it the dimensions of multiplicity, singularity, the event. Once the 'Foucauldian' elements have been properly integrated, biopower 'is another name for the real subsumption of society under capital, and both are synonymous with the globalized productive order'.[10] As we shall see, Negri's approach to biopolitics as a Janus-faced notion – both a mark of the most endemic control and a sign of a new insurgent subjectivity – is closely tied to the historico-political paradox of real subsumption, which can be said to pervade all his later work. For it is within real subsumption that power at once 'unifies and envelops within itself every element of social life' thereby undoing the bases of mediation proper, but 'at that very moment reveals a new context, a new milieu of maximum plurality and uncontainable singularization – a milieu of the event'.[11] Over and over again, biopower and 'biopolitical production' thus appear not just in terms of a Marxian theory of socialisation, but as bywords for the fusion of domains hitherto considered functionally separate into a single field of production and antagonism, without transcendent measure and without an outside.

Hardt and Negri can thus write that the 'powers of production are in fact today entirely biopolitical; in other words, they run throughout and constitute directly not only production but also the entire realm of reproduction';[12] or – in *Multitude*'s effort to encompass the latest round of military interventions and occupations under a biopolitical aegis – that 'in a sort of concert of convergence of the various forms of power, war, politics, economics and culture in Empire become finally a mode of producing social life in its entirety and hence a form of biopower'.[13] This idea of a biopolitical convergence of hitherto distinct domains of human activity also affects the political universals that Foucault sought methodologically to undermine with his inquiry into political reason,[14] so that civil society, for instance, is said to be 'absorbed in the state, but the consequence of this is an explosion of the elements that were previously coordinated and mediated in civil society'.[15] It is within this unmediated

8   Hardt and Negri 2000, p. 23.
9   Hardt and Negri 2000, p. 25.
10   Hardt and Negri 2000, p. 365.
11   Hardt and Negri 2000, p. 25.
12   Hardt and Negri 2000, p. 364.
13   Hardt and Negri 2004, p. 334.
14   Barry et al. 1996.
15   Hardt and Negri 2000, p. 25.

or immeasurable explosion that Negri discerns the traits that prefigure – within what he daringly dubs a 'materialist teleology' – a social and political ontology of the 'common': the 'destruction of the separation between public and private', the 'nomadism and the flexibility of labour-power, the new configuration of the social as the structure of the common (in all its biopolitical dimensions), the emergence of mass intellectuality'.[16] The whole of (Hardt and) Negri's later thought is thus characterised by a tension between the vision of a biopower that 'regulates social life from its interior, following it, interpreting, absorbing it, and rearticulating it'[17] and that of a biopolitics from below, as it were, which, 'through the cohesion of a network of singularities',[18] and the powers of 'love' and 'poverty', produces a new common world against biopower.

I will return below, via Foucault, to this dichotomisation between biopower and biopolitics. At this juncture, it is important to note that, whichever sign they take, whether positive or negative, these categories are aimed at affirming the termination of any mediation and any dialectic (between public and private, state and civil society, and so on). In an earlier text, appended to his *The Politics of Subversion*, Negri, following the thesis that under conditions of real subsumption capitalist power increasingly manifests itself as sheer command and terroristic crisis, declared: 'Mediation is dead. The production of goods takes place through domination. The relationships between production and reproduction, between domination/profit and resistance/wages cannot be harmonized'.[19] This quasi-Manichean disharmony persists at the heart of the theory of the multitude. Ironically employing an über-dialectical category, Hardt and Negri configure this death of mediation in terms of the opposition between two *totalities*: on the one hand, 'the totality of right and the State, the tendency toward the affirmation of an imperial right and a new sovereignty that extends over the global set of social, economic, juridical and political relations of our planet' and, on the other hand, and 'at the same time, in the same logical space, there is the insurgency against this right and against this new imperial authority'. In other words, we have the confrontation between two unmediated totalities, one involving Empire's new biopolitical sovereignty, and the other for which 'the total object is not power but rather what Spinoza called "the democratic absolute"'. This second totality, then, the concern of a 'dogmatic science of desire' is anti-dialectical, anti-teleological and anti-transcendental.[20]

---

16   Negri 2003c, p. 223.
17   Hardt and Negri 2000, p. 23.
18   Negri 2003c, p. 188.
19   Negri 2005a, p. 183; see also Chapter 10 in this volume.
20   Hardt and Negri 2002, p. 196.

But if power 'is always domination with the common, that is, within the biopolitical common', and 'in the biopolitical, the name of politics understood as command is dispelled',[21] how are we to understand the unmediated antagonism which is supposed to define our biopolitical age? Surely, a (bio)power that regulates life from the inside – that 'takes care' of it, micro-managing the individual and collective capacities and infirmities of its population – cannot be simply relegated to the status of transcendent command? Despite Hardt and Negri's attempt to view depict capitalist imperial power as parasitic on the constituent 'love' of the multitude, it is not clear that the supposed fusion of distinct domains into a biopolitical continuum can really permit us to isolate, within the operations of the production and reproduction of life, a collective communist subject that would not be pervaded, incited and restricted by innumerable *dispositifs* of biopolitical control. If Negri's philosophy can be best understood as the shifting, unstable attempt to de-dialecticise class struggle and immerse proletarian subjectivity into a plane of immanence, it is not certain that: (1) it can withstand the non-mediated micropolitics of biopower, with its dissolution of clearly distinguishable class subjects; (2) it can proceed on the basis of the spectral thesis of two totalities, which are 'not only opposed but also *asymmetrical,* not only asymmetrical but also *atopic* – that is, they constitute different places'.[22] Supposing that law and the state are increasingly employing biopolitical instruments, and thus governing life 'from within', in what sense can the life of the multitude ever *separate* itself from the insidious control of forms of power that eschew classical mediation? It is not impertinent to ask, for example, if the destruction of the public/private barrier, lauded by Negri, is not actually in the first instance a repressive and exploitative tool, rather than an augur of red dawns to come.

Should we then follow Rabinow and Rose's advice and disregard Hardt and Negri's use of biopower as 'encompassing, totalising', 'a superficial description of certain aspects of our present, framed within the kind of towering worldview that other theorists of postmodernity have proclaimed a thing of the past'?[23] The authors of *Empire* are hardly apologetic about their penchant for grand ontological narratives. Where Rabinow and Rose wish further to refine the analytical purchase of biopolitics on the present via notions such as 'risk politics' and 'molecular politics',[24] investigating the modalities of subjectivation that

---

21   Negri 2003c, pp. 214, 256.
22   Hardt and Negri 2002, p. 197.
23   Rabinow and Rose 2003, pp. 5, 6.
24   Rose 2001, p. 1.

accompany the new genetic medicine,[25] Hardt and Negri emphatically declare that the context of any analysis 'has to be the very unfolding of life itself, the process of the constitution of the world, of history'.[26] Is this to say that their use of terms like biopower and biopolitics is merely an illegitimate hypostasis of Foucault's nominalist methodology?

At this point, it is worthwhile delineating the steps leading to Hardt and Negri's appropriation of Foucault's concept, their 'totalisation' of biopolitics, together with the theoretical and methodological resistances that Foucault's work might present to such a totalisation. The key moves in the appropriation-transformation of Foucault's concept of biopolitics appear to be the following:

– biopolitics is subjectivised and linked to the Marxian notion of 'living labour';
– biopolitics is viewed no longer as an internal articulation of the governmental practices and rationalities of biopower, but as its antagonist;
– the periodisation of biopolitics is transformed.

The problem with criticisms such as Rabinow and Rose's is that they ignore Hardt and Negri's explicit treatments of this shift, which are revealing both concerning their own project and as an index of the distance they take from Foucault.

3   The Biopolitical Subject Of Living Labour

In *Il potere costituente* (translated into English as *Insurgencies*) and *Time for Revolution*, among many other texts, Negri has affirmed the centrality of the Marxian notion of living labour to his entire enterprise. Rather than a simple *capacity*, or the sum of all physical and intellectual attitudes existent in corporeality, disciplined for and dominated by the imperatives of capital, for Negri living labour is a veritable ontological principle of production, which can autonomise itself from capital, engaging in constant processes of self-valorisation. As he writes: 'The theme proposed by Marx is the omniexpansive creativity of living labour. Living labour constructs the world, creatively modelling, *ex novo*, the materials it touches. ... Its projection onto the world is ontological, its prostheses are ontological, its constructions are constructions of new being: the first result of this indefinite process is the construction of the subject'.[27] In this regard, Negri, consistently with his previous work, wishes to move beyond the

---

25   Rabinow and Rose 2003.
26   Hardt and Negri 2000, p. 30.
27   Negri 2002a, p. 403.

strict confines of philosophical anthropology and think, within and beyond Marx, a humanism that incorporates the lessons of anti-humanism.[28] That is why he opts for a maximal interpretation of Marx's famous statement on living labour: 'Labour is the living, form-giving fire; it is the transitoriness of things, their temporality, as their formation by living time'.[29] Incidentally, this means giving short thrift to Marx's argument, also from the *Grundrisse*, whereby the productivity of living labour only exists as incited and disciplined by capital:

> The use value which the worker has to offer the capitalist, which he has to offer to others in general, is not materialized in a product, does not exist apart from him at all, thus exists not really, but only in potentiality, as his capacity. ... As soon as it has obtained motion from capital, this use value exists as the worker's specific, productive activity; it is his *vitality* itself, directed toward a specific purpose and hence expressing itself in a specific form.[30]

The worker's 'own' vitality here appears as a result of the capital relation imposed upon him, not as a pre-existent productive drive that capital merely 'captures'.

Now, what is the role of living labour when Hardt and Negri come to their treatment of Foucault?[31] Despite Foucault's seminal contribution to a theory of social reproduction under conditions of Empire, Hardt and Negri chastise him for a 'structuralist epistemology' that sacrifices the 'dynamic of the system' and 'the ontological substance of cultural and social reproduction'.[32] Beneath the somewhat slapdash use of the epithet 'structuralist', lies the idea that Foucault, despite, or because of his attention to biopolitical 'modes of subjectification'[33] is incapable of postulating a productive ontological subject beneath historical

---

28   Hardt and Negri 2000, p. 91.
29   Marx 1973, p. 361.
30   Marx 1973, p. 267, my emphasis; Assoun 1999.
31   Despite Hardt and Negri's foregrounding of the significance, in moving beyond Foucault, of the new political theory of value and the new theory of subjectivity they draw from the legacy of *operaismo* – formulated in terms of the centrality of immaterial and affective labour to a critical appropriation of biopolitics – in this chapter I opt for philosophical abstraction and deal only with the issue of 'living labour' *per se*, eschewing a critique of its empirical figures. I think this is warranted by Hardt and Negri's description of the dimension added by workerist and post-workerist thought as lying in the examination of the 'immediately social and communicative dimension of living labour in contemporary society' (Hardt and Negri 2000, p. 29).
32   Hardt and Negri 2000, p. 28.
33   Rabinow and Rose 2003, p. 4.

transformations. Of course, the point is that this is not a passing peccadillo in Foucault's case, but rather, as indicated above, a methodological and theoretical decision. When Hardt and Negri complain that, were we to ask Foucault 'who or what drives the system, or rather, who is the *bios*, his response would be ineffable, or nothing at all',[34] they ignore the fact that Foucault's methodology rejects *in principle* the very question they wish to pose to it, especially since the idea of 'the system', for better or for worse, is precisely one of the universals that his genealogy and analytics of political reason is seeking to suspend.

Moreover, when Hardt and Negri seek to infuse the fire of living labour into Foucault's biopolitics, they bypass the thorny issue of Foucault's own relationship to this very concept. Notwithstanding Foucault's explicit, if unexplored, link between biopolitics and capitalism, cited by Hardt and Negri,[35] his stance towards labour was in the main profoundly dismissive. Already in *The Order of Things*, the Marxist analysis of labour had been depicted as introducing 'no real discontinuity' vis-à-vis the work of Ricardo, a conjunction of 'the historicity of economics', 'the finitude of human existence' and 'the fulfilment of an end to History', which bore all the limits of that episteme. Foucault's verdict was harsh: 'Marxism exists in nineteenth-century thought like a fish in water: that is, it is unable to breathe anywhere else'.[36] Only Nietzsche, for Foucault, truly broke with this nineteenth-century paradigm.

Even when – buoyed by a certain sympathy for Marxist (or more precisely, Maoist) politics which was more a product of his engagement with the after-effects of May '68 than an immanent theoretical development – Foucault sought to make his methodology complementary rather than antagonistic to Marxism, the concept of labour was still portrayed as an obstacle. Lecturing in Brazil in 1974, Foucault argued that Marxism's traditional concern with the exploitation and alienation of labour, viewed as the concrete essence of man, must be put aside if we are to recognise the artificiality of labour itself, and the fact that 'the capitalist system penetrates far more deeply into our existence' than Marxists are willing to countenance. This is because 'for there to be surplus-profit, there must be sub-power', a 'capillary, microscopic political power ... fixing men to the apparatus of production. ... The link between man and work is synthetic, political; it is a connection operated by power' – sub-power, not the 'State apparatus, nor the class in power, but the ensemble of small powers, small institutions situated at the lowest level. What I have tried

---

34   Hardt and Negri 2000, p. 28.
35   Hardt and Negri 2000, p. 27.
36   Foucault 1989, p. 285.

to do is the analysis of sub-power as the condition of possibility of surplus-profit'.[37] Though Negri has certainly tried to incorporate the 'death of man' into his reinvention of revolutionary humanism (hence the turn to authors such as Deleuze and Guattari, and his own conceptualisation of the 'man-machine'), and is attracted by the concept of biopolitics primarily in order to offset the penetration (real subsumption) of society by capital, he does not seem able to appropriate Foucault without positing, via an ontologised notion of living labour, a class subject, the multitude. What is more, even when it comes to biopolitics, Negri, unlike the Deleuze of the societies of control, or even his erstwhile collaborator Lazzarato,[38] does not wish to follow Foucault in bypassing sovereignty and the State altogether and focusing his analytical attention on the proliferation of biopolitical micro-institutions. For this, as I have alluded to above, would clash with the thesis, crucial to Negri's work from the late 1970s onwards, that the capitalist function has become parasitical, and therefore appears as pure crisis and command, in other words as *war*.[39]

---

37   Foucault 2001, p. 1490. See Toscano 2014a for further commentary on this text. Marx himself was not insensitive to the 'biopolitical' dimension inherent to the functioning of capital as a social relation. In the *Grundrisse* he writes of how capital must 'replace the production costs of the living labour capacities, in other words, must keep the work-ers alive as workers' (Marx 1973, p. 359). In an essay which, from a critical and liber-tarian Marxist standpoint, provides an acute argument for the trans-historical character of capitalist 'biopolitics', Nate Holdren – making incisive use of feminist literature – has detailed, through an analysis of 'simple circulation', the way in which the very relation-ship between labour-power as commodity, money (wages), and the means of subsistence is deeply biopolitical, and, what is more, how the continuous and violent enclosure of non-capitalist forms of life into these circuits (Marx's 'so-called primitive accumulation'), provides a truly materialist insight into a critique of 'biopolitical' economy. His conclusion is that 'the expansion of value production effected by the terms biopolitics and biopower demonstrates something about the concept and material existence of capitalism itself, something true for the entirety of the epoch of capitalist production, from its beginnings to the present' (Holdren 2011). Following this line of argument, one could even suggest, fol-lowing David Harvey, that contemporary 'biopolitical grievances' (Hardt and Negri 2004, p. 285) be rethought as anti-imperialist struggles against 'accumulation by dispossession' (Harvey 2003). For a pioneering account of these questions, see Mies 1986.

38   Lazzarato 2005. In the past few years Lazzarato's work has distanced itself from the Fou-cauldian conception of power, recovering a Leninist and revolutionary inspiration. See Lazzarato 2021.

39   Negri 2003a, p. 72. The question of the relationship between war and biopolitics is one that exceeds the remit of this essay. Yet we can see that Negri's characteristic oscillation between crisis/command, on the one hand, and regulation/production, on the other, is also present in this theme. Thus, though war, and in particular nuclear war, is presented as the emblem of capital's incapacity to sustain political mediations and of its terroristic resort to pure fear and command (Hardt and Negri 2004, p. 18; Negri 1987; Negri 2005a),

4   From Biopolitics to Class Struggle and Back Again

Now, Negri is perfectly aware that the bulk of Foucault's work on biopolitics approaches it as a technology of power dealing with a population, 'an ensemble of living beings who present particular onto/biological traits and whose life is susceptible to being controlled with the purpose of insuring, together with a better management of labour-power, an orderly growth of society'.[40] However, he discerns within the work of Foucault a tension between the delineation of biopolitics as a science and rationality of the police (*Polizeiwissenschaft*) and the attempt to generate 'a political economy of life in general'; between the treatment and maintenance of populations and the notion of a general ontological fabric that straddles the division between state and society. The question is: 'Must we think politics as an ensemble of biopowers deriving from the activity of governing or, on the contrary, to the degree that power has invested life, does life too become a power?'[41] Negri evidently wishes to bracket, as cumbersome 'structuralist' remnants, Foucault's nominalist or anti-universalist propaedeutic, lending instead the analytic of biopolitics the full ontological weight which he accords to living labour.

Biopolitics is therefore to be recast as 'a power that expresses itself from life, not only in work and language, but in bodies, affects, desires, sexuality' and this powerful 'life' is to be grasped as 'a counter-power, a force, a production of subjectivity that presents itself as a moment of de-subjection'.[42] Like Lazzarato,[43] Negri also wishes to generate a new distinction between biopolitics and biopower at a remove from Foucault's own (whereby, as noted above, biopolitics is the populational component of an overall biopower). This terminological realignment means that biopower is on the side of subjection and control, while biopolitics is rethought in terms of subjectivity

---

Negri also tries to conceptualise what Chomsky has debunked as the 'new military humanism' in terms of a legitimating, biopolitical intervention and a new, continuous 'regulating' war (Hardt and Negri 2000; Hardt and Negri 2004, p. 22). It may be noted that despite the often cosmetic proliferation of NGOs – which are 'completely immersed in the constitution of Empire; they anticipate the power of its pacifying and productive intervention of justice' (Hardt and Negri 2000, p. 36) – and sundry biopolitical entrepreneurs, contemporary military ventures, with the truly biopolitical misery they bring in their wake (looted hospitals, busted sewers, intermittent electricity ...), hardly fit the ideal type of imperial biopolitics. Important insights on all of these questions are to be found in Alliez and Lazzarato 2018.

40   Negri 2003a, p. 79.
41   Negri 2003a, p. 80.
42   Negri 2003a, p. 81.
43   Lazzarato 1997 and 2002.

and freedom. However, unlike Lazzarato in his more Foucauldian vein, Negri's gamble is that, via the ontologised concept of living labour, this conceptual shift can take place without sundering a commitment to revolutionary Marxism. Against the 'soft' biopolitics of risk, or, even worse, the use of Foucauldian discourse as a machine against welfare policies, Negri's gambit is that, via the infusion of living labour, we can realise that 'biopolitics is an extension of class struggle'.[44] This idea of biopolitics as an extension or even (following Negri's reading of real subsumption) an intensification and culmination of class struggle, requires that Foucault's concept be presented as one that may be complemented (rather than displaced or abolished) by a Marxian analysis of class and its composition. Thus, Hardt and Negri write that when Foucault 'discusses biopower he sees it only from above ... as the prerogative of sovereign power', but that 'when we look at the situation from the perspective of labour involved in biopolitical production, on the other hand, we can begin to recognize biopower from below'.[45] Now, though there are certainly profound and stimulating ambiguities in the relationship between sovereignty, on the one hand, and both biopower and biopolitics, on the other,[46] it is strange to argue that Foucauldian biopower is the 'prerogative of sovereign power' since, as we noted, Foucault's methodological starting point for the study of governmental practices was based on questions such as 'What if the sovereign didn't exist?' Moreover, Hardt and Negri's confidence in the autonomy of this biopolitical subject or 'biopower from below' seems unwarranted if we consider that the existence of capillary, micro-political forms of linking sub-power to surplus-profit constantly puts such autonomy in doubt. If labour under capitalism is the result of political *syntheses* that demand a plurality of institutions – not all (or most) of them encompassed by the sovereign or the state – and if, following Foucault, even a resistant biopower from below would engender its own insidious mechanisms of self-management and self-control, can we really be so confident that the new, biopolitical class struggle can simply be formulated as yet another righteous battle between immanence and transcendence? And what of Foucault's provocative suggestion that the concept of class *struggle* is not unrelated to the polemical and biopolitical history of racism?[47]

But what does it mean to say that biopolitics is an 'extension' of class struggle? On the one hand, it suggests that biopower, 'the tendency for sovereignty

44   Negri 2003a, p. 83.
45   Hardt and Negri 2002, p. 197; Hardt and Negri 2004, pp. 94–5.
46   Esposito 2004, p. 38.
47   Foucault 2003, pp. 83, 261; Elden 2002.

to become power over life itself'[48] is, in line with Negri's workerist allegiance to the anteriority of constituent power and the 'primacy of proletarian subjectivity',[49] a consequence of the potent struggles whereby insurgent multitudes have forced an increasingly polyvalent and micro-physical response by capitalist power. But, on the other, the very emergence of a biopolitical regime, the regime of the real subsumption of *life* (and not just society) under capital, means that 'biopolitical' class struggle bears little resemblance to its traditional forms. In effect, it is no longer the struggle between classes but the struggle of a class endowed with a seemingly limitless and protean 'composition' against *dispositifs* of power that are not unequivocally located at the heart of the bourgeoisie, or even of a transnational capitalist class. The struggle seems to take the guise of a direct fight against the 'classification' of living labour by biopower, where the former is driven by a surplus of immanence that no power can ever really exhaust or tame: 'Our innovative and creative capacities are always greater than our productive labour – productive, that is, of capital. At this point we can recognise that biopolitical production is on the one hand *immeasurable*, because it cannot be quantified in fixed units of time, and, on the other hand, always *excessive* with respect to the value that capital can extract from it because capital can never capture all of life'.[50] If living labour and biopolitics are synthesised in the concept of biopolitical production, then this concept is endowed with formidable ontological import: 'Biopolitical production is a matter of ontology in that it constantly creates new social being, a new human nature'.[51] But is the mere invocation of the excess of living labour sufficient? Can a new narrative of class struggle rest on the incessant reference to the struggle of immanence against transcendence, of creativity against capture?

The problem is once again that this dichotomisation of biopower (either into two variants, one oppressive the other insurgent, or into biopower versus biopolitics) papers over, without really subjecting them to sustained criticism, some of the key tenets of Foucault's account. To begin with, the idea that biopolitical rationality can eschew the dimension of sovereignty or state-power, and work at a micro-institutional and intra-subjective level. If that is the case, then what 'side' are these institutions and biopolitical operators on? What lends them their class marking? How are biopolitical strategies from above and from below concretely distinguished? More starkly, if production is increasingly becoming the production of social life, who or what is doing the

---

48   Hardt and Negri 2004, p. 334.
49   Callinicos 2005, p. 139; Toscano 2003.
50   Hardt and Negri 2004, p. 146.
51   Hardt and Negri 2004, p. 348.

producing? To simply argue, as Hardt and Negri sometimes seem to do, that all the creativity is on the side of living labour, is implausible on their own terms – after all, don't they themselves write that 'the various forms of power, war, politics, economics and culture in Empire become finally a mode of producing social life in its entirety'?[52] And that 'biopolitical' corporations 'produce producers'?[53] If power is productive, as our Foucault 101 would have it, then this surely counts – regardless of the protocol that may help us tell them apart – *both* for biopower from below and biopower from above, through all their strategic or tactical confrontations. A purely parasitic biopower is a contradiction in terms. Moreover, the very technologies of biopower, and even more of the 'societies of control' (two distinct paradigms that Hardt and Negri tend to blur), cannot by any means be regarded as forms of transcendental measure that merely reduce the immeasurable excess of the multitude. On the contrary, one might even think that it is the excess of biopower itself, of the myriad mechanisms of regulation and securitisation, which defies measure. If biopolitical rationalities are best understood in terms of multiplicities conducting the conduct of other multiplicities, then it is difficult to see how we could stop biopower from above from constantly bleeding into biopower from below, in an intricate topology that makes the retention of a Marxist concept of antagonism tenuous at best. Thus, if the term 'biopolitical' indicates 'that the traditional distinctions between the economic, the political, the social, and the cultural become increasingly blurred',[54] how can we affirm the clarity of the line separating the two opposing sides within a global class struggle, a struggle that would appear to take the guise of a global civil war?

5   Periodisation and Production

Foucault's relationship with history is notoriously complex. We have already cited his anti-historicist methodological provisos. We could add that, in terms of biopolitics and biopower, it is possible to discern in his work a shift from a more 'epochal' treatment of the term – namely in the first volume of *History of Sexuality*, where biopower seems to signal a shift away from sovereignty and representation – to a far more localised and methodologically cautious one, such as we find, for instance, in the treatment of the link between neoliberal rationality and the biopolitical. Negri's injection of the concepts of living labour

---

52   Hardt and Negri 2004, p. 334.
53   Hardt and Negri 2000, p. 32.
54   Hardt and Negri 2004, p. 109.

and class struggle into the paradigm of biopolitics, and its articulation with the Marxian notion of real subsumption (perhaps the touchstone of Negri's entire project), also has significant consequences for the historicity of the biopolitical. On one level, when Negri enlists Foucault to think the new mechanisms of social reproduction, biopower emerges to qualify the novelty of an imperial power which, devoid of simple localisation and detached from a purely national context, works through the social from within. Biopower would thus characterise a shift in the dominant paradigm of power.[55] On another level, however, in particular when Hardt and Negri refer to 'biopolitical production', a far more momentous point is being put forward – to wit that *only now*, in a situation of fully-fledged real subsumption, have the biopolitical traits that *always already* determined living labour come to the fore, only now have they been fully invested by an insurgent political subjectivity.

Thus, the very perspicuous argument according to which the inherently and trans-historically biopolitical character of capitalism as such trumps Hardt and Negri's impressionistic and voluntaristic thesis of a 'biopolitical stage of capitalism',[56] appears short-circuited: yes, capital has always involved a 'biopolitical' social relation, but only now, when the economic is a concentrated version of the political[57] can this relation be subjectively assumed in full. In this regard, Paolo Virno has produced a remarkable theory, beginning from the reduction of biopolitics to labour-power qua capacity, of this insertion of metahistory into the present. According to Virno, it is only today that labour-power manifests its full pertinence as a social and political concept, inasmuch as the regime of immaterial labour, by directly investing the linguistic capacities of the worker's

---

55   The link between biopower and the Deleuzian periodisation of societies of discipline and societies of control is chronologically rather tricky. If we stick to Foucault, in fact, the disciplinary training of bodies (anatomo-politics) and the statistical governance of populations (biopolitics) are two sides of one power-complex, that of *biopower*, so that the shift is simply one of emphasis within one figure of power. Hardt and Negri instead wish to stress a shift from modern disciplinarity to postmodern biopower, which manifests itself in the society of control. As they write, 'when power becomes entirely biopolitical, the whole social body is comprised by power's machine and developed in its virtuality' (Hardt and Negri 2000, p. 24). Or, in a more metaphysical vein, Negri declares that, in 'the period of the man-machine command becomes biopolitical control … control is inserted into the temporal ontology of the common, i.e. of life' (Negri 2003c, p. 256). Whilst this vocabulary of virtuality seems attractive in a temporal treatment of biopolitics (see also Lazzarato 1997), I suspect that, much as Negri's notion of productive power is not compatible with Virno's capacity or Agamben's treatment of potentiality, the notion of the virtual is far too Bergsonist to really gel with Negri's Spinozism of bodies and affects.

56   Holdren 2011.

57   Negri 2005a, p. 215.

living labour-power qua commodity, reveals the real paradox of labour-power –
which is that it is precisely when it is 'transcendental' possibility that is being
sold that the *bios* of the empirical body of the labourer, the ineliminable sub-
strate of the purchased *dynamis*, becomes crucial.[58] Labour-power is thus a
'not-now subject to supply and demand',[59] and the body is controlled and
manipulated as its simulacrum or bearer. What's more, to the very extent that
the object of capitalism is pure capacity, the body becomes the site of strategies
of measurement: 'to obtain the only good that he desires, power [*potenza*], the
capitalist offers a remuneration that corresponds to the maintenance of that
which instead has no value, life'.[60] What is the historical meaning of this predicament? According to Virno – much of whose work is devoted to this very
problem – prior to the onset of immaterial or post-Fordist capital, our capacities, which is to say our 'biological invariant' (our 'non-specialization, neoteny,
lack of a univocal environment'[61]) only came to the fore in the midst of catastrophic anomalies, social states of exception, that is, when the immunising
and compensatory pseudo-environments furnished by culture faltered or col-
lapsed. The destruction of these pseudo-environments by the icy calculations
of advanced capitalism bring our indefinite species-being, our generic essence,
ever more to the fore: 'amorphous potentiality, i.e. the chronic persistence of
infantile characteristics, does not threateningly emerge in the midst of a crisis,
but pervades every aspect of the most trite *routine*'.[62] And it is precisely in
this situation, where there is a premium on 'flexible' capacities, that norms
(or controls) proliferate and becomes ever more plastic, as well as more insidious.[63] There is a clear isomorphy here with the argument made by Marx in
the *Grundrisse* regarding both labour and money, of which Marx writes: 'this
very simple category ... makes a historic appearance in its full intensity only in
the most developed conditions of society ... when it is economically conceived
in this simplicity, "labour" is as modern a category as are the relations which
create this simple abstraction'.[64]

But, as we have already noted, Negri's focus on living labour, rather than
on labour-power per se, is based on the desire to move beyond a 'naturalist'
discourse of capacities and towards a veritable ontology of production. This,

---

58   Virno 2002b.
59   Virno 1999, p. 121.
60   Virno 1999, p. 127.
61   Virno 2003, p. 167.
62   Virno 2003, p. 170.
63   Virno 2003, p. 173.
64   Marx 1973, p. 103.

incidentally, is the reason for his criticisms of positions such as Virno's, which he regards as putting too much emphasis on the linguistic.[65] But what does the turn to living labour mean for the issue of periodisation? In a very rich philosophical reflection on the figure of the 'political monster', which begins with a critique of the 'eugenic' character of Western rationality (theory as *good breeding*), Negri has tried to depict the process whereby the monster, as a plebeian figure of commonality and power that could not be brought under the rational control of a good origin and proper breeding, moves from the margins to the system's core: 'Mobilised en masse in the wars of the nineteenth and twentieth century, the *monster* becomes the true *subject*, both *political* and *technical*, of the production of commodities and the reproduction of life. *The monster has become biopolitical*.'[66] In this same text, Negri affirms that 'power has always been power over life, biopower', and that, viewed through the lenses of antagonism, of biopolitical class struggle, 'the entirety of development has been dominated by this insubordination of life (the power [*potenza*] of life) against power [*potere*] (domination over life). ... Today however, rather than with the umpteenth revolt of *potenza* against *potere*, we are faced with common affirmation and the (probably irreversible) victory of *potenza*. The biopolitical monster is now centre stage. ... The monster has become hegemonic in biopolitics'.[67] This statement, and the startling optimism underlying it, entail a move beyond the far more sober and ambivalent estimation of biopolitics in terms of the nexus of capitalism and human capacities put forward by Virno, and the transfiguration of the biopolitical into a kind of subjective apotheosis of the multitude. A victory, nothing less.

Whereas for Virno contemporary capitalism enjoins us to hone the tools of naturalism, linguistics and philosophical anthropology, for Hardt and Negri, 'in the biopolitical world where social, economic and political production and reproduction coincide, the ontological perspective and the anthropological perspective tend to overlap'.[68] As Brett Neilson has suggested in an incisive article that seeks to untangle – through Virno's theoretical intercession – the dispute between Agamben and Negri, this biopolitical debate turns out to orbit far more around grounding philosophical categories, and in particular categories of modality, than it does around issues of social or political analysis. Whereas for Agamben Negri's constituent power remains caught, despite itself, in an Aristotelian matrix (and therefore in the biopolitics of sovereignty and con-

---

65   Hardt and Negri 2000, pp. 29, 364.
66   Negri 2001a, p. 191.
67   Negri 2001a, pp. 192–3.
68   Hardt and Negri 2000, p. 388.

stituted power) by its incapacity 'to think the existence of potentiality without any relation to Being in the form of actuality',[69] Negri views Agamben's account of bare life as an unacceptable concession to the negativity of power and a betrayal of any Spinozist politics of collective joy and desire. Virno is championed here by Neilson for combining a novel reading of Aristotle, against the grain of Agamben's own, with a radical theory of biopolitical capitalism, which, though it chimes with Hardt and Negri's concern with the labour of the multitude, is able better to identify the 'philosophical' specificity of capitalism as a mode of social organisation that 'gives the discrepancy potential/act an extraordinary pragmatic, empirical and economic importance. Capitalism *historicizes metahistory*'.[70]

Now, without going over the texts admirably dealt with by Neilson, I'd like briefly to complement his treatment by touching on a couple of texts published by Negri since, which might allow us to home in on the crux of the philosophical dispute over the biopolitical. In a critical portrait of Agamben as a figure permanently caught between an affirmative ethical moment and Heideggerian morbidity (with the latter most frequently getting the upper hand), Negri returns to their differend in terms that should by now be familiar. First of all, skating over the rather controversial nature of the distinction itself, Negri imposes upon Agamben the dichotomous grid of biopolitics and biopower that defines his own vision of the class struggle over life: 'in his definition of *biopolitics*, Agamben not only denies that this concept can be isolated, outside and beyond *biopower*, but he also denies that the biopolitical can be conceived as a dichotomous field as well. For Agamben, the logic of the biopolitical field is, at best, a field of forces that is bipolar and transitive: home and city, *zoé* and *bios*, life and politics flow from one to the other, and are situated within an ever-reversible flow. In this way the absolute neutralisation of the biopolitical is imposed'.[71] What does this neutralisation entail? For Negri, it signifies the evacuation from biopolitics of living labour conceived of as a 'productive force', Marx's form-giving fire. Negri's opposition to this suspension of production in Agamben is couched in terms of a struggle over the very meaning of ontology. Showing the extent to which any ontology stripped of a constructive, fiercely subjective dimension is for him unacceptable, a reactionary or defeatist travesty, Negri declares that 'Agamben's exclusion of the productive determination from the concept of biopolitics not only precludes a definition of biopolitics

---

69   Neilson 2004, p. 66.
70   Neilson 2005, p. 75.
71   Negri 2006b.

but even prevents us from grasping the concept of being'.[72] And he fingers the culprit: Heidegger, whose massively influential treatment of the metaphysics of subjectivity in his *Nietzsche* lectures neutralised the formation of a radical political ontology, opening up a 'funereal conception of being'[73] in which ethics is divorced from ontological construction and constitution. In Spinoza instead we have 'the only creative alternative in modernity', grounding the conception of 'productive being, of a being as indefinite singularisation, reproduction and, therefore, construction of new being'.[74] The verdict is clear: 'One cannot place oneself ambiguously between Spinoza and Heidegger'.[75] Even Agamben's ethical gestures towards a 'coming community' and 'forms-of-life' that would subtract themselves from the lethal production of bare life by sovereign power do not seem to placate Negri's Spinozist demands. Either ontology is both political and productive,[76] or we are left with the merely negative and formal shadow play of Power, the mystification of our collective social life.

6   Vitalism and Social Ontology

Having tried to trace the key passages, and manifest tensions, in Negri's appropriation of the concept of biopolitics, I would like to conclude with some reflections on its philosophical and methodological repercussions. To begin with, we can note the explicit shift from a localised analytical register to that of a global totality, albeit an 'insurgent' one. Almost all of Foucault's methodological provisos are jettisoned, in the creation of a revolutionary grand narrative (a narrative of 'victory'!), in which, as I have sought to show, 'biopolitics' not only spans all the facets and agents within the new globalised scenario, but it also immerses them into a single onto-political continuum. Though Hardt and Negri do employ the concept in a more empirical vein, for instance to identify actors (NGOs, Indymedia, the Indian protesters against the Narmada dam, etc.) who seem no longer to let themselves be placed in a definite 'sphere' – who struggle not just over labour, but over 'life itself' – its principal role is that of 'blurring' hitherto distinct domains. Even more than the pivotal notion of 'real subsumption', for Negri biopolitics signals the impossibility of maintaining any stable distinction not just between domains of analysis but between explan-

---

72   Negri 2006b.
73   Negri 2005b.
74   Negri 2006b.
75   Negri 2005b.
76   Negri 2001a, p. 201.

atory stances, and even organisations (for instance, the figure of the 'party' seems to fall with the biopolitical indistinction between the social, the political and the vital). Thus, it is in its internal role in Negri's own discourse – as a discourse that seeks to transcend disciplinary divisions, together with distinctions between discursive genres (for example, the explanatory and the prophetic) – that we should look for the actual application of the concept of biopolitics (whose 'empirical' use instead rarely transcends the itemisation and description of different ways in which life is governed). Besides its significant and instructive departures from Foucault, this totalising use of the concept brings with it a whole raft of questions. Among them is of course that of whether this 'interbreeding' of the Marxian discourse of real subsumption, class struggle and living labour, with the Foucauldian inquiry into the social reproduction of life, doesn't have the unfortunate effect of blunting both. So that, for instance, Marxian class struggle is undermined by the microphysical dispersion of biopowers, and Foucauldian biopolitics loses its *raison d'être* in passing from a specific rationality of government (with its attendant and mutating technologies) to an ontological master signifier.

In line with these concerns, some commentators have sought to tar Negri with a vitalist brush.[77] The polemical distancing of dialectics and the option for a muscular ontology of immanence, driven by a strong subjectivist element, might easily lead one to such a conclusion. Thus, for Alex Callinicos, 'central to Negri's ontology is not liberty, but Life'.[78] Leaving aside the fact that these two terms are incessantly conjoined in Negri's work – so that, I believe, he would find the one senseless without the other – the accusation of vitalism, with its inevitable anti-political, or even reactionary irrationalist overtones, does not quite hit the mark. First of all, contrary to what Callinicos intimates, Negri does not simply adopt Deleuze's ontological commitments (which, incidentally, are not straightforwardly 'vitalist'[79]). To the contrary, though Hardt and Negri (questionably) interpret Deleuze and Guattari's *A Thousand Plateaus* as 'a properly poststructuralist understanding of biopower that renews materialist thought and grounds itself solidly in the question of the production of social being', they chide them for their incapacity to really grasp the social determinations, organisations and institutions – not to mention the forms of subjectivity – which structure this production of social being. Enraptured by 'tendencies towards continuous movement and absolute flows' their treatment

77   Balibar in Neilson 2004; Callinicos 2005, p. 144.
78   Callinicos 2005, p. 121.
79   See Toscano 2006b.

of biopower is, in the last instance, 'insubstantial and impotent'.[80] Similarly, the political deficit that besets the 'materialist vitalist' lineage of Nietzsche-Bergson-Deleuze is to be found in their shared incapacity to think an ontologically innovative *decision*, since, even though they 'correctly allude to the production of resistance and to the dynamic of a becoming-multitude (of singularities)', they tend to end up with 'a mere rejoicing in the banal duration of life'.[81]

This criticism of the vitalist lineage echoes in its form Negri's quarrel with Agamben, in which he declared: 'There is no bare life in ontology, like there is no social structure without ordering, or word without signification. The universal is concrete'.[82] The 'savage ontology' of vitalism, as Foucault teaches, 'discloses not so much what gives beings their foundation as what bears them from an instant towards a precarious form and yet is already secretly sapping them from within in order to destroy them'; it is an 'ontology of the annihilation of beings'.[83] This vitalist *thanatos* is alien to Negri's democratic Spinozist vision whereby 'the political is the ontological power of a multitude of cooperating singularities'.[84] Though Negri does occasionally stray from the materialist determination of 'living labour' to speak of life 'as such', even then his position does not treat it as an independent principle[85] or a mystical force in its own right. Rather, 'life is nothing other than the production and reproduction of the set of bodies and brains'.[86] In this respect, Hardt and Negri, especially when they write about the *machinic* character of biopolitics, are far closer to Deleuze and Guattari's *Anti-Oedipus*, with its equation 'NATURE = PRODUCTION', than to Deleuze's more Bergsonist texts. We should also not ignore the profound if anomalous *humanist* impetus at the core of Hardt and Negri's work, which, unlike that of Lazzarato earlier writing,[87] is unaffected by Deleuze's calls for a philosophy of 'anorganic life'. In the end, their notion of life is invariably social, constructed, collective.

To say that the work of Hardt and Negri is not classically vitalist is not to suggest that their biopolitical recasting of the form-giving fire of living labour is beyond reproach. This is especially so when they frame their argument in

---

80   Hardt and Negri 2000, p. 28.
81   Negri 2003c, p. 251.
82   Negri 2001a, p. 193.
83   Foucault 1989, p. 303.
84   Negri 2002a, p. 411.
85   Assoun 1999.
86   Hardt and Negri 2000, p. 365.
87   Lazzarato 1997.

terms of the concept of 'generation': 'Generation is the *primum* of the biopolit-ical world of Empire. Biopower – a horizon of the hybridisation of the natural and the artificial, needs and machines, desire and the collective organisation of the economic and the social – must continually regenerate itself in order to exist. Generation is there, before all else, as basis and motor of production and reproduction'.[88] As I have suggested above, this 'always already' of generation – which, in a manner not entirely alien to a Hegelian philosophy of history, is only appearing 'now' – risks evacuating the molecular ambivalence of a biopolitics, that, at least in Foucault, had cast some doubt on the ontological anteriority of bases and motors. What's more, with its confidence in an invisible but irrevers-ible victory, the Negrian notion of biopolitics does away with the ambiguity in Marx's own treatment of the vitality of labour, set into motion, not by the impetus of its own excessive and autonomous desire, but by capital. The life of labouring bodies and brains might indeed be 'what infuses and dominates all production'.[89] Even so, and especially if we take seriously Foucault's study of the capillary and subjectifying mechanisms of biopolitical 'sub-power', it might be far too early to shout victory, and never too late to recognise that the vitality of many of these bodies and brains carries a very strong dose of heteronomy.

---

88   Hardt and Negri 2000, p. 389.
89   Hardt and Negri 2000, p. 365.

CHAPTER 13

Art against Empire

Unlike law, which acknowledges in the 'decision' determined by place and time a metaphysical category that gives it a claim to critical evaluation, a consideration of the police institution encounters nothing essential at all. Its power is formless, like its nowhere-tangible, all-pervasive, ghostly presence in the life of civilized states. And though the police may, in particulars, appear the same everywhere, it cannot finally be denied that in absolute monarchy, where they represent the power of a ruler in which legislative and executive supremacy are united, their spirit is less devastating than in democracies, where their existence, elevated by no such relation, bears witness to the greatest conceivable degeneration of violence.

BENJAMIN 1996, p. 243

∴

Toni Negri and Éric Alliez's intervention on the Second Gulf War, 'Peace and War',[1] is a dense text, teeming with allusions and ellipses, calls to arms and abrupt conceptual foreshortenings of entire politico-philosophical regimes. In this respect, it is a singular stylistic exemplar of what Deleuze and Guattari designated as the *stratigraphic* time of philosophy. In *What is Philosophy?*, they declare that: 'Philosophical time is thus a grandiose time of coexistence that does not exclude the before and after but *superimposes* them in a stratigraphic order'.[2] And yet, while never reneging on the virtuosity of the concept (as witnessed by a whole host of 'portmanteau notions': the 'Project of perpetual world war', 'the imbalance of terror', 'the common sense of the Unworldly' ...), this almost frenzied mustering of a vast intellectual archive on the part of Alliez and Negri is in no way intended as a mere show of erudition. First, the text is an intervention bound to a very definite site – that of an art exhibition in which it was literally projected. Far from designating it as a catalogue piece, this

---

1 Alliez and Negri 2003.
2 Deleuze and Guattari 1994, p. 59.

'site-specificity' accounts for both its mannerisms and its urgency. The latter is determined by a deceptively simple question: what is the artist to do today, in a situation that some have termed that of a *global civil war*? Or, in the paradoxical terms of Hardt and Negri's *Empire*, what is the place of art in the non-place of contemporary global capital and its apparatuses of control? Looking more closely, this question, which might at first appear to belong to the rich tradition of twentieth-century interrogations concerning the link between politics and aesthetics, is revealed as profoundly ontological in character and intimately driven by the constructive force of a material desire for emancipation (what the authors, somewhat provocatively, term a 'teleology of liberation'). By conceiving artistic practice as a 'Combat against War', Alliez and Negri wish to bestow shape and colour upon what they regard as the 'subject' of a radical politics: the 'multitude' as a tendency towards communism and as the present experience of a practical vitalism.[3]

But we need to take a step back. Not to acknowledge the *collaborative* nature of this text would constitute a serious omission, and this not for the simple reason that it concludes on a veritable chant bearing on the political force of a *cooperative* multitude. In effect, 'Peace and War' constitutes a distillate and synthesis (or to be more faithful, a *hybrid*) of two distinct and distinctive intellectual projects. On the one hand, we have Negri's long-standing attempt to articulate a communist ontology of living labour, joining a critical Marxism filtered through the insurrectional practice of the Italian *autonomia* movement to the analysis of capital, power and subjectivation offered by the works of Foucault and Deleuze and Guattari. On the other, Alliez's effort to draw from the resources of Deleuze's Bergsonism and Deleuze and Guattari's reflections on the percept and the brain – as well as from a strikingly original traversal of the history of philosophy through the prism of the political ontology of time[4] – a comprehensive recasting of the link between an expressionist aesthetics and a constructivist philosophy.[5] Besides their common friendships and conceptual affinities with Félix Guattari and Gilles Deleuze, Alliez and Negri share an enduring commitment to a rebirth of philosophical materialism and to what could be termed a counter-genealogy of modernity. Incidentally, it is worth noting that both authors have a rich history of such collaborations, as attested to by Alliez's work with Guattari, Isabelle Stengers and Michel Feher, amongst others, and Negri's research with Antonella Corsani, Maurizio Lazzarato, Yann-Moulier

---

3 Alliez 1998.
4 Alliez 1996 and 1999.
5 Alliez 2003.

Boutang, as well as his widely known book-length projects with Guattari (*Communists Like Us*) and Michael Hardt (*The Labour of Dionysus, Empire, Multitude, Declaration, Assembly*). Perhaps this drive to speculative cooperation has been best exemplified in their participation in the journals *Futur Antérieur* and *Multitudes*, which they have arguably turned into singular experiments with what Marx, in the 'Fragment on Machines' of his *Grundrisse*, dubbed the General Intellect: collective cognition as a subject of production.

There is a basic matrix at the heart of this counter-genealogy and of the theses put forward in 'Peace and War'. In a Marxian vein, it can be discerned in the thesis that the creative power of living labour is ontologically primary vis-à-vis its transcendent capture as operated by the measure of value in its monetary form. Succinctly: *resistance precedes power*. In a Deleuzian vein, this matrix is founded on the affirmation of a univocal, expressive and differential being – a being defined in terms of *virtual multiplicity* – over against the transcendent mechanisms of representation, classification and identity. In the political and juridical terms with which the first half of 'Peace and War' is preoccupied, the key distinction is accordingly that between *constituent* and *constitutive* power.[6] Given the dynamic antagonism between a constructive-expressive being and its domination by an extraneous measure (its homogenisation by the money-form and associated mechanisms of discipline and/or control), the pressing question is which configuration governs the antagonism between a productive force of *subjectivation* – determined as both multiple and singular – and an exploitative instance of *subjection*. Negri's work on Machiavelli,[7] Descartes,[8] and, above all, Spinoza,[9] is aimed at articulating this matrix in the shape of the struggle between the two names of power: *potestas*, the constitutive moment of construction, *potentia*, the constituted moment of domination.

In light of this originary political and ontological duality, the following question arises: how does the *agon* between *potestas* and *potentia* – this intense battle between a creative power and its exploitation – concretely play itself out in the relationship between peace and war? How can an alternative genealogy of political modernity *from the point of view of the multitude* – of its desire for liberation and of its recurrent neutralisation at the hands of sovereign power – allow us to situate the stakes of action and organisation in a time of endemic belligerence, in which both the rhetoric and the *modus operandi*

---

6   Negri 2000.
7   Negri 2000.
8   Negri 1970.
9   Negri 1992.

of warfare appear as definitively *out of joint*? Alliez and Negri choose to map the matrix of antagonism onto a schematic periodisation of the ontology of war, which is inseparable *de jure* from the sequence and stratification of political regimes. At base, we have three moments: (1) the Hobbesian inception of political sovereignty, reducing an unruly *multitude* to a unitary *people*; (2) the 'classical-modern' ideal of the relationship of peace and war, in which the former functions in principle as a regulative horizon of political rationality, while the latter is the *de facto* instrument for the genesis of social cohesiveness; (3) the hypermodern (postmodern or imperial) regime of war in which it becomes a genuine *ordering power*, while 'peace' – now entirely immanent to, or a function of, war – is revealed as a motor of conflict: a demand for *security* that continually generates that capillary form of warfare that provides the only substance for the state of exception which defines our present.[10] In these three political regimes of war we witness the shift of the relationship between order, monetary circulation and figures of subjectivation. In brief, tracking the relationship between peace and war functions as a prism through which to grasp the various manners in which the sovereign instance of *potestas* has attempted to control, channel and evacuate the creativity of *potentia*. At all junctures within this schematisation, war is revealed as a crucial operator, permitting an instance of sovereign control to force its hegemony over an essentially heterogeneous multiplicity of singularities. Reducing the multitudes to a people through fear and contract; erecting a hegemonic state apparatus on the ominous background of military-industrial mobilisation; invoking the phantasm of an infinite justice in order to animate the expedience of the economic order via the ubiquity of 'police' actions: we are presented with (at least) three figures through which the movement of war quells the social peril posed by the unbound productivity of a political subject that is itself not sovereign. The latter is a subject that, in the Schmittian sense, does *not* decide on the state of exception but rather *is* the exception, precisely to the extent that it exceeds any economic or sociological measure.

Throughout, war over-determines peace, meaning that any autonomous ontological consistency accorded to the latter is purely phantasmatic. What determines our current situation, then, is not so much the disappearance of any coherent project of pacifism, as much as the fact that all strategies – whether practical or ideological – for maintaining a demarcation between the two terms have withered away, consigning us to a state of affairs in which 'everything happens as if peace and war were so tightly enmeshed that they no longer form

---

10   Agamben 2002.

anything but the two faces of a single membrane projected onto the planet'.[11] What place then for artistic experience and production in this tendential 'indistinction' between peace and war? What becomes of art when it is caught up in the global drift of powers that are neither law-creating nor law-preserving (to use Benjamin's terminology)? Or, finally, how is this single membrane to be converted into a veritable *sensorium* for a novel politics of construction and perception? In an age of perpetual warfare and control, the transgression of an identifiable order is nothing if not anachronistic, and the irony of the commodity one of those luxuries that we can ill afford. Rather than an order articulated in conventions and injunctions, we are faced with war as an 'ordering power' that functions entirely in the squalid element of what Alliez and Negri term the unworldly (*l'immonde*). If to make peace into an object of our action – or even a regulative ideal – is to blind ourselves to the ontology of the present, what are the stakes of resistance? The collapse of all regulative scenarios of pacification and legitimacy opens on to the stark juxtaposition of two varieties of immanence: the unbridled immanence of an imperial war that knows no pause or boundary versus the constructive immanence of a combative cooperative subjectivation.

Based on their political ontology of war, Alliez and Negri delineate the terrain of immanence in which the constructions of sensation and the inscriptions of things ('art as a registering and composition of forces') can present themselves as the *counter-effectuation* of the destructive nihilism borne by the very real spectre of a perpetual and ubiquitous war. It is essential, however, that art delve with all its material means and sensory tactics into this nihilism. The first figure of resistance is therefore that of an immersion into the molten heart of the spectacle of violence, aimed at obliterating the iconic and perceptual structures that conceal and delay our experience of the nihilism of the present. Only starting from such an assumption of violence by the body of the artwork and the artist, in what Alliez and Negri, following Benjamin and Agamben, refer to as a 'sphere of pure means',[12] can the artistic invention of new modes of perception and new organisations of experience take place. The unworldly must be traversed without remainder, for the sake of the generation of *possible worlds* (in line with Deleuze's definition of expressionism). The roaming automatism of capital and the senseless ubiquity of imperial warfare must not simply be disarticulated 'by way of a more "profound" cosmic immersion into the materials of sensation'[13] – these same materials must be fashioned into the very real

---

11   Alliez and Negri 2003, p. 110.
12   Alliez and Negri 2003, p. 114.
13   Ibid.

vectors and components for the construction of collective forms of existence and production subtracted from the blackmail of security and the perceptual lures of a fragile and anxious commercial peace. Alliez and Negri thus propose a deeper, more inhuman (cosmic) indistinction than the one offered by the hypermodern regime of war, thereby introducing a passage to a politics of the multitude that would be freed from any simulacrum of control and, above all, from any instance of sovereignty or *potestas*. The term *exodus* should not mislead: the absence of any political order that could regulate or articulate the violence of war and the institutions of peace means that there are no stable coordinates for antagonism. The immanence of capital and the dis-location of imperial control mean that 'being-against' is completely inseparable from the active creation of spaces in which antagonism is possible. This is what to 'take leave by constituting'[14] means. By the same token, no dialectic governs this antagonism: the generalisation of the state of exception entails that *mediation* and *transcendental legislation* are disseminated into the violence and opportunism of the imperial police. In the same way that the mantra of the day is 'We don't negotiate with terrorists', it is altogether exact to say that, given the current political and ontological conditions of antagonism, *you can't negotiate with Empire*. It is precisely this refusal of dialectics and the concomitant sober assumption of the violent ontology of the present that make Alliez and Negri's figure of the artist into both a singular variant and an emblem of that *subject of resistance* that is capable of *inventing peace*; the subject, at once larval and ubiquitous, named *multitude*. Against the indistinction of democracy and policing that Benjamin diagnosed so acutely a century ago, and which defines the neutralisation of all common avenues of political conflict and negotiation in today's states of exception, Alliez and Negri propose a wager: to mobilise all the constructive forces of an inherently collective subjectivation – from the inhuman materials of sensation to the innovative energy of cooperative cognition – in order to construct a politics of immanence that would finally be capable of neutralising the lethal violence of imperial capitalism and the false peace of parliamentary democracy, for the sake of a radical emancipation from the fetters of sovereignty. It is at this level that Alliez and Negri are no longer concerned with the interaction of politics and aesthetics as separate domains but direct our attention instead to an underlying *ontological* and *constructivist* impetus: the affirmation of a new and common world produced by antagonism in 'Exodus, Secession and the Combat Against War'.[15]

---

14   Alliez and Negri 2003, p. 115.
15   Ibid.

The Sensuous Religion of the Multitude: Aesthetics and Abstraction

> At the same time, we hear so often that the great masses must have a *sensuous religion*. Not just the great masses, the philosopher needs it too. Monotheism of reason and of the heart, polytheism of the imagination and of art, this is what we need! Here first I shall speak of an idea which, as far as I know, has never before entered anyone's mind – we must have a new mythology, this mythology however must stand in the service of the ideas, it must become a mythology of *reason*.
>
> The Oldest Systematic Programme of German Idealism (1796–97), quoted in Negri, *Fabbriche del soggetto* (1987)

• • •

> Something in Italy is keeping us all alive.
>
> SCRITTI POLITTI, 'Skank Bloc Bologna' (1978)

• •
•

The ICA, Tate Britain, the Serpentine Gallery ... In a phenomenon now so common as to almost pass unremarked, Antonio Negri and the 'tradition' or 'school' of Italian autonomist or post-workerist Marxism[1] have made their appearance in all these London venues, eliciting in some the disabused aperçu that revolutionary theory has become yet another domain to be incorporated and digested by an increasingly omnivorous curatorial practice. A more affirmative (*malgré soi*) view of art as a point of transit, rather than a terminus, of political thinking and practice was proposed by Peter Osborne, co-organiser of the 'Art and Immaterial Labour' conference at Tate Britain: 'With the decline of inde-

---

1 For a persuasive questioning of the idea of a continuum spanning workerism, post-workerism and autonomist Marxism, see Bologna 2003.

pendent Left political-intellectual cultures, the artworld remains, for all its intellectual foibles, the main place beyond the institutions of higher education where intellectual and political aspects of social and cultural practices can be debated, and where these debates can be transformed'.[2] Though it is doubtful that Negri, considerably more sanguine than Osborne about the possibilities of revolutionary change in the present, would concur, it is difficult to gain-say the idea that the presence of Negri in the 'artworld' bears some relation to said 'decline'. In what was otherwise an event in equal parts misconstrued and mistranslated – Negri's 2007 talk in Eliasson and Thorsen's temporary pavil-ion at the Serpentine, 'hosted' by Hans-Ulrich Obrist – the Italian philosopher, after having charmingly reminisced about picking peas in Omskirk in the late 1940s, in his hitchhiking days, irreverently noted that his main piece of writ-ing on art, the letters from December 1988 collected in the 1990 volume *Art and Multitude*, was principally spurred by financial concerns. In exile, without a passport or a proper work permit, art just paid better (and, one imagines, was more likely to pay under the table). Aside from the welcome break with the usual reverential etiquette with which philosophers approach the arts, fre-quently verging on kitsch, I think it is worth delving further into these writings by Negri, and their later sequels, not just for the angle they might afford on the metamorphoses of his work, but for the indications they harbour for an attempt to think through the politicising *and* depoliticising potentialities of the recent 'turn' to art by a number of prominent radical theorists, a turn, one might maliciously and parenthetically note, not entirely alien from the much-debated turn to religion. If we do accept that the issue of decline, or even defeat, has something to do with it, is there a way of approaching the politico-philosophical concern with art and aesthetics in ways that do not reduce it to a surrogate for politics, a last refuge or redoubt for radicals bereft of a hori-zon of realisation? (Or, to inject a dose of healthy vulgarity into our material-ism, in need of a paycheque: it is no secret that para-academic intellectuals, or indeed translators, often have very expedient reasons to turn to the art-world.)

Tell me how you survived the 1980s and I'll tell you who you are. This might be an apt adage for the handful of contemporary radical theorists from the 1960s levy (1950s, in Negri's case) who have garnered such attention in the last decade from younger generations learning to cope with and contest neolib-eralism. If the likes of Negri, or Badiou, or Rancière, garner deserved interest and admiration today, it is also because they succeeded in inventing concep-

---

2   Osborne 2007.

tual configurations that permitted them to traverse a period of punishing reaction that either destroyed or co-opted many of their erstwhile comrades. And, though Negri above all has been led to declare that 'the winter [of reaction and counter-revolution] is over',[3] the disparate philosophical *maquis* of the eighties might still hold some lessons for those of us who still feel the chill of the neoliberal offensive. In this respect, *Art and Multitude*, translated into French with the addition of two letters (1999, 2001) and a presentation (from 2004), is a fascinating and important document.[4] In particular, it evinces the way in which the problems of art (in a rather polysemic way, straddling aesthetics, the production of artworks and artefacts, and even a theory of the productive imagination) represent a testing-ground for a revolutionary political thought that seeks to reconstitute itself in the midst of a situation that appears, for all intents and purposes, stripped of the traditional footholds for transformative and emancipatory politics, or worse, in which the very memory of struggle has been scoured from the minds and bodies of a pulverised and disconnected multitude. Though Negri rejects the Pasolinian thesis of an 'anthropological genocide', and eschews Debord's 'integrated spectacle' as well as its demotic, post-punk counterparts – think of Mark Stewart's abrasive indictment of Thatcherism's 'Passivecation Program' – *Art and Multitude* interestingly remains, together with texts like *Labour of Job* and *Factories of the Subject*,[5] not a pessimistic book, but one in which the revolutionary imagination is steeped in the realities of suffering and despair, and even wrestles with the prospect of a political annihilation of ontology itself, in the guise of nuclear conflict.[6] 'Ethics', a term that recurs throughout Negri's writing of the eighties, beginning with the Spinoza book, written in the prisons of Rovigo, Rebibbia, Fossombrone, Palmi and Trani, is perhaps the name for this constitution of hope in the midst of social devastation and political defeat – a theme that Negri had already broached in his *Political Descartes*,[7] which dramatises the search by

---

3   *L'inverno è finito* is the title of a collection of Negri's writings edited by Giuseppe Caccia and published by Castelvecchi in 1996. The subtitle is 'Writings on the denied [*negata*] transformation (1989–1995)', book-ended by the fall of the Berlin Wall on the one hand, and the French strikes and social movements of 1995, but also suggesting the ambivalence of the supposedly finished winter, or the fragile character of the spring (Negri 1996a; English translation: Negri 2013a).

4   Quotations are from the French edition: Negri 2005c. English translation: Negri 2011b.

5   Negri 1987 and 2002d.

6   The chapter of *Fabbriche del soggetto* concerned with the radicality of this ontological negation, and the manner in which it opens up a horizon of ethical and political contingency, is significantly entitled 'No Future'.

7   Negri 2006c.

a defeated class (the bourgeoisie, in this case) for a theoretical foothold from whence action may be taken up again within a hostile world, a world where one's adversaries, for the time being, hold sway.

Before immersing ourselves in *Art and Multitude*, it is pertinent to note that Negri is no stranger to the domain of art, and to the latter's imbrications with politics. In one of the letters that make up the book, addressed to the artist Manfredo Massironi, he alludes to his collaboration with the 'Gruppo N', active in Padua between 1959 and 1964, a contributor to the Op Art movement. He speaks of their experiments with the 'orgiastic Taylorisation of art', and the practice of making art non-mysterious by demonstrating its productive character, freeing it from aesthetic or market-driven mystifications. This 'deconstruction' of art is portrayed as revealing the living, human substance of labour. In his *Du retour. Abécédaire biopolitique* (translated as *Negri on Negri*) he reminisces about his connections with the IUAV, Venice's radicalised school of architecture,[8] in the 1960s, and about his participation, alongside the communist composer Luigi Nono and the painter Emilio Vedova, in the blocking of the Venice Biennale.[9] To get a sense of the occasion, it is worth quoting the mainstream account of these events, in an article entitled 'Violence Kills Culture' published in *Time* on 28 June 1968: 'Gone altogether were the champagne glasses, the busy art politicking and the horde of wealthy patrons who normally flock to the chic pre-opening parties in the palazzos along the Grand Canal. Instead, the opening of the 34th Venice Biennale had become a social and artistic shambles. This dubious achievement was yet another milestone in this spring's overlong marathon of student rebellion'. Unsurprisingly, given the importance of Venice in Negri's political biography, the Biennale, which the *Time* article comically refers to as 'the art world's equivalent of the Olympics', also features in *Art and Multitude*. First, with reference to Rauschenberg's exhibition in 1963, identified as a moment when reality could be held fast and, echoing the Brecht of 1937, turned violently, in a demystifying manner, against the dominant powers. The Biennale then returns in the letter from 2001, a rather sombre, if stoically revolutionary, text, in which Negri narrates his astonishment at 'such a void of formal invention', such an absence of the force of beauty – 'and if the beautiful is not form, what is it?', he asks.[10] The whole experience is likened to walking through a cemetery, but also linked to a problem and preoccupation arising from Negri's thinking about the real

---

8   Negri 2004. On the relations between IUAV and workerism, see Day 2005.
9   Negri 2004, p. 168.
10   Negri 2005c, p. 7.

subsumption of society under capitalism: 'How is it possible that, in a world that has been conquered by absolute immanence, artworks can still exist?'[11]

Though Negri does not tackle it head on, a strand within his own political universe, the so-called libertarian tendency within autonomism – coming to the fore in the movement of '77, especially in Bologna with the journal A/traverso, animated by Franco Berardi (Bifo), and associated with phenomena like 'Mao-Dadaism', the 'metropolitan Indians', and free radios – could be seen as an openly negative response to this question. The so-called 'desiring' and 'creative' side of the movement was driven by a heady mix of heretical Marxism, Deleuze and Guattari, and a passion for new technologies, articulating criticisms of the Leninism of *Autonomia organizzata* that Negri would later metabolise. In the editorials of A/traverso, for instance, attention to the existentially transformative dimension of the movement, its 'ethico-aesthetic' tendency, to quote Guattari, is linked to a dissemination of militancy across the social factory. The seemingly a- or anti-political is recoded as a politicisation of the entire sphere of collective life: 'Dissolution is the innovative form of social action. ... Appropriation and liberation of the body, collective transformation of interpersonal relations are the way in which today we reconstruct a project against factory work, against any order founded on performance and exploitation'.[12] Political writing itself becomes infused with aesthetic, even demiurgic content; no longer simply the production of the right slogan and the meditation on the correct line, it becomes poetic, or even mythopoietic: 'A writing capable of giving body to the tendency, to incarnate the tendency as desire, to write into collective life the possibility of liberation'.[13] The vision forwarded by this section of the movement was one of autonomy qua secession and sedition, creation of 'other spaces' that would force systemic transformations without any dialectic of recognition. As one can read in an A/traverso article from 1975: 'Capitalism as a system of domination is destined to continue living for a very long historical period. This does not mean that communism is pushed forward in time, farther away: communism lives contemporaneously, in and against, as the organisation of social forces in liberation, as the form of their liberation. But it is not communism that resolves problems; it raises with urgency the questions that the system is forced to respond to if it wants to survive. This power as partisan autonomy, and not as a government over the whole of society, is the power that we should exercise'.[14]

---

11   Ibid.

12   '"A/traverso" (Quattro frammenti)', in Bianchi and Caminiti 2004, pp. 181, 182.

13   Ibid., p. 182.

14   Ibid., p. 185.

As the '77 movement bursts, with all of its well-known contradictions (resistance of the industrial working class and anticipation of a network society, Leninist revival and libertarian carnival), the very notion of politics is more and more put into question. 'Politics', the editors of A/traverso write, in unmistakably Deleuzo-Guattarian language, 'is reductive, it restores the dictatorship of the Signifier in the face of the desiring web of a-signifying desire'.[15] The question that arises then is of knowing whether, having broken with the classical schemas of party militancy, a 'strategy of desire' is possible, understood as 'the composition of desiring flows in a direction which is that of liberation'.[16] This strategy seems to involve a withdrawal from political representation, leaving the machinations of control and the exigencies of management to a power that becomes almost self-referential, losing its grip on society and life. The examples provided of the 'strategy of desire' are instructive, as they all concern the sensible forms of political action, and more specifically the transformations within (political) language itself. A/traverso tells of a political assembly where the juxtaposition of reformists and revolutionaries is broken by a militant who re-enacts the suicide of a young proletarian who had been confined to a madhouse; a woman gets up and shouts 'I sell wallets!', 'staging her rage at her unemployment'; someone else reads out a surrealist newspaper, only to reveal that he is quoting from *L'Unità*, the PCI daily. We can also read about this collective communist 'performance':

> Bologna, Monday 16 May 1977. The police ban the demo on piazza Verdi in the city centre and starting attacking any gatherings. Thousands of comrades in single file, one after the other. It's not a demo, but it is. It does not oppose force to force, and yet it is indestructible, if you break it at any of its points, it immediately reconstitutes itself. It is capable of bringing needs and desires to the street, of reconquering a possibility of collectivisation in a cadaverous city. It is a way to pick up the thread of an emancipatory gestural expressiveness, a way of recomposing dissent into proposal, of transforming the proposal into a subject that traverses the class. It is not a question of making ostentatious show of a force that does not exist, because the capacity for transformation does not lie in force but in the historical maturity of a society that refuses the performance of work and in the intelligence that makes this refusal possible. With all our rage and all our intelligence. But also, with all our weakness and all our melancholy.[17]

15   Ibid., p. 187.
16   Ibid.
17   Ibid., p. 191.

At the time, such a strategic and libidinal aestheticisation of politics was the object of some famous observations by Umberto Eco in the Italian press. Writing for the mass-circulation weekly *L'Espresso*, Eco, striking a note of dissent from the generally dismissive or even vitriolic attacks on the movement (among others by PCI intellectuals such as the former workerist Asor Rosa, who put forward the theory of the 'two societies', in which the rebelling youths were treated as lumpen pawns of neoliberal modernisation), tried to account for the illegibility of its political codes by the traditional establishment, both left and right. What is striking for our purposes is how Eco explicitly links the 'illegibility' of the movement to that of the avant-gardes in previous historical moments. But he goes further. The generation that has burst on the scene in 'Year 9' (with 1968 as Year 0) has both sublated and relayed an otherwise exhausted avant-garde culture.

> The new generations speak and live in their everyday practice the language (i.e. the multiplicity of languages) of the avant-garde. High culture strove to identify the trajectories of avant-garde language, looking for them where they had lost themselves in dead ends, while the practice of the subversive manipulation of languages and behaviours had abandoned limited editions, art galleries, arthouse cinemas and had cut itself a path with the music of the Beatles, the psychedelic images of *Yellow Submarine*, the songs of [Enzo] Jannacci, the dialogues of Cochi [Ponzoni] and Renato [Pozzetto], as John Cage and Stockhausen were filtered through the fusion of rock and Indian music, and the walls of the city more and more resembled a painting by Cy Twombly. ... There are now more analogies between a songwriter's lyrics and Céline, or between a discussion in an assembly of marginals and a Beckett drama, than between Beckett and Céline, on the one hand, and [mainstream artistic and theatrical events] on the other.[18]

This also explains why most of the formal and existential innovations of the movement of '77 did not have the 'artworld' as their arena, and were more likely to be found in the dark exuberance of Andrea Pazienza's comics or in the prog-jazz of Area, whose Greek-born lead singer Demetrio Stratos modelled his vocal experimentations on the Artaud of *To Have Done with the Judgment of God*.[19]

---

18   Umberto Eco, 'C'é un'altra lingua, l'italo-indiano', in Balestrini and Moroni 1997, p. 610.
19   See Mauro Trotta, 'Andrea Pazienza o le straordinarie avventure del desiderio', in Bianchi and Caminiti 2004, on the link between the Italian '77 and the Anglo-American punk '77. See also Keir, 'When Two Sevens Clash', available at: https://libcom.org/article/when-two

Why this detour, especially as the 'creative' wing of '77 – despite its frequent reference to recognisably 'Negrian' notions, above all 'the tendency' – was in many respects at odds with Negri's political and theoretical practice of the late 1970s? In part, because the aesthetic reflections that occupy Negri at the close of the eighties are difficult to understand without the experience of the repression, co-option and dissipation of the transformative *élan* crystallised in that tumultuous year. Accordingly, '77 appears as a watershed, ambiguously positioned between the 'desperate resistance of forms of sociality that emerged in the period of industrial maturity' and 'the first awareness and representation of a transformation in a "mental" direction of working activity and of the overall social cycle', sundered between 'hypermodernist projection' and 'resistance against the hypermodern nightmare', to quote Bifo.[20] '77 is also viewed, in terms not devoid of the parochial, Italo-centric rhetoric that sometimes afflicts the autonomist left, as the transition-point to a postmodern phase. Almost as a verification of the workerist thesis of the productive primacy of proletarian struggle, the counter-revolutionary, anti-political and consumerist desert of the 1980s is understood as the perverted co-option of the very possibilities – for cooperation, technological change, and a new political anthropology of desires and needs – that the movement of '77 had anticipated, in all its contradictoriness. Negri's *Art and Multitude*, alongside other texts of this period, can thus be read as an attempt to recover the constituent energies of '77 during a period of crushing defeat and of rapid, but seemingly depoliticising, cultural upheaval. I want to consider Negri's contribution in terms of three axes: periodisation, abstraction, and imagination.

The periodising drive in Negri's work has been the subject of much critical attention, being variously faulted for its partiality, abstraction, teleology and one-dimensionality. Some have even regarded it as a form of prophetism – an insight to which we shall return.[21] Negri's work is indeed identifiable with a

---

-sevens-clash-punk-and-autonomia. The movement in Bologna also registered in post-punk, as evidenced by Scritti Politti's 1978 single 'Skank Bloc Bologna' (with the 'bloc' irreverently referencing, as does their garbled name, Antonio Gramsci). See Reynolds 2005. Negri himself points to the importance of punk in *Art and Multitude*: 'Punk is a very high moment of hallucinated realist affirmation. The punk dystopia is the sensation of a possible catharsis and the certainty of the impossibility of its execution' (Negri 2005c, p. 77).

20 Franco Berardi (Bifo), *'Pour en finir avec le jugement de dieu'*, in Bianchi and Caminiti 2004, p. 173.

21 See Graeber 2008 for a critical review of the 'Art and Immaterial Labour' conference. While Graeber raises some damning, and in many respects persuasive, doubts about the category of immaterial labour, and justifiably questions the obsession with novelty in

parade of hegemonic figures of antagonistic labour-power: professional worker, mass worker, social worker, immaterial labourer, cognitive worker, multitude (with the last three or even four in many ways melding together into the 'postmodern' figure of antagonism). At its most elementary, the gesture of periodisation, as enacted by Negri, allows him to posit the 'objective' leverage-point, within the material tendencies of capitalist production (and within class composition in particular) for a revolutionary offensive that is irreducible to these determinations but which must nevertheless always, axiomatically, strike at the strongest link in the capitalist chain (a link which in the latest phase of his work appears ubiquitous, nomadically crisscrossing the 'smooth space' of Empire). This periodisation always exceeds the merely sociological or political-economic; its role is not just to capture the tendency, and thus anticipate the capitalist counter-offensive, but to recompose or even summon forth the very subject it is describing. There is nothing particularly unique in this mix of social description and political prescription – in varying guises it accompanies the whole of Marxism, and revolutionary thought more broadly. Negri's specificity lies perhaps in the emphasis that he openly places on the mythopoietic character of this operation (this sets him apart, for instance, from the dialectical form of periodisation proposed by Jameson). That Negri's approach should be well-suited to the joint periodisation of art and politics – witness both *Art and Multitude* and his intervention at the 'Art and Immaterial Labour' colloquium – is also not mysterious. We could even hazard that the upsurge of new emblematic figures, which in turn synthesise the mutations of production and the potentialities of politics, is itself modelled on a particular interpretation of artistic modernity, and even shares with some theories of modernism a certain logic of purification, acceleration or radicalisation (such that the contemporary immaterial labourer would be the most unencumbered manifestation of living labour, its embodied apotheosis). Likewise, Negri maintains a fidelity to the 'biopolitical' theme of the 'new man' that brought together artistic modernism and revolutionary politics (think of the invocation of the radical transformation of 'the coagulated *Homo sapiens*' in Trotsky's *Literature and Revolution*).[22]

---

post-workerist theory – which he links to the theme of prophecy – I think his account of periodisation over-stresses the notion that Negri's concern lies with the convergence between political and artistic vanguards, with the latter understood in terms of transgressive or subversive formal innovation. As I hope to show, the theme of abstraction is much more pertinent than those of subversion or innovation for understanding the uses of art in Negri.

22   Trotsky 1960, p. 254.

Negri's periodisation of the modern correlation of art/labour/politics, which he recognises is nothing if not schematic, is as follows: 1848–70, the rise of a worker's movement, centred on the *professional worker* and aesthetically dominated by *realism*; 1871–1914, capital's reaction against increasing contestation intensifies the division of labour, while workers develop ideologies of self-management, and *impressionism* is the dominant aesthetic for the depiction and analysis of experience; 1917–29, the victory of the Russian Revolution and the soviets heralds a period of expressionist and experimental abstraction, 'an abstraction which is a representation of and participation in the abstraction of labour';[23] 1929–68 sees this abstraction becoming methodical, but also developing into mass art and accompanying the Fordist figure of the 'mass worker'; 1968 to the present: art is politically opened onto the problems of the *social worker*, and becomes inseparable from a political aesthetics of experience.[24]

Despite what might at first appear as a kind of reductivism of relations of (artistic) production to the mode of production, and to the protagonists of the labour-process in particular, it is clear that the principle of correlation here is not that of base/superstructure, but rather stems from an expressive ontology of labour, conceived as a mobile ground wherein both art and politics find their source. As Negri declares: 'Art is a collective labour, its matter is an abstract labour'.[25] It is labour, and its form-giving fire, that expresses itself in these correlations of art and politics. As Negri writes in a text that returns to the thematics (and periodisations) of *Art and Multitude*, 'It is in labour that the world is dissolved and reconstructed – and possibly the artworld too'.[26] In other words, it is the ontological valence of art as labour that subtends the vagaries of periodisation, to the extent that art 'refers us back to this creative act that constitutes labour in its originary essence', that 'artistic work is the index of man's inexhaustible capacity to turn being into excess and to free labour'.[27] What's more, inasmuch as this ontological character of labour is understood

---

23   Negri 2005c, p. 63.
24   It is interesting to note that periodisation for Negri is not just a form of cognitive mapping but can even qualify an actual aesthetic experience. Negri notes such an epiphany of periodisation, so to speak, when he declares, in his 1999 letter, following his attendance at a performance of Pina Bausch and a production of *Hamlet* by Nekrošius: 'The transition is over' (p. 16).
25   Negri 2005c, p. 57.
26   Negri 2008a, p. 21.
27   Negri 2005c, pp. 69–70. Though art is often described by Negri in terms of excess, it is in turn exceeded by the ontological dimension of power: 'Our power is greater than our capacity to express ourselves' (p. 13).

not just as production, but as linguistic communication and cooperative creativity, art, like labour, is granted an irrepressible political positivity: 'Art is, so
to speak, always democratic – its productive mechanism is democratic in the
sense that it produces language, words, colours, sounds that cluster together
into communities, into new communities'.[28] What subtends Negri's periodisation is the positing of a dimension of creativity always in excess of the measures
of capital and command – even when capital tries to capture in distribution
what escapes it in production. This is also why staggered periodisations that
would treat art as a memory or mourning of moments of politicisation have
little attraction for Negri. In this perspective, art is not a special reservoir of
autonomy, but the manifestation of an ontology of labour, or even of 'creativity'
or 'life' *tout court*, which tends toward the indiscernibility between work, political work and the work of art. The thesis of a conflictual coexistence between
living labour and its deadening capture in the mesh of capitalist valorisation
is what leads Negri to try to track the modes through which such labour might
separate itself, constructing varieties of exodus and 'red bases' of experience
and sensation, but also what makes him so impervious to the warnings of critical theory against affirmative culture. In later writings, for instance his text on
Koolhaas's *Junkspace*, this excess of living over dead labour is explicitly linked
to the 'biopolitical power of the multitude': 'All available energies are put to
work, society is put to work: *Junkspace equals* society of work. In this exploited
totality, in this injunction to labour, there lives an intransitive freedom, irreducible to the control that seeks to ply it'.[29]

But periodisation is inextricable from a gamble on the present, from an
estimation of the affordances that action may find in the phase or the conjuncture. Negri's periodisation is no different in this regard, and the key date,
unsurprisingly, is '68. It is at this point that the upsurge of abstraction that Negri
had associated with the period between the Wall Street crash and the events of
May, switches into something else. As he notes in 'Metamorphoses', the 1929–
68 period is one

> in which abstraction and production are intertwined: the abstraction
> of the current mode of production and the representation of possible
> worlds; the abstraction of the image and the use of the most varied mater-
> ials; the simplification of the artistic gesture and the geometric destruc-
> turing of the real, and so on and so forth. Picasso and Klee, Duchamp and

---

28 Negri 2005c, p. 71.
29 Negri 2008b, p. 220.

Malevich, Beuys and Fontana, Rauschenberg and Christo: we recognise in them artists sharing the same creative experience. A new subject and an abstract object: a subject capable of demystifying the fetishised destiny imposed by capital.

But this period, which Negri had defined as 'analytic' – just as analytic was the practice of the Gruppo N, which he himself described as a 'Taylorisation' of art – is terminated by the events of '68, which in turn give rise to the kind of post-Leninist molecular avant-garde embodied and celebrated by Bifo and A/traverso. According to Negri, it is with '68 that a whole new set of questions opens up for contemporary art: 'How does the event arise? How can passion and the desire for transformation develop, *here and now*? How is the revolution configured? How can man be remade? How can the abstract become subject? What world does man desire and how does he desire it? What are the forms of life taken by this extreme gesture of transformation?'[30] One might note, however, that in the Italian case – given the consuming pull of political militancy and clashes with the state – the biunivocal correlation between the artistic and the political suggested by Negri's periodisation does not entirely materialise, and that it is only really with '77 that an aestheticisation of politics and the everyday, as well as a diffuse experimentalism in youth and mass culture, really comes to the fore. It is difficult to know if 'contemporary art' has much of a role to play here.

Just as Negri split the period of 'abstraction' into expressionist and analytic variants, with '29 as the watershed, so we might think, through his work, the internal periodisation of a post-68 period, with an all-consuming politicisation taking centre-stage until the mid-70s, the surging forth of 'the last avant-garde', to cite Eco, in and around '77, and the metabolising and corruption of this moment in the benighted eighties, what Negri's letters refer to as 'this tired epoch'. It is this last moment that I want to consider in more depth. For it is glancing back at the period which followed the counter-revolutionary offensive of '79 (a year bringing together the 'Volcker shock'[31] and Negri's own incarceration at the height of the Italian state's repressive onslaught), that Negri's letters of the late eighties affirm the pertinence of the category of the postmodern – a term, it should be noted, which Negri insisted on employing even when its discursive fortunes waned considerably.

---

30   Negri 2008a, p. 22.
31   Named after Federal Reserve Chairperson Paul Volcker's decision to hike up interests rates massively to curb inflation. The Fed's monetary policies instigated the 1980–2 recession and a steep increase in US unemployment.

For Negri, the postmodern – which is explicitly coded as global – marks a modernity that has detached itself from the progressive teleologies and functionalism of modernisation (though he will try to reinfuse it with the temporality of the event, it also seems to represent a spatialisation of experience, an annihilation of revolutionary time by capitalist space). But this 'abstract second nature'[32] demands to be subjectively assumed, its world of artifice and surfaces is the only 'real'. It is here – though in considerably more tentative tones than in *Empire* and later works – that the leitmotiv of the disappearance of the outside, of an inexorable immanence is broached. As Negri puts it: 'I subscribe to the postmodern to the extent that I think its experience as the truth of abstraction, the recognition of abstraction as a condition of experience'.[33] There is no alternative *from* the world, only an alternative *in* the world. The 'ontologisation' of the postmodern, the overturning of Baudrillardian hyper-reality into a field of struggle and transformation that may still be fundamentally schematised through the Trontian lens of a primacy of working-class resistance and autonomy – this is Negri's programme following the defeat and counter-revolution of the 1980s, and in many respects the clue to his further trajectory, including in the volumes written with Michael Hardt. But postmodern abstraction is first of all experienced as a desert and a defeat, as a 'a gigantic spectacle of absolute indifference',[34] and it is this dimension that explains Negri's interest in artistic labour and experimentation as resources for the reconstitution of a revolutionary terrain in the midst of defeat, one that would allow for the 'deepening of our soul in the abstract'.[35] But this is a deepening to be delineated in the harsh light of reaction, in full awareness of the defeat of the 'red decade' as a period that Negri tellingly describes as a 'hyperrealist delirium, an American surrealism: even more, even more, life and bodies could be recreated, reinvented. Resistance had become alternative. The world belonged to us'.[36] But the 'dead calm' of the eighties is the bearer of a form of abstraction where 'every collective antagonistic subject [has] definitively disappeared', to be replaced by the commodity abstraction alone, by the tautological dominion of the market – that 'great circulatory machine' which 'produces the nothing of subjectivity'.[37] It is in the midst of this rout, which for Negri seems to affect being itself, that revolutionary thinking needs to install itself, scouring the seemingly meaning-

---

32   Negri 2005c, p. 69.
33   Negri 2005c, p. 34.
34   Negri 2005c, p. 45.
35   Negri 2005c, p. 37.
36   Negri 2005c, p. 36.
37   Negri 2005c, p. 44.

less surfaces of capitalism for elements that might allow for a recomposition of antagonistic, class politics: 'The postmodern is therefore the market. We take the postmodern for what it is – a destiny of dejection – and the postmodern as its own abstract and strong limit – the only world that is possible today. ... A world of ghosts, but a true world. The difference between reactionaries and revolutionaries consists in this: the first deny the massive ontological emptiness of the world, while the second affirm it'.[38]

How then is one to confront the derealisation that marks the 1908s, gathering enough strength to reinvent the very possibility of reinvention, now that the world emphatically seems *not* to belong to 'us' (or indeed when the us itself has been disseminated, atomised, pulverised)? It is here that Negri's reflections dramatise a kind of postmodern passion, in an openly Christian sense. The language itself is unmistakable: 'We have to live and suffer the defeat of the truth, of our truth'.[39] And further: 'Here is an authentic Christian moment in our existence: to be capable of a radical break with our reality, of an abandonment and absence that put us once again in contact with the other, with the abandoned friend, with the now dissipated real – to accept the abstraction of the world, to endure its coldness, the desert of the passions'.[40] The postmodern, and its seemingly de-ontologising thrust, is to be accepted as a 'true abstraction of the real', but in order to then reconstitute the real on this desert of experience itself. Periodisation is always marked by decisions of discontinuity, but here in particular Negri wishes to signal a caesura with the succession of periods. There is no longer 'reconstruction' but only 'constitution' in this a-teleological, disorienting space. The main challenge for a resurgent constituent power is this: to take on the seemingly nihilistic, 'meaningless' abstraction of postmodernity, the disjunction of sign and meaning, the loss of any measure of value, and turn it into something other than a counter-revolutionary 'passage to powerlessness'.[41] (It is interesting here that in *Art and Multitude*, Negri praises the 'early' Baudrillard of the catastrophe of signs and the collapse of value, wishing to maintain his subversive charge and forestall the turn to paralysing calm and implosion in the French theorist's work of the 1980s.) But if abstraction – the 'real abstraction' of capitalism – is *the* horizon of postmodernity, what kind of foothold can there be for revolutionary action? As Negri puts it: 'How can we construct, or even think the event, on this abstract terrain which is the only one we frequent?'[42]

---

38 Negri 2005c, p. 48.
39 Negri 2005c, p. 37.
40 Negri 2005c, p. 38.
41 Negri 2005c, p. 42.
42 Negri 2005c, p. 88.

To paraphrase Nietzsche's notes on European nihilism, when it comes to the thematic of abstraction, it seems that Negri's design is to transmute a passive into an active postmodernism. Despite the denial of teleology, however, there is a clear operational direction to his proposal, even a method: 'Reality is shown in its abstraction, then critically emptied of meaning, and finally reconstructed according to lines of semantic reorientation'.[43] This passage is from Negri's letter to Nanni Balestrini, a crucial figure for the melding of the postwar Italian avant-garde and heretical workerist Marxism (consider in particular the books *Vogliamo Tutto* and *Blackout*, potent collages of political antagonism, or Balestrini's 1968 collaboration with Luigi Nono, *Contrappunto dialettico alla mente*, followed by Nono's own 1969 *Non consumiamo Marx*, let us not consume/use up Marx). Writing to Balestrini, Negri praises the *nouveau roman* as 'a realism of the abstract'.[44] The quandary of art in the postmodern would thus lie for Negri in the invention of an unprecedented realism, a non-representational realism, capable of rearticulating the present into something other than a system of global indifference. There are echoes here of one of Althusser's most intriguing texts, the short essay on Luigi Cremonini, which investigates the passage from 'abstract painting' to 'painting the real *abstract*', that is real relations which *qua* relations are necessarily abstract.[45] Abstraction is no longer an operation, but the very element in which politics and labour operate: 'The abstract is our nature, the abstract is the quality of our labour, the abstract is the only community in which we exist'.[46]

It is here that, despite the cautions about the impossibility of reconstruction in postmodernity, Negri acknowledges the political inspiration that may be drawn from the history of abstract art. In this respect, *Art and Multitude* contains a crucial declaration, which formulates a hermeneutic of art as a privileged domain for thinking through the politicisation of labour, the passage from cooperation to communism:

> I love art from the moment it made itself abstract – ever since, in abstraction, it showed a new quality of being, the participation of the singularities of labour in a single ensemble, which is precisely an abstract ensemble. Art has always anticipated the determinations of valorisation; it has therefore become abstract by following a real development, creating a new world through abstraction. In order to be an ontological experience,

---

43   Negri 2005c, p. 77.
44   Negri 2005c, p. 74.
45   Althusser 1995, p. 596; Toscano 2014b.
46   Negri 2005c, p. 39.

art does not need a concrete being. With the invention of the abstract, nature and the world have been entirely replaced by art. The modern is this abstraction, this participation of the labour of each singularity and its interchangeability – an abstract community.[47]

Crucially, 'abstract labour', which Marx had qualified in terms of its commensurability and homogeneity, 'socially necessary labour as calculated in exchange-value',[48] is transubstantiated into the bearer of 'singularities' that are living, but not necessarily 'concrete' (since, in this 'abstract second nature', use-value seems to have become obsolescent or residual). Abstract art (a term whose precise extension in Negri's account is difficult to pin down with precision) would thus allow us a way into thinking the political constitution of a community stripped of natural determinants, a 'monstrous' community, to use a term dear to Negri, which is born from within a fully socialised world, the world without an outside of 'real subsumption'.[49]

'Singularity' is the pivotal notion here. The overcoming or neutralisation of the postmodern – understood as the meaningless hegemony of the market – depends on the possibility of passing from an *indifferent* abstraction to a *singular* abstraction. In the letter addressed to Giorgio Agamben, Negri insists on the possibility of thinking the escape from this hegemony, no longer in the guise of the limit or the sublime but in terms of the passage from the ideal to the singular. Here Negri seems to revive a Schellingian philosophy of art, as the 'ontological singularity of art' is envisaged in terms of 'a Platonic idea that constructs itself and exhibits, through its extension into matter, an exemplar'. But, as he goes on to explain, this exemplar 'is irreducible to the idea, because it develops the singular. Art is irreducible to mediation. ... Art is both the creation and reproduction of the singular absolute'.[50] There would be much to say about these dense, and somewhat perplexing passages. What I want to underscore is the significance, which is also evident in Negri's more explicitly political writings, of this passage from ideality to singularity, this transfiguration of abstraction that displaces it from the domain of commensurability, homogeneity, and calculability and towards the idea of a composition, or 'community'

---

47 Negri 2005c, p. 33. The modern here is not simply juxtaposed or antecedent to the post-modern, insofar as the latter is, as already noted, 'the modern that has detached itself from modernisation'.

48 Marx 1990, p. 992.

49 On the monstrous in, or as, art, see Negri 2007. For a general philosophical treatment of the question of monstrosity, see Negri 2001a.

50 Negri 2005c, p. 54.

of singularities, a commonality of differences devoid of a common measure. It is on these grounds that Negri declares that 'art is the anti-market to the extent that it opposes the multitude of singularity to uniqueness reduced to a price'.[51] In a manner that is not really spelled out by *Art and Multitude*, art would thus hint towards the possibility of *another abstraction*: 'Abstract painting is a parable for the ever-renewed pursuit of being, the void and power. ... Art is the hieroglyph of power [*puissance*]'.[52] As Negri's work developed after his original letters on art, this emphasis on the composition of singularities into an abstract community, a multitude, grew ever more insistent.

While the motif of a communism that wouldn't be founded on a normative or organic commensuration of its components is a potent one – and shared, at this baseline level, by thinkers as distant as Badiou, Derrida or Nancy – what remains opaque is, if not the definition, then at least the function or physiognomy of 'singularity' as the crux of this discourse. The aversion to sundry political naturalisms and normative humanisms is not mysterious, and bears a noble and distinguished pedigree, but how is this concept of singularity not to either regenerate an inevitably mystical limit or smuggle in a political anthropology of the individual? If nature and mediation are to be equally eschewed, what is the ontological consistency of this paradoxical notion of singularity – whose very definition or specification would *ipso facto* dissipate it? And what criterion, if any, can demarcate true, affirmative and potent singularities from their simulation and circulation by the market? Just as Horkheimer and Adorno spoke of pseudo-individuality, is there not a proliferation of pseudo-singularities now, even if we accept the obsolescence of the culture industry and the passage to cognitive capitalism?[53]

But perhaps the idea of another abstraction, and of the role that art, broadly construed, plays for Negri, is best understood in terms of another dimension of his work of the 1980s: the concern with ethics. Like his friend and comrade Guattari, in *Art and Multitude* Negri is trying to present us with an 'ethico-aesthetic paradigm', albeit one that would serve as the prelude for a renascent revolutionary politics. Or rather, ethics is the name for the very activity of recomposing the bases for a radical, transformative politics. The faculty linking ethics to politics by way of aesthetics is *imagination* – a concept that bears

---

51   Negri 2005c, p. 55.

52   Negri 2005c, p. 54.

53   I think that Negri's contention that 'Adorno's model has exhausted itself', to the extent that 'indignation' at commodification and manipulation is no longer possible, underestimates the dialectical resilience of the theme of pseudo-individuality, whether it leaves us indignant or not. See Negri 2007, p. 48.

the traces, in Negri's work, of Heidegger's reading of Kant. In the midst of the panorama of postmodern indifference that Negri paints, where counter-revolutionary capitalism is like an arid desert scored by rocky ranges, 'we move on these planes looking for impossible ruptures'. Imagination is the power that traverses the seeming void of market abstraction 'in order to determine an event of rupture'.[54] Imagination is what strives to turn the meaninglessness of capitalism into something 'monstrous', a 'cosmic palpitation'.[55] What is striking about these texts is that, though they never really abandon the methods of tendency and class composition that innervate Negri's mature work, they display in such a stark and extreme manner the seeming chasm between the inanity of the market, on the one hand, and the unlikely upsurge of an antagonistic alternative, on the other. At times, as in the letter to Agamben, this is put starkly: the 'lightning-flash of liberation', writes Negri, is not given 'dialectically, but mystically'.[56]

This non-dialectical attempt of the imagination to conjure the event and break the spell of global indifference, making contact with the 'materiality of the true',[57] pervades Negri's letters, and anticipates the formulations of books like *Kairòs, Alma Venus, Multitudo*. Another text from the 1980s, *Fabbriche del soggetto*, further excavates this question of ethics, revealing the importance of the inaugural and revolutionary insights of German idealism for the Negri of this period. In the midst of an epoch where the only available meaning is reduced to a kind of empty tautology, where the vanishing of measure also heralds the dissipation of revolutionary energies, Negri turns to the 'Oldest Systematic Programme of German Idealism', decreeing that the only way out of the seemingly inescapable horizon of a terminal defeat lies in 'the attempt to identify what today could be a new mythology of reason, of freedom, a transcendental aesthetic that would not be trapped in the nets of an extorted mediation'.[58] Once again, ethics, understood as the practice of communism here and now ('communism comes first', writes Negri, it is not the outcome of a transition), is articulated as the response to a postmodernity, which is painted as a nihilist evacuation of meaning in the market-driven circulation of signs: 'Indifference is the tendency. The more this world develops, the more it matures and perfects itself, the more it becomes indifferent'. In an experience that intermingles 'the globality of production, the senselessness of communication and

---

54   Negri 2005c, p. 49.
55   Negri 2005c, p. 51.
56   Negri 2005c, p. 52.
57   Negri 2005c, p. 53.
58   Negri 1987, p. 31.

the absolute contingency of action', in which the horizon of mutually assured nuclear destruction has made possible 'the destruction of being' itself, the constitution of an ethical base is for Negri the only way to begin to reconstitute experience, to give birth to a 'new transcendental aesthetic'.[59]

Later, this 'ethico-aesthetic' preamble to a resurrection of politics will be given a specifically corporeal inflection. In his letter of 1999 to Raúl Sanchez – the one polemically singled out by Alain Badiou in *Logics of Worlds* as an exemplar of 'democratic materialism' – Negri explicitly links this singularisation to corporeality, declaring that 'we postmoderns' know that the body 'is the machine in which production and art are inscribed', that abstraction has become 'the living matter (that is the content and the motor) of each of our expressions, determined and concrete. ... There where the abstract subsumed life, life has subsumed the abstract'.[60] Whereas in Deleuze singularity appears as a stringently inhuman and sub-representational notion, here it is indexed on the body, seemingly concretising an otherwise undefinable term in a phenomenological direction, but in a manner strangely entangled with the very dimension of abstraction, with 'an abstract power that becomes a prosthesis of the body'.[61] Thus, the previously vain avant-garde desire for the dissolution of aesthetics into a universal poetics of bodies or a politics of art is 'today' a mutation-in-progress. This is Negri's postmodernity: 'poetics becomes an ontological power, a tool of the becoming-concrete of the abstract'. With the postmodern, we are, according to Negri, on the edge Spinozist intellectual love, of 'a determinate appropriation of the abstract totality', as the postmodern mutates into 'singularity which imposes itself on universality, corporeality emerging as an irreducible multitude, the holder (and producer) of its own law'.[62]

The unreconciled dialectic of artistic and political autonomy, so central to the critical aesthetic theory of Adorno and his epigones, is abolished by Negri in favour of a kind of ontological self-legislation (or self-valorisation) of living labour. What was *always already* at stake (the form-giving fire of labour) *only now* attains to its full power, in labour's epochal 'passage from the massive abstraction of its value to the immaterial singularisation of its express-

---

59   Negri 1987, pp. 43, 45. See also Negri 2008a, where he also stresses the ethical moment: 'By recapitulating the productive and the ontological, the event and the common, art thus could (perhaps it simply must) give ethical meaning to this predicament, helping us to construct that multiple paradigm in which being for the other, being in the common, triumphs. ... Art defines itself as form of life, characterised by poverty at its base, and by revolutionary will at the apex of the becoming-swarm' (p. 25).

60   Negri 2005c, pp. 17–18.

61   Negri 2005c, p. 19.

62   Negri 2005c, pp. 21, 24.

ive power'.[63] As I've already noted, it is this non-dialectical transubstantiation of the postmodern, crystallised in the notion of singularity, which leaves the most questions pending in Negri's encounter with art, especially since we are seemingly bereft of criteria – other than those of a kind of poetic phenomenology of *potentia* – to discern true singularity from its mere simulacrum, and perhaps more importantly, to conceive of how the generalisation of singularity avoids collapsing into the indifference of abstraction. The queries are many, but the problem posed by Negri is certainly worthy of the attention of anyone concerned with the present fate of political aesthetics: how is a communist politics (and political aesthetics) born amid a system of real abstractions which tends towards indifference? What forms of sensation and creation can withstand capital's corrosion, and construct the autonomy of living labour, without devolving into nostalgia or furthering that self-same indifference?

There is much to contest both in the ontology and in the periodisation of labour that subtend Negri's treatment of art.[64] What I've tried to do in these reading notes to *Art and Multitude* is simply to identify what I think is their dominant theme, that of the resurrection of an emancipatory politics in the midst of postmodern abstraction. Written at a political nadir, these letters, alongside other texts from the same period, are unique in displaying the peculiar relationship of politics to art in phases of ebb or defeat. Negri's emphasis on ethics and the mythology of reason, on the need to fashion a 'sensuous religion' for a people to come, does not just reveal an important dimension of his thinking – whose prophetic or performative element has often been noted but rarely examined – it allows us, in a period that is perhaps more akin to Negri's 'winter years' than he would wish to countenance, to think through the very ambivalence that haunts the notion of an 'abstract community': at once the promise of a politics capable of confronting capital on its terrain, and the menace that collective agency will remain fettered to those forms of abstraction that capital subsumes.

---

63 Negri 2005c, p. 29. On the ontology that underlies this model of periodisation, see Chapter 12 in this volume.

64 For some very important critical remarks on the relevance of Negri's autonomism to a thinking of art after the readymade, which identify his principal limitations in the 'positivization of the negative power of labour', see Roberts 2008, pp. 210–15.

Prison, Revolution and Counter-Revolution

> The counter-revolution of the capitalist entrepreneur today can only operate strictly within the context of an increase in the coercive powers of the state. The 'new Right' ideology of laissez-faire implies as its corollary the extension of new techniques of coercive and state intervention in society at large.
>
> NEGRI 1988; quoted in Gilmore 2022, p. 245

∴

I want to reflect on the three terms that make up the title we've chosen for this celebration of Toni Negri's work, on the occasion of his ninetieth birthday. To my mind, the only fitting way to celebrate Negri's life and thought is to reflect on how it remains a vital contribution – both catalyst and compass – for thinking in and against our present, including the presence within it of fascist potentials and anti-fascist exigencies. In the process, we will also perforce address the other keyword, *communism*, present in the title of the international (or 'translocal') series to which this meeting belongs: 'The Irrepressible Lightness and Joy of Being Communist'.

I have also chosen this specific prism because of how overwhelming – given Negri's sheer productivity and range – it is to talk across the whole of his oeuvre, which begins with extremely dense and philologically accomplished works of historical and intellectual analysis on German historicism and neo-Kantian legal theory, only to enter into a Marxist orbit, particularly oriented toward questions of state theory, in the 1960s. Our thematic focus here also operates a kind of periodisation: I want to dwell on writings in the decade between 1973 – not just the year of the oil crisis, or the coup in Chile, but of the dissolution of Potere Operaio, the one party-like revolutionary political organisation to which Negri belonged – and 1983, the year of Negri's exit from prison, election to Parliament, and flight into a French exile that would last until his return to Italy, and prison, in 1997.

This is an incredibly rich period and – for reasons that reflect quite damningly on our own moment – still a very pertinent one with which to think the present, notwithstanding all the intervening mutations and variations in the relations of power and the forms of resistance. In retrospect, it is a period that we now recognise as that of the violent inception of a lasting order that ordinarily, albeit in disputed ways, goes under the heading of neoliberalism. This phase can be understood, as Michael Hardt has argued, as one marked by a deep asymmetry of powers; it is also a formidable period of counter-revolution, though one that I think requires us to rethink both what we understand by counter-revolution and indeed what we understand by revolution.

This was of course also a problem that imprisoned intellectuals of the Black liberation movement in the United States, like George Jackson and Angela Davis, were contending with in their own struggles to define exactly what fascism meant. Davis, for instance, leaned towards but also transformed a formulation that Marcuse himself had borrowed from an Italian anarchist intellectual of the 1920s, Luigi Fabbri, *preventive counter-revolution*. For Marcuse and Davis that was the figure taken by fascism after the movements of the 1960s.[1] You could say it is one of the definitions of fascism that it is possible to draw from Negri's coeval work.

But maybe I can take a step back and very briefly recall my own initial encounter with Negri and his work. I first came across the work – rather than across Negri as a public figure – in the 1990s, during my undergraduate studies in New York. Specifically, on a remainder table at the Strand Bookshop where I found a hardback copy of *The Savage Anomaly*, in Michael Hardt's translation. This was shortly after reading and being transformed or corrupted, or whatever the right term might be, by reading Gilles Deleuze's *Nietzsche and Philosophy* and deciding to abandon the vague notion that I would study social psychology. But Negri was somebody who for a child or young person in the Italy of the 1980s would certainly have been present, if in all kinds of peculiar and spectral ways, not least as a weirdly caricatured figure in national newspapers and as an object of a phobic allergy from your parents' Communist Party-voting friends. What really struck me and has stayed with me from reading *The Savage Anomaly* was the way that Negri – even just as a historian of philosophy, which is what I read him as notwithstanding a peripheral sense of his political position – linked *crisis and method*. His was a way of reading philosophy that was historical but not historicist, that managed to think crisis as something that traversed philosophical texts in their relationship to the political upheavals that criss-crossed those texts' social worlds. But crisis was also something that was generated in and by concepts themselves. All of a sudden, this seemingly smooth and imposing system of Spinoza's *Ethics* was shown to be riven by all

---

1   See Toscano 2023.

sorts of silent fractures and momentous shifts. At the time this was totally fascinating, absorbing and truly formative. It was only later that I saw how this
was really a political method of reading that stemmed from hard-won lessons
learned in the arena of struggle.

I think that this notion of a crisis method or method of crisis can also shed
light on our own nexus of revolution, counter-revolution, and prison. From the
start of Negri's teaching – which focused on what Italian academia referred
to as the 'doctrine of the state' – down to his scholarly and political work of
the 1970s, prison – in the sense of the juridical and carceral dimensions of
the repressive state apparatus, not just the physical institution itself – was
something that occupied his writing and thinking well before the 7 April 1979
indictment that led him and so many of his comrades into captivity, accused of
fomenting insurrection and numerous other crimes against law, order and the
state. Roughly in the decade before his arrest, Negri concerned himself with the
mutations in the state's modalities of criminalisation, policing and incarceration – especially from the side of what we could call a critique of the political
economy of law. It is in this period that Negri participates in important seminars on Marxism and the criminal question,[2] plays a salient role in critical
legal journals and publications,[3] and engages with some of Foucault's theses
on the origin of the prison – including in a striking response to the preface that
Foucault had written to a collection by Bruce Jackson on prisons in Arkansas.[4]

So, prison is already something integral to Negri's thinking in this time of
incipient revolution and gathering counter-revolution. An interesting avenue
into this conjuncture can be found in Negri's *Pipeline* – a text, originally published in 1983, that is part theoretical balance-sheet and part novel of letters.
Its subtitle is indeed 'letters from Rebibbia' – one of the prisons in which Negri
was held – even though he also tells us that these letters were not actually sent
and are a fictional reconstruction rather than an empirical document. There is
a remarkable passage in one of these letters that also speaks to the theme of an
asymmetry of power that Hardt has stressed as a central motif in Negri's work.
Evoking the New York City blackout of 1977, dramatised as a kind of revolutionary epiphany, Negri writes:

> Here, at this conjuncture, we can understand entirely the so-called emer-
> gency. This word, by some strange lapsus of the system, still maintains its

---

2 Negri 2012.
3 Negri 2015.
4 Negri 1982.

originary strength and purity: it is a noun conveying the idea of emergence, of the new, of innovation. Power appropriates and distorts its meaning and, out of hatred for the dynamism of transformation and for the sudden happiness of becoming, it blocks it into a concept of *state*: the state of emergency, the state of necessity. To destroy the emergence. *Rechtsputsch*. Emergency becomes exception, a Schmittian essence, for every advocate of the immobility of power and of its metaphysical nature. And then, blackout – the blackout of news and information – another magic watchword of those circumstances – power needs secrecy in order to gather the forces of antidemocratic repression – the dirty character of the state in its most basic essence cannot be allowed to be seen. *Blackout* – there's another paradoxical lapsus, before it becomes a deliberate mystification – we recall the blackout in New York, the carnival of reappropriation that broke out the preceding year – do you remember the incredible beauty of the spectacle, *cher* David? And now the blood pact between cruelty and stolidity took 'emergency' and 'blackout' as its weapons, decreed the (unjustifiable) finalities of constitutional order, and decided on a counterattack. To destroy the new movement.[5]

We can glean from this passage a very rich line of interpretation. Namely, how do we think through the intensification of the repressive and authoritarian facets of the capitalist state? What does it mean to discern its fascist potentials not as a kind of aberrant contingency – which would be the liberal standpoint – or a structural predisposition – say in Giorgio Agamben's treatises on the state of exception – or even a kind of metaphysical predisposition of the state? This would be a process of fascisation understood as a response or reaction to social movements for liberation and to the specificity of the innovations and indeed emergences (and emergencies) they bodied forth.

So what happened in the 1970s – together of course with the defeats, failures and pathologies immanent to movements themselves, including in various turns to armed struggle, themes elaborated upon in Hardt's important political panorama of the decade, *The Subversive Seventies*[6] – can be understood as a systematic effort to convert *emergence* – as in the upsurge of new subjects, of new modes of collective living, even the emergence of new experiences of and new desires for communism, what at the time Henri Lefebvre invoked as a movement of use-value and of 'users'[7] – into *emergency*, namely into emer-

5   Negri 2014, p. 197 ('Letter Eighteen: Moro').
6   Hardt 2023.
7   Lefebvre 1970.

gency laws, states of exception, counter-insurgency, counter-terrorism, law and order, strategy of tension, state terror. I think this face-off of sorts, this confrontation between emergence and emergency is one of the expressions of what I think is for Negri a broader, and we could say 'ethical' transformation in the deeper social, political and economic logic of the capitalist societies that we inhabit. In the 1970s, Negri will talk about this in terms of the increasing centrality of a logic of war, of separation, of antinomy and of asymmetry between powers, or between the state and workers' movements very widely and heretically construed.

So, there's a materially based, political-economic story to be told about the intensification of antagonism and repression. This is not just something accidental; it's not just because there's sordid or bad people at the helm of the Italian state, say. For Negri, the exacerbation of social war, and of the state's repressive drive construed as a directly economic factor, have to do with the end of any kind of coherent, rational dialectic between capital and labour, or between capitalist expansion and the intrinsic development of workers' movements and forms of proletarian life.

This working hypothesis is particularly interesting now, because I think we do find ourselves in a moment when, increasingly, even people who had arguably a more dialectical or more traditional understanding of the relationships between capital, labour and crisis will argue that we now live in a period of 'political capitalism',[8] in a period when capitalist relations appear as products of concentrated political will, where profit is a product of political and juridical decisions and we inhabit what are supposedly neo-feudal forms of appropriation and domination,[9] and so on. All these related efforts to name an excess of the political over the economic in our own moment resonate with theoretical postulates and critical acts of recognition advanced not just by Negri, but by all sorts of communist collectives and militant intellectuals in the 'Italian laboratory' of the 1970s. The hypothesis was that value-formation had come to be predicated on political command and on political violence. Already in this period, Negri was presenting so-called neoliberalism as this authoritarian and juridical imposition of a market logic – something that has been advanced by some of Negri's most dogged critics, positing that neoliberal rule is best conceived as a strategy of civil war.[10]

---

8   Seaton 2023.
9   Rikap 2023.
10   Dardot et al. 2021; Toscano 2023a.

The corollary to this argument is that – contra a certain traditional Marx-ism – law, the legal or the juridical, and indeed even the repressive, are no longer necessary-but-unproductive dimensions of capitalism. Rather, they are *directly productive*. In one of the texts from *Macchina Tempo*, Negri puts it starkly: judges make laws so capitalists can make profits. Law is not just a neces-sary mediation or frame, it is directly involved in political economy; it does not just regulate but constitutes and commands valorisation. It is highly sig-nificant that these reflections of Negri from the 1970s and early 1980s play an important role in the theoretical work of Ruth Wilson Gilmore, whose writ-ings on the shift from the welfare to the warfare state as the political-economic crisis-context for what we've come to call mass incarceration home in on this counter-revolutionary dynamic of the crisis-state. Gilmore quotes from Negri's 1980 'Crisis of the Crisis-State', written from Trani special prison:

> By transition from 'welfare' to 'warfare' state I am referring to the internal effects of the restructuration of the state machine – its effect on class rela-tions .... Development is now planned in terms of ideologies of scarcity and austerity. The transition involves not just state policies, but most par-ticularly the structure of the state, both political and administrative. The needs of the proletariat and of the poor are now rigidly subordinated to the necessities of the capitalist reproduction .... The state has an array of military and repressive means available (army, police, legal, etc.) to exclude from [the arena of bargaining or negotiating] all forces that do not offer unconditional obedience to its austerity-based material con-stitution and to the static reproduction of class relations that goes with it.[11]

Gilmore mobilises Negri's framework to grasp the mutations of the US racial state and its seeding of new fascist potentials. As she writes in an essay respond-ing to the conjuncture of the Rodney King beating and the 1992 Los Angeles uprising:

> The 'static reproduction of class relations' is a complicated enterprise. It is hardly accomplished simply from the top down, even with the might of the state's coercive apparatus. A significant proportion of the people whose relations are reproduced must concretely consent to the arrange-ment, however displaced their understanding. In the US, where real and

---

11   Negri 1988, pp. 181–2.

imagined social relations are expressed most rigidly in race/gender hier-archies, the 'reproduction' is in fact a production and its by-products, fear and fury, are in service of a 'changing same': the apartheid local of Amer-ican nationalism.[12]

It was also in the context of the theorisation of the crisis-state, during neolib-eralism's inception in the 'years of lead', that Negri himself tried to rethink the question of fascism in terms of an analysis of the transformations of capital and of its relation to the juridical, grasped through the prism of a phenomenology of class struggle. In this regard, Negri makes a unique contribution to a debate on new fascisms that had preoccupied militant intellectuals across the world in the wake of 1968.[13] In a text entitled 'Fascism and Law: An Experiment in Method' included in *Macchina Tempo*, a collection published when he was still incarcerated – a text that also tries to frame the new authoritarianism through a thorny discussion of interest and Volume 3 of *Capital* – Negri begins with a formal definition which I think remains quite generative in tackling our own political and analytical conundrums.

Negri distinguishes 'democracy' and 'fascism' in terms not of ideology but of their political relation to class struggles, while treating the liberal legality of the *Rechtstaat* as something that can cover both 'democratic' and 'fascist' orders. As he writes:

> By *democracy* I understand that (constitutional) political regime (be it liberal or socialist) in which power structurally consists in the relation between capitalist development and the development of workers' strug-gles. By *fascism* I understand instead, in an initial approximation, the registering of the break between the cycle of workers' and proletarian struggles, on the one hand, and the cycle of capitalist development, on the other, and therefore the political (state) institutionalisation of the break, from the standpoint of capital.[14]

The emergence of a new fascism is thus intimately linked to the passage from a planner-state to a crisis-state, where (internal and external) warfare comes to subsume welfare. Speaking elsewhere of his own trial and imprisonment for the crime of 'armed insurrection against the powers of the State', Negri would

---

12   Gilmore 2022, p. 158.
13   Toscano 2023b.
14   Negri 1982, p. 170.

have occasion to note the juridical continuities between Mussolini's Fascist regime and the post-war republican order.[15]

So, fascism is a recognition, a violent and consequential recognition, of the fact that there is no virtuous dialectic between workers' struggles and capitalist development, and moreover that capitalist development must be imposed through juridical and repressive means in order for valorisation to be secured and reproduced. To my mind, this remains a provocative and useful insight to work with – not because it obliges us to think that neoliberalism and fascism are indistinguishable, but because it gives us a lens through which to bring into focus a more structural and more materialist understanding, if you will, of why fascism might again be a concrete possibility. Not just due to perverse ideologies or bad personnel or malicious projects but because there is a social logic at work – what Negri at the time termed logics of separation and logics of war – and because there are impasses to the reproduction of capitalist relations that make these either overt or less overt forms of fascism impossible.

By way of conclusion, I wanted to note something else that we can draw from this moment in Negri's work – which in the Italy of the time was a violently vexed question, that of a critical distance towards a certain anti-fascist tradition and a certain anti-fascist reflex. That reflex is one that takes fascism as a political threat in the sense of a movement or an ideology that is a clear and present menace and therefore demands that one ally oneself, even against one's usual political instincts, with those who appear to be fighting against the movements and ideologies and personnel called fascists, whilst never actually addressing the underlying structures or potentials that make that fascism possible. I think this is where one could play on the famous Horkheimer quip from the late 1930s, the refusal to hear any talk of fascism from those who refuse to talk about capitalism. From the perspective of Negri's writings of the 1970s, which resonate with so much of his later work, we could say that anyone who talks to you of anti-fascism but refuses to talk about communism is producing a truncated, lopsided discourse. By way of antidote, we can read Negri's texts on communism and insurrection alongside his critical explorations of the nexus of fascism, law, and the prison. Indeed, we can read these texts retrospectively – as I've already suggested with my references to Gilmore's work – within an abolitionist horizon. So much is crystallised in a combative tract from 1980, *Communism and War*, where Negri declares:

---

15   Negri 1988, p. 122.

the proletarian constitution applies all possible procedures to guarantee individual and group happiness within mass administration [a term that Negri employs positively]. Once the proletariat has destroyed every separate figure of power, once we have witnessed the vanishing from the scene (and hopefully and if possible from the historical memory of humankind) of all special organs of capitalist oppression – not a single prison will ever rise again after the Communist destruction of the Bastille! But also no other specialized power that cannot be subordinated to collective knowledge and to the egalitarian circulation of use values.[16]

An affirmative thinking of a constituent communism is soldered here to the collective effort to delineate an intelligent countermovement to the fascistic dimensions of our capitalist present. It still indicates the right direction of travel. It is also a good antidote to those generic, consensual proposals to resist the rise of authoritarianism that share with gradualist schemes for prison reform the profound limitations of a liberal-democratic frame, one whose ultimate function is to pacify partisanship and to silence struggles, while ignoring capital's profoundly conflictual dynamics.

---

16   Negri 1980.

CHAPTER 16

A Communist Life: Toni Negri (1933–2023)

'The free person thinks least of all of death, and his wisdom is a meditation not on death but on life'. Toni Negri, who died in Paris at 90 on 16 December 2023, turned this dictum of Spinoza into an ethical and political lodestar. The conclusion of the third and final instalment (*From Genoa to Tomorrow*) of his intellectual autobiography, *Story of a Communist* features a moving speculation on aging as a rejoicing in life and a paring down of action. Negri offers the overcoming of death – a resolutely atheist and collective idea of eternity – as the substance of his thought, politics, and life. He reflects: 'And yet the possibility of overcoming the presence of death is not a dream of youth, but a practice of old age; always keeping in mind that organising life to overcome the presence of death is a duty of humanity, a duty as important as that of eliminating the exploitation and disease that are death's cause'.

Drawing perhaps on the distant memory of his own youthful Catholic activism, Negri extracts the materialist and humanist kernel of the resurrection of the flesh against all the miserable cults of finitude and being-towards-death. Negri's lifelong war on the palaces was founded on the conviction that power, *potestas*, is nourished by a hatred of bodies and fixed in the threefold fetish of patriarchy-property-sovereignty. The apparatchiks and administrators of the concept love that empty syllogism 'every man is mortal', which, Negri contends, lies at the base 'of the hatred of humanity, of that hatred that every authority, every power produces in order to affirm and consolidate itself: power's hatred for its subjects. Power is founded on the introduction of death as an everyday possibility into life – without the threat of death, the idea and practice of power could not obtain. ... Power is the continual effort to make death present for life'.

For Negri, freedom was a collective struggle against this lethal power, a fight against the fear of death, against terror, power's currency. As the communist poet Franco Fortini had it in his rendering of the *Internationale*, *chi ha compagni non morirà* (those who have comrades will not die). Beyond the scholarly mastery of the history and theory of philosophy, law and the state, beyond the interminable yet urgent search for the revolutionary subject, beyond the enormously influential phenomenologies of capital's power – from planner-state to crisis-state to Empire – at the core of Negri's life and work was the idea that philosophy is inseparable from a practice of collective liberation, or from communism understood as a 'joyous ethical and political collective passion that fights against the trinity of property, borders and capital'. This passion was something that Toni radiated. If anything marked him out among both militants and professors, it was a kind of boundless curiosity, a generous desire to hear about and learn, in detail, from anyone genuinely involved in a struggle for liberation that he always saw in the most capacious terms (or as he would say in *From Genoa to Tomorrow*: 'global, as an interweaving of the international and the intersectional'). His was not the cliché of a pacified wisdom – he could be combative, convoluted, contrary. But an irrepressible enthusiasm for liberation granted him a rare unruly youthfulness, even in old age. If wisdom can coincide with a joyful scorn for the powerful, with what Spinoza termed indignation, 'a Hate toward someone who has done evil to another', then Toni was wise indeed. That joy and that indignation saw him through a decade of captivity and 14 years of exile, untold caricature and calumny, as too many from his generation turned state's witness, literally and figuratively.

Both in print and in person, Toni had a critical reputation for optimism verging on fancy, especially when it came to his vision of the multitude – forged with his close friend and co-author Michael Hardt in a quartet of books that marked a season in the global left's intellectual life. Many late devotees of the party-form doggedly ignored that for Hardt and Negri the multitude is a new name both for organisation and for the working class beyond the assembly line. But the accusation of optimism also overlooked that Toni – unsurprisingly for someone who experienced the ravages of war as a child and the brutalities of prison as an adult – nursed a deep conviction in the need to confront the realities of spiritual and bodily suffering. His essay on the biblical Book of Job and his study of Giacomo Leopardi were both aimed at thinking through poetry's materialist ability to confront tragedy, pain, nihilism, and to make worlds from the experience of meaninglessness, failure, or defeat. While Toni's Marx was above all the one of the *Grundrisse* – of 'real subsumption' and the 'General Intellect' – there is a line from the *Paris Manuscripts* of 1844 that resonates with this materialist ethics and poetics of the body, when Marx writes that man is 'a suffering being, and because he feels his suffering, he is a passionate being'.

This passion for a common freedom, lived through suffering but oriented towards a joy defying death, is the point where communism and philosophy, liberation, and ethics, met for Negri – in his writing as in his life. It is no accident that he devoted the very last pages of his autobiography, his parting words, to the fight against the fascism that engulfed his own childhood and now threatened to return. The multitude's weakness and fear, he warns us, is once again making room for a terror that wants the apotheosis of property, patriarchy and sovereignty, that wishes all expressions of joy prohibited. 'Fascism', Negri tells us, 'rests on fear, produces fear, constitutes and constrains the people in fear'. Against fascism's watchword, 'long live death', Toni built a life of thought, comradeship, love and struggle. I can't think of a better way of honouring it than transcribing the final paragraph of his autobiography:

> In the resistance to fascism, in the effort to break its domination, in the certainty of doing so, I have written this book. All that is left, my friends, is to leave you. With a smile, with tenderness, dedicating these pages to the virtuous men and women who preceded me in the art of subversion and liberation, and to those who will follow. We have said that they are 'eternal' – may eternity embrace us.

Note on the Texts

Chapter 1 was originally published in *Think Again: Alain Badiou and the Future of Philosophy*, edited by Peter Hallward (London: Continuum, 2004), 138–149. This material is reprinted with permission from Bloomsbury Publishing Plc.

Chapter 2 was originally published as 'Marxism Expatriated: Alain Badiou's Turn', in *Critical Companion to Contemporary Marxism*, edited by Jacques Bidet and Stathis Kouvelakis (Leiden: Brill, 2007), 529–48.

Chapter 3 was originally published as 'From the State to the World? Badiou and Anti-Capitalism', *Communication & Cognition*, 37, 3 & 4 (2004): 199–224.

Chapter 4 was originally published as 'Can Violence Be Thought? Reflections on Badiou and the Possibility of (Marxist) Politics', *Identities: Journal for Politics, Gender and Culture*, 5, 1 (2006): 9–38.

Chapter 5 was originally published as 'The Bourgeois and the Islamist, or, The Other Subjects of Politics', *Cosmos and History: The Journal of Natural and Social Philosophy*, 2, 1–2 (2006): 15–38.

Chapter 6 was originally published as 'Emblems and Cuts: Philosophy In and Against History', *Symposium: Canadian Journal of Continental Philosophy*, 12, 2 (2008): 18–35.

Chapter 7 was originally published as 'Politics in Pre-Political Times', *Politics and Culture*, 3 (2014).

Chapter 8 was originally published as 'A Spectre is Not Haunting Europe', in *Badiou and the State*, edited by Dominik Finkelde (Baden-Baden: Nomos, 2017).

Chapter 9 was originally delivered as a talk at a two-day symposium on Badiou's *The Immanence of Truths*, 1–2 October 2018, Théâtre La Commune (Aubervilliers).

Chapter 10 was originally published in *The Italian Difference: Between Nihilism and Biopolitics*, edited by Lorenzo Chiesa and Alberto Toscano (Melbourne: re.press, 2009).

Chapter 11 was originally published as 'Factory, Territory, Metropolis, Empire', *Angelaki: Journal of Theoretical Humanities*, 9, 2 (2004): 197–216. Reprinted by permission of Taylor & Francis Ltd, https://www.tandfonline.com on behalf of 2004 *Angelaki: Journal of Theoretical Humanities*.

Chapter 12 was originally published as 'Always Already Only Now: Negri and the Biopolitical', in *The Philosophy of Antonio Negri, Vol. 2: Revolution in Theory*, edited by Tim Murphy and Abdul-Karim Mustapha (London: Pluto, 2007). Reproduced with permission of Pluto Press through PLSclear.

Chapter 13 was originally published as 'Art Against Empire: On Alliez and Negri's "Peace and War"', *Theory Culture & Society*, 20, 2 (2003): 103–8.

Chapter 14 was originally published as 'The Sensuous Religion of the Multitude: Art and Abstraction in Negri', *Third Text*, 23, 4 (2009): 369–82. Reprinted by permission of Taylor & Francis Ltd, https://www.tandfonline.com on behalf of 2009 *Third Text*.

Chapter 15 is the edited transcript of a talk delivered in a panel with Michael Hardt on the occasion of Negri's 90th birthday, hosted by Philip Wohlstetter and Red May Seattle, as part of 'The Irrepressible Lightness and Joy of Being Communist' – Translocal Lecture Series on the Political Philosophy of Toni Negri, at Mini Mart City Park, Seattle, 12 July 2023.

Chapter 16 was originally published in *Sidecar*, 21 December 2023, https://newleftreview.org/sidecar/posts/a-communist-life

I thank the abovementioned journals, publishers and editors for permission to republish these texts.

Bibliography

Achcar, Gilbert 2004, 'Eleven Theses on the Resurgence of Islamic Fundamentalism', in *Eastern Cauldron: Islam, Afghanistan, Palestine and Iraq in a Marxist Mirror*, London: Pluto Press.

Agamben, Giorgio 1995, *Homo Sacer. Il potere sovrano e la nuda vita*, Turin: Einaudi.

Agamben, Giorgio 2000, *Means Without End: Notes on Politics*, Minneapolis: University of Minnesota Press.

Agamben, Giorgio 2002, 'L'État d'exception', *Le Monde*, 11 December.

Alliez, Éric 1996, *Capital Times*, Vol. 1, Minneapolis: University of Minnesota Press.

Alliez, Éric 1998, 'Deleuze, vitalisme pratique', *Les Études Philosophiques*, 2: 245–50.

Alliez, Éric 1999, *Les Temps capitaux*, Tome 11, Vol. 1, Paris: Cerf.

Alliez, Éric 2003, *The Signature of the World: What is the Philosophy of Deleuze and Guattari?* London: Continuum.

Alliez, Éric and Antonio Negri 2003, 'Peace and War', *Theory, Culture & Society*, 20, 2: 109–18.

Alliez, Éric and Maurizio Lazzarato 2018, *Wars and Capital*, translated by Ames Hodges, New York: Semiotext(e).

Althusser, Louis, 1977, 'On the Twenty-Second Congress of the French Communist Party', trans. Ben Brewster, *New Left Review*, I/104 (July–August): 3–22.

Althusser, Louis, 1978, 'Il marxismo come teoria "finita"', in *Discutere lo Stato. Posizioni a confronto su una tesi*, Bari: De Donato, pp. 7–21.

Althusser, Louis, 1995, 'Cremonini, peintre de l'abstrait', in *Écrits philosophiques et politiques. Tome 11*, Paris: Stock/IMEC.

Althusser, Louis, 2006, 'Marx in His Limits', in *Philosophy of the Encounter. Later Writings, 1978–1987*, edited by Oliver Corpet and François Matheron, trans. G.M. Goshgarian, London: Verso, pp. 7–162.

Althusser, Louis, 2016, *Les Vaches noires. Interview imaginaire (le malaise du XXIIe Congrès). Ce qui ne va pas, camarades!*, edited by G.M. Goshgarian, Paris: PUF.

Arendt, Hannah 1963, *On Revolution*, London: Penguin.

Assoun, Paul-Laurent 1999, 'Vie/vitalisme', in *Dictionnaire critique du marxisme*, edited by Georges Labica and Gérard Bensussan, Paris: PUF.

Badiou, Alain 1966, 'L'autonomie du processus esthétique', *Cahiers Marxistes-Léninistes*, 12–13: 77–89.

Badiou, Alain 1967, 'Le (re)commencement du matérialisme dialectique', *Critique*, 240: 438–46 (Translated in Badiou 2012b).

Badiou, Alain 1969, *Le Concept de modèle. Introduction à une épistemologie materialiste des mathématiques*, Paris: François Maspéro.

Badiou, Alain 1975, *Théorie de la contradiction*, Paris: Seuil.

Badiou, Alain 1980, *Jean-Paul Sartre*, Paris: Potemkine.

Badiou, Alain 1982, *Théorie du sujet*, Paris: Seuil.

Badiou, Alain 1983, 'Les 4 dialecticiens français. Pascal, Rousseau, Mallarmé, Lacan', *Le Perroquet*, 22: 1/11–12.

Badiou, Alain 1984, 'La figure du (re)commencement', *Le Perroquet*, 42: 1/8–9.

Badiou, Alain 1985a, *Peut-on penser la politique?* Paris: Seuil.

Badiou, Alain 1985b, 'Robespierre, significations (à propos du livre de Jean-Philippe Domecq, *Robespierre derniers temps*)', *Le Perroquet*, 47: 1/10–11.

Badiou, Alain 1986, 'L'usine comme site événementiel', *Le Perroquet*, 62–3: 1–6. An English translation has been published in 2006, *Prelom*, 8, available at: http://www .prelomkolektiv.org/eng/08.htm.

Badiou, Alain 1987, 'À bas la société existante! (1)', *Le Perroquet*, 69: 1–3.

Badiou, Alain 1988, *L'Etre et l'événement*, Paris: Seuil.

Badiou, Alain 1990a, 'L'entretien de Bruxelles', *Les Temps Modernes*, 526: 1–26.

Badiou, Alain 1990b, 'Saisissement, dessaisie, fidélité', *Les Temps Modernes*, 531–3, 1: 14–22.

Badiou, Alain 1991a, *D'un désastre obscur (Droit, État, Politique)*, Paris: L'Aube.

Badiou, Alain 1991b, 'L'être, l'événement, la militance' (interview with Nicole-Édith Thévenin), *Futur Antérieur*, 8, available at: http://www.multitudes.net/L-etre-l-eve-nement-la-militance/.

Badiou, Alain 1992, *Conditions*, Paris: Seuil.

Badiou, Alain 1993, *L'éthique. Essai sur la conscience du mal*, Paris: Hatier.

Badiou, Alain 1996–97, *Théorie axiomatique du sujet*, unpublished seminar manuscript, available at: http://www.entretemps.asso.fr/Badiou/96-97.htm.

Badiou, Alain 1997a, *Saint Paul. La foundation de l'universalisme*, Paris: PUF.

Badiou, Alain 1997b, *Calme bloc ici-bas*, Paris: P.O.L.

Badiou, Alain 1998, *Abrégé de métapolitique*, Paris: Seuil.

Badiou, Alain 1999, *Manifesto for Philosophy*, trans. by Norman Madarasz, Albany: SUNY University Press.

Badiou, Alain 2001, *Ethics*, trans. by Peter Hallward, London: Verso.

Badiou, Alain 2002a, 'Prefazione all'edizione italiana', in *Metapolitica*, Napoli: Crono-pio.

Badiou, Alain 2002b, 'One Divides into Two', *Culture Machine*, 4, available at: http:// culturemachine.net/index.php/cm/article/view/270/255.

Badiou, Alain 2003a, *On Beckett*, edited and translated by Alberto Toscano and Nina Power, London: Clinamen Press.

Badiou, Alain 2003b, *Infinite Thought: Truth and the Return of Philosophy*, edited and translated by Oliver Feltham and Justin Clemens, London: Continuum.

Badiou, Alain 2003c, 'Beyond Formalisation – an interview', *Angelaki*, 8, 2: 111–36.

Badiou, Alain 2003d, 'The Caesura of Nihilism', paper delivered at the Society for European Philosophy, University of Essex, 10 September, unpublished manuscript.

Badiou, Alain 2004a, *Theoretical Writings*, edited and translated by Ray Brassier and Alberto Toscano, London: Continuum.

Badiou, Alain 2004b, 'Some Replies to a Demanding Friend', in *Think Again: Alain Badiou and the Future of Philosophy*, edited by Peter Hallward, London: Continuum.

Badiou, Alain 2004c, 'Las democracias están en guerra contra los pobres' (Democracies are at war against the poor), *Revista Ñ.*, available at: http://edant.clarin.com/suplementos/cultura/2004/10/23/u-854775.htm.

Badiou, Alain 2004d, 'Foucault: continuité / discontinuité', *Le célibataire. Revue de psychoanalyse*, 9.

Badiou, Alain 2005a, *Le Siècle*, Paris: Seuil.

Badiou, Alain 2005b, 'The Triumphant Restoration', translated by Alberto Toscano, *positions: east asia cultures critique*, 13, 3: 659–62.

Badiou, Alain 2005c, *Metapolitics*, translated by Jason Barker, London: Verso.

Badiou, Alain 2005d, 'Democratic Materialism and the Materialist Dialectic', translated by Alberto Toscano, *Radical Philosophy*, 130: 20–4.

Badiou, Alain 2005e, 'An Essential Philosophical Thesis: "It is Right to Rebel Against the Reactionaries"', *positions: east asia cultures critique* 13, 3: 669–77 (This is an extract from Badiou 1975).

Badiou, Alain 2005f, 'Interview with Alain Badiou', *The Asheville Global Report*, 20 April, available at: http://www.lacan.com/badash.htm.

Badiou, Alain 2006a, *Being and Event*, translated by Oliver Feltham, London: Continuum.

Badiou, Alain 2006b, *Logiques des mondes*, Paris: Seuil.

Badiou, Alain 2006c, 'Interview with Alain Badiou', *Carceraglio*, available at: http://scentedgardensfortheblind.blogspot.com/2006_10_15_scentedgardensfortheblind_archive.html#116103479719156657.

Badiou, Alain 2006d, *Polemics*, translated by Steve Corcoran, London: Verso.

Badiou, Alain 2007, *The Century*, translated by Alberto Toscano, London: Polity Press.

Badiou, Alain 2008, *Logics of Worlds (Being and Event, 2)*, translated by Alberto Toscano, London: Continuum.

Badiou, Alain 2011a, *Le réveil de l'histoire. Circonstances 6*, Paris: Lignes.

Badiou, Alain 2011b, 'Le socialisme est-il le réel dont le communisme est l'idée?', in *L'idée du communisme, II. Conférence de Berlin, 2010*, edited by Alain Badiou and Slavoj Žižek, Paris: Lignes.

Badiou, Alain 2012a, *The Rebirth of History*, translated by Gregory Elliot, London: Verso.

Badiou, Alain 2012b, *The Adventure of French Philosophy*, edited by Bruno Bosteels, London: Verso.

Badiou, Alain 2013, 'Our Contemporary Impotence', *Radical Philosophy*, 181: 43–7.

Badiou, Alain 2014a, *Images du temps présent, 2001–2004*, Paris: Fayard.

Badiou, Alain 2014b, *Parménide. L'être 1 – Figure ontologique, 1985–1986*, Paris: Fayard.

Badiou, Alain 2015a, *À la recherche du réel perdu*, Paris: Fayard.

Badiou, Alain 2015b, *Métaphysique du bonheur reel*, Paris: PUF.

Badiou, Alain 2017, *Que signifie "changer le monde"?*, Paris: Fayard.

Badiou, Alain 2018a, *Petrograd, Shanghai. Les deux révolutions du XXe siècle*, Paris: La Fabrique.

Badiou, Alain 2018b, *L'immanence des vérités. L'être et l'événement, 3*, Paris: Fayard.

Badiou, Alain 2018c, *Can Politics Be Thought? / Of an Obscure Disaster: On the End of the Truth of the State*, translated and introduced by Bruno Bosteels, Durham, NC: Duke University Press.

Badiou, Alain 2023, *Mémoires d'outre-politique (1937–1985)*, Paris: Flammarion.

Badiou, Alain and François Balmès 1976, *De l'Idéologie*, Paris: Maspero. [English translation by J.E. Morain: https://www.negationmag.com/articles/on-ideology-badiou-balmes]

Badiou, Alain and Maria Kakogianni 2015, *Entretien Platonicien*, Paris: Lignes.

Balestrini, Nanni and Primo Moroni, with Sergio Bianchi (eds.) 1997, *L'orda d'oro. 1968–1977. La grande ondata rivoluzionaria e creative, politica ed esistenziale*, 2nd edition, Milan: Feltrinelli.

Balibar, Étienne 1979, 'État, parti, transition', *Dialectiques*, 27: 81–92.

Balibar, Étienne 1991, 'Es Gibt Keinen Staat in Europa: Racism and Politics in Europe Today', *New Left Review*, 186: 5–19.

Balibar, Étienne 1992a, 'Foucault and Marx: The Question of Nominalism', in *Michel Foucault Philosopher*, edited by Timothy Armstrong, New York: Harvester.

Balibar, Étienne 1992b, *Les Frontières de la Démocratie*, Paris: La Découverte.

Balibar, Étienne 2001, 'Gewalt', in *Historisch-Kritisches Wörterbuch des Marxismus*, Band 5: Gegenöffentlichkeit bis Hegemonialapparat, edited by Wolfgang Fritz Haug, Hamburg: Argument Verlag.

Balibar, Étienne 2009, 'Reflections on Gewalt', *Historical Materialism*, 17, 1: 99–125.

Barry, Andrew, Thomas Osborne and Nicholas Rose (eds.) 1996, *Foucault and Political Reason: Liberalism, Neo-Liberalism and the Rationalities of Government*, Chicago: University of Chicago Press.

Benjamin, Walter 1996, 'Critique of Violence', in *Walter Benjamin Selected Writings, Vol. 1: 1913–1926*, edited by Marcus Bullock and Michael W. Jennings, Cambridge, MA: Harvard University Press, pp. 236–52.

Bensaïd, Daniel 2004, 'Alain Badiou and the Miracle of the Event', in *Think Again: Alain Badiou and the Future of Philosophy*, edited by Peter Hallward, London: Continuum.

Bianchi, Sergio and Lanfranco Caminiti (eds.) 2004, '"A/traverse" (Quattro frammenti)', in *Settantasette. La rivoluzione che viene*, 2nd edition, Roma: DeriveApprodi.

Bologna, Sergio 1997, 'La percezione dello spazio e del tempo nel lavoro indipendente', in *Il lavoro autonomo di seconda generazione*, edited by Sergio Bologna and Andrea Fumagalli, Milan: Feltrinelli. Also available at 'Erewhon', http://erewhon.ticonuno .it/arch/rivi/vita/bologna.htm.

Bologna, Sergio 2003, 'A Review of *Storming Heaven: Class Composition and Struggle in Italian Autonomist Marxism*', *Strategies: Journal of Theory, Culture and Politics*, 16, 2: 97–105.

Borio, Guido, Francesca Pozzi and Gigi Roggero 2004, *Futuro anteriore. Dai "Quaderni rossi" ai movimenti globali: ricchezze e limiti dell'operaismo italiano*, Rome: Derive-Approdi.

Borio, Guido, Francesca Pozzi and Gigi Roggero 2005, *Gli operaisti*, Roma: Derive-Approdi.

Bosteels, Bruno 2001, 'Alain Badiou's Theory of the Subject: The Recommencement of Dialectical Materialism? (Part I)', *Pli: The Warwick Journal of Philosophy*, 12: 200–29.

Bosteels, Bruno 2002, 'Alain Badiou's Theory of the Subject: The Recommencement of Dialectical Materialism? (Part II)', *Pli: The Warwick Journal of Philosophy*, 13: 173–208.

Bosteels, Bruno 2005a, 'Post-Maoism: Badiou and Politics', *positions: east asia cultures critique*, 13, 3: 575–634.

Bosteels, Bruno 2005b, 'The Speculative Left', *South Atlantic Quarterly*, 104, 4: 751–67.

Bosteels, Bruno 2005c, 'Can Change Be Thought? A Dialogue with Alain Badiou', in *Alain Badiou: Philosophy and Its Conditions*, edited by Gabriel Riera, Albany: SUNY Press.

Bosteels, Bruno 2011, *Badiou and Politics*, Durham, NC: Duke University Press.

Brassier, Ray 2000, 'Stellar Void or Cosmic Animal: Badiou and Deleuze on the Dice-Throw', *Pli: The Warwick Journal of Philosophy*, 10: 200–16.

Brassier, Ray 2004, 'Nihil Unbound: Remarks on Subtractive Ontology and Thinking Capitalism', *Think Again: Alain Badiou and the Future of Philosophy*, edited by Peter Hallward, London: Continuum.

Burgat, François 2003, *Face to Face with Political Islam*, London: I.B. Tauris.

Callinicos, Alex 2005, *The Resources of Critique*, London: Polity.

Cleaver, Harry 2000, *Reading Capital Politically*, 2nd edition, London: AK Press.

Cole, Juan 2003, 'Al-Qaeda's Doomsday Document and Psychological Manipulation', available at http://interlinkconsulting.com/Bonus_Info/Doomsday%20Document- -Atta's%20Letter%20and%20Al%20Qaeda--Comment%20by%20Dr.%20Juan%2 0Cole.pdf.

Collettivo Politico Metropolitano 1970, *Lotta sociale e organizzazione nella metropolis*, available on the web at 'Autonomia Proletaria': http://www.autprol.org/public/news /doc000331401011970.htm.

Corradi, Cristina 2005, *Storia dei marxismi in Italia*, Roma: Manifestolibri.

Dardot, Pierre, Haud Guéguen, Christian Laval and Pierre Sauvêtre 2021, *Le choix de la guerre civile. Une autre histoire néolibéralisme*, Lux: Montréal.

De Giorgi, Alessandro 2000, *Zero Tolleranza. Strategie e pratiche della società di controllo*, Rome: DeriveApprodi.

De Giorgi, Alessandro 2002, *Il governo dell'eccedenza. Postfordismo e controllo della moltitudine*, Verona: Ombre Corte.

Deleuze, Gilles 1990, *Pourparlers*, Paris: Minuit.

Deleuze, Gilles and Félix Guattari 1994, *What is Philosophy?* London: Verso.

Eco, Umberto 1995, 'Ur-Fascism', *The New York Review of Books*, 42, 11: 12–15.

Elden, Stuart 2002, 'The War of Races and the Constitution of the State: Foucault's *"Il faut défendre la société"* and the Politics of Calculation', *boundary 2* 29.1: 125–151.

Esposito, Roberto 2004, *Bíos. Biopolitica e filosofia*, Torini: Einaudi.

Euben, Roxanne L. 1999, *Enemies in the Mirror: Islamic Fundamentalism and the Limits of Modern Rationalism*, Princeton: Princeton University Press.

Feltrin, Lorenzo and Devi Sacchetto 2021, 'The work-technology nexus and working-class environmentalism: Workerism versus capitalist noxiousness in Italy's Long 1968', *Theory and Society* 50: 815–835.

Ferrari Bravo, Luciano 2000, *Dal post-fordismo alla globalizzazione*, Rome: Manifestolibri.

Ferrari Bravo, Luciano 2001, 'Homo Sacer. Una riflessione sul libro di Agamben', in *Dal Fordismo alla globalizzazione*, Roma: Manifestolibri.

Fischer, Sibylle 2004, *Modernity Disavowed: Haiti and the Cultures of Slavery in the Age of Revolution*, Durham, NC: Duke University Press.

Fortini, Franco 1971, 'Non si dà vera vita *se non* nella falsa', in *Contro l'industria culturale. Materiali per una strategia socialista*, Bologna: Guaraldi.

Fortunati, Leopoldina 1981, *L'arcano della riproduzione. Casalinghe, prostitute, operai e capitale*, Venezia: Marsilio Editori.

Foucault, Michel 1989, *The Order of Things*, London: Routledge.

Foucault, Michel 1994 [1972], 'Sur la justice populaire. Débat avec les maos', in *Dits et écrits*, Paris: Gallimard, pp. 340–69.

Foucault, Michel 2001, 'La vérité et les formes juridiques' (1974), in *Dits et écrits I, 1954–1975*, Paris: Gallimard.

Foucault, Michel 2003, *Society Must Be Defended*, London: Penguin.

Foucault, Michel 2004, *Naissance de la biopolitique. Cours au Collège de France, 1978–1979*, Paris: Gallimard/Seuil.

Fumagalli, Andrea, Christian Marazzi and Adelino Zanini 2002, *La moneta nell'Impero*, Verona: Ombre Corte.

Gilmore, Ruth Wilson 2022, *Abolition Geography: Essays Towards Liberation*, edited by Brenna Bhandar and Alberto Toscano, London: Verso.

Graeber, David 2008, 'The Sadness of Post-Workerism', *The Commoner*, April, available at: http://www.commoner.org.uk/?p=33.

Gramsci, Antonio 1998, *Selections from the Prison Notebooks*, London: Lawrence & Wishart.

Griffin, Robert 1993, *The Nature of Fascism*, London: Routledge.

Griffin, Robert 2003, 'The Palingenetic Core of Generic Fascist Ideology', in *Che cos'è il fascismo?* edited by Alessandro Campi, Rome: Ideazione, pp. 97–122, also available at: https://www.libraryofsocialscience.com/ideologies/docs/the-palingenetic-core-of-generic-fascist-ideology/index.html.

Guha, Ranajit 1999, *Elementary Aspects of Peasant Insurgency in Colonial India*, Durham, NC: Duke University Press.

Hacking, Ian 2002, *Historical Ontology*, Harvard: Harvard University Press.

Hallward, Peter 2003, *Badiou: A Subject to Truth*, Minnesota: Minnesota University Press.

Hallward, Peter 2005, 'The Politics of Prescription', *South Atlantic Quarterly*, 104, 4: 769–89.

Hardt, Michael 2023, *The Subversive Seventies*, Oxford: Oxford University Press.

Hardt, Michael and Antonio Negri 2000, *Empire*, Cambridge, MA: Harvard University Press.

Hardt, Michael and Antonio Negri 2002, '"Subterranean Passages in Thought": *Empire*'s Inserts', *Cultural Studies*, 16, 2: 193–212.

Hardt, Michael and Antonio Negri 2004, *Multitude: War and Democracy in the Age of Empire*, New York: Penguin.

Harootunian, Harry 2015, *Marx After Marx: History and Time in the Expansion of Capitalism*, New York: Columbia University Press.

Harvey, David 1999 [1982], *The Limits to Capital*, 2nd edition, London: Verso.

Harvey, David 2000, *Spaces of Hope*, Berkeley: University of California Press.

Harvey, David 2002, *Spaces of Capital*, London: Routledge.

Harvey, David 2003, *The New Imperialism*, Oxford: Oxford University Press.

Hobsbawm, Eric J. 1965, *Primitive Rebels: Studies in Archaic Forms of Social Movement in the 19th and 20th Centuries*, New York: W.W. Norton.

Holdren, Nate 2011, 'A Biopolitical Stage of Capitalism?' *What in the Hell ...?* blog, https://crashcourse666.wordpress.com/2011/11/26/biopolitical-capitalism-2/

Jameson, Fredric 1988, 'Marxism and Historicism (1979)', in *The Ideologies of Theory*, Vol. 2: *The Syntax of History*, Minneapolis: University of Minnesota Press.

Jameson, Fredric 1996, 'Five Theses on Actually Existing Marxism', *Monthly Review*, 47 (11): 1–10.

Jameson, Fredric 2002, *A Singular Modernity: Essay on the Ontology of the Present*, London: Verso.

Klein, Naomi 2000, *No Logo*, London: Flamingo.

Koolhaas, Rem 1994, *Delirious New York: A Retroactive Manifesto for Manhattan* [1978], New York: Monacelli.

Koselleck, Reinhart 2006, 'Crisis', *Journal of the History of Ideas*, 67, 2: 357–400.

Kouvelakis, Stathis 2004, 'Marx et sa critique de la politique. Des révolutions de 1848 à la Commune de Paris, ou le travail de la rectification', available at: http://www .europesolidaire.org/spip.php?page=spipdf&spipdf=spipdf_article&id_article=259 6&nom_fichier=ESSF_article-2596.

Kouvelakis, Stathis 2005, 'Sérialité, actualité, événement, notes sur la Critique de la raison dialectique', in *Sartre, Lukács, Althusser: des marxistes en philosophie*, edited by Stathis Kouvelakis and Vincent Charbonnier, Paris: PUF.

Krasivyj, Dan 1994, 'For the Recomposition of Social Labour', *Riff Raff*, 2, translated by Steve Wright, also available at https://libcom.org/library/recomposition-social -labour-riff-raff.

Kumar, Krishan 1995, *From Post-Industrial to Post-Modern Society*, Oxford: Blackwell.

La Boétie, Étienne de 2015, *The Politics of Obedience: The Discourse of Voluntary Servitude*, Auburn: The Mises Institute.

Laclau, Ernesto and Chantal Mouffe 1985, *Hegemony and Socialist Strategy*, London: Verso.

Lacoue-Labarthe, Philippe and Jean-Luc Nancy 1997, *Retreating the Political*, edited by Simon Sparks, London: Routledge.

Lardreau, Guy and Christian Jambet 1975, *L'Ange*, Paris: Grasset.

Lardreau, Guy and Christian Jambet 1978, *Le Monde*, Paris: Grasset.

Lawrence, Bruce (ed.) 2005, *Messages to the World: The Statements of Osama Bin Laden*, London: Verso.

Lazarus, Sylvain 1996, *Anthropologie du nom*, Paris: Seuil.

Lazarus, Sylvain 2005, 'Dans quel temps de la politique sommes nous? (éditorial)', *Le Journal Politique*, 2.

Lazzarato, Maurizio 1997, 'Per una ridefinizione del concetto di "bio-politica"', in *Lavoro immateriale. Forme di vita e produzione di soggettività*, Verona: Ombre Corte.

Lazzarato, Maurizio 2002, 'From Biopower to Biopolitics', translated by Ivan A. Ramirez, *Pli: The Warwick Journal of Philosophy*, 13: 100–11.

Lazzarato, Maurizio 2005, 'Biopolitique / bioéconomie', *Multitudes*, 22. An English translation by Arianna Bove is available at: http://www.multitudes.net/Biopolitics -Bioeconomics-a/.

Lazzarato, Maurizio 2021, *Capital Hates Everyone: Fascism or Revolution*, translated by Robert Hurley, New York: Semiotext(e).

Lebovici, Renée 1983, 'Shangaï et Gdansk', *Le Perroquet*, 29–30.

Lefebvre, Henri 1969, *The Explosion: Marxism and the French Upheaval*, translated by Alfred Ehrenfeld, New York: Monthly Review Press.

Lefebvre, Henri 1970, *Manifeste différentialiste*, Paris: Gallimard.

Lemke, Thomas 2001, ' "The Birth of Bio-politics": Michel Foucault's Lecture at the Collège de France on Neo-liberal Governmentality', *Economy and Society*, 30, 2: 190–207.

Lih, Lars T. 2007, ' "Our Position is in the Highest Degree Tragic": Bolshevik "Euphoria" in 1920', in *History and Revolution: Refuting Revisionism*, edited by Mike Haynes and Jim Wolfreys, London: Verso.

Lordon, Frédéric 2015, *Imperium. Structures et affects des corps politiques*, Paris: La Fabrique.

Lordon, Frédéric 2022, *Imperium: Structures and Affects of Political Bodies*, translated by Andy Bliss, foreword by Alberto Toscano, London and New York: Verso.

Lotringer, Sylvere and Christian Marazzi (eds.) 1980, *Autonomia: Post-Political Politics*, Semiotext(e) Interventions Series, Vol. III, No. 3, New York: Semiotext(e).

Löwy, Michael 2000, 'From Captain Swing to Pancho Villa: Instances of Peasant Resistance in the Historiography of Eric Hobsbawm', *Diogenes*, 48: 3–10.

Mallarmé, Stéphane 2007 [1897], *Divagations*, translated by Barbara Johnson, Cambridge, MA: The Belknap Press of Harvard University Press.

Mandarini, Matteo and Alberto Toscano 2006, 'Antonio Negri and the Antinomies of Bourgeois Reason', introduction to Antonio Negri, *The Political Descartes: Reason, Ideology and the Bourgeois Project*, translated by Matteo Mandarini and Alberto Toscano, London: Verso.

Mandarini, Matteo 2009, 'Beyond Nihilism: Notes Towards a Critique of Left-Heideggerianism in Italian Philosophy of the 1970s', *Cosmos and History: The Journal of Natural and Social Philosophy*, 5 (1): 37–56. Mann, Michael 2005, *Fascists*, Cambridge: Cambridge University Press.

Marramao, Giacomo 2003, *Il passaggio a occidente. Filosofia e globalizzazione*, Turin: Bollati Boringhieri.

Marx, Karl 1973, *Grundrisse*, translated by Martin Nicolaus, London: Penguin.

Marx, Karl 1990, *Capital: Volume I*, translated by Ben Fowkes, London: Penguin.

Marx, Karl 1992, *Early Writings*, translated by Rodney Livingstone and Gregor Benton, London: Penguin.

Marx, Karl 2002, *Il Capitale, Libro I, Capitolo VI Inedito*, edited by Bruno Maffi, Milan: Etas.

Marx, Karl and Frederick Engels 1989, *Collected Works, Volume 24*, London: Lawrence and Wishart.

Marx, Karl and Frederick Engels *Collected Works, Volume 45*, London: Lawrence and Wishart.

Massari, Roberto 1998, *Il terrorismo. Storia, concetti, metodi*, 3rd edition, Bolsena: Aracne.

Meillasoux, Quentin 2002, 'Nouveauté et événement', in *Alain Badiou. Penser le multiple*, edited by Charles Ramond, Paris: L'Harmattan.

Mezzadra, Sandro 2006, *Diritto di fuga. Migrazioni, cittadinanza, globalizzazione*, 2nd edition, Verona: Ombre Corte.

Mies, Maria 1986, *Patriarchy and Accumulation on a World Scale*, London: Zed.

Moghadam, Val 1987, 'Socialism or Anti-Imperialism? The Left and Revolution in Iran', *New Left Review*, 166: 5–28.

Nancy, Jean-Luc 1991, 'La Comparution', in *La Comparution (politique à venir)*, edited by Jean-Luc Nancy and Jean-Christophe Bailly, Paris: Christian Bourgois, pp. 49–100.

Negri, Antonio 1970, *Descartes Politico o della ragionevole ideologia*, Milan: Feltrinelli.

Negri, Antonio 1980, *Il comunismo e la guerra*, Milan: Feltrinelli.

Negri, Antonio 1982, *Macchina tempo. Rompicapi Liberazione Costituzione*, Milan: Feltrinelli.

Negri, Antonio 1987, *Fabbriche del Soggetto. Profili, protesi, transiti, macchine, paradossi, passaggi, souversioni, sistemi, potenze: appunti, per un dispositivo ontologico*, Livorno: Secolo XXI.

Negri, Antonio 1988, *Revolution Retrieved: Writings on Marx, Keynes, Capitalist Crisis and New Social Subjects (1967–1983)*, translated by Ed Emery and John Merrington, London: Red Notes.

Negri, Antonio 1989, *Marx Beyond Marx: Lessons on the Grundrisse*, edited by Jim Fleming, translated by Michael Ryan, Maurizio Viano and Harry Cleaver, New York: Autonomedia.

Negri, Antonio 1990, 'De la transition au pouvoir constituant', *Futur Antérieur*, 2, available at http://www.multitudes.net/De-la-transition-au-pouvoir/.

Negri, Antonio 1992, *The Savage Anomaly*, Minneapolis: University of Minnesota Press.

Negri, Antonio 1996, *L'inverno è finito. Scritti sulla trasformazione negata (1989–1995)*, edited by Giuseppe Caccia, Rome: Castelvecchi.

Negri, Antonio 2000, *Insurgencies*, Minneapolis: University of Minnesota Press.

Negri, Antonio 2001a, 'Il mostro politico. Nuda vita e potenza', in *Desiderio del mostro*, edited by Ubaldo Fadini, Antonio Negri and Charles T. Wolfe, Roma: Manifestolibri.

Negri, Antonio 2001b, 'Terreni di mezzo', *Posse*, October: 197–207.

Negri, Antonio 2002a [1992], *Il potere costituente. Saggio sulle alternative del modern*, 2nd edition, Roma: Manifestolibri.

Negri, Antonio 2002b, 'La moltitudine e la metropoli', *Posse*, October: 309–17. Also available at https://www.mail-archive.com/rekombinant@autistici.org/msg00105.html.

Negri, Antonio 2002c, 'Oltre i confini della società del controllo', *il manifesto*, 15 June.

Negri, Antonio 2002d [1990], *Il lavoro di Giobbe*, Rome: Manifestolibri.

Negri, Antonio 2003a, *Guide. Cinque lezioni su Impero e dintorni*, Milan: Raffaele Cortina.

Negri, Antonio 2003b, *L'Europa e l'Impero. Riflessioni su un processo costituente*, Rome: Manifestolibri.

Negri, Antonio 2003c, *Time for Revolution*, translated by Matteo Mandarini, London: Continuum.

Negri, Antonio 2004, *Negri on Negri: In Conversation with Anne Dufourmentelle*, London: Routledge.

Negri, Antonio 2005a [1989], *The Politics of Subversion: A Manifesto for the Twenty-First Century*, London: Polity.

Negri, Antonio 2005b, 'The Political Subject and Absolute Immanence', in *Theology and the Political: The New Debate*, edited by Creston Davis, John Millbank and Slavoj Žižek, Durham, NC: Duke University Press.

Negri, Antonio 2005c, *Art et multitude. Neuf lettres sur l'art*, Paris: Atelier/EPEL.

Negri, Antonio 2006a, *I libri del rogo*, Rome: DeriveApprodi.

Negri, Antonio 2006b, 'The Discreet Taste of the Dialectic', in *Sovereignty and Life: Essays on Giorgio Agamben*, edited by Matthew Calarco and Steve DeCaroli, Stanford: Stanford University Press.

Negri, Antonio 2006c, *The Political Descartes: Reason, Ideology and the Bourgeois Project*, translated by Matteo Mandarini and Alberto Toscano, London: Verso.

Negri, Antonio 2007, 'Art and Culture in the Age of Empire and the Time of the Multitudes', translated by Max Henninger, *SubStance*, 112, 36: 48–55.

Negri, Antonio 2008, 'Metamorphoses', translated by Alberto Toscano, *Radical Philosophy*, 149: 21–5.

Negri, Antonio 2009a, 'The Italian Difference', in *The Italian Difference: Between Nihilism and Biopolitics*, edited by Lorenzo Chiesa and Alberto Toscano, Melbourne: re.press.

Negri, Antonio 2009b, 'Some Thoughts on the Use of Dialectics', *Chto Delat*, 3, available at http://chtodelat.org/b8-newspapers/12-47/some-thoughts-on-the-use-of-dialecti cs/.

Negri, Antonio 2011, 'La construction du commun: un nouveau communisme', in *L'idée du communisme, II. Conférence de Berlin, 2010*, edited by Alain Badiou and Slavoj Žižek, Paris: Lignes.

Negri, Antonio 2012 [1977] 'Il marxismo e la questione criminale', in *La forma stato. Per la critica dell'economia politica della Costituzione*, Milan: Baldini Castoldi Dalai.

Negri, Antonio 2013a, *Winter is Over: Writings on the Transformation Denied, 1989–1995*, New York: Semiotext(e).

Negri, Antonio 2013b, 'From the End of National Lefts to Subversive Movements for Europe', *Radical Philosophy*, 181: 26–32.

Negri, Antonio 2014 [1983], *Pipeline: Letters from Prison*, translated by Ed Emery, Cambridge: Polity.

Negri, Antonio 2015, *Storia di un comunista*, edited by Girolamo De Michele, Milan: Ponte alle Grazie.

Negri, Antonio 2017, *Galera ed esilio. Storia di un comunista*, edited by Girolamo De Michele, Milan: Ponte alle Grazie.

Negri, Antonio 2020, *Da Genova a domani. Storia di un comunista*, edited by Girolamo De Michele, Milan: Ponte alle Grazie.

Negri, Antonio et al. 1993, *Benetton et Sentier. Des enterprises pas comme les autres*, Paris: Publisud.

Negri, Antonio and Judith Revel 2008, 'Inventer le commun des hommes', *Multitudes*, 31, available at http://www.eurozine.com/articles/2008-05-13-negri-fr.html.

Negri, Antonio and Jean-Marie Vincent 1991, 'La pensée affaiblie', in *"Le gai renonce-ment"*, supplement à *Futur antérieur*, Paris: L'Harmattan.

Neilson, Brett 2004, *'Potenza Nuda?* Sovereignty, Biopolitics, Capitalism', *Contretemps*, 5: 63–78.

Notes from Nowhere (ed.) 2003, *We Are Everywhere: The Irresistible Rise of Global Anti-capitalism*, London: Verso.

Osborne, Peter 2007, 'What is to be Done? (Education)', *Radical Philosophy*, 141: 33, available at https://www.radicalphilosophy.com/dossiers/what-is-to-be-done-educ ation.

Peyrol, Georges (aka Alain Badiou) 1982, 'Brèves notes sur le terrorisme', *Le Perroquet*, 10, 6–7.

Peyrol, Georges (aka Alain Badiou) 1983, '30 moyens de reconnaître à coup sûr un vieux-marxiste', *Le Perroquet*, 29–30: 5–6. English translation in 2006, *Prelom*, 8, available at: http://www.prelomkolektiv.org/eng/08.htm.

Platonov, Andrei 2011, 'On the First Socialist Tragedy (1934)', *New Left Review*, 69: 30–2.

Potere Operaio 1971, 'Che cos'è potere operaio', *Potere Operaio*, 45.

Power, Nina and Alberto Toscano 2009, 'The Philosophy of Restoration: Alain Badiou and the Enemies of May', *boundary 2*, 36, 1: 27–46.

Rabinow, Paul and Nikolas Rose 2003, 'Thoughts on the Concept of Biopower Today', available at: http://www.lse.ac.uk/sociology/pdf/RabinowandRose-BiopowerToday 03.pdf.

Rabouin, David, Oliver Feltham and Lissa Lincoln (eds) 2011, *Autour de Logiques des mondes d'Alain Badiou*, Paris: Editions des archives contemporaines.

Rancière, Jacques 1992, *Les mots de l'histoire*, Paris: Seuil.

RETORT (Iain Boal, T.J. Clark, Joseph Matthews, Michael Watts) 2005, *Afflicted Powers: Capital and Spectacle in a New Age of War*, London: Verso.

Reynolds, Simon 2005, *Rip It Up and Start Again: Postpunk 1978–1984*, London: Faber & Faber.

Rikap, Cecilia 2023, 'Capitalism as Usual?' *New Left Review*, 139: 145–60.

Roberts, John 2008, *The Intangibilities of Form: Skill and Deskilling in Art After the Readymade*, London: Verso.

Rose, Nikolas 2001, 'The Politics of Life Itself', *Theory, Culture & Society*, 18, 6: 1–30.

Sacchetto, Devi and Gianni Sbrogiò (eds) 2009, *Quando il potere è operaio. Autonomia e soggettività politica a Porto Marghera (1960–1980)*, Roma: manifestolibri.

Sandevince, Paul (aka Sylvain Lazarus) 1984a, 'La politique sous condition', *Le Perroquet*, 42: 1–3.

Sandevince, Paul (aka Sylvain Lazarus) 1984b, 'Les formes de conscience', *Le Perroquet*, 42: 5–6.

Sandevince, Paul (aka Sylvain Lazarus) 1984c, 'La fin des références', *Le Perroquet*, 42: 10.

Sartre, Jean-Paul 1968, *Search for a Method*, New York: Vintage.

Saunders, Frances Stonor 2000, *Who Paid the Piper? The CIA and the Cultural Cold War*, London: Granta.

Seaton, Lola 2023, 'Reflections on "Political Capitalism"', *New Left Review*, 142: 5–27.

Shari'ati, Ali 1979, *On the Sociology of Islam*, translated by Hamid Algar, Oneonta: Mizan Press.

Sivanandan, A. 1989, 'All that melts into air is solid: the hokum of New Times', *Race & Class*, 31.3: 1–30.

Streeck, Wolfgang 2014, *Buying Time: The Delayed Crisis of Democratic Capitalism*, London: Verso.

Szondi, Peter 2002, *An Essay on the Tragic*, translated by Paul Fleming, Stanford: Stanford University Press.

Tafuri, Manfredo 1976, *Architecture and Utopia: Design and Capitalist Development*, translated by Barbara Luigia La Penta, Cambridge, MA: MIT Press.

Tafuri, Manfredo 1987, *The Sphere and the Labyrinth: Avant-Gardes and Architecture from Piranesi to the 1970s*, translated by Pellegrino d'Acierno and Robert Connolly, Cambridge, MA: MIT Press.

Tomba, Massimiliano 2007, 'Differentials of Surplus-Value', *The Commoner*, 12: 23–37, available at http://www.commoner.org.uk/12tomba.pdf.

Toscano, Alberto 2006a, 'Anti-antitotalitarianism' (on Michael Scott Christofferson's *French Intellectuals Against the Left: The Antitotalitarian Moment of the 1970s*), *Radical Philosophy*, 139: 52–5.

Toscano, Alberto 2006b, *The Theatre of Production: Philosophy and Individuation between Kant and Deleuze*, Basingstoke: Palgrave.

Toscano, Alberto 2011, 'Mao and Manichaeism: An Episode in the Politics of Purity', *Parallax* 17.2 (2011): 49–58

Toscano, Alberto 2014a, 'What is Capitalist Power? Reflections on Truth and Juridical Forms', in *Foucault and the History of Our Present*, ed. Martina Tazzioli, Sophie Fuggle and Yari Lanci, Basingstoke: Palgrave Macmillan.

Toscano, Alberto 2014b, 'Materialism Without Matter: Abstraction, Absence and Social Form', *Textual Practice* 28.7: 1221–40.

Toscano, Alberto 2015, 'Taming the Furies: Badiou and Hegel on *The Eumenides*', in *Badiou and Hegel: Infinity, Dialectics, Subjectivity*, edited by Antonio Calcagno and Jim Vernon, Lanham, MD: Rowman & Littlefield/Lexington Books.

Toscano, Alberto 2016a, 'A Structuralism of Feeling?' *New Left Review*, 97: 73–93.

Toscano, Alberto 2016b, 'Limits to Periodization' (on Joshua Clover's *Riot. Strike. Riot*), *Viewpoint*, 6 September, https://www.viewpointmag.com/2016/09/06/limits-to-peri odization/

Toscano, Alberto 2017, *Fanaticism: On the Uses of an Idea*, 2nd edition, London: Verso.

Toscano, Alberto 2021, 'A Time of Riots and Martyrs: Alain Bertho's Anthropology of the Present' (review of *Le temps des émeutes* and *Les enfants du chaos/The Age of Violence* by Alain Bertho), *historical materialism*, https://www.historicalmaterialism .org/book-review/time-riots-and-martyrs-alain-berthos-anthropology-present

Toscano, Alberto 2022, '"Everything can be made better, except man": On Frédéric Lordon's Communist Realism', *Radical Philosophy*, 2.12: 19–34.

Toscano, Alberto 2023a, 'Shifting Currents', *New Left Review*, II/140–1: 181–90.

Toscano, Alberto 2023b, *Late Fascism: Race, Capitalism and the Politics of Crisis*, London: Verso.

Tronti, Mario 1971, *Operai e capitale*, 2nd edition, Turin: Einaudi.

Tronti, Mario 1980a, 'The Strategy of Refusal', in *Autonomia: Post-Political Politics*, edited by Sylvère Lotringer and Christian Marazzi, New York: Semiotext(e).

Tronti, Mario 1980b, *Il tempo della politica*, Roma: Editori Riuniti.

Tronti, Mario 1992, *Con le spalle al futuro. Per un altro dizionario politico*, Roma: Editori Riuniti.

Tronti, Mario 1998, *La politica al tramonto*, Torino: Einaudi.

Tronti, Mario 2001, *Cenni di castella*, Fiesole: Cadmo.

Tronti, Mario 2006, *Operai e capitale*, 3rd edition, Rome: DeriveApprodi.

Trotsky, Leon 1960 [1924], *Literature and Revolution*, Ann Arbor: University of Michigan Press.

UCFML 1983, 'Le Marxisme comme politique', *Le Perroquet*, 29–30: 1–3.

Virno, Paolo 1999, *Il Ricordo del presente. Saggio sul tempo storico*, Torino: Bollati Boringhieri.

Virno, Paolo 2002a, *A Grammar of the Multitude*, translated by Isabella Bertoletti, James Cascaito and Andrea Casson, New York: Semiotext(e).

Virno, Paolo 2002b, *Esercizi di esodo. Linguaggio e azione politica*, Verona: Ombre Corte.

Virno, Paolo 2003, *Quando il verbo si fa carne. Linguaggio e natura umana*, Turin: Bollati Boringhieri.

Virno, Paolo 2004, *A Grammar of the Multitude*, New York: Semiotext(e).

Virno, Paolo and Michael Hardt 1996, *Radical Thought in Italy: A Potential Politics*, Minneapolis: University of Minnesota Press.

Wallerstein, Immanuel 2003, *The Decline of American Power*, New York: The Free Press.

Wolff, Kurt H. (ed.) 1964, *The Sociology of Georg Simmel*, New York: The Free Press.

Wood, Ellen Meiksins 1998, *The Retreat from Class: A New 'True' Socialism*, 2nd edition, London: Verso.

Wright, Steve 2002, *Storming Heaven: Class Composition and Struggle in Italian Auto-nomist Marxism*, London: Pluto.

Wright, Steve 2006, 'There and Back Again: Mapping the Pathways Within Autonomist Marxism', paper delivered at the Cambridge conference 'Immaterial Labour, Multitudes and New Social Subjects: Class Composition in Cognitive Capitalism', 29–30 April, available at http://www.geocities.com/immateriallabour/wrightpaper2006.html.

Wright, Steve 2007, 'Back to the Future: Italian Workerist Reflect Upon the Operaista Project', *ephemera*, 7, 1: 270–81.

Zanini, Adelino and Ubaldo Fadini (eds.) 2001, *Lessico postfordista*, Milan: Feltrinelli.

Žižek, Slavoj 1998, 'Psychoanalysis in Post-Marxism: The Case of Alain Badiou', *The South Atlantic Quarterly*, 97, 2: 235–61.

Žižek, Slavoj 1999, *The Ticklish Subject*, London: Verso.

Žižek, Slavoj 2006, *The Parallax View*, Cambridge, MA: MIT Press.

Žižek, Slavoj 2007, 'Badiou: Notes from an Ongoing Debate', *International Journal of Žižek Studies*, 2, 1: 28–43, available at: https://zizekstudies.org/index.php/IJZS/article/view/37/34.

Index of names